Twentieth Century
Industrial Archaeology

Twentieth Century

Industrial Archaeology

Michael Stratton
and **Barrie Trinder**

First published 2000
by E & FN Spon
11 New Fetter Lane, London EC4P 4EE

Simultaneously published in the USA and Canada
by E & FN Spon
29 West 35th Street, New York, NY 10001

E & FN Spon is an imprint of the Taylor & Francis Group

© 2000 Michael Stratton and Barrie Trinder

The right of Michael Stratton and Barrie Trinder to be identified as the
Authors of this Work has been asserted by them in accordance with
the Copyright, Designs and Patents Act 1988

Designed and typeset in 9.3/12.5pt Palatino by Gavin Ward Design Associates
Printed and bound in Great Britain by
St Edmundsbury Press, Bury St Edmunds, Suffolk

British Library Cataloguing in Publication Data
A catalogue record for this book is available from the British Library

Library of Congress Cataloging in Publication Data
A catalog record for this book has been requested

ISBN 0-419-24680-0

Contents

Foreword
by Sir Neil Cossons

The world came of age in the twentieth century. It was a century endowed at its outset with immense industrial power, widespread prosperity, and emerging technologies that were to affect the lives of every person on the planet. But that same inheritance held the seeds of tragedy, in unresolved issues of influence and position in Europe, and in a capacity for annihilation made possible by the very industrial pre-eminence that had brought such wealth. It was to take three world wars, two of unimaginable carnage and horror and a third – the Cold War – that threatened imminent global extinction, to exorcise the ghosts of that nineteenth century legacy. By the twentieth century's end, the transformation in political, economic and social structures had been so universal that the American historian Francis Fukuyama could contemplate it as 'the end of history'.

Those changes were felt in Britain as keenly as anywhere. At the dawn of the twentieth century Britain was the leading world power, her influence and authority rooted in industrial, mercantile and imperial supremacy. By its end, the empire on which the sun never set had evaporated and she had become a less than enthusiastic partner in a European consortium of nations which history had taught her to view with circumspection. What had been the first industrial nation in the eighteenth century and 'workshop of the world' in the nineteenth was by the end of the twentieth a more democratic place, pluralistic and prosperous, but a place in which industry played a diminishing part in building the wealth of the nation.

But changes in the landscape of twentieth century Britain, urban and rural, were no less dramatic than they had been in the great age of industrialisation, on the contrary. New industries and the urban diaspora, the arrival of the motor car and the diesel lorry, of air travel and the aviation industry, of new building technologies based on reinforced concrete and prefabrication, of the filling station, the cinema and the out-of-town shopping centre all combined to alter the face of the nation irrevocably and irreversibly. Such was the impact of these seismic shifts in the social geography of Britain that by the 1990s regeneration of those urban landscapes that had suffered progressive decay as they were denuded of people and industries had become a national priority. So called 'brown field' areas, mostly in and around the old industrial heartlands of the Midlands and the North, were to be the places where people would live and work in the future, taking pressure off the countryside and reviving the fortunes of urban life. A key part of this new approach to planning and investment is 'regeneration through heritage', the recognition that many of the buildings on which urban and industrial living had been built a century and more ago themselves afforded opportunities not simply for re-use but as keys to reviving and maintaining the social fabric of communities.

The industrial archaeology of the twentieth century is the archaeology of paradox, signalled by the arrival of the cult of 'recency' in our understanding of history, the realisation that the past is being created around us day-by-day and that we can all be active players in ensuring that yesterday can be used to benefit and fashion tomorrow. The recent past is, in a very real sense, the context within which we play out our lives. These are themes Michael Stratton well understood. They are reflected in much of the work of English Heritage of which in April I had the privilege to become Chairman. And it is a particular pleasure to see English Heritage, through the National Monuments Record, be so closely associated with this book.

In his Preface, Barrie Trinder accords Michael Stratton the distinction of having conceived the idea of *Twentieth Century Industrial Archaeology*. Michael died of myeloma, shortly before his forty-sixth birthday, at the end of April 1999. He was in every sense a twentieth century man. He grew up in north London alongside the Great Northern main line. He studied at the universities of Durham, Sheffield and Leicester before moving to Ironbridge as a research student of the University of Aston in the late 1970s. He saw, in the buildings and landscapes around him, what none of the rest of us could see. And, his interests and enthusiasms, his profound knowledge and scholarship, equipped him as nobody else to commentate with authority on the twentieth century world. His research and publication on terra cotta, on the archaeology of the British car factory, on the aviation and electricity generation industries, were just a few of the more tangible reflections of his insatiable curiosity and his appetite for revealing the invisible, the obscure or just the unknown to wider audiences. But above all it was Michael's perception of the aesthetics of his contemporary surroundings and the masterly way in which he could stand outside conventional wisdom in order to confer value upon the recent past at a time when fashion dictated otherwise that will for me be the most abiding memory of his contribution to industrial archaeology. As a colleague at Ironbridge in the late seventies and thereafter as someone whose friendship I valued and intellect I admired Michael has made a lasting contribution to our understanding of the world in which we live.

Neil Cossons
April 2000

Preface and acknowledgements

The idea for this book was Michael Stratton's. The outline was sketched while awaiting a train at Kettering Station in June 1996. It was Michael who sought a publisher and convinced the Royal Commission on the Historical Monuments of England (now merged with English Heritage) to support the venture.

Michael and I jointly taught postgraduate programmes in industrial archaeology at the Ironbridge Institute between 1982 and the end of 1994 when Michael left to take up a post at the University of York. We soon realised that the archaeology of the twentieth century needed a different approach from that of the Industrial Revolution, and developed such an approach when from 1986 the course was divided into modules. Michael ceased to teach specifically twentieth-century topics after he moved to York, although he continued to research certain aspects, which he did with alacrity. After moving to University College Northampton in 1996 I was able to continue specific programmes on the subject, both at that institution and in the School of Continuing Studies at the University of Birmingham. I am grateful to the numerous students who have stimulated the thinking that has gone into the book.

We spent much of 1998 working on the book, and planned most of the illustrations during a two-day spell at the National Monuments Record Centre, Swindon, in mid-December of that year. Within a month Michael was stricken with the illness from which he died on 29 April 1999. He was determined that the project should continue, and had written some parts of the book and approved others before he died. The book has been completed during the summer and autumn of 1999 in the hope of achieving its objective of publication during the conference of the International Congress on the Conservation of the Industrial Heritage (TICCIH) in August 2000.

Rather too much of 1999 has been spent at the word processor and not enough, as we had planned, in fieldwork. The book does nevertheless reflect a great deal of fieldwork undertaken during the past twenty years. Michael was stimulating company in any landscape, and I particularly cherish his delight in the bizarre environment of the former Royal Ordnance Factory at Thorp Arch on a November afternoon in 1998. We would doubtless have argued about many points in the text, and the book will be the poorer for the lack of those debates. I trust nevertheless that Michael would have approved of the book in its final form, and that it will be a worthy part of the splendid legacy that he has bequeathed to scholarship.

I would like to record my gratitude, first, to Annabel Stratton, both for her composure and for her gentle encouragement of the project.

The book draws on the work of many of our former students at the Ironbridge Institute, particularly that of Jane Bennett, Bob Brooks, Alan Bryant, Richard Butterfield, David Cant, Paul Collins, Tony Crosby,

Mark Davey, Tanya English, Sharon Hall, Rob Kinchin-Smith, Michael New, Claire Pudney, Stuart Shaw, Larraine Wilde and David Worth. Two other ex-students, Mark Watson, now of Historic Scotland, and David Eve of Kent County Council, have provided helpful information. I would like to thank also John Edmunds, Ian Grant, Ann and Michael Harrison, Doug Jamieson, Patrick McDermot, Brian Malaws, Derek Merfield, Clifford Morris and Tony Parks, all members of my classes at the University of Birmingham's School of Continuing Studies, for their help with the project.

Several people read the text, or parts of it, during the summer of 1999, and I would like to record my gratitude to Kathy and Tony Herbert, Dr Peter Wakelin, Dr Garry Campion, John Powell, Julian Temple and John McGuinness for their invigorating comments. Any errors of fact or judgement that remain are entirely my responsibility. I am grateful also to my colleague Professor Peter King of University College Northampton for his steady encouragement of the project and to Sir Neil Cossons for writing the Foreword.

Thanks are due also to Tom Hassall, Secretary of the Royal Commission at the time when the publication of the book was agreed, and to Wayne Cocroft, Keith Falconer and Robin Taylor, formerly of the Commission but now of English Heritage, for their valued support. The book's subject is Great Britain, not England, and I wish, therefore, to record my gratitude to Hilary Malaws and Medwyn Parry of the Royal Commission in Wales, to Miriam McDonald and Miles Oglethorpe of the Royal Commission in Scotland, as well as to the secretaries of those Commissions for their help with the illustrations. Thanks are due also to Derek Elliott of the Welsh Office, and to John Swannick for help with photographs.

The task of completing this text has been emotionally draining and time-consuming, and my greatest debt is to my wife Barbara Trinder, who has shown much patience and understanding during a long, work-dominated summer.

Finally, this remains Michael Stratton's book. The structure is that which he agreed, and it incorporates many of his ideas, including the use of the Great Western Main Line between Paddington and Swindon to provide a synopsis of the whole book. To work with Michael was intellectually stimulating. It was also great fun. I hope that the completed book reflects both these aspects of his personality.

Barrie Trinder
November 1999

Abbreviations

ABC	Associated British Cinemas	LNER	London & North Eastern Railway
ac	alternating current	LNWR	London & North Western Railway
AEC	Associated Equipment Company	LPTB	London Passenger Transport Board
BA	British Airways	LSWR	London & South Western Railway
BAC	British Aluminium Company	MG	Morris Garages
BEA	British European Airways	MOD	Ministry of Defence
BISF	British Iron & Steel Federation	MW	megawatt
BMC	British Motor Corporation	NALGO	National & Local Government Officers' Organisation
BOAC	British Overseas Airways Corporation	NCB	National Coal Board
BP	British Petroleum	nd	not dated
BSA	Birmingham Small Arms	NMRC	National Monuments Record Centre
BSAA	British South American Airways	OCL	Overseas Containers Ltd
CEGB	Central Electricity Generating Board	P&O	Peninsular & Oriental
CPRE	Council for the Preservation (later, Protection) of Rural England	PLUTO	pipe line under the ocean
		PVC	polyvinyl chloride
CWS	Co-operative Wholesale Society	RAF	Royal Air Force
DC	direct current	RCAHMS	Royal Commission on the Ancient & Historical Monuments of Scotland
GCR	Great Central Railway		
GLC	Greater London Council	RCAHMW	Royal Commission on the Ancient & Historical Monuments of Wales
GWR	Great Western Railway		
HMSO	Her Majesty's Stationery Office	RCHME	Royal Commission on the Historical Monuments of England
HMV	His Master's Voice		
HST	High Speed Train	RSJ	rolled-steel joist
ICI	Imperial Chemical Industries	SECR	South East & Chatham Railway
IWT	Inland Water Transport	SAA	small arms ammunition
JCB	J. C. Bamford	SS	Standard Swallows
LBC	London Brick Company	TICCIH	The International Congress on the Conservation of the Industrial Heritage
LBSCR	London, Brighton & South Coast Railway		
LCC	London County Council	USAAF	United States Army Air Force
LMSR	London Midland & Scottish Railway	USSR	Union of Soviet Socialist Republics
		WD	War Department

Chapter one

Introduction

'Archaeology' and 'the twentieth century' are terms that do not easily co-exist. 'Archaeology' has associations with Stonehenge and with the excavation of Roman villas, and 'industrial archaeology' is traditionally linked with the period between the Seven Years War and the Great Exhibition, with Cromford, Blaenavon, New Lanark, the Albert Dock and Swindon. Yet one twentieth-century archaeological site of some importance in British history was by the 1990s already displayed in much the same way as the Roman villa at Chedworth or the foundations of Richard Arkwright's second mill at Cromford. In the Old Port of Montreal visitors can observe the outline of the concrete foundations of a thirty-two-storey grain elevator erected in 1912, together with associated fragments of rubber belting, twisted steelwork and rusting electric motors. The conserved ruin conveys a vivid sense of the scale of the Canadian grain trade and, indirectly, of its impact on Great Britain, and provides enlightening evidence of the new materials of the early years of the century. The elevator encapsulates the fundamental, if elementary, concept on which this book is based – that our understanding of the twentieth century is increased by an awareness of its archaeology, of the artefacts, images, structures, sites and landscapes of the past 100 years.

1.1
The site of Elevator No. 2 in the port of Montreal, a thirty-storey concrete structure, built in 1912, when Montreal handled more grain than any other port in North America. The remains of the elevator are preserved as an archaeological site by Le Vieux Port de Montréal.

(Photo: Barrie Trinder)

1.2
The buildings on the
Pier Head at Liverpool
illustrate the
constructional
possibilities of the early
twentieth century. The
Liver Building (left) was
designed, by W. Aubrey
Thomas, on the
Hennebique system, and
built between 1908 and
1911. The cladding is of
grey stone. The Cunard
Building (centre) was
built in 1915 with a
Truscon frame. The
headquarters of the
Mersey Docks & Harbour
Board (right) was built in
1907 to the design of
Arnold Thornley, with a
Baroque dome supported
on a steel frame supplied
by Dorman Long.

(Photo: A. F. Kersting)

The book has several starting-points. The first is the proposition that our understanding of any event or sequence of events is increased by an awareness of its physical context, something which is lacking in many conventional twentieth-century historical studies, for example in the kind of business history written from a head-office viewpoint, that conveys no sense of a company's factories, shops or warehouses. Yet events took place in real landscapes, in structures which can be studied either in the field or through maps and pictures. Factories produced real products which survive, if nowhere else, in museums. Houses and flats were built for real people who exercised in them their aesthetic taste, made love, raised children, and installed appliances made in real factories. Some historians follow conventional wisdom in deploring certain aspects of the twentieth century – the monotony of work in car factories or the horrors of living in tower blocks, for example. We have tried to write from first-hand experience of sites and landscapes, and have consciously taken a sceptical, irreverent and sometimes counter-intuitive attitude to received views of twentieth-century artefacts and places. In this respect we acknowledge as a starting-point the writings of the late Reyner Banham, who was excited by and recognised the merits

of Cummings ice-cream vans, container ports and the power stations of the Trent Valley.[1]

We are consciously attempting to work in the tradition established in the 1950s by Maurice Beresford and W. G. Hoskins, that archaeologists and historians should help people to understand their everyday surroundings. Beresford, chronicler of industrial Leeds and an inspiration for all who study history on the ground, wrote in 1957 about journeys along boundaries, among deserted villages, through parks and to Elizabethan marketplaces. We offer journeys along by-passes, among ordnance factory buildings, through industrial estates and to Elizabethan power stations, and share with Beresford some expeditions to new towns.[2] Similarly we are inspired by the work of the late W. G. Hoskins. We share his pleasure in the English landscape, in trying to recognise 'every one of its details name by name, in knowing how and when each came to be there, why it is just that colour, shape or size, and not otherwise, and in seeing how the various patterns and parts fit together to make the whole scene'. Hoskins saw the landscape in musical and architectural terms, and strove 'to isolate the themes as they enter, to see how one by one they are intricately woven together and by what magic new harmonies are produced ...

[to] perceive the subtle variations on a single theme'. We do not share Hoskins's view of the twentieth century. We are unhappy with his opinion that the word 'overspill' is as 'beastly as the thing it describes' – he would surely not have written 'the people whom it describes'.[3] Whatever the ancient field and settlement patterns obliterated by the airfields of the Second World War, the remnants of runways, accommodation blocks and control towers are monuments to an heroic resistance to Fascism. The England of the Nissen hut, the 'prefab' and the arterial by-pass may not be beautiful, but it merits analysis. The Britain of Grangemouth, Port Talbot, Trafford Park, Billingham and Drax has transformed our way of life in the past century, raising most people's living standards to levels unimagined in 1900. The Britain of Letchworth, Gretna and Roehampton, of the Spitfire, the *Queen Mary*, the Cheltenham Flyer, the Mini-Minor and the E-type Jaguar, includes themes as harmonious as any to be heard in Hoskins's more distant centuries. Nevertheless, we are wholly in agreement with Hoskins that the pace of change in the twentieth century was unprecedented, that surging economic growth, whatever its causes, unleashed far-reaching changes in every aspect of material culture.

Our third objective is to provide a context for some of the specialised studies currently being undertaken by industrial archaeologists of particular aspects of twentieth-century history. The royal commissions in England, Scotland and Wales have been responsible in recent years for much innovative recording: of the explosives industry, of road transport, of the monuments of coal mining and the operation of coal mines. Some of the reports of the Monuments Protection Programme have been concerned with sites of recent date relating to industries which are centuries old, like lime-burning, ceramics and non-ferrous mining; and some, like the study of power stations, are concerned largely with the twentieth century. Such studies will in due course change our views of twentieth-century industry. This book is intended to enable them to be seen in a wider setting.

We hope also to identify some of the sites which encapsulate the developments of the last 100 years, and to begin to set an agenda for future investigations. The pioneering works on industrial archaeology of the 1960s and the early 1970s, by the late Kenneth Hudson, and by Neil Cossons and Angus Buchanan, brought to public attention the most significant sites and structures of the classic Industrial Revolution period.[4] In the last thirty years our understanding of that period has been increased by studies of textile mills, primitive railways, canals, potbanks, ironworks, domestic manufactures and coalfield landscapes. Following in this tradition, we hope to show why such places as Trafford Park, Letchworth, Dungeness, Clydebank and Bridgend demand our attention and repay archaeological analysis, and why, for reasons of historical scholarship as well as of basic humanity, we should be grateful that Slough was not destroyed by friendly bombs, as envisaged in John Betjeman's poem.[5] Many characteristic features of twentieth-century Britain have already disappeared, or are now represented only by chance survivals, to which we shall draw attention. We hope to take our readers into parts of Britain with which they may not be familiar, areas that may be despised, even by those who live in them. Like Maurice Beresford in 1957, we see our journeys as the starting-points for those of other people.

1.3
Derelict petrol pumps with a sign for the long-extinct Cleveland brand of petrol, photographed at Darlaston near Wolverhampton in 1998.

(Photo: Clifford Morris)

Finally, we hope that this study will engage and add an archaeological element to some historians' debates on twentieth-century Britain. The chapters are centred not on sectors of industry but on historical themes, some of them perhaps historical clichés. We examine, from the archaeological viewpoint, a series of propositions: that twentieth-century industry has been shaped by science and by the international transfer of technology; that the quality of British industrial technology has declined relative to that of other countries; that the two world wars have been decisive factors in the history of the past 100 years; that the inter-war years and the period from 1955 to 1973 were times of 'great rebuilding'; that the service sector of industry has grown at the expense of the manufacturing sector.

Debates on twentieth-century Britain take place within many disciplines. In the research for this book we have gained understanding from the work of political, social, economic and urban historians, and from historians of architecture, technology and science; from sociologists, planners, architects, engineers, social anthropologists and psychologists. We owe particular debts to several scholars. Kenneth Hudson not only set an agenda in the 1960s for studying the archaeology of the Industrial Revolution but published in the late 1970s the first studies of twentieth-century industrial archaeology.[6] We disagree profoundly with some aspects of Hudson's approach, but we acknowledge with gratitude his pioneering role. All students of twentieth-century Britain must regard with awe Charles Loch Mowat's *Britain between the Wars*, perhaps the best textbook on any period of our island's history. It shows an awareness of landscape and process with which we have strong sympathies. We admire equally the same author's classic micro-study of a rural branch railway in the Welsh Borderland.[7] Our third particular debt must be to Arthur Marwick, from whose studies of twentieth-century society, and of the impact of war upon it, we have gained much stimulation.[8]

If, as we contend, our understanding of the development of industry between 1700 and 1850 has, over the past thirty years, been extended by archaeological analysis, it is pertinent to ask how this has been achieved. Some developments have come through straightforward quantification, by bringing together the evidence of maps, documents, pictures and fieldwork and asking how many establishments there were of particular kinds at particular times, by doing what the prehistorian with no evidence other than fieldwork data might do with burial mounds or rectangular enclosures. Our knowledge of textile mills, potbanks in north Staffordshire, domestic weaving premises in lowland Lancashire and ironworkers' housing in South Wales, to give but four examples, has been profitably enlarged by these means. Second, our understanding has grown by developing typologies.[9] Demonstrating that there was a distinct type of medium-lift steam pumping engine has increased our knowledge of the canal system.[10] Comparative studies, contrasting evidence from Aberdeen, Leeds, Whitehaven and Shrewsbury, have shown that the majority of the first iron-framed buildings in the textile industry were used for processing flax, and have begun to reveal how flax-spinning complexes were organised.[11] Spatial analysis of settlements where domestic and factory production co-existed is revealing much about the process of industrialisation, whether in the spinning and weaving of cotton in Preston, lacemaking in Nottinghamshire, or boot- and shoemaking in Northamptonshire.[12] The physical evidence of any period of history is not negated by a profusion of documentary sources. The student of Roman Britain will examine the ruins of Wroxeter as well as the writings of Tacitus. Offa's Dyke is as effective a testimony to the authority of Saxon kings as the Anglo-Saxon Chronicle. Lincoln Cathedral and Caernarfon Castle as well as the Pipe Rolls and monastic cartularies enrich our knowledge of the Middle Ages. The twentieth century can scarcely be different. All sensible people can agree that archaeological and documentary knowledge should be integrated, and we strive for such integration here. But there is something to be gained from putting ourselves in the position of the prehistorian and asking narrowly archaeological questions – what could we learn about twentieth-century society, if we had no other source of information, by studying Clydebank or Longbridge, or the aircraft factory at Hawarden or the front at Blackpool? If we accept that historical understanding is advanced by continuing debate, such exercises will be illuminating, for so often the reasoned analysis of material culture throws up questions that are entirely different from those generated by documentary research.

It is easy to assume that twentieth-century industrial buildings were 'functional' and that they had few architectural merits. We contend that twentieth-century factories display precisely the same tensions as industrial buildings of earlier periods. Some were built to accommodate particular technologies, and some simply to provide space and services for any potential user. Some designers of factories simply made their buildings conform politely with their settings. Some were more ambitious. A sequence of 'flagship' buildings, designed to make strong architectural statements, ran through the century: the Wallis, Gilbert & Partners factories on the Great West Road of the 1930s, Battersea Power Station of 1933, British Nylon Spinners, Pontypool, of 1948, the Brynmawr rubber factory of 1950, Maerdy Colliery of 1948–53, at Swindon the Reliance Controls building of 1965, and the Inmos factory of 1982 at Newport.[13] At the opposite architectural extreme, the most basic forms of industrial structure have also changed. Huts used by builders and others closely resemble the containers used by the transport industry. They can be craned from the backs of lorries to create instant settlements, while containers discarded by transport companies are used for storage in many contexts.

The settings of factories also have changed. In 1900 Ebenezer Howard's idea that industry should be confined to defined zones within a community was novel. The success of industrial estates like those established from 1887 by the Scottish CWS at Shieldhall, and above all the Trafford Park estate, developed from 1896, set a pattern for industrial zoning, which was an integral part of the plan for Letchworth, the first Garden City (see Chapter 8). The pattern was continued in the 1920s and 1930s, most famously at Slough, but also at Park Royal and other military sites of the First World War, and in 1938 was adopted by government, which supported the establishment of trading estates designed to relieve unemployment at Team Valley in Co Durham, Treforest in South Wales, and North Hillingdon, Glasgow.[14] After the Second World War the advisability of placing industry within particular zones became one of the basic assumptions of planning policy.

1.4
Trafford Park. The buildings highlighted were those occupied by Metropolitan Vickers Ltd at the conclusion of the Second World War.

(Ironbridge Gorge Museum Trust)

Industrial archaeologists have shunned the twentieth century. The standard work on the Bristol region, published in 1969, has little to say about Avonmouth (see Figure 1.5), and a recent study of Devon ignores the county's dairy industry.[15] In this respect archaeologists have tended to follow received opinion, and to despise prefabs, tower blocks, and factories that can be seen to symbolise Britain's industrial decline. We would contend that on the contrary the archaeological record of the twentieth century bears witness to remarkable economic, social and technological vitality, that it is evidence which merits analysis. Twentieth-century buildings deserve to be studied without preconceptions. Factories are not all anonymous, and housing bears much evidence of regional and local practices. Some twentieth-century industrial complexes are gigantic, but can nevertheless be analysed. We do not flinch from the challenge of evaluating the archaeological record of the twentieth century, and contend that there is within society at large a hunger for the kind of understanding which the archaeologist can bring to the physical remains of the past 100 years. We see this book as a means of setting an agenda which in the course of time will take different forms, but we are confident that the study of the artefacts, images, structures, sites and landscapes of the twentieth century can add significantly to our understanding of the recent past, and that archaeological evidence often provides a stimulating challenge to conventional wisdom.

1.5
The industrial landscape
of the port of
Avonmouth,
photographed in 1986.

(Crown copyright. NMR)

Notes and references

1 R. Banham, 'Sundae Painters', 'Flatscape with
   Containers', 'Power of Trent and Aire', in P. Barker
   (ed.) *Arts in Society*, London: Fontana, 1977,
   pp. 159–63, 250–9.

2 M. Beresford, *History on the Ground*, London:
   Methuen, 1971, pp. 19–22.

3 W. G. Hoskins, *The Making of the English Landscape*,
   London: Hodder & Stoughton, 1957, pp. 19, 231–3.

4 R. A. Buchanan, *Industrial Archaeology in Britain*,
   Harmondsworth: Penguin, 1972; N. Cossons, *The BP
   Book of Industrial Archaeology*, Newton Abbot: David
   & Charles, 1975; K. Hudson, *Industrial Archaeology:
   An Introduction*, London: John Baker, 1963.

5 'Slough', in J. Betjeman, *John Betjeman's Collected
   Poems*, London: John Murray, 1983, pp. 22–4.

6 K. Hudson, *Food, Clothes and Shelter: Twentieth
   Century Industrial Archaeology*, London: John Baker,
   1978; K. Hudson, *Where We Used to Work*, London:
   John Baker, 1980.

7 C. L. Mowat, *Britain between the Wars 1918–1940*,
   London: Methuen, 1955; C. L. Mowat, *The Golden
   Valley Railway: Railway Enterprise on the Welsh Border
   in Late Victorian Times*, Cardiff: University of Wales
   Press, 1964.

8 A. Marwick, *The Deluge*, London: Bodley Head, 1965;
   Britain in the Century of Total War, London: Bodley
   Head, 1968; *The Home Front: The British and the Second
   World War*, London: Thames & Hudson, 1976; *War,
   Peace and Social Change in Twentieth Century Europe*,
   Milton Keynes: Open University, 1989. See also
   A. Marwick (ed.) *Total War and Social Change*,
   Basingstoke: Macmillan, 1988.

9 A. Calladine and J. Fricker, *East Cheshire Textile
   Mills*, London: Royal Commission on the Historical
   Monuments of England, 1993; C. Giles and I. H.
   Goodall, *Yorkshire Textile Mills*, London: HMSO for
   Royal Commission on the Historical Monuments of
   England, 1992; M. Williams, *Cotton Mills in Greater
   Manchester*, Preston: Carnegie for the Royal
   Commission on the Historical Monuments of
   England, 1992; D. Baker, *Potworks: The Industrial
   Architecture of the Staffordshire Potteries*, London:
   Royal Commission on the Historical Monuments
   of England, 1991; J. G. Timmins, *Handloom Weavers'
   Cottages in Central Lancashire*, Lancaster: University
   of Lancaster Press, 1977; J. B. Lowe, *Welsh Industrial
   Workers' Housing 1775–1875*, Cardiff: National
   Museum of Wales.

10 J. Andrew, 'Canal Pumping Engines', *Industrial
   Archaeology Review*, 1993, vol. 15, pp. 140–59;
   M. Stratton and B. Trinder, *Industrial England*,
   London: Batsford, 1997, pp. 56–61.

11 B. Trinder, 'Ditherington Flax Mill – a Re-evaluation',
   Textile History, 1992, vol. 23, pp. 189–224; M. Watson,
   'Broadford Works, Aberdeen: Evidence for the
   Earliest Iron-Framed Flax Mills', *Textile History*, 1992,
   vol. 23, pp. 225–42; K. A. Falconer, 'Fireproof Mills –
   the Widening Perspectives', *Industrial Archaeology
   Review*, 1993, vol. 16, pp. 11–26.

12 N. Morgan, *Vanished Dwellings: Early Industrial
   Housing in a Lancashire Cotton Town, Preston*, Preston:
   Mullion, 1990; G. Campion, 'People, Process and the
   Poverty-Pew: A Functional Analysis of Mundane
   Buildings in the Nottinghamshire Framework-
   Knitting Industry', *Antiquity*, 1996, vol. 70, pp.
   847–60.

13 M. Stratton and B. Trinder, *Industrial England*,
   London: Batsford, 1997, pp. 56–61.

14 Ibid., pp. 114–18.

15 R. A. Buchanan and N. Cossons, *The Industrial
   Archaeology of the Bristol Region*, Newton Abbot:
   David & Charles, 1969; M. Bone and P. Stanier,
   A Guide to the Industrial Archaeology of Devon, Telford:
   Association for Industrial Archaeology, 1998.

Chapter two

M any of the materials from which the everyday artefacts of the 1990s were made would not have been recognised in the early years of the twentieth century. New forms of steel and of plastic were developed in the course of the century. Concrete, aluminium and asbestos became familiar in many contexts, while there were many innovations in the ways in which traditional materials – glass, wood, paper and ceramics – were used. The purpose of this chapter is to outline some of the more significant changes, and to highlight some of the key sites where developments took place.

A new material culture

Iron and steel

Steel was one of the most influential materials of the twentieth century. Its low cost and capacity for development enabled it to outlast new materials which challenged it in particular contexts. It provided the frames for skyscrapers

2.1
The steel plant at
Ebbw Vale in 1948.

(Crown copyright/MOD)

and was used in many forms in large-scale chemical plants, and in great bridges. Politicians were heavily involved in the industry for much of the twentieth century. Steelmaking was controlled by government in both world wars, and government prompting led to the construction of new works in the 1930s at Shotton (SJ 3070), Ebbw Vale (SO 1708) and Corby (SP 9089). It was the Prime Minister, Harold Macmillan, who announced on 18 November 1958 that the cabinet had decided to build not one new integrated works with a strip mill but two, at Llanwern (ST 3786) and Ravenscraig (NS 7756).[1] The steel industry was nationalised in 1951, denationalised in 1953, renationalised in 1967 and privatised in 1988.

Mild steel – that is, iron with a carbon content of 0.1–0.2 per cent – was first made by Sir Henry Bessemer (1813–98) in 1856. It largely supplanted wrought iron, a characteristic material of the nineteenth century, which could not be made in bulk. Output of wrought iron was already declining in 1900. It had fallen to around a million tonnes a year by 1914, never exceeded 600,000 tonnes afterwards, had diminished to 54,000 tonnes by 1938, and ceased completely in the 1970s.

The constructional potential of steel was beginning to be recognised in 1900. The Forth Bridge, completed in 1889, was its principal advertisement. Steel had been accepted in shipbuilding in the 1880s, and its properties were coming to be appreciated in building.

Steel frames were used in the Great Northern Railway's warehouse in Manchester (SJ 836977) in 1898, in the Midland Hotel in the same city and the Westinghouse engineering works at Trafford Park (SJ 792962) in 1900, and in the Mathias Robinson (now Debenhams) store in Stockton-on-Tees about 1901. In 1904 the Engineering Standards Association set regular standards for steel joists used in building, and the London County Council (General Powers Act of 1909) – often called the Steel-Frame Act – permitted the use of curtain walling in steel-framed buildings. While it applied only to London, it stimulated the use of steel in construction throughout the country. In 1900 the steelmakers Dorman Long opened a new 8-acre (3ha) site for fabricating constructional steel adjacent to their Teesside works.[2] Steel is made from cast iron, the product of the blast furnace (and from scrap). There were over 600 blast furnaces in the United Kingdom in 1900, at 149 different works, and just over 400 were in blast during that year. Some of them were very old. Most were sited on the coalfields, and were charged with locally mined ore and coke made from locally raised coal, although some were situated in areas like Northamptonshire which had ore but no coal. An increasing proportion of the ore used in blast furnaces was being imported. The number of blast furnaces steadily diminished through the century as the capacity of individual furnaces grew: 427 in 1927, 190 in 1939 and 89 in 1967. In 1999 there were just 15 furnaces at four integrated steelworks near the coast, at Margam (SS 7886), Llanwern (ST 3786), Scunthorpe (SE 9111) and Redcar (NZ 5525), dependent entirely on imported ore and coal. The furnace at Redcar, first lit in September 1979, is one of the largest in the world, with a nominal capacity of 10,000 tonnes per day. Nevertheless, it operates on the same basic principles as had the most archaic of the furnaces working in 1900.[3]

No twentieth-century blast furnace is actively preserved, although several much older furnaces that were still operating in 1900, like those at Blaenavon (SO 248093) and Blists Hill (Ironbridge: SJ 693033), are conserved as monuments, and good examples of twentieth-century furnaces are preserved in Germany and the United States. New steam engines were still being installed to blow air into blast furnaces in the early years of the twentieth century. At the

2.3
Lightweight steel
construction – the Dome
of Discovery at the
Festival of Britain, 1951.

(Crown copyright. NMR)

Priorslee furnaces (SJ 702099) of the Lilleshall
Company in Shropshire two vertical compound
engines to the design of Edward Allis & Co. of
Milwaukee were installed in 1900 and worked
until the furnaces were finally blown out in
1959. The barring engine, used to set the
flywheel in motion, is preserved at Ironbridge.
During the twentieth century electric blowers
became standard, just as mechanical charging
of raw materials, first employed at Scunthorpe
in 1905, replaced the filling of furnaces with
hand barrows. By the 1990s the burden charged
to furnaces was a semi-fused cake of ore and
coke called sinter, the first British sinter plant
having been built at Scunthorpe in 1934.
All furnaces built in the twentieth century
employed hot blast, and their stacks were
therefore surrounded by tall cylindrical Cowper
stoves, in which refractories, heated by waste
gas, raised the temperature of the air being
blown into the furnaces.[4]
   During the first eighty years of the twentieth
century a substantial proportion of the iron
ore used in blast furnaces in the UK was home

2.4
A blast furnace with its
Cowper stoves at the
Margam Steelworks at
Port Talbot.

(Crown copyright. NMR)

produced, much of it from Jurassic deposits in Oxfordshire, Northamptonshire, Rutland, Leicestershire and Lincolnshire, counties which still bear many marks of quarrying on a large scale. From 1900 to 1938 annual output varied between 10,000,000 and 15,000,000 tonnes, except for the years affected by strikes, 1921–22 and 1926, and a trough at the depths of the Great Depression in 1931–33. The nature of quarrying, and of the railways which served the quarries, is shown at Irchester Country Park near Wellingborough (SP 9166), at Hunbury Hill (SP 7358) near Northampton, and at the Rutland Railway Museum, Cottesmore (SK 886137). Large quantities of ore were moved by the main-line railways, the principal traffics being from High Dyke (SK 940284) near Grantham to Scunthorpe, from Banbury to South Wales and Bilston (SO 9395), and from the Wellingborough and Kettering areas to Stanton (SK 4368) and Teesside. There were similar movements of imported ore to inland ironworks, from Tyne Dock (NZ 3565) across the grain of Co Durham to Consett (NZ 0951), and from Newport to Ebbw Vale.

Steel was made from iron in 1900 in Bessemer converters, an example of which stands at the entrance to the Kelham Island Museum (SK 352882) in Sheffield, or in open-hearth furnaces, of which none survives in Britain. From the early 1950s these two methods were eclipsed by the basic oxygen, or Linz Donawitz, process employed in the 1990s at the four major integrated plants. A vessel, or converter, of up to 350-ton capacity, was charged with scrap and molten iron before oxygen was blown through it from a water-cooled lance, setting off a vigorous chemical reaction. The process was precisely monitored, and by blowing through other gases, or adding small quantities of other metals, quality could be strictly controlled. The process was first used in Britain at Ebbw Vale, in 1960. Much of the steel is continuously cast by pouring it from a ladle through a tundish into a copper mould from which it is drawn with the profile of the billet or slab required. Continuous casting was first used as early as 1946 in Britain, at the Low Moor works in Yorkshire, and was employed in the 1990s at all four integrated plants.

The concentration of bulk steelmaking at the four integrated plants led to large-scale closures of steelworks in the second half of the twentieth century. Parts of some older works, like the coating plants at Ebbw Vale and Shotton, the tube mill at Corby, the rail mill at Workington, and the rolling mill at Shelton, Stoke-on-Trent, continued to operate with steel brought in from elsewhere, but some works closed completely, and whole communities were transformed. The closure of the Ravenscraig works at Motherwell in 1993 marked the end of steelmaking in Scotland.[5] Consett, in upland west Durham, an isolated community whose *raison d'être* was steel, turned to light industry and was best known in the 1990s for expensive snack foods. The site of the Round Oak steelworks in the Black Country was occupied by the Merry Hill shopping centre (SO 921876).

Most steel was rolled, and tandem rolling mills, in which billets pass continuously through successions of rolls, were some of the largest industrial structures created in the twentieth century. The universal mill, one in which the top, bottom and sides of a piece of steel are rolled simultaneously, was first used for producing plates in 1878. Henry Grey (1849–1913) showed in the early years of the twentieth century that it could be applied to the rolling of H-beams, or rolled-steel joists (RSJs). All large rolling mills in 1900 were steam driven, and some remained so past the middle of the century; but more sophisticated forms of rolling depended on electric power. Continuous

2.5
The long-distance movement of home-produced iron ore – a former GWR 2-8-0 locomotive No. 2849, north of Cropredy, Oxfordshire, with a load of iron ore from quarries near Banbury en route to blast furnaces in South Wales, probably to Ebbw Vale, July 1961.

(Photo: Barrie Trinder)

A new material culture

wide-strip rolling, producing the coils of thin steel used in motorcar bodies and domestic appliances, as well as in tin plate, was developed in the United States, and first applied in the UK at Ebbw Vale in 1938. Continuous rolling was also applied to the manufacture of joists (or girders), and the mile-long medium-section mill which forms part of the Anchor plant at Scunthorpe, built in 1970–73, was one of the most awe-inspiring sights in industrial Britain.

Steel castings were of great importance in many aspects of engineering in the twentieth century. One of the principal plants was that of F. H. Lloyd & Co. at Wednesbury (SJ 988972), alongside the M6 motorway; it closed in the 1980s, and was replaced by IKEA and other large stores. The company's products in the 1930s included locomotive driving wheels and buckets for earthmoving equipment, and it produced many parts for tanks during the Second World War.[6]

Tubes were another influential steel product of the twentieth century. Tubes could be made by spinning cast iron, a process invented by a Brazilian in 1914. A plant using this process began operation in 1922 at the historic works of the Stanton Iron Company in Nottinghamshire.[7] Only concrete pipes are now made on the site, but the communal buildings of the mid-twentieth century – the training centre, the exhibition centre and the sports club – remain as evidence of a particular phase of industrial culture. The alternative process is seamless tubemaking, in which a solid billet of steel is pierced and elongated in a special form of rolling mill, developed by the brothers Mannesmann in Germany in 1891. The most significant British plant was built in 1934 at Corby, a Northamptonshire village where there had been some small blast furnaces. New furnaces were built, together with a plant producing steel by the basic Bessemer process, which suited local ores, together with a tube mill, in 1999 the only surviving part of the plant. About one-third of the 4,000 employed there migrated from declining steelworking communities in Lanarkshire, and Corby retains a Scottish culture. Corby was designated a new town in 1949, when it was difficult to attract labour to the steelworks, and many of its buildings are characteristic of the first generation of new towns. The furnaces and

steel plant closed in 1980 and the tube mill subsequently used steel from Teesside. Much of the land quarried in the first half of the twentieth century was left unfit for agricultural use, and Corby retains amid its modern industrial estates many marks of its steelmaking past: quarry faces, remnants of mineral railways, and large areas flattened for freight terminals or the storage of motorcars.[8]

One of the most rapid revolutions in the iron and steel industry was in the manufacture of tinplate – steel (or previously wrought iron), rolled thin, and coated with tin for use in the canning industry. In 1900 tinplate was made, largely by manual labour, in scores of small works, chiefly in the western part of the South Wales coalfield. Just one example remains of an old-style tinplate works with its equipment, at Kidwelly (SN 421078), while groups of buildings used for tinplate production survive at the Old Castle works, Llanelli, and at Treforest. In 1938 coils of thin steel for tinplate manufacture began to be produced in a continuous strip mill at Ebbw Vale, but the principal change came after the Second World War when electrolytic tinning was combined with continuing rolling, first at Ebbw Vale, then at Trostre (SS 5299). Subsequently, new methods of coating have been developed, producing, for example, the steel sheeting used to clad many late twentieth-century factory buildings.

2.6
The rolling mill complex at Trostre in 1995.

(Crown copyright. Royal Commission on the Ancient and Historical Monuments of Wales)

Stainless steel, more than any other form of the metal, can be regarded as a characteristic twentieth-century material. The making of special steels of all kinds has for centuries been centred on Sheffield. Carbon steels, used particularly for cutting tools, were being made in 1900 by the crucible process, which dated from 1740, and the even older cementation process. Both continued on a diminishing scale until mid-century. The older processes were replaced by electric arc and electric induction furnaces. During the First World War a 400-metre-long melting shop, 'the anvil of South Yorkshire', was built at the Templeborough works, Rotherham (SK 4595), to house fourteen open-hearth furnaces; it was rebuilt in the 1960s to accommodate six 100-ton electric arc furnaces. There were proposals in 1999 to make it the centrepiece of a multimedia extravaganza about steelmaking. The two most important varieties of special steel being made in 1900 were tungsten alloy steel, developed in the 1860s by R. F. Mushet (1811–91), and manganese steel, perfected by Sir Robert Hadfield (1858–1940) in 1887. Stainless steel, initially an alloy of iron with carbon and chromium, was the invention of Harry Brearley (1871–1948) in 1913. It transformed the chemical and food industries, proved an attractive building material, and appeared in most homes in washing machines, work surfaces, razor blades, cutlery and the Scandinavian-style dishes and plates fashionable in the 1960s, the best British examples of which were made from 1928 by the Old Hall Tableware Company at unfashionable Bloxwich, near Walsall.

Concrete

Concrete, like steel, was just gaining acceptance as a constructional material in 1900. The first generation of significant concrete buildings used the constructional technology of reinforcement with steel developed by the Frenchman François Hennebique, and energetically promoted in Britain by Louis Gustave Mouchel. It is generally accepted that the first reinforced concrete industrial building in Britain was Weaver's Mill in Swansea, built

by Mouchel in 1893 and demolished in the early 1980s. Three small sections of the concrete frame are preserved, one outside the supermarket which now occupies the site, and one in the Science Museum, London. The CWS warehouse on the riverside at Newcastle upon Tyne, dating from 1897–1900, is probably the oldest surviving concrete-framed building in Britain.

2.7
The use of concrete in buildings – the Boots factory at Beeston, designed by Sir Owen Williams, in the course of construction, completed in 1932.

(Crown copyright. NMR)

2.8
Probably the oldest surviving concrete-framed building in Britain – the Co-operative Wholesale Society's warehouse of 1897–1900 on the Quayside at Newcastle upon Tyne.

(Crown copyright. NMR)

The CWS was also responsible for the construction, in 1901, of a concrete grain silo at its nearby mill complex at Dunston and, in 1909, for the adjacent concrete Renaissance-style soap works. In 1903 in Detroit Julius Kahn, brother of the architect Albert Kahn, perfected a new system of concrete construction which was brought to Britain by a third brother, Moritz Kahn, who established the Truscon Company in London in 1907. In 1912–13 Truscon established a works at Trafford Park, and by 1920 claimed that 90 per cent of multi-storey factories being built in Britain were of reinforced concrete construction, stressing that the Kahn system enabled the installation of large windows, admitting daylight, the cheapest and healthiest illuminant, and that users of the system included the Ford Motor Company, responsible for 'the new gospel of Mass Production'. Outstanding examples of buildings using the system include the Arrol-Johnston motorcar factory in Dumfries of 1912–13 (*see Chapter 5*) and the Birmingham Small Arms (BSA) factory in Munitions Road, Birmingham. Concrete frames were employed in many twentieth-century factories, notably in the frontage buildings of the 'by-pass' factories of the inter-war period designed by Wallis, Gilbert & Partners.[9] The mid-century possibilities of concrete construction are best displayed at the research station of the Cement & Concrete Association at Wexham, Buckinghamshire (TO 9983), which includes a variety of structures built between 1947 and the early 1970s. The motorways built in the last four decades of the twentieth century utilised concrete technology on a large scale, both in bridges (*see Chapter 9*) and in complex intersections like Almondbury, where the M5 meets the M4, or Spaghetti Junction in Birmingham.

Many unheroic applications of concrete were equally important. Concrete platform frames and fence panels were essential in the creation of the Southern Electric railway network, and elegant bus stop posts incorporating panels where timetables could be displayed were erected all over London by the London Passenger Transport Board (*see Chapter 9*). Concrete was extensively used in Royal Ordnance Factories during the Second World War (*see Chapter 7*), and in the prefabs of the late 1940s and the tower blocks of the 1950s and 1960s (*see Chapter 8*). Public utilities used many concrete pipes, spun from 1920 at the Stanton Ironworks, which in 1937 began to manufacture concrete standards for street lights. Main-line railway track came to be carried on concrete sleepers after the Second World War.

Aluminium

Aluminium had a chequered history in the twentieth century. Aluminium alloys were essential in aircraft construction from the 1930s, and remain so today. In other spheres the metal has faced, and sometimes lost to, competition from steel or plastics. At Shipshaw, northern Quebec, adjacent to one of the elegant hydro-electric power stations which provide power for the colossal aluminium plant at Jonquière, stands a 150m (490ft) span aluminium bridge, completed in 1950. The development of steel technology is perhaps the most potent reason for the failure of engineers to use aluminium for large-scale construction, but there is a small British parallel. In 1955 an aluminium version of the cantilevered lifting accommo-dation bridge, characteristic of the southern section of the Oxford Canal, was built at Hardwick, Banbury (SP 455417), by apprentices from the nearby Northern Aluminium works. The lane which it carried became in due course a link road to a motorway, and the bridge was removed and now spans the Somerset Coal Canal at its junction with the Kennet and Avon Canal, south of Bath (ST 784625). By the 1990s aluminium was no longer used for tubes containing toothpaste and similar substances, nor for inexpensive household utensils.

2.9
The CWS soapworks at Dunston, Gateshead, designed by L. G. Ekins and built in 1909. The building was used for most of its working life as a leather-processing plant.

(Photo: Barrie Trinder)

Aluminium is reduced, by processes which demand large quantities of electric power, from alumina (pure aluminium oxide), which in turn is made from bauxite. All of the first aluminium smelters in Britain were linked with hydro-electric power stations in the highland zone; at Foyers (NH 4921) from 1894 until 1967; in Scotland, at Kinlochleven (NN 1861) from 1907 and Lochaber (NX 9270) from 1929; and at Dolgarrog (SH 7766) in North Wales from 1908 until 1944. From 1917 the Scottish works, all built by the British Aluminium Company, drew their alumina from a plant at Burntisland in Fife. During the Second World War an attempt was made to produce aluminium in South Wales. An alumina plant was established at Newport, and reduction works built at Rheola, near Neath, and Port Tennant, Swansea. The former (SO 840040) was designed to generate its own power using anthracite duff, but the power units had not been delivered from Switzerland by the outbreak of the Second World War, and it was dependent on the National Grid for its electricity. It ceased work in 1943, was converted to a strip mill in 1948, and is now used by Consolidated Coal plc for packing coal. Two ranges of north-lit sheds, with steel lattice frames, stand with other buildings in what was once a Georgian ornamental park, whose lodge house still stands, together with a range of exotic trees, on the far side of the property. An aluminium wire works was established in 1946 in the former smelter at Port Tennant (SN 6793). In the mid-1960s the government, concerned that only a small proportion of the aluminium used in Britain was home produced, encouraged the construction of new smelters at Holyhead (SH 2681), drawing power from the nearby Wylfa nuclear power station (SH 3593), at Blyth (NZ 2989), using power from a coal-fired station, and at Invergordon (NH 7168) in the Scottish Highlands. The latter produced metal for only ten years after its commissioning in 1971.

Other works were concerned with the production of aluminium alloys, and with the shaping of the metal by rolling, casting or extrusion into forms in which it could be usefully employed. The oldest rolling mill in Britain, renowned for the quality of its finish, and employing hand-rolling techniques as late as the 1950s, was at Milton, Stoke-on-Trent. Its operations were transferred to Rheola in a

2.10
Turbines in the power house at the hydro-electric generating station at Kinlochleven in 1991.

(Crown copyright. Royal Commission on the Ancient and Historical Monuments of Scotland)

perceptively analysed move in 1964. The first aluminium extrusion press was installed at Milton in 1911. In 1955 it was still working at the BAC plant at Warrington, which had been built in 1913–14, and also operated rolling mills. The Northern Aluminium Company's factory at Banbury (opened in 1931 and renowned for its role in the manufacture of aircraft during the Second World War) had a rolling mill and an extrusion plant, and also made aluminium 'paste' for use in paint. The function of the plant has changed, but its principal buildings remain. Several important plants were built during the Second World War, including a BAC rolling mill at Falkirk, making alloy sheets for aircraft, completed in 1944, a foundry at Friar Park, West Bromwich, which made castings for aero engines, and an extrusion plant at Kitts Green, Birmingham.[10]

2.11
The cell room in the aluminium smelting works at Kinlochleven in 1991.

(Crown copyright. Royal Commission on the Ancient and Historical Monuments of Scotland)

Asbestos

The reputation of asbestos soared and diminished in the twentieth century. It was 'the miracle among minerals' in 1945, but the carcinogenic nature of blue asbestos fibres reduced its applications. Asbestos was already used in Britain in 1900, chiefly for fire-resistant packing materials and for insulation. Soon afterwards asbestos cement was introduced from Austria. British Uralite, a mixture of asbestos from the Ural Mountains with 30 per cent chalk, and a gelatinous silica used as a binder, enjoyed a spell of popularity as a building material in the first decade of the century. Several firms began to make building materials before the First World War, among them Bell's United Asbestos at Harefield, Middlesex (TQ 050888), from 1909, Turner Bros at Trafford Park from 1912 and British Fibro-Cement at Erith from 1913. Corrugated asbestos sheets were first made in Britain in 1924 at the Turner factory at Widnes, and the first asbestos cement pipes in 1927. Other important works were at Spotland in Rochdale, declared in 1947 to be 'the home of the asbestos industry', at Huddersfield, at Washington, Co Durham, and at Slough, where Bells United Asbestos produced partitions for Royal Navy ships in the Second World War. Asbestos was and is used in many factories making brakes and clutches for motor vehicles, belting and insulating materials.

The greatest emotions were aroused by the use of asbestos as a cheap building material, as wall panels or roofing tiles. A study of the Cornish coast in 1930 commented: 'One material produced in this country on a large scale since the war, namely, asbestos, had done more than any other to encourage "jerry building" and the disfigurement of rural England.' A bandstand in a park at Swindon was perhaps the most prestigious asbestos structure.[11]

Synthetic fibres

Synthetic fibres are also a characteristic twentieth-century material, although traditional branches of the textile industry continued to grow in the early years of the century, and the steel-framed, concrete-floored cotton mills, some powered by the last generation of mill engines and some by electricity, built between 1900 and 1914, some even in the 1920s, in Bolton, Oldham and Stockport, are among the most impressive of British industrial buildings. Several small factories were already producing rayon or artificial silk by 1900. The British Viscose Company had begun production at Erith in 1892, the New Artificial Silk Company at Wolston, Coventry, in 1898, and United Cellulo Silk Spinners at Great Yarmouth before 1900. C. F. Cross (1855–1935) of British Viscose had developed, at Kew, and patented a process for making viscose rayon, which in 1904 was purchased by Courtaulds Ltd, the Essex silk manufacturers. Courtaulds became one of the dominant companies in the textile industry, with over 2,000 employees in Coventry by 1914, the majority of them women. Most buildings of the Courtauld factory (1905) at Foleshill, Coventry (SP 349831), remained in the 1990s, although they had been adapted to other uses. The filament was produced from wood pulp in single-storey buildings with high ceilings, to mitigate the danger from the highly unstable carbon disulphide (CS_2) used in the process, whereas the multi-storey spinning mills are much like buildings used for that purpose in other branches of the textile industry. Rayon was made by various firms at thirty-six different factories between 1905 and 1939, but sixteen had closed by the latter date. Rayon stockings first went on sale in Britain in 1912.[12]

Cellulose acetate, another source of rayon, which was also used as the dope applied to canvas on the first generations of aircraft, was not made in commercial quantities in Britain before the First World War. In 1916, with government prompting, the Swiss Cellonite Company and its British partners established British Cellulose (British Celanese, from 1923), which constructed a large plant to make dope at Spondon, Derbyshire (SK 4034). It began production in 1917, and after the Armistice went over to make acetate rayon yarn, first produced there in 1921, and rayon garments. The company was taken over by Courtaulds in 1957.[13]

Nylon, the invention of the Du Pont Corporation chemist Wallace Hume Carothers (1896–1937) in 1928, first appeared in Britain during the Second World War – as parachutes, and the stockings that were traditional gift of American servicemen to British females. Manufacturing rights in Britain were acquired from 1 January 1940 by British Nylon Spinners, a company jointly owned by ICI and Courtaulds, which used a shell-filling factory of the First World War at Lockhurst Lane, Coventry, and part of an ICI paint factory at Stowmarket (TM 0558) to supply government demands. After the Second World War British Nylon Spinners built a new factory at Pontypool (SO 310023), on the site of the hutments of the Glascoed Royal Ordnance Factory (see Chapter 7), which began production in 1946. Designed by Sir Percy Thomas & Son, this elegant and imposing monument to a confident period in British industrial history is set among lawns and trees, and remains in production operated by the Du Pont Corporation, although some buildings are now tenemented. The company also opened a plant at Doncaster in 1955, in a factory previously used by another company for synthetic-fibre production, and in 1959 took over a former aircraft factory at Hucclecote, Gloucestershire (SO 8816) (see Chapter 7), that was still occupied by Du Pont in 1999.[14] There have been many subsequent developments in synthetic fibres, some of which are reflected in structures, like the single-storey building (c. 1960) across the road from William Strutt's historic North Mill at Belper (SK 346479), constructed to accommodate one process in the manufacture of Crimplene, which was used for a time for cotton spinning before it passed out of the textile industry.

Plastics

Plastics form another group of largely despised new materials of the twentieth century. A plastic is a substance that contains, at some stage, long chains of carbon atoms or arrangements of carbon atoms with oxygen, hydrogen and other atoms that can be shaped without losing their cohesion, and that keep the new forms given to them. Natural plastics like shellac and bitumen, a form of which was once used for the black stoppers on beer bottles, have a long history. One of the principal plastics manufactured in 1900 was Xylonite, a development of celluloid, first demonstrated in 1862 by Sir Alexander Parkes (1813–90). The British Xylonite Company, established in 1877, employed about 2,000 people in east London and Suffolk by 1914. Casein plastics, made by hardening milk solids with formaldehyde, were introduced in Britain in 1907 and known as 'Erinoid', since the solids were derived from Irish milk. Casein knitting needles were produced on a large scale during the First World War for the knitting of soldiers' comforts.[15]

Plastics technology advanced rapidly during the First World War, as demonstrated by the building of the cellulose acetate factory at Spondon (see above). In the inter-war period most of the compounds used in the production of plastics were derived from compounds distilled from coal, but from the late 1940s oil refineries became the principal source. Bakelite, patented in 1907 by the Belgian Leo Baekeland (1863–1944), and made from phenol formaldehyde, usually produced by distilling coal tar, was widely used in motorcars, electrical insulation and radio sets. The main producers were the Damard Lacquer Company and Mouldrite Ltd of Croydon, but ICI constructed a new bakelite plant at Huddersfield in 1929, and took a 51 per cent holding in Mouldrite in 1933. Bakelite was always brown in colour, but from 1928 the British Cyanide Company began to use urea-formaldehyde to create 'Beetle' plastics in bright greens, yellows and oranges. A more water-resistant plastic, melamine, that could be used for coating tables or work surfaces in kitchens, became available in 1938. A very different kind of plastic, Cellophane, was increasingly used in packaging, and in 1935–37 the British Cellophane Company, a joint venture of La Cellophane SA and Courtaulds, built an extensive plant at Bridgwater, Somerset (ST 310382), which employed 3,000 people.

Two important new plastics were developed in Britain in the inter-war period. Perspex, or acrylic sheet, was patented by ICI scientists in 1932, and was used for aircraft windows and cockpit canopies in the Second World War, and for numerous other purposes in peacetime. Polythene was discovered by other ICI researchers in 1933, and its production began at Wallerscote, Northwich (SJ 645748), in 1939.

It was used during the Second World War as an insulator. Polythene buckets and bowls for household use were first put on sale in 1948. Polyvinyl chloride (PVC) and polystyrene were developed in Germany and the United States, and became familiar in Britain after the Second World War.[16]

If plastics are despised, they were used nevertheless for the manufacture of some key twentieth-century artefacts: the 78 rpm gramophone record, made of shellac until 1933, the 33 rpm (long-playing) vinyl record introduced in 1952, audio- and video-cassettes, sunglasses, the polypropylene chair designed by Robin Day for Hille in 1962 (of which over 12 million were made), the blow-moulded bottle for washing-up liquid or soft drinks introduced in the 1970s, and the wheely-bin. Plastic artefacts have been comprehensively analysed by Mossman and are displayed in the Science Museum. The University of Wolverhampton organised an exhibition of 'Plastics Antiques' as early as 1977. Most raw materials are the products of the largest chemical plants and oil refineries, and are distributed in tankers or in drums to be moulded, extruded, laminated or blown, in more than 4,200 plastics factories, most of them unremarkable buildings on industrial estates in all parts of Britain. The philosopher Roland Barthes found particular pleasure in the plant used in such factories: 'A dream machine, all tuby and rectangular ... effortlessly converts a heap of greenish crystals into bright fluted trays to put on a dressing table'.[17]

New ways with traditional materials

Traditional materials were manipulated in new ways during the twentieth century. Wood appeared as chipboard, plywood and hardboard, and wood pulp was the raw material for synthetic fibres and other products. The manufacture of glass in its many and varied forms was transformed. Vitrolite, the coloured glass much used in shop fascias, was produced by the British Vitrolite Company, established in 1932. The production of flat glass was revolutionised by the float glass process developed in the 1950s by Pilkingtons of St Helens.[18] The manufacture of rubber, paper, copper and ceramics has similarly been transformed. Space expeditions depend on ceramic tiles, produced by one of the oldest technologies known to man. Manipulative techniques have also changed. In 1900 hydraulic transmission systems were bulky and used mainly in ports and railway yards, and in big cities for operating passenger lifts and presses for textiles. Developments in the Second World War stimulated their widespread use, often in miniaturised forms, in motorcars, earthmoving equipment, pit props and, above all, in aircraft.[19] The computer, the origins of which go back to the work of Charles Babbage (1792–1871) in the 1830s, was energetically developed during the Second World War in association with the application of radar technology and code-breaking, and received further impetus during the arms race in the Cold War. Its influence by the late 1990s seemed all-pervasive (see Chapter 6).

Notes and references

1 D. Burn, The Steel Industry 1939–59: A Study in Competition and Planning, Cambridge: Cambridge University Press, 1961, p. 645.

2 M. Stratton, 'New Materials for a New Age: Steel and Concrete Construction in the North of England, 1860–1939', Industrial Archaeology Review, 1999, vol. 21, pp. 5–24.

3 Steel Times, The British Steel Corporation Teesside Division, London: Fuel & Metallurgical Journals, 1979; P. Riden and J. G. Owen, British Blast Furnace Statistics 1790–1980, Cardiff: Merton Priory Press, 1995.

4 W. K. V. Gale, Iron and Steel, London: Longman, 1969, pp. 84–111.

5 A full photographic record and documentation of the last phases of operation at Ravenscraig was made by the Royal Commission on the Ancient and Historical Monuments of Scotland, and is held at the Commission's Edinburgh headquarters.

6 P. Collins and B. Trinder, The Archives of F. H. Lloyd & Co. of James Bridge, Wednesbury: A Report Compiled for the Triplex Lloyd Group, Telford: Ironbridge Institute, 1988.

7   V. Lewis, *The Iron Dale*, Nottingham: Stanton
    Ironworks Co., 1959.

8   Sir F. Scopes, *The Development of Corby Works*, Corby:
    Steward & Lloyd, 1968; Burn, op. cit., pp. 254–60.

9   Stratton, op. cit., pp. 14–22.

10 The Times, *British War Production 1939–45*, London:
    The Times, 1945; British Aluminium Company,
    *The History of the British Aluminium Co. Ltd
    1894–1955*, London: British Aluminium Company,
    1955; A. Fox, *The Milton Plan*, London: Institute of
    Personnel Management, 1965; G. G. Drummond,
    The Invergordon Smelter: A Case Study in Management,
    London: Hutchinson Benham, 1977.

11 The Times, op. cit., p.15; A. D. King, *The Bungalow:
    The Production of a Global Culture*, London: Routledge
    & Kegan Paul, 1984, pp. 171, 185. We are also
    grateful to John McGuinness for information
    on the Harefield site.

12 K. Hudson, *Food, Clothes and Shelter: Twentieth
    Century Industrial Archaeology*, London: John Baker,
    1978, pp. 58–75.

13 D. C. Coleman, 'War Demand and Industrial
    Supply: The "Dope Scandal" 1915–19', in *Myth,
    History and the Industrial Revolution*, London:
    Hambledon, 1991, pp. 39–51; C. Chant, *Science,
    Technology and Everyday Life 1870–1950*, London:
    Routledge, 1989, pp. 121–2.

14 Royal Institute of British Architects, *Industrial
    Architecture: The Book of the Exhibition and Conference*,
    London: RIBA, 1949, pp. 6–9; W. J. Reader, *Imperial
    Chemical Industries: A History*, vol. 2, Oxford: Oxford
    University Press, 1975, pp. 374–5.

15 Reader, op. cit., pp. 340–4; K. Hudson, *The
    Archaeology of the Consumer Society*, London:
    Heinemann, 1983, pp. 36–7.

16 S. Mossman, *Early Plastics: Perspectives 1850–1950*,
    Leicester: Leicester University Press, 1994; Reader,
    op. cit., pp. 354–6; Chant, op. cit., pp. 118–27.

17 Quoted in P. Barker, *Arts in Society*, London:
    Fontana, 1977, p. 8.

18 T. C. Barker, *The Glassmakers: Pilkingtons – the Rise
    of an International Company 1826–1976*, London:
    Weidenfeld & Nicolson, 1977.

19 L. T. C. Rolt, *The Dowty Story*, London: Newman
    Neame, 1962.

Chapter three

Industrial revolutions

energy

Sources of energy are the foundation of any industrial economy, and energy has been the most politicised of twentieth-century industries. Cabinets were involved in labour disputes in coal mining in 1912, 1921, 1926, 1972, 1974 and, most notoriously, in 1984–85. The British government held a substantial share in the Anglo-Persian Oil Company (Anglo-Iranian from 1935, British Petroleum from 1954) from 1914 until 1990. Followers of one political dogma in the 1940s nationalised the coal, gas and electricity industries, perceiving them to be the commanding heights of the economy, and politicians of a different persuasion privatised them in the 1980s. The building of nuclear power stations in the 1950s was part of the British nuclear weapons programme. The 'dash for gas' of the 1990s has a political as well as an economic rationale, and in 1999 was the subject of discussion between the highest echelons of the British and United States governments. Energy is of all industries the most exposed to international pressures. Its costs are determined as much by exchange rates as by wages and the price of equipment. The industry changed dramatically in the last forty years, particularly in the last fifteen years of the century. Imports of coal from Australia and Latin America, the extraction of oil and gas from offshore wells, attempts by electricity companies to supply domestic consumers with gas and by gas companies to supply electricity – all would have appeared bizarre before 1960. The purpose of this chapter is to examine the archaeological evidence for the changes in the industry.

Coal

Home-produced coal was the principal source of energy in Britain during most of the twentieth century. The growth of coal mining was one of the mainsprings of the Industrial Revolution of the eighteenth century, and coal mining was a huge industry in 1900, providing over 200 million tonnes of coal a year that served as fuel for the steam engines which provided the power for most factories, for the locomotives which worked the country's railways, for the merchant marine and fishing fleets, for gas production, and increasingly for the generation of electricity. In 1900 over 40 million tonnes of coal was exported, a total which increased by more than 50 per cent before the outbreak of the First World War.[1] Many of the country's transport resources – railways, coastal shipping, canals and, in Yorkshire, rivers – were devoted to the movement of coal. The mining labour force was increasing in this period, reaching a peak in excess of 1.13 million, almost all of them male, and comprising about 9 per cent of Britain's male labour force, in the early months of 1914. Coal mining was one of the principal battlegrounds of the class war. While much of the archaeological record of coal mining has disappeared, enough remains to substantially enhance our understanding of its past.

Coal mining was a very local industry. While there was much in the common experience of working underground that was universal, the cultures of particular coalfields, even of particular villages, were powerful, distinctive, and usually historically determined. They might be shaped by isolation, by struggles to create communal institutions, by housing of mean quality, although some miners' houses represented the best practice of their time, and by an inheritance of industrial relations that was often bitter at a national level but sometimes amicable within the region or the village. A group of sociologists noted in 1957:

> Coal mining unites all its workers in an experience of dark and dirty conditions and of industrial battles unknown in other industries; it also divides them through highly developed local customs.... The colliers' skill, seniority and even knowledge of technical terms are often not transferable from pit to pit, let alone village to village, district to district or coalfield to coalfield.[2]

The varied inheritances of the British coalfields were expressed in their archaeology. At Seaham, Sunderland, in South Shields and Blyth, coal was conveyed to the coast in railway wagons which discharged their loads, through bottom doors from staithes or coal drops, into the holds of ships. At Cardiff, Newport, Penarth, Barry and Swansea, box-like wagons were lifted on hoists from which their coal was dropped on to waiting vessels. These methods were historically determined, the development of two systems of primitive railways whose seventeenth-century origins on Tyneside and in Shropshire were described in 1970 by Dr Michael Lewis.[3]

Coal mining was an industry of small units. In 1913 there were 2,648 active collieries, owned by 1,439 companies, an average of less than two each. Some owners were conglomerates like the Butterley Company or the Lilleshall Company which also operated blast furnaces, brickyards and engineering works. Some had been formed to exploit aristocratic resources – two of the twenty largest coal companies were the estates, respectively, of Lord Lambton and Lord Londonderry. Some, like Ocean Coal or Powell Duffryn in South Wales, were the result of entrepreneurial flair. Many companies were modest concerns, supplying local domestic markets and providing fuel for a brickworks or limekiln. Only 70 pits employed more than 2,000 miners. The average pit had just over 400 workers and produced a little less than 11,000 tonnes of coal a year. In the whole of the United Kingdom only 408 conveyers were used, and only 652 cutting machines, the latter producing about 8 per cent of the nation's total output. The coal industry in 1914 was, according to Professor Supple, in the travails of decline, caused principally by excess capacity, and the level of output of 1913, more than 287 million tonnes, was never equalled.[4]

Production of coal slumped during the First World War but rose in the early 1920s, the highest annual output of the decade being 267 million tonnes, in 1924. The General Strike and the prolonged miners' strike which followed it reduced both output and manpower. The highest annual output of the 1930s was 240 million tonnes, in 1937. The labour force in the industry declined in the early part of the First World War, but by the end of the war it again exceeded a million and with the return of miners from the forces reached an all-time peak of 1.25 million in 1920. There were still more than a million miners when the General Strike began on 3 May 1926, but thereafter numbers declined steadily to little more than 0.75 million in 1936, and less than 0.70 million at the end of the Second World War. Conventional wisdom sees the inter-war period as one of acute depression in the mining industry. Many of the communities where unemployment rates were highest – Merthyr, Jarrow, Maryport,

Motherwell – were in the coalfields. A minister reported to the cabinet in 1942 that 'Miners tend to see present events in the light of the history of their own community and of their experience as miners.... The last thirty years, seen through the miners' eyes, have been a period of decline and frustration.' An American observer in 1944 noted 'the bad feeling and antagonism which pervade the industry and which manifests itself in low morale, non-cooperation and indifference ...'. A senior civil servant wrote in 1945 of 'so much disorder and dilapidation on the surface ... the appearance of the colliery premises can hardly fail to affect the psychology of all employed at the mine'.[5]

Yet not all pits were disordered and not all were in depressed regions. Parts of the coal industry, like the anthracite region of south-west Wales, the Dukeries and the Doncaster region, were prosperous. The number of collieries fell from 2,507 in 1924 to 1,870 in 1938. The mean annual production, which in 1924 was slightly less than before the First World War, rose to around 12,000 tonnes. Electric power was increasingly used in pits in the early years of the century. The proportion of coal cut mechanically rose from 28 per cent in 1929 to 59 per cent in 1938, while 917 cutting machines were responsible for 61 per cent of the national output. The rate of mechanisation highlighted regional differences. By 1939, 91 per cent of the coal produced in Northumberland and 92 per cent of that mined in north Staffordshire was cut mechanically, but only 42 per cent of that in Co Durham and 26 per cent of that in South Wales.[6]

Archaeological studies can identify both the archaic and the progressive tendencies within the coal industry. The discipline can contribute only marginally to an understanding of working conditions underground, through the study of tools and machines allied to oral and documentary evidence. The museums at Caphouse (SE 254165), near Wakefield, and Big Pit, Blaenavon (SO 238087), provide an unforgettable sense of the darkness, dampness and creaking roofs common to all underground workings, but convey nothing of the dust, noise and urgency of producing coal. The history of the flameproof diesel locomotive, used underground in many twentieth-century mines, is portrayed in the industrial museum in Leeds, the city in which it was developed and

manufactured. Photographic evidence from the period before nationalisation is rare, although there is a short but impressive sequence showing coal being cut by hand in Humphrey Jennings's *Diary for Timothy*, and more recent underground scenes are portrayed in the photographs by John Cornwell held by the Royal Commissions. The best archaeological record of surface workings, the photographs taken by the late George Watkins held by the National Monuments Record, provides evidence of how much very ancient plant was being used well into the twentieth century. An American engineer, wandering through the Blists Hill mines of the Madeley Wood Company at Ironbridge in 1912, was astonished to find Newcomen and Heslop steam engines of the late eighteenth century still working,[7] while the Newcomen engine of 1795, preserved at Elsecar (SE 390002), Yorkshire, operated regularly until 1923, and the vertical winding engine of 1855 displayed at Beamish (NZ 216544) ceased work only in 1963.

Surface buildings of the twentieth century are preserved in the three national mining museums – at Caphouse in England, Blaenavon's Big Pit in Wales and the Lady Victoria Colliery (NT 334637), Newtongrange, in Scotland – at the scheduled site at Chatterley Whitfield (SJ 848512), and at smaller mining museums at Ashington (NZ 2787) and Cefn Coed (SN 785035). Some other twentieth-century surface buildings are conserved, and others have been adapted to new uses. In the Wyre Forest coalfield in south Shropshire the pithead baths, mechanical workshops and weighbridge house remain of Highley Colliery (SO 754842), all dating from the inter-war period and all in industrial use, while a variety of small brick buildings mark the site of Billingsley Colliery (SO 715843), most of them probably dating from the time when the pit was taken over by Powell Duffryn in 1908. Many of the buildings of Llanbradach Colliery in the Rhymney Valley (ST 148897), including a power hall, a winding house, workshops and a fan house, remain in use for other purposes, chiefly for scrapping cars.[8] Similar buildings from collieries closed before 1970 can be found in most British coalfields – those in Lancashire are detailed by Rees.[9] In the 1970s some sites of closed collieries, like that at Bersham in North Wales, were consciously developed as

3.1 *(left)*
Billingsley Colliery,
Shropshire, in the early
years of the twentieth
century.

*(Photo: Shropshire Records
& Research Unit)*

3.2 *(right)*
A surviving early-
twentieth-century
building at Billingsley
Colliery, Shropshire,
photographed in 1994.

(Photo: Barrie Trinder)

industrial estates, but in the last twenty years of the century most mine structures were erased from the landscape when production ceased.

The most impressive monuments of collieries are headstocks.[10] Some were still being built of pitch pine in 1900, but the use of timber for new structures was forbidden in 1911. Many wooden headstocks remained in use, the last in South Wales operating until 1964, and one survives at Caphouse. Most surviving twentieth-century headstocks are of steel. In South Wales there are examples at the Big Pit and Cefn Coed museums, and at Penallta. The headstock of Bersham Colliery in North Wales (SJ 311492) remains, as do other surface buildings. There are other steel examples at Snibston Discovery Park (SK 417144) near Coalville and at Caphouse, and a monumental structure at Lady Victoria.

Some of the engines used for working winding gear also survive. They include a Grant Richie engine of 1900 at Ashington, a Worsley Mesnes engine of 1914 at Chatterley

Whitfield, and a 3,300hp Yates & Thom engine of 1912, which stands adjacent to a soaring steel headstock, at Astley Green Colliery, Tyldesley (SD 705001). An electric winding house in the Arts and Crafts style of about 1912 survives, alongside the pithead baths, at Ledstone Luck Colliery in Yorkhire (SE 429307). One of the best groupings of colliery buildings is at Pleasley, Nottinghamshire (SK 499644), where two steam engines, a Worsley Mesnes of 1874 and a Markhams of 1924, which worked until 1986, remain alongside a steel headframe of 1901, another frame encased in brick and concrete and the tall chimney of the demolished boiler house. Another is at Navigation Colliery, Crumlin (ST 211989), a 'flagship' colliery built in a stylish manner between 1907 and 1911, where two winding-engine houses, a pumping-engine house, stores, offices and workshops could still be seen in 1999.

The most productive collieries in South Wales through the twentieth century were sunk soon after 1900, and many had central power

3.3
The headstocks at
Chatterley Whitfield
Colliery, Stoke-on-Trent,
photographed in 1993.

(Crown copyright. NMR)

halls, accommodating steam engines for winding, pumping, working ventilation fans, compressors and underground haulage engines, and generating electricity, all supplied with steam from a central boiler plant. An outstanding example survives at Penallta (ST 139958), alongside two steel headstocks. It was built by the Powell Duffryn Steam Coal Company in 1906–9. Other examples remain at Lower Navigation, Abersychan (SO 254040), and Ynysmaerdy near Llantrisant (ST 033840).

Demands for particular qualities of coal became increasingly stringent during the twentieth century, and screens (to separate lumps of coal by size) and washeries were built at most collieries. The complexities of the systems by which coal was taken from the tops of shafts to screening and washing plants are illustrated at Lady Victoria Colliery, and the screens building remains at Caphouse. Most washeries were substantial buildings designed to absorb vibration, with steel frames, infilled with brick panels. The process of treating coal on the surface was analysed at Taff Merthyr Colliery (ST 103990) by Malaws, who devised a series of six drawings which, combined with text and flow diagrams, explain the principal stages in the process:

▌ raising coal and stone extraction

▌ preliminary coal grading

▌ raw coal treatment (washing)

▌ fines separation

▌ preparation of treated coal for market

▌ shale disposal and reclamation of surface water.[11]

Electric power was increasingly being employed in collieries in the first decade of the twentieth century, after the Mines Inspectorate in 1904 approved the use of alternating current underground. A generating station built in 1906 to provide power for local mines remains at Philadelphia, Co Durham (NZ 335520), flanked by streets named 'Voltage Terrace' and 'Electric Crescent'.

Soon after 1900 in Germany it became compulsory for colliery owners to provide baths for their miners, but such installations were rare in Britain before 1920. A baths built in 1908 at Stanley Colliery, Derbyshire, was

3.4
The pithead baths built at Ifton Colliery, St Martin's, Shropshire, adapted to new uses after the pit closed in 1967. Photographed in 1992.

(Photo: Barrie Trinder)

3.5
Interior of the pithead baths at Caphouse Colliery, Yorkshire.

(Crown copyright. NMR)

designed more for leisure than for ablutions. The first building in which miners were able to bathe and dress in their non-working clothes was built in 1913 at Gibfield Colliery, Coalpit Lane, Atherton, Lancashire (SK 665033). It was used in 1999 as a motor-repair workshop, but green and cream tiles still line its interior and glass bricks remain in its walls. The first pithead baths in South Wales was installed at Deep Navigation, Treharris (ST 1097), in 1916. The Mining Industry Act of 1920 provided for the creation of a Miners' Welfare Fund, sustained by a penny per ton levy on output, which provided money for, among other things, baths at pits where miners agreed to sustain part of the cost. Over 100 had been built by 1930, but the pace of building in the ensuing decade was slow, and in 1945 there were only 348 built with money from the fund, and 16 provided by the colliery companies themselves, while there were still more than 1,600 pits. Many pithead baths were built in brick in a distinctive Modernist style derived from the work of the Dutch architect Willem Marinus Dudok (*see Chapter 9*). The same fund provided for the social centres called Miners' Welfares to be found in many colliery villages. A considerable number survive from the inter-war period, together with some from the years after nationalisation. There are examples at Elemore (NZ 355454) and Easington in Co Durham, built respectively in 1933 and 1937, and at Alveley (SO 753842) and Ifton (SJ 323363) in Shropshire.

'This colliery is now managed by the National Coal Board on behalf of the people', read a widely displayed poster dated 1 January 1947. In some respects much changed with nationalisation. Best practices were extended to pits where they had hitherto been unknown, and the standardisation which came with public ownership has left an archaeological record. Concrete towers carrying Koepe winders were erected at many pits, together with washeries, and workshops for maintaining the complex cutting machines and conveyors used underground, while pithead baths, canteens and medical centres were constructed at every colliery of consequence. The larger new pits had the characteristic features of 'flagship' industrial buildings. The colliery at Maerdy (SS 963000) in the Rhondda Fach was rebuilt in 1948–53, and linked underground to mines in the adjacent Rhondda Fawr. It was regarded as 'the first material realisation of the bright new future planned by the newly nationalised coal industry'. Its winding houses were in a Modernist style with continuously glazed walls. Three gardeners were employed to keep up its grounds in its early years. It was closed in 1990 and, in spite of protests, demolished immediately. Nationalisation brought few changes to the industrial relations of a conservative industry. It was remarked of Featherstone in 1957: 'The old system of industrial relations characterised by a fundamental conflict between management and men is kept healthily functioning.'[12] The class war was not fought daily in every colliery, nor even in every coalfield. Archaeological study can now add but little to our knowledge of mining technology, but the evidence of both alienation and deference which may be observed in mining communities can increase understanding of the industry's tortuous social history.

A colliery was only part of a landscape of extraction, much of which remains when mining operations cease. The fabric of mining communities is likely to be the most enduring monument of Britain's principal source of energy during three centuries. There is a popular archetype of the pit village: an assemblage of terraces, with a few shops, a school and possibly an institute, one or more places of worship, and open space, some of it pitches for football, rugby league or rugby union, and some of it garden ground, punctuated by pigsties, pigeon crees and improvised shelters for forcing the growth of rhubarb or leeks. The majority of miners did not live in this kind of community. Many lived in urban surroundings alongside those who followed other working-class occupations in towns like Sunderland, Bradford, Barnsley, Wakefield, Burnley, Wigan, St Helens, Dudley, Coventry, West Bromwich and Kilmarnock. At the outbreak of the First World War about 12 per cent of miners, of whom about half were in Northumberland and Co Durham, lived in company accommodation.

In the South Wales valleys there were few company houses, and in the early twentieth century as many as 20 per cent of miners there were owner-occupiers. The linear settlements of the Valleys are distinctive mining communities, their principal features being chapels, many of them with separate doors for men and women, and institutes, like the vast building of 1895 which dominates the town of Blaenavon (SO 250089), or that of 1917 from Oakdale, a new village established in 1907 by the Tredegar Iron & Coal Company, which has been removed to the Welsh Folk Museum at St Fagan's.[13] The many houses built in the Valleys in the early years of the twentieth century followed largely traditional patterns, although Oakdale was built in the Garden City style, and the settlement built in the 1920s for Taff Merthyr Colliery (ST 106980) was actually called Garden Village.

Some of the saddest communities in the region are those constructed in the post-war era on the lower sides of the mountains. The archaeology of the Valleys highlights many paradoxes. Socialist idealism and deference may both be observed in the centre of Tredegar (SO 141088), where a building named after Aneurin Bevan stands alongside a cast-iron clock tower erected in memory of the Duke of Wellington. In Senghenydd (ST 114911) another clock tower, at the centre of the shopping area, commemorates the dead of two world wars, relatively small numbers in comparison with the 439 who died in an explosion in the Universal Colliery on 14 October 1913 and the 81 who perished in a similar accident in 1907, commemorated by an inscription beneath a miniature colliery headstock almost hidden behind trees near the Westside Primary School.

D. H. Lawrence (1885–1930) described a characteristic English coalfield landscape around 1900 in the opening paragraphs of *Sons and Lovers*:

> down the valleys of the brooks from Selby and Nuttall, new mines were sunk until soon there were six pits working ... six mines like black studs on the countryside, linked by a loop of fine chain, the railway.... The Bottoms consisted of six blocks of miners' dwellings, two rows of three, like the dots on a blank-six domino, and twelve houses in a block.... The houses themselves were very decent ... between the rows, between the long lines of ash pits, went the alley, where the children played and the women gossiped and the men smoked ...[14]

Long terraces of this kind had been built in the nineteenth century and continued to be built in mining villages until 1914. The Ashington Coal Company in Northumberland, owner of some of the most productive new pits in the north-east, which happened to be at a distance from existing communities, built 837 houses between 1898 and 1904, and had completed more than 2,500 by 1914.[15] After the First World War new and potentially productive pits were being sunk in places which for the most part, like Ashington, were remote from older settlements, particularly in Nottinghamshire and south Yorkshire.

Seven new pits were sunk in the Dukeries region of Nottinghamshire in the 1920s, by companies like Staveley, Butterley and Bolsover, which were involved in ironmaking and brickmaking, as well as in mining.[16] The government gave guarantees for much of the investment in the pits, and in 1922 the principal companies became partners in the Industrial Housing Association, which, with support from the Public Works Loans Board, built 12,000 houses in the region between 1922 and 1928. The colliery villages of the Dukeries and south Yorkshire were designed as 'model' communities, with the intention that, for a century or more, they would accommodate stable communities in which mining would be the hereditary male occupation. Curiously, plotland-like shanties built to accommodate sinkers and builders remained in occupation at Bilsthorpe until the 1960s, and at Ollerton until 1978.

The Dukeries coalfield is one of the best places to observe the archaeology of the twentieth-century coal industry. The village of Whaley Thornes (SK 5371), near Langwith, represents the industry in the early years of the century: grim terraces named after Sir John French, Earl Jellicoe and Robert Falcon Scott, which suggests that they were built about 1914. Many of the houses were boarded up in 1999. The site of the colliery is now a children's playground, alongside the Robin Hood Line, the re-animated railway from Nottingham to Worksop, beyond which a landscaped slag heap covers the site of a munitions factory of the First World War. To the north and east lie the villages built for the pits sunk in the 1920s: Ollerton (SK 6668) with Boughton (SK 6768), Edwinstowe (SK 6266), Clipstone (SK 5862), Bilsthorpe (SK 6460), Blidworth (SK 5956) and Harworth (SK 6291) with Bircotes (SK 6291). The collieries at Clipstone, Edwinstowe (Thoresby) and Harworth were still working in 1999. The housing in most exceeds the standards of all but the best local authority dwellings in other parts of Britain. Houses in pairs or groups of four are set along curving avenues, with spacious gardens. The villages mark a break with the past. As the *New Statesman* remarked in 1927:

> Here in the open land of the Dukeries, the narrow meanness of the owners has been discarded. They have shown a wider outlook – a realization of the social importance of cleanliness, of the social value of comfort, which marks an almost revolutionary tendency in their class.

Clipstone has a huge central green with an Anglican church at one end and a Methodist chapel at the other. The stubs walls around the green, made by pouring concrete on blast-furnace slag held in place by narrow-gauge rails, indicate the links of the builders, the Bolsover Company, with the iron trade, and suggest that building materials were distributed across the site by rail, as on the larger LCC estates (see Chapter 8). Some houses at Blidworth have elements of cosmetic timber framing, or pantiled roofs. Timber framing, bow windows, polychrome brickwork and pantiles are in evidence at Bircotes. Tiles laid flat form the lintels of ground-floor windows at Edwinstowe and Clipstone. The cinema at Edwinstowe is half-timbered with a high, thin central gable and is now an antiques centre, while that at Bilsthorpe serves as a late-opening store, that at Ollerton as a bingo hall and those at Harworth and Blidworth as snooker clubs. Miners' Welfare buildings remain prominent, as do public houses, that at Bilsthorpe still bearing the name Stanton Arms, having been built by the Stanton–Staveley company. The Dukeries landscape abounds in paradox. The sites of collieries closed since the strike of 1984–85, including Bevercotes (SK 6973), the show-piece colliery of public ownership in Nottinghamshire, have been completely cleared, although some buildings of the colliery at Blidworth, which closed before the strike, have been adapted to new uses. Waste heaps are being disguised by large-scale earthmoving operations. Some have been returned to agricultural use but that at Ollerton was scheduled in 1999 to become the Sherwood Energy Village. The greatest irony is to be observed at Edwinstowe, where on the edge of the village, almost within sight of the working colliery, is the Sherwood Forest Visitor Centre, where tourists are entertained by costumed outlaws with bows and arrows, together with a fairground, a youth hostel, a craft centre and a business innovation centre.

The landscape of the twentieth-century Yorkshire coalfield shows similar patterns. Around Doncaster most of the pit villages follow a similar style, derived from the Garden City movement, to those of the nearby Dukeries. New Rossington (SK 6098), only 4 miles from the most northerly of the Dukeries pits at Harworth, is built around a pit sunk in 1916 and still working in 1999. The village is built in two groups of concentric circles around greens, on one of which stands a large Romanesque church. The presence of Pentecostal and Roman Catholic as well as Methodist buildings illustrates the diversity of religious practice in the community. A colossal public house – the Royal – stands on Queen Mary Road. Immediately north of Doncaster is Bentley (SE 5606), where the pit, sunk in 1905–8, was closed in 1994, closure being followed by the demolition, a year later, of the innovative Hennebique concrete screens. The 'New Village' is in the familiar Garden City style, although there are two much earlier terraces adjacent to the site of the pit, and Bentley West End (SK 5605), nearer the centre of Doncaster and on the opposite side of the A19, is a grid of rather grim terraces which belong in spirit if not in date to the nineteenth century. About 2 miles further north lies Woodlands (SE 5307), part of the village of Adwick le Street, built to accommodate miners from Brodsworth Main Colliery, its pit sunk in 1905–8, then the largest coal mine in Britain. Woodlands was designed by Percy Houfton, winner of the Cheap Cottages Competition at Letchworth (see Chapter 8). The lay-out is spacious and the architectural detailing carefully contrived. Some faintly flared gables, reflecting the outline of the winning cottage at Letchworth, can be observed. On the A638 road stands an extraordinary building, adorned with white faience, in which a picture house – as cinemas were often called – is twinned with a billiard hall. Similar settlements surround other collieries in the Doncaster area, like those at Dinnington, Maltby and Armthorpe. Older colliery villages to the east, towards Barnsley, consist chiefly of brick terraces, while about 14 miles north-west of Doncaster lies Featherstone (SE 4120), an archetypal mining settlement of the old style, which grew rapidly in the first half of the twentieth century, about 1,000 houses being erected between 1891 and 1911, and a further 1,300 between 1911 and 1953. Featherstone was 'Ashton', the subject of the sociological study Coal Is Our Life, published in 1957 when its population was around 14,000, of whom 3,700 were active miners. It was celebrated for its rugby league club and its brass bands, as the place where soldiers shot two miners during an industrial dispute in

and the communal buildings include an International Miners' Mission opened in 1928 (TR 240527). The 10-mile-long aerial ropeway which linked Tilmanstone Colliery (TR 298505) with Dover harbour was one of the longest in Britain.[18]

The coal industry's influence is pervasive in many parts of Britain. In Bedwellty Park, Tredegar (SO 142085), are displayed two colossal lumps of coal, one of 15 tonnes, cut for the Great Exhibition of 1851, but not taken to the Crystal Palace because it was too heavy, and one of 2 tonnes which featured in the Festival of Britain in London in 1951. When collieries closed, their waste tips were usually rounded down or even taken away. Some, like that at Aberfan which slipped and killed more than 100 children in 1966, were positively dangerous. J. B. Priestley, looking in 1936 at the perpetual fires which smothered the village of Shotton, Co Durham, with sulphurous fumes, pertinently remarked: 'I hope it will always be there, not as a smoking tip, but as a monument to remind happier and healthier men of England's old industrial greatness.'[19] Two surviving waste tips in North Wales form an archaeological record which raises many questions. The tip at Bersham (SJ 312482), a growling presence about the A483, is a monument to the enterprise which enabled one of the owners of Erddigg, the nearby National Trust house, to spend endless time fantasising about his servants, while that at Gresford (SJ 335538) broods over the scene of an underground explosion which killed more than 260 miners in 1934.

1893, and for its reputation in Yorkshire as 'a dirty hole'. Many of the worst of its nineteenth-century houses, occupied in the 1950s, have been cleared, and mining in the immediate vicinity has ceased, but Featherstone is still a settlement of long, unadorned terraces, unmistakably a mining village, if a large one.[17]

The most purely twentieth-century coalfield is in Kent, a series of enclaves in the Garden of England reputedly populated by political militants. The sinking of pit-shafts began just before the First World War, and large-scale operations began in the 1920s at Snowdown (TR 247513) and Betteshanger (TR 338529). Both collieries worked until the 1980s, when winding-engine houses and workshops were left standing after closure, together with a pithead baths at Betteshanger. There are also earthworks at Cobham (TW 687695), where coal was extracted for a short time in the 1950s, workshops at Stonehill (TR 271456), where operations were abandoned in 1920, and a winding-engine house and workshops at Guilford (TR 281469), where a full set of colliery buildings was constructed in 1919–20, but abandoned in 1921. The colliery village at Betteshanger resembles in many respects those in the Dukeries and in the Doncaster region, with semi-detached houses facing inwards on a circular road which incorporates the institutes and pithead baths. The 'New Town' of Aylesham, built from 1927 to accommodate miners from Snowdown, is also in Garden City style. The original 250 houses are of five basic types, some being of concrete construction,

3.6
The billiard hall and cinema building at Woodlands near Doncaster, Yorkshire.

(Photo: Barrie Trinder)

3.7
Garden City-style housing of the 1920s at Whinney Lane, Boughton, in the Dukeries coalfield, Nottinghamshire.

(Photo: Barrie Trinder)

All coal mined on a significant scale in Britain before the Second World War came from shaft mines, or adits. Open-cast working was confined to shallow excavations by miners seeking for domestic fuel during lengthy strikes or in the depths of the Depression. Nevertheless, large-scale open-cast (or strip) mining was well established in Germany and the United States, and the demands of the war led to the beginning of operations in Britain. Surface extraction of coal began in November 1941. One of the first sites to be worked was at Blaenavon, where local people remember the role of the Canadian Army, which, as in other parts of the country, made available diamond drills and men skilled in working them. Much of the earthmoving machinery employed was imported from the United States. Open-cast workings produced 1.3 million tonnes of coal in 1942, rising to 8.65 million tonnes in 1944. The official historian concluded that they had played 'a vital part in balancing the national coal budget during the later years of the war'.[20] Open-cast operations continued under public ownership, and by the 1960s were sometimes seen, as in the development of the new town of Telford, as restoring utility to land made derelict by earlier generations of shaft mining. Only the workings at Blaenavon (SO 2310) are wholly unrestored, and they are being retained in that state. Later schemes have left few recognisable traces in the landscape other than new field boundaries, marked by fences rather than hedges, running across artificial slopes.

Coal was the principal source of feedstocks for the chemical industry before the Second World War. Plants for the destructive distillation of coal, in which coke for iron and steel works or other forms of smokeless fuel were produced, together with recovered by-products, consumed nearly 20 million tonnes a year immediately before 1914, and reached a peak of 21.9 million tonnes in 1937. Before 1914 much of the coke used in British iron and steel works was made in beehive ovens in which the tar was wasted. During the First World War, when the need for explosives, picric acid (trinitrophenol) and TNT (trinitrotoluene) required huge quantities of benzene, toluene and phenol, while the cordite used as a propellant required acetone, new plants were constructed in which the by-products could be recovered. Such plants typically had unloading facilities for coal wagons, concrete bunkers and screens in which coal and coke were stored, graded and blended, and by-product plants which consisted partly of brick buildings and partly of mazes of pipes and stills. The number of beehive oven plants was declining even before 1914, but fell sharply during the war. Significantly, the industry's professional body, the Coke Oven Managers' Association, was formed in 1915.

Wharncliffe Silkstone works, notable for its timber-loading bunkers, was one of the by-product recovery plants which pre-dated the First World War. It opened in 1898 and was closed in 1957. Royston works (SK 375122) had 180 ovens by 1901, became the Monckton Coal & Chemical Company in the 1920s, and was renewed by British Coal in 1976–79. One of the plants built with financial assistance from the Ministry of Munitions was at Orgreave Colliery near Rotherham (SK 423874), where three banks of beehive ovens were replaced by 108 Koppers Regenerative ovens which were intended to provide coke for the United Steels Company and benzol for the Ministry, although the plant was not commissioned until 1920. Subsequently tar from other ovens operated by United Steels was processed at Orgreave, which passed into the ownership of British Steel and was the scene of ferocious confrontations during the miners' strike in 1984. Orgreave Colliery and the coke ovens closed in 1990 and most of the structures were demolished. Avenue works at Wingerworth, Chesterfield (SK 394675), was

3.8
The Avenue coke works and by-product recovery plant near Chesterfield, photographed in 1993.

(Crown copyright. NMR)

built by the National Coal Board in 1956, on the site of a colliery closed in the 1930s, to produce domestic smokeless fuel and to process tar from other coking plants in the region. The core of the plant was its 106 American-designed ovens. The plant closed in the mid-1990s. There were numerous other works in the productive east midlands and Yorkshire coalfields, as well as several in South Wales. One of the largest in Yorkshire was the Manvers Main Company, whose works were threaded by passenger trains between York and Sheffield. South Yorkshire Chemical Works at Parkgate, Rotherham, was established in 1919, and in due course came under the ownership of the NCB. The Coalite Company, established in 1917, made smokeless fuels by a low-temperature process, and recovered by-products, at plants at Barugh, near Barnsley, opened in 1928, at Askern, near Doncaster, which operated from 1928 to 1986, at Bolsover (SK 462715), opened in 1936 and still operating in 1999, and at Grimethorpe, opened in 1965. The landscape at Mountain Ash, south of Aberdare, was dominated until the 1980s by a colossal coke plant. Numerous iron and steel works had their own coke ovens, and sent the crude tar recovered to larger specialised processing plants.

Except for the coke ovens within the integrated steel complexes at Port Talbot, Llanwern, Scunthorpe and Redcar, the only by-product recovery plants remaining in use in 1999 were the coke works at Cwm, Llantwit Fardre (ST 066861), opened in 1957, where the two wooden cooling towers are listed, the works at Royston, and Coalite's works, near Chesterfield. Sites of by-product recovery plants are toxic, difficult to understand, and aesthetically unappealing. None is likely to be preserved, although some token structures may be retained; and, since productive seams of coal remained unexploited beneath many of them, open-cast mining may be an appropriate means of bringing the land back into use. The photographic record made by the Royal Commissions will be one of the few records of an unlovely but important twentieth-century industry.[21]

In the nineteenth century the usual way of using coal to produce mechanical power was through the agency of a steam engine. Electric power was already in use by 1900 – the first cotton mill in Lancashire to be powered by

3.9
The water-pumping engines at Kempton Park, London, built in 1929 by Worthington Simpson, an indication that steam-engine construction continued during the inter-war period.

(Water Authorities Association)

electricity was Falcon Mill, Bolton, built between 1904 and 1908, and the first Yorkshire woollen mill was Beck's Mill at Keighley, in 1907.[22] Nevertheless, steam engines continued to be built until the 1930s, but it is impossible to be certain when the last new steam engine was installed. Nor can a precise date be given for the last regular use of a steam engine. In 1980 there were certainly steam engines in daily use, at collieries and in pumping water and sewage, but it is doubtful that any remained working in 1990. George Watkins (1904–89), a boilerman in a Bristol gasworks, toured Britain by motorcycle from the 1930s until 1979 recording steam engines working at 1,525 sites. The significance of steam power installed in the twentieth century is shown by a selection of his records:

1045. Dorman Long, Britannia Works, Teesside. Cogging mill: Davey engine of 1904; No. 1 mill, Davey engine of 1905; No. 2 mill, Galloway engine, undated.

1075. Colne Valley Spinning Co., Titanic Mill, Westwood, Linthwaite. 800 hp tandem engine by Mark Shaw of Milnthorpe, designed by J & E Wood, made after J & E Wood closed. Started April 1912. 20 ropes drive machinery on six floors from an 18 ft flywheel.

1114. Fox Bros., Uffcolme Mill, Cullompton. Pollett 320 hp horizontal cross compound engine, with flywheel drive to floors, 1910.

1329. Sutton Manor Colliery. No. 1 shaft, Fraser Chalmers cross compound engine of 1907; No. 2 shaft, Yates & Thom cross compound engines of 1914.

1345. Walton Colliery, West Yorkshire. No. 2 shaft, Robey engine of 1922–23.

1355. Colditch Colliery, Newcastle, Staffs. No. 1 shaft, engine by Worsley Menes, 1918; No. 2 shaft also engine by Worsley Mesnes, 1917, moved from Victoria Pit.

1389. Taylor's Forge, Trafford Park. Tyre mill, with steam hammers and 3-stage tyre rolling mill, installed c 1923, rolling mill worked by three 3-cylinder compound engines by Lamberton of Coatbridge.

Gas

For about two-thirds of the twentieth century coal was destructively distilled to produce gas and coke in almost every town in Britain. Up to 20 per cent of the coal used in Britain was delivered to gasworks by rail, or sometimes by canal, or even by horse and cart or lorry from the nearest railhead. Gas, having been stored in a gasholder, was piped to local commercial and domestic consumers. Coke from a small works would be carted away for local use, but that from large works might go by rail to distant markets. Ammoniacal liquors, iron sulphate and tar would be despatched, by means appropriate to the quantities produced, to various branches of the chemical industry. Teachers of chemistry found visits to gasworks useful demonstrations of the practical value of their subject, and sufferers from chest complaints were advised that they would find spells in retort houses therapeutic. Nevertheless, most people shunned gasworks, not least because of the pervasive unappealing aroma of hydrogen sulphide. There were many more than 1,000 gasworks in 1900, of which some

were parts of large industrial concerns, the biggest of them the Gas Light & Coke Company in London, while others were exemplars of all that was best in municipal enterprise, like the gas undertaking in Birmingham, whose offices now form part of the city's art gallery, and some tiny concerns in places as small as Rhayader, St Just and Raunds. A slow process of consolidation took place during the inter-war period, as larger companies took over smaller ones, closed their works and laid connecting pipes to supply their networks. The Gas Act of 1948, which nationalised the industry, brought 1,050 works under the control of twelve Area Gas Boards.

Production of gas trebled between 1875 and 1920, largely due to the increased domestic consumption stimulated by a series of innovations: the penny-in-the-slot meter introduced in 1889 made it possible for poorer families to use gas; the Potterton water heater was introduced in 1905, columnar radiants in gas fires in 1905, grid radiants in 1925 and the Ascot water heater in 1932.[23]

There were several important innovations in the technology of gas production at the larger works in the 1920s and 1930s. Klönne-type gasholders were introduced from Germany, and mechanical handling systems, coke oven style retorts and tower purifiers were built at some works. After nationalisation the industry was speedily rationalised. The number of gasworks fell to 428 by 1960, while the mains system, enabling the networks radiating from closed works to be fed from others, was steadily extended. Consumption doubled between 1948 and 1973.

The gas industry was transformed in the eighteen years between 1959 and 1977. The first stage of the transformation, which can be traced in the landscape in several places, was a search for new sources of gas. 'Lurgi' plants using a new process to obtain gas from coal were built at Westfield in Fife, and at Coleshill, Warwickshire, the latter working from 1962 until 1969. At Avonmouth a plant was commissioned in 1965 to make gas using the Gas Recycle Hydrogeneration (GRH) method, derived from an ICI process to produce hydrogen-rich gas for ammonia production using light distillate feedstock (ldf) as its raw material. A similar Catalytic Rich Gas process was installed in 1964 at the gasworks at Bromley by Bow, and another, which began to operate in 1967, on the

site of the old corporation gasworks at Tipton
(SO 958923) in the Black Country. The South
Eastern Gas Board began to take supplies from
the BP oil refinery on the Isle of Grain in
1959–60, and refinery gas from Stanlow was
fed to North Western Gas at Ellesmere Port.
Another works, at Bicester (SP 585218),
Oxfordshire, blended naphtha, delivered by rail
from Parkeston Quay, but had a very short life,
receiving its first tankers on 19 February 1968
and its last on 13 June 1969. A jetty for natural
gas tanker ships was constructed on Canvey
Island (TQ 7783) and took its first delivery of
gas from the United States, brought by the
Methane Pioneer, in 1959. In 1963 supplies from
America were augmented by gas from North
Africa delivered by the *Methane Progress* and
Methane Princess, and a trunk pipeline was
constructed, with several branches, to take
gas from Canvey Island to Leeds.[24]

With hindsight, these developments prove
to have been short-term expedients. In 1959,
while the Canvey Island terminal was being
built, a huge field of natural gas was discovered
near Groningen in The Netherlands, suggesting
the probability that there would also be gas in
the British portion of the North Sea. Exploration
licences were issued in 1964, gas was struck
at West Sole, 40 miles off the mouth of the
Humber, in 1965, and the first gas was piped
ashore at Easington, Humberside, in 1967, and
fed through a pipeline to Totley, near Sheffield,
into the trunk line from Canvey Island to Leeds.
Conversion of domestic appliances to burn
natural gas began in the same year at Burton
upon Trent, and was completed in 1977. The
trunk pipeline network was extended and
totalled over 3,000 miles by 1980, and was
controlled from a centre at Hinckley opened
in 1970. Compressor stations, powered by noisy
gas turbines which had to be sound-proofed,
were built at Ambergate, Alrewas, King's Lynn,
Peterborough and Churchover in 1970–72.
More were added as the pipeline network was
extended. Only eighty-one gasworks remained
in 1973, and all, including the non-traditional

works of the 1960s, had closed by 1977. The key points in the gas supply industry came to be the shore terminals for offshore gas at Canvey Island, at Easington, Humberside (TA 4019), at Bacton (TG 3233), Norfolk, opened in 1967–68, at Theddlethorpe (TF 4688), opened in 1972–73, and at St Fergus (TNK 1054), near Peterhead, opened in 1975–76. Barrow-in-Furness, serving the South Morecambe field, opened in 1985, and Point of Ayr (SJ 1285), serving the Liverpool Bay platforms, in 1995. The gas industry was privatised in 1986, and its constituent companies no longer confine themselves to the supply of gas (*see below*).[25]

The key features of the gas industry are its networks, national and local. Much is hidden, and is revealed only by signs at the edges of fields indicating the existence of pipelines, by radio masts which control the system, by a few buildings sealed off from the world, and when holes are dug in roads. Gas technology, and the artefacts used in local networks and in the home, are well illustrated in the Museum of Science and Industry in Manchester. The principal surviving features from the pre-1967 industry that remained in use for thirty years or so were about 600 gasholders, some of them of pre-1900 date, in which natural gas was stored as readily as was coal gas. All are due to be replaced by high-pressure storage in underground pipes by 2004. Some examples –

like those at King's Cross and Battersea – which have become accepted parts of industrial landscapes, are likely to be retained, but in 1999 the Klönne-type gas holder at Swan Village, West Bromwich (SO 991923), was demolished, fulfilling the wishes of local residents, although it was all that remained of an historic gasworks, and had been one of the most prominent features of the Black Country landscape. The preserved gasworks at Fakenham (TF 218298) and Biggar (NT 042379) illustrate effectively the technology employed at gasworks in small towns, but can convey nothing of the atmosphere and activity of such large works as Swan Village, or Saltley in Birmingham, Kensal Green in north London or East Greenwich in south London. The largest of all gasworks was begun in 1869–70 at Becton (TQ 4481), located near the eastern terminus of the Docklands Light Railway. A ski slope descends the waste tip.

Onshore oil

The most significant inland sources of oil in Britain were the shales mined in West Lothian and adjacent parts of Fife. A substantial industry around Bathgate, Burntisland and the present-day New Town of Livingston was created by James ('Paraffin') Young (1811–83), who realised that oil could be distilled from the shales by heating them in retorts, producing vapours which could be refined to produce ammonium sulphate, naphtha, lamp oil, candles, motor spirit and the black tar used in road building. Spent shales were deposited on tips called 'bings', which are the most obvious archaeological evidence of the industry, but some was used in road building. The industry passed its peak of production, 3.5 million tonnes, in 1913, when it was already showing signs of decline. There were nine oil shale works in 1900 but only seven by 1910. All were amalgamated in 1918 as Scottish Oils, which two years later became part of the Anglo-Persian company, later BP. In 1933, 13 mines supplied shale to five crude oil plants, which in turn supplied their products to a central refinery at Pumpherstone (NT 0769). Petrol was supplied in the inter-war period

3.11
Battersea Power Station, as completed in 1933, before the addition of two chimneys after the Second World War.

(Crown copyright. NMR)

Industrial revolutions:

through pumps whose signs bore the curiously ambiguous inscription 'Scotch'. The scale of production diminished after the Second World War, and shale mining ceased in 1962. The industry's history is illustrated by displays of artefacts at the Almond Valley Country Park (NT 088686).[26]

A petroleum well was successfully drilled at Hardstoft, near Mansfield, in 1919, and during the 1920s and 1930s prospecting took place in several parts of Britain. The east midlands oilfield, principally in Nottinghamshire, but with some wells in adjacent parts of Leicestershire, Yorkshire and Lincolnshire, was energetically developed during the Second World War, production rising from 16,000 tonnes in 1940 to 112,000 tonnes in 1943. Daily trainloads of crude oil were despatched for refining at Pumpherstone (*see above*).[27] Oil is still extracted in the region, and unattended 'nodding donkeys' can be seen in operation at wells like those at Bothamsall (SK 6773) and Plungar (SK 7633). The significance of the industry is best appreciated at the Duke's Wood nature reserve (SK 6860), where several 'nodding donkeys' have been preserved in clearings, and there is a monument to the oilmen from Oklahoma who developed Nottinghamshire oil production during the Second World War. Subsequently, oilfields were developed in Dorset, at Wytch Farm and Kimmeridge, despatching crude oil by train to Llandarcy.

3.12
A working oil well at Bothamsell, Nottinghamshire, photographed in 1999.

(Photo: Barrie Trinder)

Oil from overseas

The modern internationally focused oil industry dates its beginnings from the discovery of crude oil at Titusville, Pennsylvania, in 1859, although there were parallel contemporary developments in eastern Europe. In the nineteenth century the industry had been concerned chiefly with oil for lighting, but by 1900 the demand for motor spirit was evident, as was the use of oil as fuel for ships. The Admiralty decided in 1914 that the ships of the Royal Navy should burn oil rather than coal, and in consequence Winston Churchill gained parliamentary sanction for the government to take a substantial share in the fledgling Anglo-Persian Oil Company.

The value of imports of petroleum did not exceed £6.7 million in the first decade of the century, but soared to £63.9 million in 1918. During the 1920s and 1930s most oil for the British market was partially refined near to the wells from which it was raised: Iranian oil at Abadan, oil from Iraq at Haifa in Palestine. The resultant 'topped' crudes, from which the lighter fractions had been removed, were treated at refineries in Britain, like those established by Shell in the 1920s at Shellhaven (TQ 7582) in the Thames Estuary, Stanlow (SJ 4375) on Merseyside and Ardrossan (NS 2242) on the Clyde Estuary. The Anglo-Iranian company decided in 1916 to establish a refinery on a site near Swansea that was named Llandarcy (SS 7195) after William Knox D'Arcy (1849–1917), the acknowledged founder of the company. Government support was withdrawn in 1917, but the refinery began operation in 1922. It was followed in 1924 by a refinery at Grangemouth (NS 9581) on the Forth. Both dealt with crude oil, but their output was modest in the inter-war period. The refinery at Fawley (SU 4404) on Southampton Water dates from 1921, when a site of 670 acres (270ha) was purchased by the Atlantic, Gulf & West Indies Oil Company. It was operated by Standard Oil from 1927. Other refineries of the period included one at Ellesmere Port built by Lobitos, and the Manchester refinery at Barton on the edge of Trafford Park, which was intended chiefly for lubricating oils, as was a plant at Stanlow built for the RAF by Shell, which began to operate in July 1940.

3.13
A spherical storage tank for highly inflammable materials at the Shellhaven oil refinery, Essex.

(Crown copyright. NMR)

The oil industry was transformed during the Second World War. The government decided to draw supplies for the United Kingdom from the Americas, rather than to bring oil from the Middle East round the Cape of Good Hope, and from April 1941 to suspend the refining of crude oil in Britain. One of the most significant developments of the wartime years was the establishment of a network of oil pipelines. The first, from Avonmouth to Aldermaston in Berkshire, was built in 1941, and was extended to Hamble and Fawley in 1942. By July of the following year a 'box' had been created across midland England, with lines from Stanlow to Misterton near Doncaster, thence to Sandy in

Cambridgeshire, Aldermaston, Avonmouth, and back to Stanlow. Branches ran from Sandy through Saffron Walden to Hetherset, for the supply of East Anglian air bases, and Thameshaven, and from Aldermaston to the Isle of Grain and to the Kent coast. A pipeline was also established from coast to coast across the central lowlands of Scotland. Storage facilities for oil products were established at Gloucester, Worcester, Stourport and Aldermaston. The best known of the pipelines, PLUTO (pipe line under the ocean), which conveyed oil to continental Europe from pumping stations at Dungeness and Sandown in the Isle of Wight, was ironically the least successful, supplying less than 8 per cent of the oil sent to the Continent between D-Day and the conclusion of the war.[28] The pipeline network was steadily extended in peacetime, and by 1999 most oil products were despatched from refineries to regional distribution depots by that means.

The refining side of the industry was transformed after the Second World War, partly because of increased demand for motor fuel but also because refineries became the principal suppliers of feedstocks to the chemical industry (*see Chapter 6*). Stanlow was enlarged and absorbed several other oil installations in the Ellesmere Port area. In 1998 it was processing 12 million tonnes of crude oil annually. Shell's other UK refinery, at Shellhaven, processed 4 million tonnes a year. Fawley was enlarged after Esso bought an additional 3,000 acres (1,200ha) of land in 1949, and a chemical plant was added in 1958. A new deep-water terminal was built in 1959 for tankers supplying Grangemouth at Finnart (NS 1888) on Loch Long. British Petroleum, as the company was known from 1954, opened a new refinery on the Isle of Grain (TQ 8675) in 1952. The refinery at Milford Haven (SR 9304), on the shores of one of Britain's most spacious deep-water harbours, opened in the 1960s. Behind their high-security fences, oil refineries appear secretive, so much so that they are scarcely mentioned in the standard works on industrial archaeology. The processes carried out are unspectacular – the only sign of activity in a catalytic cracker is likely to be an occasional wisp of steam. They have none of the drama of a rolling mill or a car assembly plant. They nevertheless deserve attention, for they were some of the most

3.14
The oil-fired power station at Connah's Quay, North Wales, photographed in 1996, the year it came into operation.

(Crown copyright. Royal Commission on the Ancient and Historical Monuments of Wales)

3.15
Electrical equipment in production and awaiting despatch at the factory of English Electric Ltd at Preston, Lancashire, *c.* 1900.

(Crown copyright. NMR)

important industrial sites established during the twentieth century, the sources of many of the products which shape our daily lives.

Offshore oil

The oil industry, like the gas industry, underwent many changes following the 1960s discovery of oil and gas in the British section of the North Sea, and in 1974 in Morecambe Bay, but unlike the nationalised British Gas, the great oil companies operated in international markets. The products of the North Sea fields could be processed in existing refineries, or exported. The archaeology of offshore oil and gas production can be divided into three segments. First, there are the platforms themselves, rarely seen by people outside the industry, but remarkable engineering achievements nevertheless. In due course platforms cease to work, and many will be disposed of during the first decades of the twenty-first century. Second, there are shore establishments where oil and gas are processed. The gas terminals are those noted above. The principal oil terminal is at Sullom Voe. A plant at Mossmorran in Scotland extracts ethane, propane and butane from natural gas liquids supplied by pipeline from St Fergus, and

despatches them, again by pipeline, for shipment from a terminal at Braefoot Bay. Third, there are those fishing ports of eastern England and Scotland, particularly Lowestoft, Great Yarmouth and Aberdeen, which were transformed into base camps for the North Sea operations. Many buildings and wharves once used for processing fish or equipping fishing boats now supply the little ships which ply to and from the oil platforms. The bustling atmosphere of herring fishing at Great Yarmouth and Lowestoft in the early years of the twentieth century is vividly conveyed in the compilation *Chasing the Herring*, produced by the East Anglian Film Archive. The atmosphere of the Scottish industry of the same period is magnificently captured in the photographs of George Washington Wilson.[29] The archaeological study of the buildings and landscapes of the east coast ports raises many questions about the way a second industry, internationally orientated and practising state-of-the-art technology, has grown from the discarded chrysalis of an industry which expanded with the steam trawler and the railway network, provided cheap nourishment for a wide segment of the population in the first half of the twentieth century, and went into decline with the disappearance of the herring from the North Sea. On the west coast, Blackpool provides the base from which the platforms in Morecambe Bay are serviced, while Hornby Dock in Liverpool serves the same purpose for the Liverpool Bay platforms.

Electricity

Electric power was a pervasive factor in twentieth-century society. It provided power for energy-hungry industrial processes. It made it possible for each machine to have its own, appropriately sized source of power rather than to be worked by a belt from line shafting. It removed the necessity to bring coal into a factory to provide heat for boilers. It created a huge demand for domestic appliances. It provided an indispensable foundation for telecommunications and computers. In the closing years of the century it was used to replicate daylight in unfenestrated factories.

3.16

A hoarding at Totley, near Sheffield, attempting to persuade householders to take an electricity supply from the city corporation, *c.* 1929.

(University of Reading: Museum of English Rural Life, CPRE Collection)

The artefacts of the industry, features of the local infrastructure and the domestic appliances of different periods are best studied in the Museum of Science and Industry in Manchester. There is a rich legacy of buildings and landscapes associated with electricity generation from the first half of the twentieth century. It is likely that there will be relatively few accessible monuments to the industry which flourished between 1950 and 1990. The scale of power generation increased in the 1950s and 1960s, creating monster installations, some of which had already reached the ends of their working lives by 1999. Redundant coal-burning stations have largely disappeared. Nuclear stations will remain, in effect, for ever.

Four principal types of power station were being built around 1900, and considerable numbers of buildings from each type survive.[30] Most used steam engines, steam turbines or gas engines to drive generators.

First, there were wholly private operations, for which that at Cragside, home of Sir William Armstrong, had set the pattern in 1878. One of the best early-twentieth-century examples is at Ashton Mill, Northamptonshire, an historic building whose corn-milling machinery was removed in 1900 to be replaced by water turbines by Gilkes of Kendal, generators made by the Electric Power Company of Wolverhampton in 1900, Blackstone oil engines which provided an alternative source of power, and pumps by Glenfield & Kennedy of Kilmarnock. From the mill water and electric power were supplied water to a large estate. The building in 1999 was the centre of the National Dragonfly Museum.

Second, there were power stations which provided power for particular industrial concerns, like that at Philadelphia, Co Durham (*see above*). Important examples are the buildings erected for generating plant at Longford Mills, Gloucestershire, in 1904, at Thwaite putty mills, Leeds, in 1901–5, at Dee Mills, Chester, in 1913, and at the carriage works in York built by North Eastern Railway around 1914.

Third, there were generating plants built to provide power for street tramways or electric railways. Kelham Island Museum in Sheffield is located in one such building, constructed in 1899. In Melbourne Street, Newcastle upon Tyne (NZ 253642), stands a building of 1901 which was both generating station and management headquarters for the city's tramways. It is ornately detailed, with high-quality wooden panelling and stained glass, and has served as a bus garage since the 1960s. The generating station in Park Road, Stalybridge (SJ 953981), built in 1903 to provide power for the Stalybridge, Hyde, Mossley and Dukinfield Transport & Electricity Board, is equally impressive. A substantial building in Accrington-style brick, immaculately laid, and topped with a brick dome, it is now used as a parts depot by an international machine tool company, and while the machinery has all been removed, the tiled interior remains little disturbed. The generating station in Old Woolwich Road (TQ 389781), built in 1902–10 to provide power for LCC's tramways, was one of the first to have a steel frame. It still generates electricity to power the Underground's trains. Another very old power station operating in 1999 was that built at Lots Road, Chelsea, in 1902–4 to provide power for trains on the District Line. All the plant was situated in a single building, 139.5m x 53.9m in extent x 43.1m high, and the station was reckoned the third largest in the world at the time of its completion. It has been much altered, and was due in 1999 to be closed and adapted to new uses.

Fourth, there were power stations intended to supply the public, some privately and some municipally operated. The electricity works in Barbican Road, Gloucester (SO 829185), built for the City Corporation in 1900, was one of several municipal undertakings to burn domestic waste to produce a proportion of its power. A power station at Tanners Bank, North Shields (NZ 363688), built for Tynemouth Corporation in 1901, has for many years served as a factory. The Carville 'A' station of 1904 at nearby Wallsend (NZ 304661) is recognised as the first to have had a central control room. The generating hall and offices of the power station built by Tonbridge Urban District Council in 1902 remain at The Slade in Tonbridge (TQ 588466), as does the building of the Weald Electric Supply Company at Hawkhurst (TQ 761305). The buildings of the plant of 1903 at Frederick Road, Salford (SJ 817994), which include an imposing generator hall in the Italianate style, were adapted as offices in 1935. A power station of 1903, built for the Derbyshire & Nottinghamshire Electric Power Company, survives at Manners Avenue, Ilkeston (SK 454423), as does one built at much the same time by the Midlands Electricity Company in Dudley Street, Wednesbury (SO 983948). The Sevenoaks power station of 1914 at Sundridge (TR 489556) was an electricity company depot in 1999. Perhaps the most substantial surviving example of an early municipal power station is that of 1896–1902 in Haven Road, Exeter (SX 920918), on the front of which are panels depicting the spirit of electricity.

The electricity industry changed utterly in the 1920s. It became a symbol of modernity, and its impact on the landscape was regretted. Pylons, 'great bare girls with nothing to hide' as a poet described them, were particularly hated. The industry may be regarded as one of the great successes of the inter-war period. Private and municipal enterprise with direction from central government created an infrastructure which sustained industry during the Second World War, and in the second half of the twentieth century provided a more constant supply than was enjoyed by most developed countries. The Electricity (Supply) Act of 1919 set up the Electricity Commissioners and provided for the creation of joint authorities which could combine to provide power economically for particular regions. It led to the building of so-called 'super stations', like those built in the west midlands – Stourport in 1927, Hams Hall 'A' in 1929 and Ironbridge in 1932 – and the Clarence Dock plant in Liverpool, commissioned in 1931. There was, however, little standardisation in the industry, and companies provided alternating or direct current at a variety of voltages. The Electricity (Supply) Act of 1926 put the industry under the overall direction of a public body, the Central Electricity Board, which was empowered to buy power from generating companies, distribute it by means of a national network, and sell it to local distribution concerns. The resulting National Grid, a 4,000-mile web of power lines sustained by pylons, distributed power from 130 of the larger generating stations by 1933. Few of the first generation of stations built to supply the grid remain intact. They were too large to be adapted to new purposes, and asbestos insulation made adaptation expensive. The exception is the 'flagship' power station of the 1930s, at Battersea, the first stage of which began generation in 1933. Battersea was a symbol of modernity, 'perpetually in London's eye', the largest unit generating electric power in Europe at the time, and the *Queen Mary* of power stations. Its foundation stone, laid on 23 April 1931, commemorating Michael Faraday's discovery of magnetic induction a century earlier, proclaimed that it was 'a landmark in the development of larger London's light and power ... another memorial of the scientific heritage derived from famous Englishmen'. The control room was floored with hardwood,

3.17
The two coal-fired power stations at Ferrybridge, Yorkshire.

(Crown copyright. NMR)

and marble panels adorned its walls. The power station's well-known outline was designed by Sir Giles Gilbert Scott. The second stage of Battersea power station was not completed until 1955. It continued in operation until 1983, and had still not been adapted to another use by the end of the century.[31]

Hydro-electric power

The generation of electricity for industry and for public supply from water power was already established by 1900, by which time the first hydro-electric station in England, at Godalming, was already 19 years old. Developments in England were on a small scale, the most significant being the power stations at Mary Tavy (SX 509785) and Morwellham (SX 446697) in Devon, opened respectively in 1932 and 1934. Most developments were in the highland zone, and the majority are accompanied by small villages for staff built in the Garden City style.

One group of stations was in North Wales. Supply to the public and to slate mines in the Blaenau Ffestiniog area began in 1902. The Cwm Dyli station began operation in 1906, supplying power principally to quarries and mines in Snowdonia, distributed on 26 miles of cable supported on wooden poles. The power station associated with the aluminium smelter at Dolgarrog (SH 771675) in the Conwy valley began operation in 1908. The dam above Dolgarrog was breached on 2 November 1925, causing the deaths of sixteen people. The principal development of the inter-war period was the power station at Maentwrog (SH 655394), for which water was impounded by a concrete dam across the Afon Prysor. Electric power was supplied to Crewe, Wrexham and other towns in the borderlands from 15 October 1928. The principal post-nationalisation developments in the region were the spectacular pumped-storage schemes at Ffestiniog (SH 678444) and Dinorwic (SH 586602), which use power generated by coal-burning stations during the hours of darkness, for which there is only limited demand, to pump water into reservoirs from which it can power turbines to generate cheap electricity during times of peak demand.[32]

3.18
The nuclear power station at Trawsfynydd, North Wales, photographed in 1996.

(Crown copyright. Royal Commission on the Ancient and Historical Monuments of Wales)

The most significant hydro-electric station in Scotland in 1900 was that powering the aluminium smelter at Foyers, which was then 6 years old. It operated until 1967, when it became part of a pumped-storage system. In 1907 British Aluminium opened its power station and smelter at Kinlochleven, which were still operating in 1999, as were the smelter and power station at Lochaber, the first stage of which began to work in 1929. Other important projects of the inter-war period were at Rannoch, a 42MW station designed by George Balfour and opened in 1930, and at Tummel, opened in 1933. In the Scottish lowlands two stations with a joint output of 15.5MW were opened in 1926 at the Falls of Clyde, a short distance upstream from New Lanark. The Scottish Hydro-Electricity Board was established in 1943 and steadily increased its annual output, from 86,915kW in 1949 to 431,385kW in 1954, 866,472kW in 1959 and 1,041,058kW in 1965. New projects included power stations at Clunie and Pitlochrie, both completed in 1950, and a pumped-storage scheme at Cruachan which began work in 1969.[33]

The most impressive hydro-electric power scheme in Scotland was that created in Galloway, at the instigation largely of Colonel William McLellan (1874–1934). The creation of the National Grid from 1926 made hydro-electric power stations more viable, since unlike coal-fired stations they can come quickly on and off load, and through the grid can readily satisfy sudden demands. Legislation setting up the Galloway Water Power Company received the royal assent in 1929. Power stations with a total output of 102MW were built at Glenlee (NX 605805), Tongland (NX 695535), Earlstoun (NX 613818), Carsfad (NX 604855) and Kendoon (NX 604876). Tunnels and dams were constructed, and lochs, principally Loch Doon, used as reservoirs. Fishing resources were carefully preserved. The scheme, then the largest hydro-electric project in Britain, came into operation in the spring of 1935. The components of the project fit comfortably into the landscape, which is ornamented by the small but strikingly elegant Modernist generating stations designed by Sir Alexander Gibb (1872–1958). To study the scheme is to understand how, even in the worst years of the inter-war Depression, it was possible to carry through a scheme that was rational in economic terms, and which did not intrude upon but even enhanced the landscape.[34]

Nationalisation and after

The electric power industry was nationalised with effect from 1 April 1948, after which the Central Electricity Generating Board was responsible for providing power, and area boards for supplying it to customers. The CEGB inherited over 300 generating plants, but invested heavily in ever-larger stations, the majority of them coal fired. By 1980 less than 100 power stations were supplying four times the load delivered at the time of nationalisation. Most of those built in the 1950s passed out of use and were demolished before the end of the century. That at Keadby, Lincolnshire, opened in 1952, the first to have six 60MW generating sets, was a pleasing building in the Festival of Britain style, but its appearance was changed by conversion to gas firing. The first large public supply station designed for oil firing, Bankside 'B', also completed in 1952, with its main building designed by Sir Giles Gilbert Scott, is now part of the Tate Gallery. Several generating plants – Grimethorpe of 1958, Bold 'A' at St Helens of 1953, Agecroft, and Rugeley – were sited to take coal by conveyor direct from adjacent collieries.

In April 1954 the Laing construction company drew attention in the trade press to its role in the construction of 'Sellafield; Britain's Plutonium Factory'. This was a remarkably frank – and accurate – description. Two years later national pride was exhibited when the Queen opened at Sellafield what was described as Britain's first nuclear power station, then called Calder Hall, and subsequently Windscale, reverting to the name Sellafield in the 1980s. Windscale was operated by the United Kingdom Atomic Energy Authority, whose core business was the manufacture of nuclear weapons, the generation of electricity being a by-product. Most of the first generation of British nuclear power stations were similarly designed to provide material for weapons intended to destroy the Communist states of eastern Europe. The first seriously commercial nuclear power station, at Berkeley (ST 660995), opened in 1962 and ceased work in 1989. Several other stations, including Bradwell, Hunterston and Trawsfynydd, have also ceased operation, and are likely to remain sealed to public access for many generations, as are the fast-breeder reactor at Dounreay on the north coast of Scotland, and the heavy-water reactor built from 1957 at Winfrith Heath, Dorset. The latter is slowly being converted to a science park where innovative enterprises benefit from the security necessary to protect structures that will be radioactive for much of the twenty-first century. Britain's nuclear stations were dependent on the reprocessing plant at Sellafield and the nearby nuclear waste dump at Drigg. The first nuclear reactor in Britain remains in a hangar in the former RAF base at Harwell in the Vale of the White Horse, a research establishment which began work in 1947 and once housed over 6,000 staff. It remained in operation on a reduced scale at the end of the century. In 1998 just under 30 per cent of the electricity consumed in Britain came from nuclear sources, a much lower proportion than in France or Belgium, and somewhat less than in Germany, Japan or Spain. The nuclear industry is seriously mistrusted, following the disasters at Three Mile Island and Chernobyl, and a fire at Sellafield in October 1957. The ring of uninviting, security-sealed concrete monoliths around the coast seems likely to be the most enduring archaeological evidence of the Cold War.[35]

The size of coal-fired power stations increased rapidly under nationalisation. Castle Donnington in 1956 was the first to have 100MW generating units. Thorpe Marsh, completed in 1964, had two 275MW sets, and was then the largest power station in Europe. Drax was built in three stages between 1965 and 1986 to utilise coal from the Selby coalfield, on a 750-acre (300ha) site in Yorkshire. Each stage involved the construction of three 600MW sets. The 2,000MW station at Didcot (SU 5191), begun in 1965, dominates the landscape of the Thames Valley. The cooling towers and 670ft (205m) stack of Ironbridge 'B' (SJ 6503) can be seen from every part of Shropshire. Ratcliffe on Soar (SK 5036) stands by the Trent where it is crossed by the M1 and the Midland Main Line railway, like a sentinel watching the entrance to

the north of England. Rayner Banham in 1970 perceptively draw attention to the economic significance and the aesthetic appeal of what he called 'the power of Trent and Aire'.[36] The traveller on the East Coast Main Line between Doncaster and York can observe Thorpe Marsh (SE 6009), Eggborough (SE 5724), Ferryhill (SE 4724) and Drax (SE 6627) in a journey of no more than twenty-three minutes. A particular paradox can be observed at Tuxford, Lincolnshire, where, south of the lane to Skegby, the East Coast Main Line is crossed by the one-time Lancashire, Derbyshire & East Coast Railway, established in 1891 to carry east midlands coal for export eastwards to Sutton on Sea on the Lincolnshire coast and westwards to Warrington on the Manchester Ship Canal. It never grew beyond a line from Chesterfield to Lincoln opened in 1896–97. It was taken over by the Great Central Railway in 1907 and in the 1920s became the lifeline of the Dukeries coalfield. Occasionally a merry-go-round train passes along the line. Beyond the bridge which carries the lane over the main line (SK 748711) a prospect opens up to the north and east of the eight cooling towers of West Burton's power station (SK 7985), another eight at Cottam (SK 8179) and five at High Marnham (SK 7180). The landscape encapsulates the conventional thinking of two eras: the turn-of-the-century belief that British coal would always supply much of the world's energy, and the scarcely questioned mid-century assumption that most of Britain's own energy requirements would be met by coal.

The tall chimneys, generating halls, boiler plants, the merry-go-round coal trains (see Chapter 9) and above all the cooling towers of that generation of power stations symbolise much about British society in the mid-twentieth century: a belief in the effectiveness of large-scale operations; an assumption that the economy established during the Industrial Revolution would change only slowly; and the authority exercised by three huge nationalised corporations responsible for coal, railways and electricity.

The electricity industry was privatised in the late 1980s, and government direction on the use of fuels has largely been abandoned. The number of power stations increased during the 1990s with the construction of relatively small gas-fired generating plants. Even smaller sources of power – wind farms and generators fired by methane from domestic waste – have also proliferated. It is doubtful that the coal-burning goliaths will generate power for very much of the twenty-first century. The structures of most of them will doubtless be demolished, but the impact they have made on the landscape will not easily be erased.

Conclusions

The archaeology of the energy industries of the twentieth century provides much evidence of sudden change, of the abandonment of certainties. For much of the century coal appeared to be Britain's prime source of energy but by 1999 the coal-mining industry, with less than twenty active deep pits, was reduced to a rump of what it had been twenty years earlier. Its social and environmental legacies will be influential in the twenty-first century. Perhaps the most enduring archaeological features of the energy industries are their networks, the National Grid, the oil pipelines first constructed during the Second World War, and the gas pipelines; at a strategic level the creation of a nationalised industry from 1959, and at a local level the legacy of numerous small-scale Victorian enterprises. It is ironic that the gas which in 1999 seemed to be the predominant source of energy, the principal source of domestic heating, the fuel for growing numbers of power stations as well as an increasingly used chemical feedstock, has such ancient roots.

Notes and references

1   B. R. Mitchell (with P. Deane), *Abstract of British Historical Statistics*, Cambridge: Cambridge University Press, 1962, pp. 120–1; B. Supple, *The History of the British Coal Industry*, vol. IV: *1913–46: The Political Economy of Decline*, Oxford: Clarendon Press, 1987, p. 89.

2   N. Dennis, F. M. Henriques and C. Slaughter, *Coal Is Our Life*, London: Eyre & Spottiswoode, 1957, p. 51.

3   M. J. T. Lewis, *Early Wooden Railways*, London, Routledge & Kegan Paul, 1970.

4   Supple, op. cit., p. 539.

5   Quoted in C. Barnet, *The Audit of War: The Illusion and Reality of Britain as a Great Nation*, London: Pan, 1996, pp. 63–4; C. L. Mowat, *Britain between the Wars 1918–40*, London, Methuen, 1955, p. 465.

6   Supple, op. cit., pp. 8–9; Mitchell, op. cit., p. 123.

7   J. S. Leese, 'Old English Power Plants', *Power* (New York), 1912, vol. 36.

8   Ironbridge Institute, *Llanbradach Colliery: Research Paper No. 101*, Telford: Ironbridge Institute, 1994. Llanbradach produced its first coal in 1894, employed 3,000 miners in 1915, and ceased production in 1961.

9   P. Rees, *A Guide to Merseyside's Industrial Past*, Liverpool: Countywise, 1991, pp. 18–19.

10 R. Thornes, *Images of Industry: Coal*, Swindon: RCHME; S. Hughes, B. A. Malaws, M. Parry and P. Wakelin, *Collieries of Wales: Engineering and Architecture*, Aberystwyth: RCAHMW, nd.

11 B. A. Malaws, 'Process Recording at Industrial Sites', *Industrial Archaeology Review*, 1997, vol. 19, pp. 75–98.

12 Dennis, Henriques and Slaughter, op. cit., p. 57.

13 G. D. Nash, T. A. Davies and B. Thomas, *Workmen's Halls and Institutes: Oakdale Workmen's Institute*, Cardiff: National Museums & Galleries of Wales, 1995.

14 D. H. Lawrence, *Sons and Lovers*, ed. D. Trotter, Oxford: Oxford University Press World Classics, pp. 5–6.

15 R. Church, *The History of the British Coal Industry*, vol. III: 1830–1913: *Victorian Pre-Eminence*, Oxford: Clarendon Press, 1986, p. 161.

16 The account of the Dukeries is based on R. J. Waller, *The Dukeries Transformed: The Social and Political Development of a Twentieth Century Coalfield*, Oxford: Oxford University Press, 1983; and Supple, op. cit., pp. 475–7.

17 R. C. K. Ensor, *England 1871–1914*, Oxford: Oxford University Press, 1952, p. 299; Dennis, Henriques and Slaughter, op. cit.

18 D. Eve, *A Guide to the Industrial Archaeology of Kent*, Telford: Association for Industrial Archaeology, 1999, pp. 28–9; Thornes, op. cit., pp. 86–8; Mitchell Engineering Group, *British Industrial and Engineering Installations*, London: Mitchell Engineering Group, 1946, pp. 83, 202.

19 J. B. Priestley, *English Journey*, London: Heinemann, 1934, p. 338.

20 W. H. B. Court, *History of the Second World War: Coal*, London: HMSO–Longmans, 1951, p. 213; K. C. Appleyard and G. Curry, 'Open-Cast Coal Production in Wartime', *Journal of the Institution of Civil Engineers*, 1946, vol. 26, pp. 331–76.

21 L. Wilde, 'A Comparative Study of Two Coking and By-Product Sites', Ironbridge Institute assignment, 1993.

22 M. Williams, *Cotton Mills in Greater Manchester*, Preston: Carnegie, 1993, p. 11; C. Giles and I. H. Goodall, *Yorkshire Textile Mills*, London: HMSO, p. 25.

23 Monuments Protection Programme, *Gas*, London: English Heritage, 1997.

24 T. I. Williams, *The History of the British Gas Industry*, Oxford: Oxford University Press, 1981, pp. 125–40; issues of the *Gas Journal* for: 15 June 1960, 21 June 1961, 15 October 1961, 12 June 1963 (Westfield); 21 March 1962, 7 November 1962, 19 June 1963 (Coleshill); 23 January 1963, 22 July 1964, 12 May 1965 (Avonmouth); 11 November 1964 (Bromley); 12 July 1967 (Tipton); W. Simpson, *The Oxford–Cambridge Railway*, vol. I: *Oxford–Bletchley*, Oxford: Oxford Publishing Company, 1981 (Bicester). We are grateful to John Powell for these references.

25 Williams, op. cit., pp. 160–9; *Gas Journal*, 14 February 1970 (Hinckley); C. Elliott, *The History of Natural Gas Conversion in Great Britain*, Cambridge: Information & Research Services, 1980.

26 G. T. Morton and D. D. Pratt, *The British Chemical Industry: Its Rise and Development*, London: Edward Arnold, 1938; J. R. Hume, *The Industrial Archaeology of Scotland*, vol. I: *The Central Lowlands*, London: Batsford, 1976.

27 Monuments Protection Programme, *Oil*, London: English Heritage, 1998.

28 D. J. Payton Smith, *History of the Second World War: Oil: A Study of Wartime Policy and Administration*, London: HMSO, p. 176.

29 M. Gray, *George Washington Wilson and the Scottish Fishing Industry*, Keighley: Kennedy, 1982.

30 Monuments Protection Programme, *Electric Power Generation*, London: English Heritage.

31 M. Stratton, *Ironbridge and the Electric Revolution: The History of Electricity Generation at Ironbridge A and B Power Stations*, London: John Murray, 1994, pp. 21–2; R. Cochrane, *Landmark of London – the Story of Battersea Power Station*, London: CEGB, 1984.

32 G. Woodward, 'Hydro-electricity in North Wales 1880–1948', *Transactions of the Newcomen Society*, 1997–98, vol. 69, pp. 205–36; E. D. Jones and D. Gwynn, *Dolgarrog: An Industrial History*, Bangor: Gwynedd Archives & Museums, 1989.

33 L. Payne, *The Hydro: A Study of the Major Hydro-Electric Schemes Undertaken by the North of Scotland Hydro-Electricity Board*, Aberdeen: Aberdeen University Press, 1988.

34 G. Hill, *Tunnel and Dam – the Story of the Galloway Hydros*, Glasgow: South of Scotland Electricity Board, 1984.

35 Calder Hall, Hunterston, Berkeley, Trawsfynydd, Bradwell, Chapelcross, Wylfa, Oldbury, Hinkley Point, Sizewell, Dungeness.

36 R. Banham, 'The Power of Trent and Aire', in P. Barker (ed.) *Arts in Society*, London: Fontana, 1977, pp. 254–62.

Chapter four

Industrial technology moves between countries in many ways. It can be carried by individuals like the Jewish chemists who fled from Hitler and Stalin to Britain and the United States, and by poor immigrants selling the food of their native countries to their hosts. It can travel through the agency of large corporations establishing branch factories, sometimes with government subsidies. It can be passed, like the cavity magnetron, from one country to another as a favour in wartime. It can be transmitted through espionage, by the observations of spies or by enticing skilled workers to emigrate. Different ways of doing things are noticed on holidays or during spells of work experience overseas. All these means of transmission have been discussed in the context of the eighteenth and nineteenth centuries by John Harris and David Jeremy.[1] All have occurred in the twentieth century. It is the purpose of this chapter to use the food industries as a case study by which to examine the various means by which industrial technology has reached Britain from overseas.

The international transfer of technology

the case of the food industries

Trafford Park

The Trafford Park industrial estate (SJ 7996) is the appropriate place to begin any study of the inward transfer of technology in twentieth-century Britain. It was established alongside the 2-year-old Manchester Ship Canal in 1896 and became the principal gateway into Britain for North American technology. An early and prominent example was the engineering works established by George Westinghouse (1846–1914), where production began in 1902. It passed into British ownership in 1917 and for much of the century was best known as Metropolitan-Vickers. The office block is almost identical to the Westinghouse headquarters building in Pittsburgh, and the principal shops were steel framed. Photographs of railway wagons being shunted into the machine shop carrying crated machine tools, unloaded from the ships that had brought them from North America, are positive evidence of the transfer of technology. Westinghouse's example was followed by other innovative companies from the United States: the American Car & Foundry Company in 1904; Owen's European Bottle Company, from Toledo, Ohio, pioneers in the mass production of bottles, in 1907; the Ford Motor Company in 1911; Truscon, suppliers of reinforced concrete beams (*see Chapter 2*), in 1913; and Harley Davidson in 1916. Many of the characteristic materials of the twentieth century were processed at Trafford Park – oil, rubber, asbestos, steel and aniline dyestuffs – and characteristic twentieth-century products included electicity generating equipment, railway locomotives, aircraft, domestic utensils, cash registers, detergents and penicillin. If any one site is an epitome of twentieth-century industrial archaeology, it is Trafford Park.[2]

Trafford Park is important also as a location for the food industry, and for the transfer of food technology. Its first significant food industry enterprise was the elevator for unloading grain from ships, built in 1898 by John S. Metcalf (1847–1912) of Chicago, reputedly 'the cleverest elevator engineer in America'. A cluster of mills was built to make use of the grain unloaded by the elevator. The

Co-operative Wholesale Society's Sun Mill was built in 1906, and by 1913 it had doubled in size to become the largest in England, while the Society had also built a grocery-packing factory alongside it. The Hovis Mill opened in 1905, the English Grain Company's mill in 1909 and the mill of J. Greenwood & Son, later Rank's mill, in the same year. The elevator and the Hovis Mill were destroyed by bombing in the Second World War, and the CWS mill by fire in 1980, and only one much-rebuilt mill remained in 1999.

Edible oils were processed at Trafford Park from 1898 when the works of N. Kilvert & Sons went into production. In 1934 a soap factory was established by the Newcastle firm Thomas Hedley & Co., which had just been taken over by the American company Proctor & Gamble. Edible oils were processed at the plant from 1936 until 1989. The works of Nichols Nagel was set up in 1911 to produce corn products including glucose, gravy browning and cornflower. It remained in production in 1999 as Cerestar, under Italian ownership. The American food processing concern H. J. Heinz had a works at Trafford Park for a short time

4.1
The international transfer of technology – machine tools from the United States being shunted into the newly erected buildings of George Westinghouse's engineering works at Trafford Park, *c*. 1902.

(Ironbridge Gorge Museum Trust)

The international transfer of technology:

from 1926, and the breakfast cereal manufacturer Kellogg commissioned a factory there in 1938.[3] Other food products made at Trafford Park included biscuits, lard and jam, while imported products stored or processed there included bacon, lamb, tea, coffee, cocoa and lard.

Grain

The British milling industry had been transformed in the last two decades of the nineteenth century by the introduction of gradual reduction roller milling technology, the most popular forms of which utilised chilled iron rolls, and incorporated purifiers to sift and grade the milled product. Roller milling systems from Germany, Hungary and the United States were installed in England in the late 1870s, and gained publicity through an exhibition at Islington in 1881. *The Engineer* reported in 1883 that 'the great rush in roller milling [had] set in', and by 1887 there were 461 mills using the roller process in the UK. The rapid growth of the new system was due to the rise of three engineering companies: J. Harrison Carter (from 1888, E. R. & F. Turner), of Ipswich, J. S. & C. J. Robinson of Rochdale, and above all Henry Simon of Manchester, a Silesian with experience of industry in Germany, Russia and France, who settled in Manchester in 1860. Large roller mills were built in the principal ports – Henry Simon alone installed seven major plants in Liverpool between 1881 and 1884. Milling plants of increasing size were being built in 1900, and continued to be constructed until the Second World War.[4]

4.2
The concrete mills and grain silos erected by the Co-operative Wholesale Society at Avonmouth, c. 1909.

(Photo: Barrie Trinder)

4.3
The Ocean Flour Mills at Birkenhead.

(Photo: Barrie Trinder)

4.4
The Homepride Mill complex at Birkenhead.

(Photo: Barrie Trinder)

Ports on the west coast were concerned principally with grain from North America. In 1899 Henry Simon built the Millennium Mills at Birkenhead for W. Vernon & Sons, installing eighty roller units. The CWS opened its mill at Trafford Park in 1906 and its concrete-framed mill at Avonmouth in 1910, extending it in 1920, 1921, 1923, 1925 and 1936. Grain was handled also at the ports of Preston and Fleetwood, and at Barry Dock, where the mill of 1906 was extensively renewed in the late 1980s, resulting in the demolition of most of the original buildings.[5]

The ports on the east coast handled chiefly hard grains imported from the Baltic. The first stage of the CWS mill at Dunston on the River Tyne was opened in 1891; ten years later the first reinforced grain silo in Britain was constructed on the site, and in 1906 the first circular grain silos in Britain, measuring 14.02m (46ft) in diameter and 21.33m (70ft) deep, designed by Mouchel, were built there. Roller mills were also located around the King George V Dock in Hull, where two blocks of concrete silos were built in 1920.[6] The Scottish CWS opened its Chancelot Mills at Leith in 1894.

The grain trade was of major importance, too, in the London docks. The main concentration of twentieth-century mill buildings was at the Royal Victoria Dock (TQ 6080), where the London Grain Elevator Company in 1898 had begun to construct corrugated iron silos, later replaced by concrete structures, on the site formerly occupied by the Thames Graving Dock. From 1905 four very large mills were constructed on the dockside. The remarkable CWS mill, built to the design of L. G. Ekins in the late 1930s and intended to supersede the Society's Silvertown Mill of 1900, was demolished, but Spiller's Millennium Mill survived, awaiting adaptation to new uses in 1999, and an elevator had also been preserved as a monument. The other concentration of mills in Dockland, on the south side of Millwall Dock, was demolished after its closure in 1980 and replaced by housing.

Roller milling was spreading to inland towns at the turn of the century. *The Miller* commented in 1896: 'Not the least significant among the signs of these times is the constant and never ending progress of the Roller System among the country mills of this land. One by one country millers are converting their mills to the most

approved Roller Systems.' Some plants continued to be extended throughout the twentieth century, like the Victoria Mills of the Whitworth company in Wellingborough (SP 902665), which opened in 1886 and now includes notable examples of both steel and concrete construction. Other examples are the works of Jordan & Co. at Holme Mill, Biggleswade, converted to roller milling in 1896, the Wansbeck Mill of 1889 at Morpeth (NZ 202858), and the Chelmsford Mill of Marriage & Co., built in 1900. Mills are prone to fire, and many provincial examples have been demolished. The roller milling process is best illustrated, although in a pre-twentieth-century establishment, at Caudwells Mill, Rowsley, Derbyshire (SK 265656).[7]

4.5
An example of an inland roller milling installation, the Whitworth mills on the River Nene at Wellingborough, Northamptonshire.

(Photo: Barrie Trinder)

Baking was changing rapidly in 1900, following an influential exhibition in 1881, but also as a result of the Food and Drugs Act of 1875, one of the objects of which was to discourage cellar bakeries. By 1900 most bakeries were equipped with at least a mechanical kneader for dough and a flour sifter. The bakery of the Kettering Industrial Co-operative Society (SP 870791), opened in 1900, provides an indication of the size of the industrial-scale establishments then being built in many towns. One of the most prominent baking firms in the north is Warburtons of

Bolton, originally grocers. The firm became involved in baking in 1907, and in 1914 Warburtons constructed a new Model Bakery, claimed to be 'the most modern in the north', utilising American technology and specialising in the Eatmore loaf. Some bakeries developed chains of shops and cafés (*see Chapter 10*). An innovation of the inter-war period was the production of loaves that were sliced and wrapped. Warburtons began wrapping bread in 1921, and in the 1930s J. Lyons & Co. were offering their 'Kut-Bread', thirty slices wrapped and sealed, at the same price as unsliced loaves.

The baking trade was transformed in the second half of the twentieth century. Production was concentrated in ever-larger units, while traditional methods were necessarily confined to small-scale bakeries. The archaeological legacy of the first two-thirds of the century consists chiefly of medium-sized bakeries that were adapted for other purposes, like that at Kettering, or the AFB works of the early 1960s in Abbey Foregate, Shrewsbury (SJ 498125).

The American practice of eating breakfast cereals became deeply rooted in British culture during the twentieth century. Shredded Wheat, the invention of the Denver lawyer Henry Perky, was first produced in the United States in 1892, and exported to Britain from 1908. From 1925 it was manufactured at a factory at Welwyn Garden City (TL 242129), most of which remained in the 1990s after many alterations and extensions. Clean and pressure-cooked grain was shredded between pairs of smooth and grooved rotating rollers, sheared into strands as it passed through rollers rotating at different speeds, combed and formed into a bed on a conveyor, then cut into shape by a rotary cutter. Shredded Wheat biscuits were originally made on a gravity flow system in a multi-storey building, but production was transferred to a single-storey range in 1939. The vacated space in the original building was used for the manufacture of bran flakes in the 1990s. The factory was a 'flagship' building whose image was vigorously promoted by the company to suggest that Shredded Wheat was linked with cleanliness and healthy living. The manufacturer's American origins were obscured by the slogan 'Britons make it – it makes Britons'. The factory had sports and social facilities, which were reduced as demand for workplace recreation diminished from the 1960s

and as playing-field space was used for factory extensions. Other products were manufactured at the plant – Shreddies from 1953, cake mixes from 1955 and Ritz Cracker biscuits, which had been imported from the USA since the 1930s, in 1961. By the 1990s Shredded Wheat, like other breakfast cereals, and indeed like many well-known foods, was marketed through links with popular culture rather than by promoting the qualities of the product itself. The factory became simply the location of production rather than a part of the image of the product.[8]

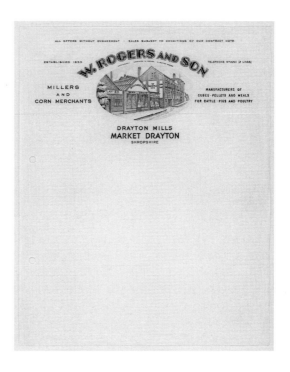

4.6
The bill-heading of another inland roller milling installation, that of W. Rogers and Son built in the 1890s at Market Drayton, Shropshire.

(Authors' collection)

The introduction of Kelloggs Cornflakes, first made at Battle Creek, Michigan, in 1908, followed a similar but later pattern. From 1924 the company began to sell products manufactured in Canada, and in 1938 set up a factory at Trafford Park, followed after the Second World War by another on the industrial estate created on the site of the Royal Ordnance Factory at Wrexham (SJ 388506).

Not all breakfast cereals were made by American companies. Force Wheat Flakes were reputedly the first British breakfast cereal, and were introduced in 1902. In 1999 they were made at a factory on Imperial Way, Watford, but the most significant archaeological legacy of the product was an artefact, the Sunny Jim cuddly toy of the inter-war period, examples of which are prized still by many long past their childhood who rarely eat wheatflakes. The manufacturers of Scotts' Porage Oats were proud that they were 'made in these wonderful mills on the beautiful waters of Leith'. The most successful British cereals company was Weetabix, which set up a plant on an ancient mill site at Burton Latimer, Northamptonshire (SP 890750), in 1932. The plant has been successively extended but is still where it is because there was a water mill on the site from Saxon times.

Biscuits were extensively eaten in the twentieth century, and formed part of many social rituals. An advertisement early in the century, showing a turbaned waiter serving a Briton in a tent somewhere in Asia, even referred to 'correct' biscuits. One of the most substantial factories of the early years of the century was that of McVitie & Price at Harlesden (TQ 205834) in north-west London. The Westons factory at Llantarnam near Pontypool (ST 306936), built in 1938 to the design of Sir Alexander Gibb & Partners, is a distinguished building in a mildly Art Deco style, which well expresses the technology employed. Flour stores at first-floor level feed materials by gravity into a mixing area below, from which biscuits proceed into a 240-ft-long building that accommodates the ovens. Perhaps the best-known company in the early years of the century was Huntley & Palmer of Reading, which by the 1930s had become, according to its historian, a very old-fashioned firm.

A partnership agreement with the London company Peek Frean in 1931 stimulated change, and a new factory building was constructed in 1937. The old companies lost their separate identities although many of their brand names continued after mergers and take-overs in the 1950s. Huntley & Palmer built a new factory at Huyton near Liverpool in 1953–55. Their Reading factory closed in 1977, to be replaced by office blocks.[9]

By 1900 biscuits had already been marketed for several decades in decorative tins, which continued to be a feature of the industry, particularly of Christmas trade, throughout the century. Collections of such tins, particularly from the decades before the Second World War, reflect many aspects of twentieth-century industrial archaeology. Images include telephone boxes, Box Brownie cameras, motorcars and trucks, military tanks, the liners *Berengaria* and *Lusitania*, and the *Flying Scotsman* locomotive. The Co-operative Wholesale Society adorned some of its tins with pictures of its biscuit factory at Crumpsall, near Manchester. A tin produced by Huntley & Palmer to commemorate the 1939 visit of the King and Queen to North America has six images of the royal family on one side, and on the other side six which symbolised 'modern achievements' at the end of the fourth decade of the century: Broadcasting House, the Mersey Tunnel, slum clearance, Malcolm Campbell's record-breaking car Bluebird, a train hauled by Sir Nigel Gresley's 2-8-2 *Cock of the North*, and, inevitably, the *Queen Mary*.[10]

4.7
A Huntley & Palmer's biscuit tin of the 1930s in the shape of a delivery van, in the Huntley & Palmer collection, Reading Museum.

(Photo: Barrie Trinder)

Sugar

The refining of cane sugar was a port industry in the twentieth century, concentrated principally in London, Liverpool and Greenock, all ports with links to the Caribbean that went back to the eighteenth century. The outstanding twentieth-century structure relating to the industry is the range of concrete parabolic-roofed tunnel-vaulted stores on Regent Road, Kirkdale, Liverpool (SJ 338935), built by Cementation in 1957 for Tate & Lyle. The Abram Lyle & Sons sugar refinery of 1881 alongside the Thames at Plaistow in east London (TQ 424799) was entirely rebuilt by Tate & Lyle between 1946 and 1955. The Portland-stone-faced office block of 1946–50, in the Classical style, displays a relief of the firm's trademark, the lion killed by Samson surrounded by bees.[11] The Tate & Lyle refinery at Greenock retained in the 1990s an eight-storey tower building topped by a cast-iron tank, and a triple-gabled sugar store.

The manufacture of sugar from beet was a wholly twentieth-century industry in Britain, one that relied not on the import of materials from the tropics but on the transfer of technology from continental Europe.[12] A beet-sugar refinery required abundant process water, a large flat site with foundations solid enough to support very large structures, usually of concrete, and, until the 1980s, access to rail transport. It also needed farmers within a fairly short radius who would contract to grow beet. The first beet-sugar factory was built at Cantley near Norwich (G 3704) in 1912. It closed during the First World War, but was re-opened by a Dutch company as the English Beet Sugar corporation in 1920. A second factory was opened by a French firm at Kelham near Newark (SK 793552) in 1921. The government offered subsidies to farmers for growing sugar beet, and nine factories opened during 1925, at Colwick near Nottingham (SK 6240), Bury St Edmunds (TL 8665), Ely (TL 5680), Ipswich (TM 1344), Spalding (TF 2524), Wissington, Kidderminster, Eynsham near Oxford and Greenock. The last two operated for only a few seasons. Four opened in 1926, at Peterborough, Cupar in Fife (NO 3714), Felsted in Essex (TL 6720) and Poppleton near York (SE 5751); four in 1927, at Allscott in Shropshire (SJ 6012), Bardney in Lincolnshire (TF 1169),

King's Lynn (TF 6117) and Selby (SE 6333); and one in 1928, at Brigg, Lincolnshire (TA 0007). There were seventeen working in 1930, of which about half were still operating in the 1990s. All originally had links with French, Dutch or German firms – the menu for the opening of the Allscott factory was in both German and English. The beet-sugar refineries came under the common ownership of the British Sugar Corporation in 1936, but the industry was deregulated in the 1980s.

Margarine

Margarine was first sold in England in the 1870s, a transfer of technology from the Chicago stockyards, which provided the beef fat for its production. A million tonnes of what was then called 'butterine' (a name that became illegal in Britain in 1887) was imported from America in 1876. After 1900, vegetable and whale oils came to be used in margarine, and close links developed with soap-making companies, which used the same raw materials. Until the First World War most margarine eaten in Britain was imported. During the first thirty years of the century there was a 'margarine war', which epitomised the always uneasy relationship in the food industry between producers and suppliers. This struggle has been described in two major works of business history, by Mathias and Wilson, and culminated in the merger in 1927 of Jurgens and Van den Berghs, the two principal Dutch firms operating in Britain, and the formation of the Unilever Company in 1929.[13]

The first significant margarine factory in Britain was opened in premises formerly used for hat-making at Godley in Cheshire in April 1889 by Otto Monsted of Aarhus, the largest margarine manufacturer in Denmark, who had close links with Maypole Dairies. During the 1890s he set up a factory at Southall to supply Maypole's shops in London and the south, but production for the whole country was concentrated there from 1914, when the Godley works was closed. In 1907 an oil works to refine coconut oil for the Southall factory was built at Erith on the Kentish marshes, to which a crushing mill for groundnuts was appended in 1914–16, both using technology developed by Monsted's company in Denmark. Jurgens's plant at Purfleet was established before the First World War and greatly extended immediately afterwards. The Van den Bergh factory was at Fulham in west London. Planters Ltd, a subsidiary of Lever Brothers, the soap company, began margarine manufacture with the purchase of the former Monsted factory at Godley, but soon afterwards transferred production to a model factory at Bromborough, near the company's headquarters at Port Sunlight. Jurgens and Van den Bergh merged as the Margarine Union in 1927, and subsequently the Southall factory was closed. The new company acquired smaller works, including two in Scotland at Ballochmyle and Dunragit. In parallel to these developments in the private sector, the Co-operative Wholesale Society in 1917 opened a margarine factory at Higher Irlam alongside the Manchester Ship Canal, and close to the Society's soap works. It was extended in 1919, and in 1922 began to produce shredded suet and lard. The archaeology of the margarine industry has yet to be investigated, but the factories at Godley, Erith, Fulham, Bromborough, Purfleet and Higher Irlam were of paramount importance in the British food industry in the first half of the twentieth century, and merit analysis. The business histories of the two great conglomerates which dominated the industry make it clear that the transfer of technology from Denmark and The Netherlands was a key factor in its growth. It remains to be seen whether this is reflected in the industry's archaeology.

Creameries

Rather more is known about the history and archaeology of dairying. The industry was revolutionised in the early 1870s with the establishment of a series of innovative enterprises – the first large-scale depot for cooling milk and despatching it by rail to London at Semley (ST 874268) in Wiltshire, the first substantial milk condenseries in Britain at Chippenham (ST 918733) and

Aylesbury (SP 827138), and the first cheese factory at Longford in Derbyshire (SK 220374) – and by the Great Western Railway's decision to begin construction, on a large scale, of vans specially designed for the carriage of milk in churns.[14] This transformation owed much to the transfer of technology. Butter manufacture was aided by the centrifugal cream separator patented in Scandinavia in 1878. The condenseries were established by the Anglo-Swiss Condensed Milk Company, set up at Cham in Switzerland by the American brothers Charles and George Page, which utilised technology originally developed by the American Gail Borden in the 1850s. The first manager of the factory at Longford, an American of Dutch extraction, utilised the American method of making Cheddar cheese.

4.8
The initials of Henri Nestlé inscribed on the condensed-milk factory he constructed in 1901 at Tutbury, Staffordshire.

(Photo: Barrie Trinder)

Many creameries (a term which can usefully be taken to mean any kind of factory concerned with the processing of milk) had already been established by 1900, and more continued to be built in the first decades of the century. The majority were located alongside railways, which enabled them to despatch liquid milk to large cities, in particular to London, or to margarine factories, as well as making cheese, butter, condensed milk or other milk products. The dominant international influence on the industry in the years before 1914 was Henri Nestlé, who had begun to manufacture a milk-based baby food at Cham, near to the Page brothers' condensery, in the late 1860s. Nestlé

established several factories in England; that at Tutbury (SK 216296) still bears the inscription 'HN 1901', indicating its owner and the year of its opening. The Nestlé corporation merged with Anglo-Swiss in 1905. The company's factories of the years immediately before the First World War are in a distinctive house style, the work of its architects' department based at its Middlewich plant. The same kind of

4.9
The can shop at the Nestlé factory at Staverton near Trowbridge, built just before the First World War ended. Note the stepped pattern in the brickwork in the end gable.

(Photo: Barrie Trinder)

4.10
The Nestlé condensed-milk factory at Ashbourne, Derbyshire. The three gables on the extreme left form part of the original boiler house of 1913, and have the same stepped pattern in the brickwork that can be observed in the company's Staverton factory (*see 4.9*) The five-storey structure in the centre dates from the Second World War and housed a spray-drying plant, used originally for the production of dried milk and subsequently for instant coffee and tea. The more modern building on the right was built to house a process for canning rice pudding.

(Photo: Barrie Trinder)

patterned brickwork, precisely laid, with relief stepped patterns beneath the gable eaves can be observed in the buildings added around 1913 to the former woollen mill acquired by Anglo-Swiss in 1897, which was the nucleus of its plant at Staverton near Trowbridge (ST 856603), and in the condensery at Ashbourne, Derbyshire (SK 177463), built in 1912–13.

Makers of cheese and butter in the early years of the twentieth century faced competition from producers in North America, The Netherlands, Denmark, northern Germany, and even Siberia. It was partly for this reason that a substantial trade developed in conveying milk by train to London, where much of it was distributed by large companies like Express Dairies. By the early years of the century the principal railway companies had established depots where milk in churns delivered by vans could be passed to the retail distributors. The Great Northern's milk sidings were just beyond the ends of the passenger platforms at King's Cross. The LNWR handled milk at Euston, the Great Western at the country end of Platform 1 at Paddington, the Great Eastern at Stratford, the LSWR at Vauxhall, and the Metropolitan at Farringdon and Willesden Green. A fossil-like trace of the siding where LBSCR milk traffic was handled was still visible in 1999 at the Victoria end of Platform 4 at Clapham Junction. Most of the railway companies built vans especially for this traffic. Several of the Great Western's Siphon vans are in the collections of preserved railways, and there is a Metropolitan Railway van at the London Transport Museum, and an LBSCR example on the Bluebell Railway. Artefacts illustrating the domestic distribution of milk displayed in the National Dairy Museum in Hampshire include perambulators, earlier examples carrying churns from which customers' jugs and bowls were filled with milk, and later vehicles designed to carry milk in bottles, mass-produced by the Libby-Owens process imported from Toledo, Ohio, just after 1900.

After the First World War the retail dairy companies opened larger bottling plants in London, like those at Wood Lane of 1934, Cricklewood of 1929, and South Morden of 1954. In 1928 glass-lined or sometimes stainless steel 3,000-gallon tank wagons were introduced. The tanks belonged to the dairy companies and the chassis to the railways. The latter, by the

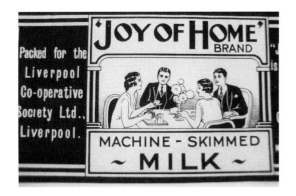

4.11
A label for canned milk
produced in the 1930s
at the creamery at
Minsterley, Shropshire,
for the Liverpool Co-
operative Society (the
label is preserved at the
library of the Ironbridge
Gorge Museum).

(Photo: Barrie Trinder)

4.12
A 3,000-gallon glass-lined
tank mounted on a six-
wheel rail chassis,
preserved by the Great
Western Society at Didcot.

(Photo: Barrie Trinder)

late 1930s, always had six wheels, after four-
wheel chassis had been found to oscillate
dangerously at speed. There were also 2,000-
gallon tanks mounted on road chassis which
could be rolled at creameries or wayside
stations on to flat railway wagons. Twelve
ex-GWR six-wheel tanks are held by various
railway preservation groups, including one
converted from a four-wheel vehicle, and one
flat truck for carrying road tanks, together with
two ex-Southern Railway vehicles, and six from
the LMS. Milk tanks travelled at speed to
London from distant parts of the railway
system, from St Erth (SW 542357), Lostwithiel
(SX 106597) and Totnes (SX 801609) on the Great
Western main line in Cornwall and Devon, from
Whitland (SN 201164), Pont Llanio (SN 652569)
and Felin Fach (SN 518575) in the far west of
Wales, from Aspatria (NY 143413) and Appleby
in Cumbria (NY 690203), and even from
Sanquhar in southern Scotland (NS 7809). In the
early 1930s two glass-lined tanks were
despatched daily from the creamery on the site
of the once-important copper mine at Ecton (SJ
096584) in Staffordshire, travelling on
transporter wagons on the (2ft 6in. gauge) Leek
& Manifold Light Railway to join standard-
gauge tracks at Waterhouses, before being
conveyed via Derby Friargate, Grantham and
the Great Northern main line to Finsbury Park.
The same train carried tanks from a creamery at
Ingestre near Stafford (SJ 977268), which by the
1990s had been obliterated from the landscape
except for the one-time manager's house. In
1936 tanks began to be conveyed from a
creamery at Dorrington, south of Shrewsbury
(SJ 480032), to a distribution depot in Rossmore
Road, just outside Marylebone Station. The
working continued into the 1970s, but by the
1990s the London depot had been demolished,

its site recognisable only by a change in the
brickwork of the boundary wall, and the
Shropshire creamery had been adapted for
other purposes. Milk trains conveying churns
in long rakes of vans continued to operate until
the Second World War, but after 1945 most milk
handled by the railways travelled in bulk tanks,
which continued to operate until 1980.

Creameries could readily be adapted to
different purposes and many manufactured
a diversity of products in the course of the
century. Many made cheese and butter. The
latter was usually cut up for sale in grocers'
shops in the first quarter of the century. One
of the pioneers in the supply of packed butter
was Frederick Adams of Leek, who in 1925
established a factory for the purpose in the
town, and in the 1930s set up his own plant
for printing wrappers. The company, having
greatly expanded and passed into Irish
ownership, opened a new factory in 1975.
Several creameries, including Ashbourne,

4.13
The derelict buildings of
the creamery at Pont
Llanio in West Wales,
photographed in 1995.
Milk in 3,000-gallon rail
tanks was regularly
despatched from this
creamery to London
until the 1960s.

(Photo: Barrie Trinder)

Dumfries, Staverton and Minsterley (SJ 375052) in Shropshire, produced condensed milk. Cow & Gate was making milk powder at Wincanton (ST 7128) as early as 1903, and during the Second World War many creameries, among them Lapford in Devon (SX 727079), Minsterley and Ashbourne, produced National Dried Milk in distinctive blue-and-white cans. Sterilised milk, supplied in swing-stoppered bottles, was developed by Anthony Hailwood in the 1890s, and was available in most big cities. The principal supplier in the north-west was the Cheshire Sterilized Milk Company, operator of the 'Garden Dairy' in Stockport, which was supplied with raw milk by road tankers from a cheese-making creamery at Aston near Nantwich (SJ 609454), purchased by the company in 1930. The subsequent history of the Aston works illustrates the kaleidoscopic changes in the dairy industry in the late twentieth century.[15] It was sold in 1954 and for a time specialised in conventional cheese production. In 1982 it became the second factory to produce the ill-fated Lymeswold soft cheese, and was subsequently adapted to make mozzarella cheese for pizza manufacturers. In 1999 the buildings were used as a bakery. Baby foods had been a creamery product since the time of Henri Nestlé. One creamery which specialised in making them in the 1960s and 1970s was at Wrenbury, Cheshire (SJ 601468), where Trufood was manufactured. The buildings by 1999 had been adapted as

a small industrial estate. The chief chemist of Ambrosia's creamery, opened in 1928 at Lapford, Devon, developed a process in 1936 for making canned rice puddings, which continued in use when the company moved to North Tawton (SS 664015) in 1974.[16] A similar process was used at the Ashbourne creamery in the early 1990s. Some creameries supplied substantial quantities of milk to margarine factories, among them that opposite the LNWR railway station at Buckingham, which despatched regular supplies to Van den Berghs at Purfleet, as well as to the Ovaltine factory at King's Langley (*see below*), in the inter-war period. In the mid-1990s the buildings were adapted as the library of the University of Buckingham (SP 695333).

At some creameries cheese was made for use in the manufacture of processed cheese. Aplin & Barrett set up a works on a First World War airfield at The Ham, Wiltshire (ST 862521), in 1925 in order to produce Chedlet processed cheese. In 1923 two Canadian salesmen opened an office in Liverpool to market processed cheese made by the method developed in Chicago by James L. Kraft. His cheese was of uniform quality and had been sold on a large scale to US forces during the First World War. Production in Britain commenced in 1926. By 1930 Kraft had a factory making Velveeta cheese at Hayes, Middlesex, which had 750 staff by 1939. Between 1936 and 1954 Kraft owned the cheese factory at Ruyton XI Towns in Shropshire (SJ 391223), and subsequently established the creamery at Merlin Bridge, Haverfordwest (SM 946143), which was still operating, although in different ownership, in the 1990s. The Kraft company supplied large quantities of processed cheese to British forces in the Second World War. By 1954 it was selling Dairylea cheese; Velveeta was re-introduced in 1955, and it had started to make margarine. In 1957 a large factory was opened at Kirkby near Liverpool, on an industrial estate on the site of a Royal Ordnance Factory, which made Philadelphia cheese and margarine, in collaboration with an oil and fats factory operated by Kraft at Trafford Park.

One of the principal changes in the dairy industry in the last forty years of the twentieth century was the introduction of 'chilled products', made possible by the spread of refrigerators to almost every household and by the development of refrigerated display cabinets

4.14
A machine used in the manufacture of butter displayed outside the creamery at Felin Fach in West Wales.

(Photo: Barrie Trinder)

in supermarkets. One of the pioneers of the trade was Arthur Hollins of Fordhall Organic Farm near Market Drayton (SJ 648329), who in the late 1950s began to make organic yogurt, previously a minority taste, and to sell in markets and later in the food halls of department stores. The large dairy companies soon became involved with chilled products. Express Dairies bought a modest company called Ski Yogurt in Haywards Heath, Sussex, and began to make yogurt at a large modern works at Cuddington, Cheshire (SJ 596712), with which it had replaced an older plant it had purchased in 1963. Cuddington, alongside the A49, was claimed to be the first purpose-built yogurt plant in Britain. A creamery at Minsterley (SJ 375052), Shropshire, established just before the First World War to supply liquid milk to Birmingham, produced butter, cheese, canned cream and canned condensed milk and dried milk until the 1960s, and was subsequently adapted to produce cottage cheese, using enclosed vessels imported from Finland, and fromage frais. Sales of chilled products depend on well-designed packaging, made by such companies as Waddingtons of Leeds, which in the early 1970s were claiming credit for the success of mousse – 'the marketing sensation of 1969'. Ironically, the largest plant for the production of chilled products operating in the late 1990s, a further example of the transfer of technology, was that of the Müller corporation from Bavaria, established outside Market Drayton (SJ 6535), which towers over the fields of Arthur Hollins's Fordhall Farm, where sales of yogurt began forty years earlier.[17]

In the early years of the twentieth century farmers delivered milk in churns to the deck of the creamery. Immediately after the First World War most dairy companies invested in ex-military lorries, which collected churns from stands at the ends of farm drives. The Staverton creamery employed army-surplus Dennis vehicles, while Albions were used at Ingestre. Bulk tankers began collecting milk from farms in the 1960s, which involved the installation of storage tanks at farms and redundancy for the milk stands at the ends of farm drives, and changes in the means by which milk was received at creameries. When a factory changed, all its supplier farms had to change with it. Bulk collection was universal in most dairying regions by the late 1970s.

The dairy industry experienced numerous organisational changes, take-overs and sales of plant in the course of the twentieth century. Some regulation of relationships between farmers and manufacturers followed, after a period of disorganisation, the establishment of the Milk Marketing Board in 1933, but the industry was deregulated in the 1980s. Many creameries have made different products at different times, and there was a tendency in the closing decades of the century for manufacturing to be concentrated in larger plants. Much investigation is needed before the industry can be understood, but its archaeology, whether the study of its buildings, its transport systems, its technology or its packaging, is a productive source of evidence.

4.15 *(top)*
The creamery at Whitland, West Wales, photographed in 1991.

(Photo: Barrie Trinder)

4.16 *(bottom)*
The creamery at Johnstown, Carmarthen, photographed in 1991, when the rail connections, across which tanks bound to and from London were shunted until the 1970s, were still in place.

(Photo: Barrie Trinder)

The international transfer of technology:

Beverages

Milk-based drinks were another product of the dairy industry. Cocoa and similar chocolate-based products were made by the major chocolate companies, but involved them in the processing of milk. Cadbury's plant at Knighton, Staffordshire (SJ 748268), on the banks of the Shropshire Union Canal, made extensive use of canal transport. The principal drinks not made by the chocolate companies were Horlicks and Ovaltine. The Horlicks factory in Stoke Poges Lane, Slough (SU 973804), was built in 1908, more than a decade before the establishment of the Slough Industrial Estate. It has a long three-storey front elevation with a crenellated tower at one end, and supposedly copied the factory built by William Horlick (1846–1940) in Racine, Michigan, to manufacture the malted milk drink he invented in 1887. Ovaltine first appeared in Britain in 1909. The Ovaltine factory of A. Wander & Sons (now Novartis) was constructed in 1913 alongside the West Coast Main Line at King's Langley in Hertfordshire (TL 079021), in the centre of an estate which produced a range of materials used in manufacturing. Until the 1980s several tableaux advertising Ovaltine stood in the fields of the Ovaltine Farm on the opposite side of the railway.

The manufacture of instant coffee began at the Nestlé factory at Hayes (TQ 129789) in 1939. The Hayes plant was originally a chocolate factory, and after it had been purchased by Nestlé a range of buildings designed by Wallis, Gilbert & Partners was built alongside the Grand Junction Canal. After 1945, supplies from Hayes were supplemented by coffee made in a four-storey tower at Ashbourne with plant installed during the Second World War for the manufacture of powdered milk. Demand was such that Nestlé decided in 1956–57 to adapt the whole of its plant at nearby Tutbury (SK 216296) to the manufacture of instant coffee. The tower in which coffee was freeze-dried in the 1990s dominates the surrounding countryside. The coffee-roasting ovens built in Emmerich on the German–Dutch border are a further example of the transfer of technology, and the packing building of 1901 that bears Henri Nestlé's initials remained in use in the 1990s.

4.17
The Nestlé factory at Hayes, Middlesex, photographed in 1995. The factory was built in 1914 for the manufacture of chocolate, and taken over by Nestlé in 1929, although the company had a substantial interest in it as early as 1919. After being used for munitions storage during the First World War, it was extended with a four-storey building alongside the Grand Junction Canal designed by Wallis, Gilbert & Partners in 1919–20. From 1939 it was used for the manufacture of instant coffee.

(Crown copyright. NMR)

The other principal supplier of instant coffee to supermarkets in the 1990s also had overseas origins. Alfred Bird, a Birmingham chemist, discovered in 1837 a means of making custard without eggs, and set up a company to produce custard and baking powder in 1843. Its existence was uneventful in the twentieth century until 1947, when it formed a link with the General Foods corporation of the United States, and acquired new premises about 100 yards from its original works in Digbeth (SP 077864) with the intention of making instant coffee. The business grew rapidly after the product was named Maxwell House in 1957, and the company had 30 per cent of the market by 1962. By that year the site was threatened by road-widening proposals, and the company decided to move to a purpose-built plant at Banbury (SP 452416) whose coffee-making tower is a prominent landmark north of the town. Its aromas can be sensed through the open windows of passing cars on the nearby M40. The old Birds custard factory remains in Birmingham, and has been adapted to new uses.[18]

The chocolate industry was distinguished in the early twentieth century by three factories – Cadbury at Bournville, Birmingham (SP 048812), Rowntree at New Earswick, York

(SE 609559), and Fry at Somerdale near Bristol (ST 656695) – that were adjacent to workers' housing, designed according to the most enlightened thinking of the time. They remained in production in 1999, although the Rowntree factory was by then part of the Nestlé conglomerate, and the Cadbury works the centre of a large international company. The most significant example of the transfer of technology in this branch of the food industry was the leasing in 1932 of land for a factory on the Slough Trading Estate by the US Mars corporation (TQ 954816). In 1999 the company continued to occupy a First World War building, but most of its very large complex dated from the early 1960s. The original intention of Forrest Mars was to make Milky Way bars, but the new Mars Bar proved to be more appealing to British tastes. The company also manufactured Chappie dog food.[19]

Beer is the most English of drinks, and in the 1990s large-scale brewing continued in towns that had for many centuries been famous for beer, in London, Edinburgh, Alloa, Burton upon Trent and Tadcaster. Brewing nevertheless changed greatly in the course of the twentieth century and some of the changes were the consequence of transfers of technology. In 1899 the Allsopp company in Burton upon Trent began making lager in their old brewery, under the direction of a Swedish brewer, E. M. Lundgren. Twenty-six large glass enamelled steel tanks were imported from the Pfaudler Vacuum Fermentation Company in Rochester, New York, together with ammonia compressors from the Buffalo Refrigeration Company, also in the state of New York. The Guinness Brewery was established in Dublin in 1759 and was exporting to England by the early nineteenth century. In 1913 the company purchased over 100 acres (40ha) of land at Trafford Park, and subsequently used part of it as a depot. The Guinness landholding was significant in the way the estate developed in the inter-war period, but it was never used for a brewery. Relationships between the British and Irish governments in the 1930s were uneasy, and Guinness feared that import duties might be imposed on Irish products. In 1933 the company decided to build a new brewery at Park Royal in north-west London (TQ 196828) on the site of the disused showground of the Royal Agricultural Society, and adjacent to the

industrial estate that was developing on a former munitions works (*see Chapter 7*). Land that was surplus to the requirements of the brewery was leased to small companies. The brewery was designed by Sir Giles Gilbert Scott, with Sir Alexander Gibb & Partners as consultant engineers. The seven principal buildings, each with a height of 30.5m (100ft), were steel framed and clad with pale ground bricks. Construction began in 1934, and the first brew was made on 21 February 1936. The distinctive strain of yeast used at the Dublin brewery since 1759 was transferred to Park Royal from Ireland. The brewery employed 1,600 people when opened and 1,200 in the early 1990s. Like many plants of the 1930s it included social facilities, tennis and squash courts, a club house, and a sports ground. The buildings were adapted in the post-war period to produce Harp Lager and Kaliber low-alcohol beer.[20]

Another significant transfer of technology, by one of the most famous European brewers, Carlsberg of Copenhagen, was the construction in 1973–79 of an extensive lager-manufacturing plant, designed by Knud Monk, on the site of several older breweries on the banks of the River Nene in Northampton (SP 755600).

In the 1990s drinkers in most public houses had a choice of beers bearing names from many parts of the world – Australia, Canada, the mid-west of the United States, Alsace, Belgium, The Netherlands, Germany and Mexico. Most such beers were manufactured at large plants in Britain, brewing technology having developed to a stage where most tastes can be replicated in any part of the world.

One of the greatest changes in diet in the last forty years of the twentieth century was the surging popularity of wine drinking, the preserve of a discriminating minority until the late 1950s. One means of popularising wine was through cheese-and-wine parties. A Shropshire grocer who supplied cheese for one such party in about 1960 recalled that the participants drank wine as if it were beer, and in consequence became very drunk. One of the first brands of wine to be widely sold was Hirondelle, which was handled in the restored kilns of the Three Mills complex in east London (TQ 383827). Off-licences were easier to obtain by the early 1970s than previously, and the principal supermarkets began to sell wine. Sainsbury decided in 1970 to begin to purchase wines bottled at source, initially from France, but then from Italy, Spain and, by the 1990s, from Australia and Latin America. Wine in many respects is just one among many supermarket lines, and even when handled by specialist chains or local wine merchants creates few distinctive archaeological features. One aspect of the increased interest in wine was the establishment of vineyards in southern Britain in the last three decades of the century.

Meat, vegetables and fish

Much of the meat eaten in Britain during the twentieth century came from overseas. Two of the most substantial structures associated with the meat trade were the lairages at Wallasey and Woodside at Birkenhead, built in the 1870s for the import of live cattle. Because of restrictions on the trade, most cattle actually imported in the twentieth century were from Ireland. The installations were used for much of the century, the Wallasey lairage closing in 1969 and that at Woodside in 1985.[21] Most meat was imported frozen, and the principal features of this part of the trade were the huge cold stores in the ports, like those in the Royal Albert Dock (TQ 4280) in London, which had been demolished by 1999.

The bacon trade was considerably influenced by the transfer of technology. The processing of bacon on a large scale was much more advanced in Denmark and the United States than in Britain in the early years of the century. The St Edmundsbury Bacon Factory at Elmswell (TL 989640) near Bury St Edmunds, the enterprise of a group of local farmers and landowners, opened in 1912, having been designed by the Danish architect M. Wendelbow Madsen. Many of the techniques practised at the Wiltshire bacon factories of C. & T. Harris of Calne (ST 9970) were learned by a member of the family at Schenectady, New York. Like other food manufacturers, producers of bacon, and of sausages, were dependent on railways prior to the 1960s. In the inter-war years C. & T. Harris distributed its products throughout Britain in the Great Western Railway's siphon vans, originally designed for carrying milk in churns,

which carried on their sides boards detailing precisely the trains in which they were scheduled to travel. Palethorpes Ltd in 1890 purchased a model brewery in Park Lane, Tipton (SO 965918), and converted it to a sausage factory. Until the works was relocated to Market Drayton (SJ 682348) in 1968, a fleet of six-wheeled vans bearing the company livery was used to distribute Palethorpe's products on passenger and parcels trains to many parts of Britain.

The growth of the H. J. Heinz corporation in Britain illustrates many aspects of the food industry. The company was founded in Pittsburgh in 1869, its main products being pickles and tomato ketchup. The founder, Henry John Heinz (1844–1919), began trading in Britain in 1886 when he started to supply Fortnum & Mason with ketchup. The company established an office in London in 1896 and moved to larger premises in Farringdon Road two years later, at which time it was simply distributing products imported from the United States, most of it to outlets catering for the same exclusive markets as Fortnum & Mason. In 1905 Heinz bought Batty & Co., makers of pickles in Peckham, and used their premises to manufacture the company's own products on a small scale. After the First World War the company moved from exclusive to mass markets. In 1925 Heinz opened its factory at Harlesden (TQ 205834) in north-west London, doubling its size after three years, and in 1928 commencing the large-scale manufacture of baked beans, its most celebrated product in Britain. The history of Heinz for much of the century was a history of its advertising as much as of its buildings. The '57 varieties' slogan, first used in the United States in 1896, became part of the English language. After the Second World War planning legislation restricted expansion in London, and in 1946 the company established a new factory in a wartime munitions works at Standish near Wigan (SQ 5610), where air-raid shelters were adapted as tasting rooms, and stores of tomato paste replaced stocks of anti-aircraft ammunition. In 1957 the first section of a new factory at Kitt Green, Wigan (SQ 5406), designed by J. Douglas Mathews & Partners to replace that at Standish, was brought into commission The architect's views of the project reveal much about changes in factory design during the twentieth century. The Harlesden factory he considered 'tailor-made to the production requirements of the time ... [though] insufficient allowances were made for the possibility of technical advances', while Kitt Green incorporated 'large uninterrupted spaces with the minimum of structural restrictions so that production plant can be installed and changed with ease'. The change from designing buildings for particular technologies to creating premises which can accommodate new systems, as yet unimagined, is profound and has affected every kind of industrial enterprise.[22]

Fish in the seas around Britain were one of the nation's greatest national resources in the early twentieth century, but after intensive exploitation they were no longer so abundant in the 1990s. Aberdeen, Hull, Grimsby, Great Yarmouth, Lowestoft and Fleetwood, the principal industrial fishing ports that had grown up in the closing decades of the nineteenth century, were supplied principally by steam trawlers and drifters, and had markets and gutting sheds on shore, railway sidings from which prime fish could be distributed across the country, and industries like meal and glue manufacture that could use the parts of fish that could not be eaten. There was a substantial export trade of preserved herring to Germany and Russia. The pattern of the industry remained much the same through the first sixty years of the century. It was dependent on the railways. The nominal destination of the long train of fish wagons that just after one o'clock left Grimsby daily in the 1950s was Whitland in West Wales (SN 2016). Only one or two wagons would actually go there, but others carried fish via the Great Central Line and Banbury to almost every town of consequence in South Wales and in southern England west of Hastings. On the East Coast Main Line fish was conveyed between Aberdeen and London in trains made up of long-wheelbase wagons which could go at the same speeds as passenger trains. The fish trains were abruptly withdrawn in the early 1960s, but their disappearance was a symptom rather than a cause of the changes in the fishing industry, and not just the consequence of competition from road transport. Fish stocks were diminishing, and customs changing. Young women from the north-east of Scotland no longer migrated to Yarmouth every autumn to gut and pack herring on the quays.[23]

Substantial changes were also brought about by the transfer of technology. The Scandinavian company Findus in 1955 began to use cold stores at Grimsby as warehouses from which to distribute food, chiefly fish products, manufactured in Scandinavia. In 1960 Findus began to make 'fish sticks' at a factory in Humberstone Road, Grimsby, using cod frozen at Hammerfest in Norway that was coated with locally produced breadcrumbs. Techniques for preserving food and for the preparation of complete meals that need a minimum of cooking in the home greatly advanced during the last forty years of the century. Grimsby remained in the 1990s one of the most important centres of food production in Britain, and not just of fish-based products, partly because of its inheritance from the nineteenth century of a thriving fish industry, but also because in the 1950s and 1960s Scandinavian companies used the town as a base from which to introduce new techniques of food manufacture to Britain. There is also a cluster of food processing works around Great Yarmouth and Lowestoft, which similarly owe their origins to the long history of fish processing on the Norfolk coast.

Individual enterprises

Much of this chapter has been concerned with large companies battling for mass markets, with take-overs, mergers and plants employing many hundreds of people. Nevertheless, some of the most significant transfers of food technology in the twentieth century were achieved on a micro scale, by individual immigrants whose collective enterprises did much to alter the British diet.

One group that left few archaeological traces was the Italians, who set up coffee houses in South Wales, and in some other mining areas, in the early years of the twentieth century. In the early 1970s it was still possible to enjoy espressos or cappuccinos together with Italian confectionery in bars in settlements no more fashionable than Brynmawr (SO 191116), Aberdare or Oakengates. The hissing of the gilded monster coffee machine at the first of these was particularly memorable. The principal trace of the Italian coffee house in the South Wales coalfield is now discernible in the names of bakery chains like Ferrari.

Italian migrants were influential also in the dairy trade. In Huddersfield, in the 1950s, Dominico Dagostino operated a retail dairy on Bradford Road and the Original Milk Bar in the Beastmarket, which closed in the 1970s. The Vighlietti and Gabrielli families were active in the town's ice-cream trade, as were Italians in many parts of Britain. In Scarborough the ice-cream trade was dominated by the Jaconelli family, who moved there in 1933 from Glasgow. Peter Jaconelli (1925–99), who had trained as an opera singer, developed national markets for his products, and helped to rejuvenate the port of Scarborough.[24] The most elegant archaeological evidence of the Italian ice-cream manufacturers is Nardini's, a Modernist roadhouse-style complex on the seafront at Largs (NS 202597), illustrated on page 188.

In Scotland Italians were also prominent in the fish-and-chips trade, most of them originating from the villages around Barga in Tuscany, and around Picinisco in the Val di Comino. They dominated the trade in Glasgow in the early part of the century, and in some establishments combined the production of fried fish-and-chips with the selling of ice-cream.[25]

In the second half of the century the greatest changes in diet brought about by individual immigrants were the consequence of Chinese and Indian restaurants, which had opened in most sizeable towns by 1960. Restaurants and still more take-away ('carry-out' in Scotland) shops proliferated, and by the 1990s they could be found in almost every settlement large enough to support half a dozen retailers. In their early years such restaurants made eating out possible for the young. The meals were inexpensive, and the venues were open late into the evenings and at weekends. The transferred technology has been modified to suit the tastes of the host country. Chicken tikka masala appears to have its origins in England rather than in Bangladesh, while balti dishes appear to have been developed in Birmingham as opposed to the sub-continent.[26] On a slightly later time scale, another significant change was the appearance in Britain of American pizza chains and hamburger chains like McDonald's and Burger King, the greatest impact of which was perhaps to introduce the habit of eating out to young children. The first McDonald's in the UK opened at Woolwich in 1974, and the 500th in Notting Hill in 1993. While the first generations of oriental restaurants have left few significant archaeological traces, the kiosks of the American chains are likely to remain distinctive features of the landscape well into the twenty-first century.

Conclusions

The food industry illustrates well the importance of the transfer of technology in twentieth-century industry, but another way of describing what has happened might, to use a cliché of the 1990s, be increasing globalisation. This is true at the level of large corporations. Britain is just one sphere of operation for Cadbury, Nestlé or Mars. But food in Britain illustrates also broader changes: the long-sustained impact of the Second World War, the power of American multinational companies, growing cultural and economic links with Europe, and diminishing trade ties with the Old Commonwealth. Similar transfers of technology could be illustrated in other industries. The food industry is interesting is that the transfer of its technology changes cultures. The hamburgers sold by McDonald's are intended to be identical wherever they are sold, but much of what has come from overseas has acquired a particular place in British culture. Fish fingers or baked beans symbolise quick, trouble-free meals and were more popular in Britain in the 1990s than in their countries of origin. The Mars Bar and the carton of yogurt became quintessential twentieth-century artefacts. Examination of the food industry shows that there is a cultural dimension to the study of industrial archaeology, a dimension extending beyond artefacts, images, structures, sites and landscapes, and that imagination is needed if it is to be fully uncovered.

Notes and references

1 J. R. Harris, *Industrial Espionage and Technology Transfer: Britain and France in the Eighteenth Century*, Aldershot: Ashgate, 1998; D. Jeremy, *Transatlantic Industrial Revolution: The Diffusion of Textile Technologies between Britain and America 1790–1830*, Oxford: Blackwell, 1981.

2 R. Nicholls, *Trafford Park*, Chichester: Phillimore, 1996.

3 The Kellogg plant is strictly speaking on the Barton Dock estate.

4 J. Tann and R. Glyn Jones, 'Technology and Transformation: The Diffusion of the Roller Mill in the British Flour Milling Industry, 1870–1907', *Technology and Culture*, 1996, vol. 37, pp. 36–69.

5 *Railway Magazine*, 1914, vol. 24, p. 139.

6 M. Stratton, 'New Materials for a New Age: Steel and Concrete Construction in the North of England, 1860–1939', *Industrial Archaeology Review*, 1999, vol. 21, pp. 18–19.

7 *The Miller*, 4 May 1896; J. Booker, *Essex and the Industrial Revolution*, Chelmsford: Essex County Council, 1974, pp. 90–2.

8 R. Butterfield, 'The Industrial Archaeology of the Twentieth Century: The Shredded Wheat Factory at Welwyn Garden City', *Industrial Archaeology Review*, 1994, vol. 16, pp. 196–215.

9 T. A. B. Corley, *Quaker Enterprise in Biscuits: Huntley & Palmer of Reading 1822–1972*, London: Hutchinson, 1972.

10 M. J. Franklin, *British Biscuit Tins*, London: New Cavendish, 1979; P. R. G. Hornsby, *Decorated Biscuit Tins*, London: Schiffer, 1984.

11 Data from National Monuments Record, Swindon.

12 D. Cant, 'The Establishment and Development of the Sugar Beet Industry in the United Kingdom 1900–1930', Ironbridge Institute, Master's dissertation, 1986.

13 This account of the margarine industry is drawn from: P. Mathias, *Retailing Revolution*, London: Longmans, 1967; C. Wilson, *The History of Unilever: A Study in Economic Growth and Social Change*, 2 vols, London: Cassell, 1954; and A. Armstrong, *The Economy of Kent 1640–1914*, Woodbridge: Boydell, 1995, pp. 121–2.

14 B. Trinder, 'The Archaeology of the British Food Industry 1660–1960: A Preliminary Survey', *Industrial Archaeology Review*, 1993, vol. 15, pp. 119–39; J. N. Slinn, *Great Western Railway Siphons: An Account of Vehicles Built for Milk Traffic*, Penryn: Pendragon, 1986.

15 The research on Aston Creamery was done by Tanya English, a student at the Ironbridge Institute 1991–92.

16 P. Sainsbury, *The Transition from Tradition to Technology: A History of the Dairy Industry in Devon*, Tiverton, privately published, 1991, pp. 39, 43, 79, 96.

17 A. Hollins, *The Farmer, the Plough and the Devil: The Story of Fordhall Farm, Pioneer of Organic Farming*, Bath: Ashgrove, 1984.

18 M. Mann, *Workers on the Move: The Sociology of Relocation*, Cambridge: Cambridge University Press, 1973.

19 M. Cassell, *Long Lease: The Story of Slough Estates 1920–1991*, London: Pencorp, 1991.

20 L. Shepherd, *Brewery Railways of Burton on Trent*, Guisborough: Industrial Railway Society, 1996, pp. 205–6; A. Bryant, 'The Guinness Brewery, Park Royal', Ironbridge Institute, assignment for the Diploma course in Industrial Archaeology, 1994.

21 K. McCarron, *Meat at Woodside: The Birkenhead Livestock Trade 1878–1981*, Birkenhead: Merseyside Port Folios, 1991.

22 S. Potter, *The Magic Number: The Story of 57*, London: Max Reinhardt, 1959, pp. 162–7.

23 B. Trinder, 'Revolutions in the Food Industry', *From Industry to Industrial Heritage: Proceedings of the Ninth International Conference on the Conservation of the Industrial Heritage, Montreal/Ottawa 1994*, Canadian Society for Industrial Heritage, 1998, pp. 114–17.

24 The research on Huddersfield was carried out by Richard Butterfield, a student at the Ironbridge Institute in 1990–91. The material on Scarborough is from the obituary to Peter Jaconelli in the *Guardian*, 17 May 1999.

25 J. K. Walton, *Fish and Chips and the British Working Class 1870–1940*, Leicester: Leicester University Press, 1992, pp. 37–8; L. Sponza, *Italian Immigrants in Nineteenth Century Britain: Realities and Images*, Leicester: Leicester University Press, 1988.

26 E. Brockes and Iqbal Wahhab, 'Spice ... the Final Frontier', *Guardian*, 4 November 1999.

Chapter five

Much of Britain's twentieth-century prosperity was derived from making ships, aircraft and motorcars. Nevertheless, by 1999 shipbuilding had almost disappeared, aircraft factories were concerned largely with making components, if large or important ones, and the principal car plants were owned by foreign companies. It is easy to use evidence from these three industries within a declinist historiography, to see them as symptoms of a deep-seated decline or an anti-technological culture fostered within the public schools and the ancient universities, of the irresponsible misuse of power by trade unions, of failures of management, or of excessive interference by governments. Evidence can readily be found of all four phenomena.

Cars, ships and aircraft

5.1
Morris cars being assembled at Cowley *c.* 1930.

(Crown copyright. NMR)

Yet within a wider context the picture may look different. At the simplest level, archaeology may show that nothing in the British motorcar industry is comparable with the research and development facilities of Mercedes Benz at Stuttgart, that some motorcars wholly lacked imagination and were badly built. Nevertheless, the British car industry was second only to that of the United States until after 1960, and exports of cars contributed notably to the post-war economic recovery. The successful manufacture of aircraft depends largely on achieving low unit costs of production, something that was scarcely possible in the 1930s. The motor and aircraft industries together succeeded during the Second World War in producing large numbers of successful aircraft. The post-war civil aircraft programme set out in the report of the Brabazon Committee seems, with hindsight, to have been ludicrously over-ambitious, although the Vickers Viscount and subsequently the BAC 1-11 were successfully sold in large numbers in world markets. Aircraft manufacture is crucially linked with military expenditure, and David Edgerton has argued that English society in the twentieth century had a strongly militaristic component, a legacy of imperialism and a consequence of the aspiration that the country should 'punch above its weight' in international affairs.[1] Shipbuilding is a notoriously volatile and footloose industry, and in the long run it is scarcely surprising that the yards on the Clyde, Tyne, Wear and Mersey that rose in the latter part of the nineteenth century have declined in the same way as those of an earlier generation in London and on the New Brunswick coast.

The received view of the shipbuilding regions is one of unemployment and depression, yet many of the world's ships of the first two-thirds of the twentieth century were indeed made in British yards.

Several consistent themes emerge from a review of the archaeology of aircraft and motorcar manufacture in Britain. First, it is evident that the two industries were closely linked. The name Rolls-Royce, shared between the nation's best-known luxury car and its most successful producer of aero-engines, is the best-known example. Second, it is clear that motorcar manufacture emerged from other industries – in many towns, from local coach-making businesses and agricultural engineering concerns, and in metalworking communities like Coventry and Birmingham, from the manufacture of bicycles and sewing machines – while some motorcar engineers received their training in locomotive works. Third, it is evident from the archaeological record that many early factories were of modest size, that while some manufacturers were building large

5.2
One of the principal shops at the shipyard of Cammell Laird, Birkenhead, photographed in 1913.

(Crown copyright: NMR)

factories others were operating what was in scale almost a domestic industry. Fourth, it is clear that many men who had received conventional upper-middle-class education were certainly not dissuaded thereby from involvement in engineering. The 'blazered classes' were interested in cars and in flying, developed a club culture associated with these activities, and often became involved in manufacturing. Fifth, the influence of two world wars can be seen at almost every significant motorcar and aircraft manufacturing site in Britain. Sixth, the two industries have been of such importance through the twentieth century that they have constantly been the subject of government intervention, and that intervention has been concerned not just with the production of munitions but with the general direction of economic policy. It is impossible in a study of this kind to focus attention on every car factory, and the state of research enables scarcely anything to be said about those that produced commercial vehicles. Some factories, like the Austin works at Longbridge (*see Chapter 7*), are discussed in other contexts. Motorcar factories are exceedingly varied. Nevertheless, they provide convincing evidence of many of the themes that characterised the industry during the twentieth century.

The artefactual record of the two industries is also important. Motorcars are preserved in large numbers. Enthusiasts' clubs keep records of and provide advice and parts for the restoration of vehicles of all sorts, from Rolls-Royces to Austin Sevens, and even models that are rarely regarded as successful, like the Austin Allegro, have their devotees. There are many museums of motor vehicles, some with extensive collections like those at Beaulieu, Coventry and Gaydon. Similarly, there are many museums of aircraft, and examples are preserved of almost every type constructed in Britain since the Second World War, but very few museums highlight the process of production. There are few preserved machine tools or presses, and no museum displays a section of a robot-less assembly line of the kind used to make cars prior to the 1980s. One of the best ways to gain an understanding of the manufacture of aircraft is to visit the restoration workshops at the Imperial War Museum, Duxford (TL 4646), which show the intricate nature of the construction of even the largest of aircraft,

although such workshops can convey nothing of the pressures of large-scale production. Aircraft museums range in scale from the RAF Museum in Hendon (TQ 220904), the Aerospace Museum at Cosford and the National Museum of Scotland at East Fortune to modest local collections with just one or two complete aircraft. Some historic aircraft are preserved by collectors. One Victor bomber is owned by an individual, who exercises it on a runway, and more than forty Tiger Moths flew to the annual rally of the marque at Woburn in 1999.

Most mass-production motorcars in the 1990s were assembled on moving tracks in large single-storey buildings with high roofs to accommodate sophisticated conveyor systems. Most bodies were welded by robots from pressed steel panels, and some phases of final assembly were also largely automated. Many parts, including complex sub-assemblies, were bought in from specialist suppliers on computer-controlled 'just-in-time' systems, with few components stored on the site. In 1900 the majority of the cars on British roads were imported, but manufacturing plants had been set up in a number of towns and the industry was beginning to grow rapidly. In the first decade of the century motorcars were assembled on trestles, a form of production still practised in 1999 at Morgan and by some small specialist producers. The first moving assembly line for motorcar chassis in Britain was developed by Ford from 1911 at Trafford Park and was fully operational by 1914, at the same time as the first at Ford's US plant at Highland Park, Detroit. In 1926 Morris at Cowley and Austin at Longbridge established chassis assembly lines. During the 1930s the major manufacturers developed 'monocoque', or chassis-less, forms of construction, utilising powered assembly lines and increasingly sophisticated systems of conveyors. The assembly line developed after the Second World War, with increasing numbers of tasks being undertaken by robots from the 1970s. The mass-production car factory of the late twentieth century, whether newly built or occupying buildings of some age, was invariably a high single-storey building. In the opening years of the century it was considered logical to build cars in multi-storey buildings, like the daylight factories constructed in Detroit by Albert Kahn.

The earliest surviving purpose-built car factory in England is probably that constructed in Guildford (SU 995495) in 1901 by the brothers John and Ray Dennis, a three-storey structure which remains, as Rodboro Buildings, close to the city centre. The building has recently been restored and is now a restaurant and pub. It proved ill-fitted for the assembly of cars, and from 1905 the company began to develop a site at Woodbridge Hill (SU 985508), on the edge of Guildford, to which production was soon transferred. From 1913 the company concentrated on the production of such specialist vehicles as fire engines and ambulances, and car production ceased. It remains a leading producer of fire engines and buses. Several other large-scale multi-storey factories were established in the Edwardian period, and from time to time British manufacturers returned to the notion in subsequent decades.[2]

Motorcar and aeroplane culture

Brooklands (TQ 068629) in Surrey is the most appropriate place to begin a survey of British motorcar and aircraft manufacture, not least because some of its buildings now form a museum illustrating aspects of both industries. Brooklands epitomises a certain tradition, that of the well-educated, well-connected gentleman, knowledgeable about technology, with funds to invest. An embanked concrete race track was established near Weybridge by the landowner Hugh Locke King in 1907. It was crossed by a steel bridge, symbolising the two new constructional materials of the early twentieth century. The year after the track was opened, A. V. Roe made there the first powered flight by a Briton in a British aeroplane. The first public demonstration of flying in Britain took place there in 1909, and in 1910 flying training commenced and was a feature of Brooklands for many years. The kiosk used from 1911 to sell tickets for pleasure flights still stands. In 1914 the Blériot company began to build aircraft at Brooklands and in 1915 Vickers commenced aircraft production in the former Itala motorcar factory within the racing circuit,

and aircraft were made there until the closure of the works in 1987. Barnes Wallis, who originated the geodetic construction used in the Wellington bomber and designed the bouncing bombs used to destroy the dams in the Ruhr, worked at Brooklands for almost forty years. The racing circuit had a strongly upper-middle-class atmosphere: 'the right crowd and no crowding.... If Henley wasn't on, if Ascot wasn't on, if the Derby wasn't running, you went to Brooklands'. The setting resembles a horse-racing course. Officials included the clerk of the course and the clerk of the scales, who weighed cars, and the early drivers wore silks like jockeys. The Aero clubhouse, opened in 1932, was designed by Graham Dawbarn, best known for his buildings at municipal airports (*see Chapter 9*). People associated with Brooklands in the inter-war period included the speed-record holders John Cobb and Malcolm Campbell, Reid Railton (1895–1977), who designed Cobb's car, and T. G. John of Alvis Cars. While the Vickers factory has been demolished, it is still possible to sense at Brooklands something of an ethos that was a significant factor in both the motorcar and the aircraft industries, an aspiration to excel, rather like that of a cricket or rugby union club, but also of an upper-middle-class exasperation at the failings of government, whether failure to subsidise Grand Prix motor racing or failure to adopt innovations in military aircraft more quickly. Underpinning such echoes one may discern a sense of fervent patriotism, like that of Barnes Wallis, but also an awareness of how the reality of wartime and the necessity of mass production overtook the pleasure flights and fun-loving races with cars that did not go particularly fast and did not kill people.[3]

The customer-orientated factory

Clement Talbot's factory in Barlby Road (TQ 238821), north-west London, also exemplifies many aspects of the motorcar industry in the early years of the century. It was designed by William T. Walker (1856–1930) and produced cars between 1904 and 1938. Its office block, in a Beaux Arts style, is in red brick dressed with Portland stone, with a *porte-cochère* beneath which potential buyers could dismount from their vehicles and proceed to a display area within, where they could see sectioned models, before ascending to a balcony from which they could view the spectacular hall in which power for the plant was generated. The hall was adorned with a huge roundal inscribed 'Sunbeam Talbot Automobile works 1903'. The office building, with the appearance of a country house, fronted workshops of concrete construction. The brand names 'Talbot' and 'Sunbeam' passed to the Rootes Group and the factory was adapted to other uses.[4]

The Argyll motorcar factory at Alexandria (NS 392807), west of Glasgow alongside the railway from Dumbarton to Balloch, reflects even greater ambitions. The Argyll car had been developed by Alexander Govan. The red-sandstone factory, designed by Charles Halley of Dumbarton, was built on a 25-acre (10ha) site and began production in 1906. Its 760ft (230m) road frontage is richly ornamented with carvings illustrating the production process, including vices and compasses, while in the pediment a car emerges from the building bearing a colossal female figure with supporters, one of whom is blowing a trumpet while another holds an anvil and gear wheels. The management suite included a lecture hall which could accommodate orchestral concerts, and there were extensive welfare facilities for shopfloor workers, who were provided with uniforms. Govan died in 1907, production of motorcars ceased in 1914, and the buildings were taken over by government for the manufacture of torpedoes. The production sheds had been demolished but the frontage buildings were restored in the late 1990s. Like Clement Talbot's factory, the Argyll works reflects the close association which early motorcar manufacturers were trying to establish with their customers. The factory was designed to impress, and to stimulate sales.

Scotland's other great motorcar factory of the early twentieth century, the Arrol-Johnston plant at Heathall, Dumfries (NY 988791), illustrates rather more fully the themes which run through the history of the industry. George Johnston, who developed the Argyll car, had trained as a locomotive engineer, and had begun production in adapted premises in Glasgow and Paisley. Thomas Charles Pullinger, who was appointed general manager in 1909, brought to the company experience in bicycle manufacture and in making motorcars in the west midlands and in Paris. He had visited Detroit, and the new works built at Dumfries in 1912–13 was a three-storey concrete-framed daylight factory, similar to those designed by Albert Kahn for Henry Ford and other Detroit manufacturers. It was designed and built by Truscon, the British company established by Moritz Kahn, brother of Albert, which had its base at Trafford Park. Each floor of the factory had specific functions. Electric power was provided by a generating plant with five gas engines. There were drinking fountains supplied by artesian wells, a health centre and a canteen with timber-framed ornamentation, rather like that used at

5.3 (left)
The Arrol-Johnston motorcar factory at Heathhall, Dumfries, photographed in 1995.

(Crown copyright. Royal Commission on the Ancient and Historical Monuments of Scotland)

5.4 (right)
A poster of c. 1910 for a Shrewsbury garage that had evolved, as did many others, from a carriage-building business. Arrol-Johnston cars, made in Dumfries, are mentioned, together with three American marques.

(Authors' collection)

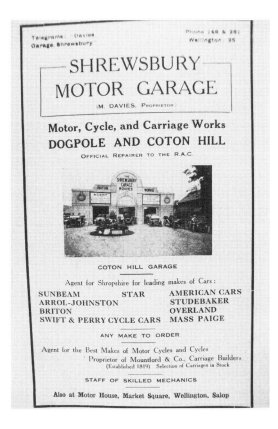

Cadbury's chocolate factory at Bournville. Some thirty-four workers' houses were constructed, though the company had intended to build 300. The site at Dumfries was chosen because it enabled the company to retain its Scottish identity while being near to English markets. Some skilled labour may also have been available since there was an earlier, short-lived, car factory in the town, the Drummond works, which produced about 125 vehicles between 1905 and 1909. Bernard Drummond, who had worked as a mechanical engineer in Berlin, took over a typical market-town foundry that had made agricultural machinery and traction engines. The buildings of the Drummond works were put to diverse uses after 1909, but remained in 1999.[5]

Aero-engines were made at the Argyll factory during the First World War, when more buildings were erected in the same style as the original. Production of cars resumed in 1919, and in 1921–22 the company made a light car, the Galloway, at a daylight factory at Tongland (NX 700939), built for munitions production during the war, powered by a hydro-electric plant, and staffed mainly by women. Production of the Galloway was transferred to Dumfries, where cars were made until 1927. The Argyll works then served different purposes and in 1999 was being used for the manufacture of green Wellington boots, while the Tongland factory was a battery chicken farm. The two surviving buildings of the Argyll enterprise are evidence of the international transfer of technology in the motorcar industry, even in its early years, of its origins in bicycle manufacture, locomotive building and market-town foundries, and of the profound influence of the world wars on the industry.[6]

The Morgan Motor Company factory at Malvern retains much of the atmosphere of an early twentieth-century works. It was established by H. F. S. Morgan, who, like George Johnston, had experience of locomotive engineering, in his case with the Great Western Railway at Swindon. He set up a garage in Malvern in 1906, and made his first car, a three-wheeler, three years later. The garage was extended, and was used for producing munitions in the First World War, but proved inadequate to increasing demand afterwards. Production was transferred to a new factory in nearby Pickersleigh Road in stages between 1919 and 1923. Morgan cars, still much in demand, are made on trestles, with ash-framed bodies. The factory retains three of the principal features of early motorcar factories: a combined machine shop and smithy; substantial wood-working facilities; and a service department, evidence of close links between manufacturer and customer.[7]

Market town and Garden City origins

The Morgan factory is an astonishing survival, based on sound engineering, close regard for customers and strong commitment on the part of both owners and the generally long-serving workforce. While its survival is unusual, it was, as the archaeological record shows, typical of many companies established in the first quarter of the twentieth century, evidence of whose existence is now provided only by factory buildings put to other uses, and in most cases by vehicles kept mobile by enthusiasts' clubs. Many garage owners in the early years of the twentieth century assembled a few cars, like that made by Charles Robinson and now displayed in Kettering museum, but factories making appreciable numbers of vehicles operated in towns which are scarcely ever linked with the motor industry: Adams in Bedford, which made cars between 1905 and 1913, Iris of Aylesbury of 1912–26, Gorden of Beverley of 1909–17, Prideaux of Barnstaple of 1907–12, Black Prince of Barnard Castle of 1919–21, Scout of Salisbury of 1905–21, and Brooke of Lowestoft of 1902–13.[8]

One of the best examples of this kind of company is that of J. H. Pick (1857–1954) of Stamford (SK 031067), a blacksmith, who had worked for Blackstone's agricultural engineering works and as a bicycle dealer. He began to make motorcars in 1899. He built a factory in Blackfriars Street in the town centre in 1903, but in 1904 disagreements with investors led him to leave the company. The building of 1903 was sold in 1906 to a printing firm which still occupied it in 1999. Pick established a new works in a former coachmaker's shop on High Street, St Martin's, one of the most elegant streets in Britain. In 1999 the factory was used as an antiques showroom. After the factory closed, Pick traded as a greengrocer from 11 High Street,

St Martin's, a premises he had also used for car production for a short time after his move from Blackfriars. All three buildings associated with the company thus survive, together with six known examples of vehicles made there, two in Britain and four in New Zealand.[9]

Stamford invites comparisons with Oxford. William Morris (1877–1963), later first Viscount Nuffield, shared some characteristics with J. H. Pick, notably his skills as a bicycle maker, repairer and agent. He began to repair bicycles at the home of his parents at 16 James Street, Oxford, and in 1901 moved to a shop at 48 High Street, where by 1905 he was operating a garage and taxi service, providing driving tuition for undergraduates, as well as making motorcycles. He extended his operations into nearby Longwall Street (SP 519064), where between 1908 and 1910 several ramshackle buildings were reconstructed as the Longwall Garage. It was there in 1913 that the first Bullnose Morris car was assembled, largely from parts made by others. The building remained a garage until 1963, and is now adapted as residential accommodation for New College, although the frontage has been retained. In 1914 Morris transferred production of motorcars to the Oxford Military College at Cowley (SP 5503), an ambitious range of buildings designed by T. G. Jackson, constructed in 1877–78 but never completed. There Morris found large spaces which were cleared of partitions. Machine tools were ranked on the ground floor and the first floor was used for assembling cars on trestles. By the 1990s both floors were used as open-plan offices, while Morris's own office was carefully preserved.

After the outbreak of war in 1914 Morris continued to produce cars, using some engines and other components imported from the United States, but by 1916 the Cowley plant was given over largely to munitions production. After the Armistice, Morris presided over the growth of one of the most successful British companies, increasing production to meet growing demand stimulated by reduced prices in the 1920s, and by exports, principally to India, Burma and Sri Lanka in the 1930s, and to Australia in the 1940s and 1950s. The company expanded in the 1920s by taking over its suppliers, including the S.U. Carburettor Company and the bodymakers

Hollick & Pratt in Birmingham; Hotchkiss et Cie, makers of engines in Coventry; and the Osberton Radiator Company in north Oxford (SP 504086). In 1925 Morris saw all-steel vehicle bodies being produced by the company established by Edward G. Budd in Philadelphia, and established a joint venture with Budd, building the plant of the Pressed Steel Company alongside the Cowley works, the first body pressings being produced in 1927. By the mid-1930s Pressed Steel was supplying bodywork for other British companies. It brought to Oxford the heaviest aspect of motor engineering, and the factory was notorious for its hazardous working conditions.

In 1937–38 more buildings were added to the Cowley site as part of the re-armament programme, and during the Second World War it produced more than 3,000 De Havilland Tiger Moth aircraft, repaired thousands of damaged military aircraft, made Merlin aero-engines, mines and military trucks to an American design, and built components for Horsa gliders and various types of fighter aircraft. The new wartime buildings were adapted to motorcar production after 1945, the outstanding success of the post-war period being the Morris Minor, introduced in 1948, which remained in production until 1971. The rationalisation of motorcar production in Britain, which began in the inter-war period with the take over by Nuffield of such companies as Riley and Wolseley, continued with the merger of Morris with Austin in 1952, creating the British Motor Corporation, in which Pressed Steel was incorporated the following year. Full integration did not follow, and further mergers, with Leyland in 1968 and with Rover in 1982, occurred. In the early 1990s the Cowley plant was changed on a dramatic scale. Production was concentrated in the former Pressed Steel plant, and the buildings of the old north and south works were demolished. Cowley in 1999 was a much smaller plant, employing far fewer people, than it had been in the third quarter of the century. The history of motorcar production in Oxford illustrates several of the key themes set out at the beginning of this chapter: the emergence of the car industry from trading in bicycles, the small scale of early production, the importance of the transfer of technology and of wartime investment by government. Comparison of the modest workshop at

Stamford with the ultra-modern plant that remained at Cowley in 1999 is evidence of another factor: the role of the gifted entrepreneur in the industry in the first half of the century. William Morris had management skills that J. H. Pick simply lacked, and those skills transformed Oxford, while Pick's enterprise made little long-term difference to the character of Stamford.[10]

A contrast with motorcar factories developed piecemeal from earlier buildings is provided by the Phoenix works in Pixmore Avenue (TL 226327), Letchworth (*see Chapter 8*), built in 1910 to accommodate a company established in north London by Joseph Van Hooydonk. The frontage building, accommodating offices and design studios, was in characteristic Garden City style, while behind it was a range of single-storey sheds with lightweight steel-framed roofs. The manufacture of Phoenix cars involved the transfer of technology from Belgium, since they used Minerva engines. Production ceased in 1922, but in 1926–27 the works was used for the manufacture of Arab cars, a venture by Reid Railton (*see above*) providing a link with activities at Brooklands. For another short spell in 1928–29 it was used by the Ascot Motor Company, set up by Cyril Pullin, who based his design on a Hungarian prototype. The building remains as evidence of one of the many characteristic twentieth-century products made in the first Garden City.[11]

Multinationals and the persistence of workshops

The works of the Ford Motor Company, widely scattered across Wales and England south of Merseyside, further illuminate the themes which run through the archaeology of the motorcar industry. The mere presence of Ford in Great Britain is evidence of the transfer of technology, and the expertise gained by Henry Ford in Detroit was brought to Trafford Park (*see Chapter 4*). Ford's factory at Trafford Park (SJ 780976), adapted from a coach works, opened on 13 October 1911, and assembly-line production of chassis began in 1914. One of the persistent characteristics of the international transfer of technology – the need to adapt to the circumstances of the host country – quickly

became evident. The factory assembled Model Ts, but the bodywork, imported from the United States, was not to British tastes, and a body-production department began operation in the spring of 1912. During the First World War some 30,000 Model Ts were produced for military use, and the factory was extended. Production was increased after the Armistice, 8,000 cars being completed in 1919 and 26,000 in the following year. By the end of the 1920s Ford employed some 3,500 people at Trafford Park, but in 1931 production and many workers were transferred to Dagenham. The factory was on the market for eight years. Part was sold in 1939, but on the outbreak of war Ford returned to Manchester to make aero-engines, and re-occupied its original factory. After 1945 the buildings passed to other uses. Some have been demolished, but the stores, machine shops, body shops and trim shops remained in 1999, used principally as a timber warehouse.[12]

The Ford Motor Company began to search for other sites in Britain from 1913, and considered and rejected two at Southampton, where in subsequent years a works producing vans was established in the former Cunliffe-Owen aircraft factory. In 1923 the company purchased a 307-acre (124ha) site at Dagenham (TQ 4981) on the Thames-side marshes, the attractions of which were deep water for mooring ships, railway links with the midlands, and the availability of labour from the huge estate that had been built by the LCC at Becontree (*see Chapter 8*). Further land was acquired in the late 1920s, and in 1929 construction began of an integrated plant, largely of steel-framed buildings, the foundations of which were concrete piles driven into the marshes. Some £5 million was invested to create a factory employing 20,000 people, with a capacity to produce 200,000 cars a year. Like the company's River Rouge plant in Detroit, Dagenham was intended to be self-sufficient, smelting iron ore in its own blast furnaces to produce pig iron for the foundry, and operating its own generating plant. Benzol from the ovens which provided coke for blast furnaces and cupolas was used to provide new cars with their first tankfuls of petrol. The plant began operation in stages from the spring of 1931. Munitions, principally vehicles, were manufactured on a large scale at Dagenham during the Second World War, but Ford's

Cars, ships and aircraft

considerable involvement in the production of aircraft and aero-engines took place elsewhere. Bodies were provided from an adjacent factory set up in 1931 by Briggs Bodies of Detroit, and taken over by Ford in 1953. It was linked to a new assembly plant by a conveyor bridge in 1959. The plant was much altered in the second half of the twentieth century. The power station, foundry and blast furnaces were demolished, and methods of production completely re-organised. The outstanding product of the Essex works was the Cortina, of which more than four million were made between 1962 and 1982. Many were still on the roads in 1999, and they are enthusiastically preserved. Dagenham was a unique plant. It was intended to be self-sufficient in a way that is unparalled within the British motor industry, and was designed from the first as a large plant by an overseas investor in a way that had no parallels until the 1980s.[13]

Ford's other passenger-car assembly plant at Halewood (SJ 4484) near Liverpool also exemplifies a particular stage in the history of the motor industry, indeed in social and economic history generally. One of the outcomes of the conventional wisdom of the mid-1940s that governments could make and implement plans for economic growth and social improvement was a widespread acceptance of the efficacy of planned industrial location. In the late 1950s and early 1960s the west midlands, the heartland of motorcar manufacturing, was perceived as suffering from over-employment and overcrowded living conditions, while other areas where traditional industries had declined, like Lancashire and Scotland, were seen as in need of investment. In consequence, motorcar companies were given incentives to set up plants in new areas but allowed few opportunities to expand their existing plants. Ford acquired land for a Merseyside factory in 1963, conveniently situated alongside a dual-carriageway and within a mile of Liverpool airport. Rail connections have always been important for the interchange of parts with Dagenham and, since the opening of the Channel Tunnel, with the Ford works at Genk in eastern Belgium. Production began in 1963 in long ranges of interconnected concrete- and steel-framed sheds. The best-known product of Halewood was the front-wheel-drive Escort, made in large numbers from 1980.[14] Halewood, with the Vauxhall plant at Ellesmere Port on the other side of the Mersey, has proved the most successful of the plants that were effectively located at the direction of government in the early 1960s.

Vauxhall's Merseyside plant (SJ 3878) was located on the site of Hooton Park airfield, used by the RAF from 1917 until 1957, of which some hangars remained in the 1990s. It began production of machined parts in 1963 and commenced the assembly of Vivas in 1964. Its future was threatened in the late 1970s but the plant's prosperity was revived with the beginning of Astra assembly in 1981. The other plants, Standard Triumph at Speke, Rootes at Linwood and BMC at Bathgate, Scotland (NS 9768), fared less well. Standard Triumph in 1959 purchased a factory at Speke that was supplying the company with bodies, and soon afterwards commenced construction of an adjacent assembly plant that was due to commence production in 1964–65, but did not actually do so until 1969. Labour relations and the transfer of bodies and engines between Merseyside and the midlands were not well managed. The assembly plant closed in 1978, by which time Standard Triumph was part of the British Leyland Group, and production of bodies ceased in 1980. By 1999 the plant had been converted to small industrial units. The Rootes Group was reluctant to move from Coventry but in the early 1960s was persuaded to build a new factory at Linwood (NS 4564) near Paisley. Bodies were provided by a Pressed Steel plant, established in a shadow factory building in 1947, which in turn drew its steel from the plant at Ravenscraig, Motherwell, itself established as the result of a government decision in 1958 (see Chapter 2). Rootes purchased the body plant in 1966. Initially the plant built the Hillman Imp, the Rootes response to BMC's Mini. Subsequently other models were made at Linwood but the plant closed in 1981, and by the 1990s was being developed as a retail park.[15]

Ford has many other plants in Britain. Commercial vehicles were produced in 1999 at Southampton, and from the 1950s until the mid-1990s the company used the former Hawker aircraft factory at Langley, Buckinghamshire, where the Hurricane and Tempest fighters were built during the Second World War, for the same purpose. A large engine plant (SS 9378) of the late 1970s stands

5.5
A Ford components
factory on the Treforest
Industrial Estate in
South Wales.

(Photo: Barrie Trinder)

alongside the industrial estate on the site of the former Royal Ordnance Factory at Bridgend (*see Chapter 7*), while on the pioneer industrial estate at Treforest (ST 1086) are two relatively small components factories, with stylish fronts, apparently of the 1950s, probably masking some of the original modular units erected on the estate from 1938.

Like the plants at Halewood and Dagenham, the Vauxhall factory at Luton (TL 1020) belongs to one of the world's largest multinational companies. The Vauxhall name, and the Wyvern logo which appears on the company's cars, originated from a marine-engine works established near Vauxhall station in south London in 1857. Car manufacture began in 1903 as the result of the interest of a manager, and sixty-four vehicles were sold the following year. Production was transferred to an existing factory at Luton in 1905. The plant was steadily expanded, and the office block, in the Queen Anne style designed by H. B. Cresswell in 1907, was fitted out in a luxurious manner reminiscent of the Clement Talbot and Argyll works. Subsequent production buildings constructed between 1911 and 1920 have diminishingly ornate detailing. In 1925 the company was taken over by the American General Motors corporation, and the factory

expanded rapidly in the 1930s. More buildings were constructed during the Second World War to manufacture military trucks and Churchill tanks, and expansion continued in the late 1940s and 1950s. The state of the plant in the 1990s reflected its place in a multinational corporation operating in a European market. Many buildings had been demolished, some land sold off, and the workforce reduced in number, but there had been substantial investment in production facilities which on the main site were concentrated on only one model.[16]

Evidence of the international transfer of technology in the motor industry at different periods of the twentieth century is provided by two distinctive groups of factories. Three large continental European manufacturers, Citroën in 1926, Renault in 1927 and Fiat in 1937, established manufacturing plants in the London area, partly as a means of overcoming import duties. The Citroën plant on the Slough Trading Estate (SU 952815) was heralded as the 'biggest factory under one roof in Great Britain', and in 1926 Citroën was the first manufacturer in Britain to produce all-steel bodies. After the fall of France in 1940 the works was taken over by government and used for the assembly from knock-down kits of Canadian military lorries. The French company resumed control after 1945, and from 1956 right-hand drive versions of the voluptuous DS19 were made at Slough, but the plant closed in 1966. Citroën's UK headquarters remains at Slough, but in other buildings, and the former assembly plant is now used by Mars. Renault built a factory on Western Avenue for similar reasons. It opened in 1927, and was much enlarged in 1958 for the production of the Dauphine model. It closed in 1961 and became a spares and service depot. The Fiat factory in Water Road, Wembley (TQ 190835), opened in 1937, also closed in 1961 and became the company's headquarters in Britain. The sites are evidence of the re-orientation of the British economy since the inter-war period. In the 1920s and 1930s, tariff duties made it advantageous for Continental companies to assemble vehicles in Britain, and Imperial Preference from the early 1930s enabled cars made in Britain to be exported to countries like Australia and South Africa without the payment of import duties. By the 1990s the ties of empire and commonwealth no longer had any economic significance, and Britain's membership of the European Community meant that cars produced in Italy or France could be imported without paying duties.[17]

In the six years 1986–92 three Japanese companies opened large purpose-built car assembly plants in Britain, all of them on sites which had been airfields. Vehicles built in Britain, unlike those assembled in Japan, could be exported to fellow members of the European Community without the payment of import duties. The Nissan plant at Usworth, Sunderland (NZ 3458), opened in 1986, occupies the site that had been used by the Royal Flying Corps from 1916, and was subsequently Sunderland's municipal airport. It was the only one of the three built in an area of high unemployment. The Toyota plant at Burmaston (SK 2930), completed in 1992, is on the site of the former Derby municipal airport (*see Chapter 9*), and works in conjunction with an engine plant on the Deeside Industrial Park in Clwyd. The Honda plant at Swindon (SU 188863), also of 1992, was on the site of a wartime shadow factory and airfield. The buildings of the three plants are not especially noteworthy, and the unique character of Japanese methods of production has to be observed as a form of process recording rather than being deduced from buildings.[18]

While all the major car-assembly plants in Britain in the late 1990s were owned by multinational companies based overseas, a profusion of small independent companies remained, showing that workshop production and the fascination for many of a club-like ambience centred around motorcars were traditions that ran right through the twentieth century. TVR, supposedly the largest independent car manufacturer in 1999, established at Blackpool in 1970, was making up to twenty vehicles a week. Other companies included Chesil Speedsters, in production at Bridport since 1979, and J. H. Classics, at Ilminster since 1987. Aston Martin at Newport Pagnell (SP 885435) and Jaguarsport at Wykham Mill, west of Banbury (SP 885435) since 1992, continued the same traditions within the context of ownership by Ford. The two traditions are expressed even more strongly in the manufacture of racing cars, where most of the consortia that construct cars for Formula One and for Indy car racing in North America are based in England, and particularly in the Thames Valley and Surrey.[19]

Coventry: a case study

Coventry was at the heart of British car production throughout the twentieth century.[20] It was in the inter-war period Britain's fastest-growing city in terms of population, expanding from around 136,000 in 1919 to 220,000 in 1939. Between 1900 and 1910 twenty-eight manufacturers established factories in the city, and it remained one of the chief centres of production in the 1990s. While Coventry was, as events in 1941 proved, dangerously open to air attack, the skills of its engineering workers dictated that it became a principal centre for munitions production in the Second World War, particularly for the manufacture of aero-engines. A peak output of 390,000 cars per annum was achieved in 1971, representing 22.4 per cent of national output, although a total of 133,000 in 1951 represented 27.9 per cent of the national production. Some of the most important buildings associated with the history of car manufacture, like the Alvis factory, were destroyed in the closing years of the century, but not without some record being made. A study of the archaeology of the motor industry in Coventry illustrates all the themes which pervade this section of the book.

The motorcar industry in Coventry in the early twentieth century grew on the basis of contemporary factory and domestic production, just like cotton production in late-eighteenth-century Lancashire and footwear manufacture in late-nineteenth-century Northamptonshire. The domestic nature of some of the first generation of car-assembly sites is illustrated by the works behind 77 Moor Street in Earlsdon (SP 319780), where cars were made by Allard & Co. between 1899 and 1902, and possibly by others in subsequent years. The works is ranged around a courtyard, with a house at one end, and consists of single-storey and two-storey sheds, some of them clad in corrugated iron. After car production ceased, the workshops were used for making motor components and bicycles, and later as a car-spraying plant. Another example of this scale of production is provided by 18 Ellys Road (SP 331801), a modest terraced house, where John Ridley produced small two-seater cars between 1901 and 1904.

Coventry was also the location for Britain's first car factory, the Motor Mill (SP 332800) in Sandy Lane, Radford, proclaimed in an advertisement of 1896, the year production commenced, to be 'the largest autocar factory in the world'. The factory was established in a disused cotton mill by a consortium inspired by Frederick Richard Simms, who in 1893 had acquired the rights to manufacture in Britain internal combustion engines employing the patents of Gottlieb Daimler, whose other members included people associated with bicycle and sewing-machine manufacture in Coventry. Daimler cars were made in a line of ground-floor workshops, while the main four-storey block was occupied by the Great Horseless Carriage Company. The works expanded during the First World War, and continued to make Daimler cars through the inter-war period, but was severely damaged during the bombing raids on Coventry in 1941, which left standing only the office block and the one-time power station on the banks of the Coventry Canal. The site was redeveloped after 1945 and the offices were refurbished in the 1990s.

The emergence of motorcar production from Coventry's earlier metal-working industries is best illustrated by the factory of Calcott Brothers in Far Gosford Street (SP 344788). The company originally made bicycles and built the factory in 1896, a date which appears in terracotta on the frontage building. Evidence of the firm's status in Coventry is provided by mosaic floors and engraved glass screens within the office block. Calcott Brothers began to make motorcars in 1913, but in 1924 the company was taken over by Singer and production in Far Gosford Street ceased two years later. The sheds used for vehicle assembly, with wooden-truss roofs carried on cast-iron columns remained in the 1990s when the premises were used by a builder's merchant. The Challenge factory in Foleshill Road (SP 335803) illustrates the same theme. The company built a bicycle factory in 1906–7, where it made cars between 1912 and 1915. The sheds used for assembly have been demolished, but the entrance building remains, with classical columns, mosaic floors and doors with stained-glass panels, evidence of the links with bicycle manufacturing, and of the need to entertain and impress potential customers. The Lea-Francis factory in Lower Ford Street (SP 339793) had a longer history – cars were made there between 1903 and 1960 – but its origins are equally characteristic. Richard Lea and Graham Francis had formed a partnership in 1896 to make bicycles, and their first car was designed by Alexander Craig, a locomotive engineer who had served an apprenticeship at Crewe. William Riley inherited a family textile engineering concern in 1870 and moved through bicycle manufacture to make cars from the late 1890s, at first in a factory on Aldbourne Road, but from 1919 in a factory at Durbar Avenue, Coleshill (SP 339819), that had been built by the Nero Engine Company during the First World War. The company was taken over by Nuffield, and production transferred to the MG works at Abingdon in 1948. The Durbar Avenue factory was occupied by a parts company in the 1990s.

Another important works linking motorcar and cycle manufacture was the Quinton factory (SP 335787), built for bicycle manufacture in 1890, purchased in 1896 by the New Beeston Cycle Company, and used to produce the motor tricycle that was the only British-built entry in the Brighton Emancipation Run in November 1896. Beeston was wound up in 1900, but between 1905 and 1931 some Swift cars were made at the Quinton factory. In its form, a symmetrical two-storey frontage block screening a range of north-lit sheds, the Quinton Works foreshadowed that of many twentieth-century car factories. The Canterbury Street factory (SP 341792) of the Singer company was built in 1891 for bicycle manufacture, with a French Chateau-style office block fronting a courtyard formed by blocks of north-lit sheds. The first Singer powered vehicles, tricycles, were made in 1905, and in the inter-war period the firm was a highly successful car manufacturer. It opened a factory in Birmingham in 1927, after which the Canterbury Street works concentrated on sports cars. The company was acquired by the Rootes Group in 1956, and car production at Canterbury Street ceased two years later. After being used by Peugeot for parts manufacture, it was empty in the early 1990s and subsequently demolished.

The importance in the history of the motor industry of companies which made car bodies rather than complete vehicles is evident from the role of Pressed Steel at Cowley and Linwood, of Briggs at Dagenham and Fisher & Ludlow in Coventry and Birmingham. The factory of Carbodies Ltd on Holyhead Road (SP 323795) in Coventry further illuminates this theme. The company was founded in 1919, provided bodies for several manufacturers in the inter-war period, expanded considerably in the Second World War, and from about 1947 began to assemble London taxis. The bodies and chassis of taxis are still made at the factory, using the traditional methods of the mid-twentieth century, and vehicles are assembled, using components made elsewhere in the west midlands and engines from Japan.

Evidence of the impact of the First World War on motorcar manufacture is provided by the former Jaguar works in Swallow Road (SP 332822). The wartime economy not only provided engineering work for car companies, but created space for future expansion. The origins of Jaguar cars were in Blackpool, where William (later Sir William) Lyons, who worked for Swallow, a firm making sidecars in Cocker Street, began in 1926 to make Swallow bodies for fitting to small car chassis like the Austin Seven. In 1928 he moved to a former shell-filling factory near Holbrook Lane on the north side of Coventry. At first he continued to make Swallow bodies, but from 1931 began to make cars, Standard Swallows, or SS cars, a name

abandoned in favour of Jaguar in February 1945. The building retained many of the features of its wartime origins, including the wooden railways used to move materials without the danger of causing sparks. Jaguar sold the premises to Dunlop in the early 1950s and it was occupied by Dunlop Aviation in the 1990s.

The Alvis plant on Holyhead Road (SP 322794), where cars were produced between 1920 and 1967, was demolished in the early 1990s but epitomised the influence of wartime conditions on motorcar manufacture. Its founder, Thomas George John, had many links with the car- and aeroplane-centred culture of Brooklands (*see above*). The main building, fronted by a three-storey office range, was built in 1936 in anticipation of orders for aero-engines. Alvis greatly expanded its activities during the Second World War, when it was producing vehicles and other munitions on twenty sites in Coventry.

The plant used in 1999 by Peugeot at Ryton-on-Dunsmoor (SP 376746) exemplifies another phase of Coventry's history. It was built by Rootes as a shadow factory (*see Chapter 7*) for the production of aero-engines on the southern edge of the city at the junction of the roads to London and Oxford. Construction commenced in June 1939, and the first engines were made early in 1940. New buildings were added in 1943, and over 6,000 people were employed in the closing years of the war. From 1945 the factory was adapted to produce cars that included the Humber Super Snipe, much used by government officials and the military, the Hillman Minx and the Hillman Avenger. The Rootes Group was subsequently taken over by Chrysler, and then by Peugeot, for whom it is a major assembly plant. The roofs of the main shops have been raised in places to accommodate new conveyor systems, but the plant retains much evidence of its wartime origins. It has a lengthy frontage along the A45, with office blocks, and an entrance hall that is decorated with some wooden panelling but is entirely unpretentious, in keeping with the sober atmosphere of the period when it was built. Camouflage paint was still visible in 1999, and a high concrete building, used for maintaining assembly-line equipment, was built in wartime to test the aero-engines produced at the factory. In the 1990s it was still possible to read the inscription 'Rootes Group Research and Development'.

Coventry's other five shadow factories remained in use in the 1990s: the other Rootes plant, the Stoke works at Humber Road (SP 352780) for stores and packaging; the Daimler works at Radford (SP 332808) for making engines; the second Daimler plant at Browns Lane (SP 300818), where the classic Jaguars of the 1950s and 1960s were built, still producing cars; the Standard factory at Fletchampstead South, Canley (SP 306776), for parts storage; and the Standard plant at Banner Lane (SP 275795) making tractors.

5.6
Standard Vanguard cars in the water-test area at the Canley factory in the early 1950s.

(Ironbridge Gorge Museum Trust)

One of the largest, and in many respects the most diffuse, complexes in Coventry is that of the Standard Motor Company, alongside the railway to Birmingham at Canley (SP 3078). The company was established in 1903 and operated from dispersed sites across the city. It was heavily involved in munitions, particularly aircraft manufacture, during the First World War, when it was able to purchase a 30-acre site at Canley. Ranges of A-frame sheds were constructed, which were replicated as car production expanded in the 1920s. The complex had many of the characteristics of a First World War factory: an ornate administration block; the three-storey red-brick Ivy Cottage, with three projecting pedimented bays and prominent quoins; a canteen, sports fields and swimming baths. More than 1,600 aircraft were built at Canley in 1916–18. The company prospered during the inter-war period, and had installed its first moving assembly line for bodies by 1922. From 1936 a shadow factory for

aero-engines was built on a golf course in a corner of the site. Two years later a steady supply of car bodies was secured when Fisher & Ludlow built a plant in the style of a shadow factory some 3 miles from Canley at Torrington Avenue, Tile Hill (SP 296780), specifically for making bodies for the Standard Flying Eight. Standard acquired Triumph in 1944, and prospered in the immediate post-war period, producing the popular Standard Vanguard and Triumph Mayflower models. In 1958–59 the company constructed a multi-storey block, often called the Rocket Range, for the production of its new Triumph Herald model. The proposed methods of production harked back to the Dennis and Arrol-Johnston buildings of the early twentieth century. Production did not begin until March 1961, and was later transferred to other buildings on the site, while problems at Canley were exacerbated by those at Speke on Merseyside (*see above*). Car production ceased at Canley in 1970, but the site became an administrative centre for the company, which in 1999 was part of the Rover group, as well as a base for parts distribution.

Aircraft

The manufacture of aircraft is a radically different industry from the production of motorcars, although it employs many of the same basic engineering techniques. Aircraft were only produced in large numbers in the two world wars of the twentieth century. After the First World War the huge factories that had been constructed, and which were still being built at the time of the Armistice, were for the most part put to other uses. While British aircraft constructors, many of them imbued with the kind of Brooklands culture described above, achieved many notable technological innovations in the 1920s and 1930s, they gained scarcely any experience of mass production, nor was that remotely possible given the small numbers of most of the aircraft types of the period that were actually manufactured. Only eight examples were built of the HP42 airliner, the archetypal British aircraft of the 1930s. The mass production of aircraft and aero-engines during the Second World War, as indicated above, was organised largely by firms accustomed to making motorcars which had gained experience of manufacture on a large scale.[21]

One of the first British aircraft builders was Alliott Verdon Roe, who had trained as a railway engineer. He made his first flight at Brooklands in July 1908. He was subsequently banished from Brooklands, and constructed aircraft in a railway arch in Hackney, duly marked with a blue commemorative plaque. Trial flights were made over the Hackney Marshes. In 1910 Roe moved to a redundant cotton mill in Ancoats, Manchester, and subsequently to another empty factory at nearby Miles Platting.

Short Brothers also used railway arches, in their case in Battersea, for constructing aircraft, but even before 1914 manufacturers were seeking buildings with large areas of uninterrupted space, in effect hangars that had been built for such other purposes as ice- and roller-skating rinks, tramcar sheds or exhibition halls. Some manufacturers began to erect purpose-built workshops for assembling aircraft, as the Shorts did at Leysdown in the Isle of Sheppey in 1909, and at Willis Avenue, Rochester, alongside the River Medway in 1913. In the same year Noel Pemberton-Belling began to assemble Supermarine flying-boats in a former boatyard at Woolston, Southampton. Claude Graham-White formed the Graham-White Aviation Company at Hendon, north London, in 1911, and built a large factory during the First World War, of which some hangars remained in 1999. The oldest purpose-built aircraft factory in England is usually reckoned to be that of the Sopwith Aviation Company in Canbury Park Road, Kingston upon Thames, which was built in 1913. It was expanded during the First World War, and again in the period of re-armament in 1935–36. After the Second World War it was occupied by Kingston Polytechnic, but passed out of academic use in 1996.

Mass-production techniques were applied for the first time to the manufacture of aircraft during the First World War, which necessitated the construction of large factories (*see Chapter 7*). Some of the fifty-eight buildings of National Aircraft Factory No. 1 remain at Waddon, Surrey (TQ 310646), near to the surviving buildings of Croydon airport, and now serve a variety of purposes. The other National Aircraft Factories –

at Aintree, Liverpool, and Heaton Chapel, Stockport – were not so large. Other exceptionally large factories in the London area were those of Sopwith at Richmond Road, Kingston upon Thames, of Handley Page at Cricklewood (TQ 240862) and of Airco at Hendon (TQ 222901). After the Armistice such large-scale manufacturing capacity was unviable. Some factories, like Airco's, closed down, and their buildings were put to other uses. Some, like the Armstrong Siddeley works at Parkside, Coventry, were adapted to make motorcars. Others, like the Gloster works at Brockworth (*see Chapter 7*), continued to be involved with aircraft production but scarcely prospered.

During the inter-war period the size of aircraft increased. It had been possible to move the mass-produced fighters of the First World War quite easily from factory to flying field, but bombers and airliners could be moved only in a disassembled state. Several firms in the late 1930s established manufacturing plants on the perimeters of the growing number of municipal airfields (*see Chapter 9*): Percival at Luton, Boulton & Paul at Wolverhampton and Airspeed at Portsmouth. Some companies, including De Havilland at Hatfield and Cunliffe-Owen at Eastleigh near Southampton, followed the fashion of the 1930s and built factories in the by-pass style, with styling office blocks fronting ranges of single-storey north-lit sheds. The first moving assembly line for the production of aircraft was installed by Phillips & Powis at its

5.7
The manufacture of aircraft wings in a factory at Pleasant Street, Liverpool, in 1918.

(*Crown copyright. NMR*)

works at Reading Aerodrome, Woodley, in 1938. The trolleys carrying fuselages ran on rails salvaged from Reading's tramway system.

During the Second World War the production of aircraft was massively expanded, and some entirely new assembly plants were constructed, a number of which remained in use by the aircraft industry, although not necessarily for assembly in the 1990s (*see Chapter 7*). Some were located at great distance from the traditional heartland of aircraft manufacture in the London area. Avro's shadow factory at Chadderton, near Oldham (SD 894064), was built in 1938–39, and produced Ansons, Manchesters and Bristol Blenheims in association with the company's works at Miles Platting, and is still used by British Aerospace, as is the factory at Woodford, Cheshire (SJ 898828), where Avro aircraft were assembled in wartime in newly constructed hangars, and where Vulcan bombers were built in the 1950s and 1960s. The Blackburn factory at Dumbarton built Short Sunderland flying-boats which could be flown off from the adjacent River Clyde.

In the post-war period much more space was needed in factories which continued to produce airliners or heavy bombers. The change in the scale of aircraft is vividly illustrated at Filton, Bristol, where three linked hangars with a combined frontage of 1,052 feet (319 metres) covering 8 acres (3.2ha) was built for the

assembly of the eight-engined Bristol Brabazon airliner with its 130ft (40m) wing-span. Production of the aircraft did not progress beyond the prototype stage, but the building accommodated the construction of the Bristol Britannia and Concorde, and was used in the 1990s for the refurbishment of Airbuses and the conversion of VC10s from airliners to tankers. Other factories that saw considerable use in the second half of the twentieth century were at Hurn, Hampshire (SZ 1098), where many Vickers Viscounts and BAC 1-11s were assembled, and at Dunsfold, Surrey (TQ 0236), a Second World War military airfield, where Hawker Hunters, Hawks and Harriers were built. Its closure was announced in 1999, the last aircraft factory in the county. During the era of the Cold War aircraft firms were increasingly involved with the manufacture of missiles, which provided employment for a high proportion of the inhabitants of Stevenage, and of some other towns.

Shipbuilding

At one level shipbuilding is very different from making cars or aircraft, employing the techniques of Victorian-style heavy engineering, even if modified in the course of the twentieth century by the substitution of welding for riveting, and of diesel engines for coal- or oil-fired steam engines or steam turbines. There are nevertheless close connections, since ships, aircraft and motor vehicles all have military value, and some firms, like Vickers and Beardmore, have been involved in all three industries.

In 1900 Britain was the principal source of the world's ships, producing about 60 per cent of the tonnage launched each year. The proportion declined in the 1920s, and in the early 1930s, as demand for new vessels evaporated, shipbuilding communities like Jarrow and Clydebank suffered severely from unemployment. The relative international position of Britain in shipbuilding declined after the Second World War, and in 1956 Japan became the world's principal supplier of ships. While the size of ships was increasing, British

5.8
The plaque commemorating the first successful flight of a jet aircraft at Brockworth / Hucclecote near Gloucester.

(Crown copyright. NMR)

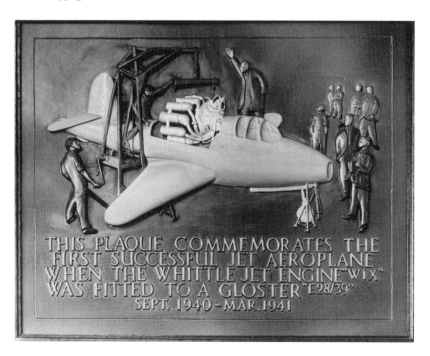

THIS PLAQUE COMMEMORATES THE
FIRST SUCCESSFUL JET AEROPLANE
WHEN THE WHITTLE JET ENGINE "WIX"
WAS FITTED TO A GLOSTER "E28/39"
SEPT. 1940 – MAR. 1941

companies failed to lay out the spacious yards necessary for their construction and to adopt the kind of standardisation necessary to bring the benefits of mass production to the industry. Shipbuilding was beset with labour problems, which stemmed from long traditions of casual labour. The industry suffered precipitate decline in the 1960s, and what remained of the industry in the 1990s was concerned principally with military vessels, specialised and generally fairly small merchant ships, and with such structures as oil and gas platforms. Nevertheless, just as there is a tradition of enthusiast involvement with motorcars and aircraft, so gentlemen are accustomed to 'mess about in boats', and the number of workers involved in building and maintaining yachts and cabin cruisers in the 1990s was very large, if difficult to quantify.

There are relatively few remains of the great shipyards of the early part of the twentieth century. Perhaps the most complete historic yard is that of Cammell Laird (Harland & Wolff) at Birkenhead (SJ 326877), while the best-preserved on Tyneside is the North East Engineering works at Wallsend. Otherwise most of the remaining structures are office blocks like those at Low Walker's yard, Newcastle, Swan Hunter, Wallsend, and the Cleveland Dockyard, Teesside.

Beardmore: a case study

By the 1990s only a platers' shed, a time office, a power-station building and some workers' housing remained of the works of William Beardmore at Clydebank (NS 493702), and most of its site was occupied by a hospital begun in 1991. Nevertheless, the history of the works illustrates much that is at the heart of this chapter.[22]

William Beardmore (1856–1936) was the son of the owner of Parkhead Forge in Glasgow, which he controlled from 1887 and where he began to roll armour plate three years later. In 1900 he acquired the shipyard in Govan formerly owned by Robert Napier, and purchased an 80-acre site at Dalmuir on Clydebank, adjacent to the shipyard that had been taken over by John Brown, the Sheffield steelmakers, in 1899. Beardmore developed a shipyard on a scale sufficiently large to build battleships, with a 150-ton crane supplied by a German company, a power station, and a gantry at the water's edge, 755ft long and 150ft high, erected by Arrols, one of only two of its kind in Britain. The works was officially opened in June 1906 with the launch of the battleship *Agamemnon*, but by that time a half-share of the company had been taken by Vickers, which feared that Beardmore, with the capacity to produce armour plate and large ships, might start to make heavy guns. From 1907 Beardmore built sheds for the construction of submarines, and during the First World War employed 16,000 workers, many travelling daily from Glasgow by train. New shops were built for the production of artillery, and fifty tanks were built during 1917. After the war new shipbuilding facilities were constructed utilising cranes from the National Shipyard at Chepstow, and the artillery shops were adapted to build and repair locomotives.

William Beardmore was a shareholder in Arrol-Johnston's motorcar factory at Dumfries, where aircraft and aero-engines were built during the First World War. This led to the construction of aircraft production facilities at Dalmuir, including sheds for seaplanes, and 487 aircraft were built there in the course of the war. They were wheeled to a nearby flying field at Robertson Park. Beardmore was invited by the Admiralty to participate in the construction of its aircraft, and the Royal Navy provided capital for structures at Inchinnan (NS 4768), one and a half miles from Dalmuir but on the opposite, southern, bank of the Clyde, that included a shed 720ft x 230ft and 122ft high (219m x 70m x 37m), built by Arrols, and completed in September 1916, as well as fabrication sheds and a hydrogen plant. Beardmore built several airships, including the R34, which made a double journey across the Atlantic in June 1919, and the R36, a civilian aircraft delivered in April 1921, damaged at its moorings two months later, which after four years' inactivity flew to Egypt in 1925. Nevertheless, the Inchinnan works closed in September 1921, and Beardmore's buildings, including the great airship shed, were demolished in 1923.

The shipyard at Dalmuir experienced increasing difficulties in the 1920s. Its last major commission was the cruiser *Shropshire*, launched in 1928 and completed in 1929. The yard closed the following year. Part was used for the processing of asbestos from 1938 until 1971.

The engineering shops were taken over by the War Office in January 1939 and under Beardmore's management produced armour plate for tanks during the Second World War. The fitting-out basin was used by John Browns, the shipbuilders, which occupied a nearby yard. The remainder of the site became a Royal Ordnance Factory, principally concerned with the repair of war-damaged ships (*see Chapter 7*). Military vehicles were produced at the site between 1951 and 1957, and cranes in the early 1960s. The land was sold in 1969, and most of the buildings demolished.

Conclusions

It is easy to use evidence from the motorcar, aircraft and shipbuilding industries to support a declinist view of the history of twentieth-century Britain.[23] It was suggested at the start of the chapter that this is a simplistic approach which can distort understanding. The case of William Beardmore, shareholder in the company that built one of the century's outstanding car plants, shipbuilder and maker of aeroplanes and airships, provides a rationale for considering these three together. The object of this chapter has been to use archaeological evidence to highlight some of the themes that run through their history in the twentieth century. There remains much scope for investigating aircraft and motorcar factories, and for using cartographic and pictorial evidence for the investigation of shipyards. We hope that we have demonstrated in this chapter the ways in which archaeological evidence can highlight individual and corporate aspirations and ambitions, triumphs and failures, and the influence upon companies and those who worked for them of the great events of the century.

Notes and references

1 D. Edgerton, *England and the Aeroplane*, London: Macmillan, 1991. See also C. Barnett, *The Audit of War: The Illusion and Reality of Britain as a Great Nation*, London: Macmillan, 1986.

2 P. Collins and M. Stratton, 'From Trestles to Tracks; The Influence of the Motorcar Manufacturing Process on the Design of British Car Factories', *Journal of Transport History*, 1988, vol. 9, pp. 198–208. See also J. Foreman-Peck, S. Bowden and A. McKinlay, *The British Motor Industry*, Manchester: Manchester University Press, 1995; R. Church, *The Rise and Decline of the British Motor Industry*, Cambridge: Cambridge University Press, 1994.

3 Brooklands Museum Trust, *The Spirit of Brooklands*, Weybridge: Brooklands Museum Trust, 1996. We are also grateful to Julian Temple, Curator of Aviation at Brooklands, for his guidance on the site.

4 P. Collins and M. Stratton, *British Car Factories from 1896*, Godmanstone: Veloce, 1993, pp. 130–2.

5 Ibid., pp. 248–51.

6 Ibid., pp. 253–5.

7 Ibid., pp. 99–101.

8 Ibid., pp. 61, 68–9, 86–7, 104–5, 162, 138.

9 Ibid., pp. 111–12; M. Key, *Pick of Stamford: A History of the Pick Motor Company*, Stamford: Paul Watkins, 1994, pp. 7–50.

10 Collins and Stratton, op. cit., pp. 145–56.

11 Ibid., pp. 102–4.

12 Ibid., pp. 93–6.

13 Ibid., pp. 118–24.

14 Ibid., pp. 134–8.

15 Ibid., pp. 78–9, 138–9, 256–7; J. Foreman-Peck, S. Bowden and A. McKinlay, op. cit., pp. 204–15.

16 Ibid., pp. 62–7.

17 Ibid., pp. 71–4, 117, 128–9.

18 Ibid., pp. 84–5, 174–7, 238–9.

19 Ibid., pp. 69–709, 87, 108–9, 145, 158.

20 The account of Coventry which follows is drawn from Collins and Stratton, op. cit., pp. 209–31, and from B. Lancaster and T. Mason, *Life and Labour in a Twentieth Century City: The Experience of Coventry*, Coventry: Cryfield Press, 1987, *passim*; and K. Richardson, *Twentieth Century Coventry*, Coventry: Coventry City Corporation, 1971, *passim*.

21 The account of aircraft factories which follows is drawn from M. Stratton, 'Skating Rinks to Shadow Factories: The Evolution of British Aircraft Manufacturing Complexes', *Industrial Archaeology Review*, 1996, vol. 18, pp. 113–44.

22 The account that follows is drawn principally from I. Johnson, *Beardmore Built: The Rise and Fall of a Clydeside Shipyard*, Clydebank: Clydebank Libraries and Museums Department, 1993.

23 Barnett, op. cit., pp. 125–58.

A characteristic image of British industry in
1900 might have been a man shovelling
coal. In 1950 it could have been a man in a
white laboratory coat looking at a test tube.
In 1999 it might be a woman using a computer
for spectrographic analysis. Industry acquired
an increasingly scientific image during the
twentieth century, and the objectives of this
chapter are to assess the archaeology of the
chemical industries which lie at the heart of
twentieth-century manufactures, to identify
some of the most important sites and the kinds
of record appropriate to concerns that have been
influential on many aspects of people's lives.

Chapter six

The age of science

6.1
The unscientific image of
the chemical industry at
the turn of the
nineteenth and twentieth
centuries: West Bank
Viaduct at Widnes.

(Crown copyright. NMR)

Billingham and Wilton on Teesside, Stanlow,
Runcorn and Widnes on the banks of the
Mersey, Llandarcy and Baglan Bay on the
eastern side of Swansea Bay, Immingham on
the Humber, and Grangemouth on the Forth are
some of the most dramatic industrial landscapes
in Britain. They reflect the fundamental
importance of the chemical industry to the
British economy of the twentieth century.
Industrial archaeologists have neglected
such plants. The only chemical works that have
been considered in the process of listing and
scheduling have been early saltworks. Petro-
chemical plants and dyeworks have scarcely
been researched, and their buildings are
unprotected; while few of the machines used in
making synthetic textiles and plastics have been
preserved in museums. Most large-scale

chemical plants clearly cannot be preserved or adapted to new uses in the same way as can disused textile mills, warehouses or railway stations. Frank Kirk in his 1998 study[1] of the ICI coal-to-oil plant at Billingham bravely suggested means by which an effective archaeological record may be made of complex twentieth-century plants.

The chemical industry has been neglected because its processes are perceived to be difficult to comprehend, and because conventional wisdom asserts that scarcely any plant of historical interest survives. We cannot attempt to analyse complexes or structures in detail, but hope to show that differing processes and plants have characteristic features and that some sites have proved to be remarkably long-lived. A works manager at May & Baker of Dagenham recalled around 1985 that he still had vessels marked 'War Department', and hence at least 40 years old. Most of the stylish buildings in the May & Baker complex date from a wave of investment just after the Second World War.

Chemical companies produced materials for other industries and for the consumer market. They operated on an increasingly international basis. In peacetime they were particularly subject to fluctuations in exchange rates, since many chemical products are standardised and can compete only on price in international markets. Wartime experience showed the danger of dependence on overseas producers, and many initiatives between the First World War and the end of the Cold War were driven by a determination to ensure that all essential chemicals could be produced in Britain. There were many international transfers of technology in the industry, and the cost of research and development dictated the evolution of international companies able to garner the necessary skills and provide the maximum returns on capital.

Most chemical complexes present a picture of both continuity and change. Sites have remained in use for many decades, sometimes for more than a century, due to a proximity to salt reserves, oil refineries, to deep-water ports, or to markets. The infrastructure of a works, the patterns of piping, the storage tanks, the offices, the transport links and social facilities may well have proved durable while the processing plant may have changed rapidly. John Harvey-Jones, chairman of ICI from 1982, saw six ethylene

crackers built on Teesside from the early 1950s and five of them shut down by the mid-1980s in what he described as a typical thirty-year life-cycle in the petrochemical business. The detailed operation of most plants changed as batch production gave way to continuous processes, then hand work to mechanical handling, and manual control to automation.[2]

Much of the nineteenth-century chemical industry was far from scientific. The production of soda ash (sodium carbonate, often called 'alkali'), used in making soap and glass, or of bleaching power was based on the empirical knowledge of processes developed by scientists like Nicolas Leblanc (1742–1806) and Charles Tennant (1768–1838), but could be wasteful of resources and polluting. The Leblanc process, for example, involved the dumping of solid calcium sulphide, which formed the white hills on Merseyside that came to be called the 'Ditton Alps', the site of a golf course in the 1990s. It might also involve the release of hydrochloric acid gas into the atmosphere. Some remnants of late-nineteenth-century plant are preserved on the banks of the Mersey at the Catalyst Museum in Widnes.

The more complex ammonia soda process developed by Ernest Solvay (1838–1922) required much greater investment of capital, but was infinitely more efficient in its use of resources. It was introduced in Britain at Northwich, Cheshire, in 1873–74 by John Brunner (1842–1919) and Ludwig Mond (1839–1909), making use of brine pumped from the salt deposits in the region, and limestone carried by rail from the Pennines. Brunner and Mond had first met in 1862 at the offices of the Hutchinson company at Widnes – in 1999, in a much altered form, the headquarters of the Catalyst Museum (SJ 513844). In the early twentieth century the company expanded from the production of chemicals into consumer products, taking over the soap manufacturers Crosfield & Gossage in 1911, and it was heavily involved in armaments production, particularly the manufacture of ammonium nitrate, during the First World War. Brunner Mond took a 25 per cent share in 1916 in the Castner Kellner (Electrolytic) Alkali Company, which in 1895 had established a works at Weston Point, Runcorn, for producing caustic soda from brine, using the process developed by Hamilton Y. Castner (1859–99), an American working in England, and an Austrian,

Carl Kellner (1850–1905), and took over the company in 1920. Brunner Mond had also established a nitrogen plant at Billingham on Teesside in 1919, with the object of supplying fertiliser to the whole British Empire.[3]

The chemical industry for much of the twentieth century was dominated by one company, Imperial Chemical Industries (ICI), formed on 7 December 1926 by a merger of four companies. Brunner, Mond & Co., headed by Alfred Mond (1868–1930), the son of Ludwig Mond and later Lord Melchett, had successfully established the Solvay process in Cheshire, and was active in various other fields. Nobel Industries Ltd, headed by the other architect of the merger, Sir Harry McGowan, originated in the 1860s when Alfred Nobel (1833–96) established a factory producing high explosives at Ardeer in Ayrshire. The production of ammunition involved the use of non-ferrous metals, and the company had developed links with the metal trades in the west midlands, and thus with motorcar manufacturers. The third company was the United Alkali Company, formed in 1891, an ailing conglomerate which had brought together many of the old-established chemical firms, chiefly on Merseyside. Originally most of its constituent firms had employed the Leblanc process, but they had diversified, and the Leblanc process was last used in Britain at the company's Allhussen works at Gateshead in 1920. The fourth constituent company was the British Dyestuffs Corporation, which had been hurriedly formed during the First World War. It was characteristic of the period that the negotiations concerning the merger between Mond and McGowan took place during a six-day voyage from New York to Southampton on the *Aquitania*. ICI was responsible for 40 per cent of the British output of chemicals. The managers of the new company saw themselves, in the 1920s and 1930s, as suppliers to other producers, hesitated to become involved in the manufacture of consumer goods, and avoided competition with their suppliers. The word 'Imperial' in the company's title was significant – Mond and McGowan adhered to the commonplace view of the 1920s that the British Empire was permanent and beneficent, and had a vision of their company as a leader in the modernisation of British industry, and as an effective competitor with the large German and

American companies also involved in many aspects of chemical manufacture. The benefits of the company's size can be seen in the increase of expenditure on research, which, in spite of problems caused by the recession, rose from £221,000 in 1926–27 to £1,034,000 ten years later. The company expanded on a massive scale during the Second World War and the preceding period of re-armament. Between 1938 and 1944 it invested over £20 million of its own resources, and over £58 million of government capital, in new plant and in the expansion of capacity at old ones.[4]

Cheshire: the heartland of inorganic chemicals

The enterprise in Cheshire established by Brunner and Mond in the 1870s proved to be the nucleus of what was still in the 1990s one of the principal concentrations of chemical manufacturing in Britain. Two of the principal works were operated in the late 1990s by a company called Brunner Mond plc, following the demerger of ICI in 1993. A survey in the 1990s revealed that many structures of historical interest remained in the Merseyside plants.[5] Few structures survived on the sites of closed works, although lime-settling beds at Plumley near Knutsford (SJ 705750) were protected for their botanical interest as a Site of Special Scientific Interest.

The ICI plant best known to industrial archaeologists is probably that at Winnington (SJ 647749), on the opposite bank of the River Weaver from the Anderton Lift. By the mid-

6.2
The Winnington works of Brunner Mond plc, formerly ICI, at Northwich, on the opposite bank of the River Weaver from the Anderton boat lift. Photographed in 1996.

(Photo: Barrie Trinder)

1990s the Winnington site incorporated parts of the adjacent Wallerscote works of 1926. The basic form of the Solvay plant dated from the first decade of the twentieth century, but the towers in use in the 1990s were built in 1952. Some of the offices and a range of washing-soda sheds dated from the nineteenth century.

The other plant using the Solvay process in the 1990s, at Lostock Gralam (SJ 683743), was built by Bowman Thompson & Co. in 1891 and was taken over by Brunner Mond in 1900. The Solvay plant in use in the 1990s dated from 1907. In 1942 Lostock Gralam began to produce Winnafill, a form of activated calcium carbonate used as a filler in rubber, sealants and plastics, and was still doing so in the 1990s with a plant that dated from 1955. The works produced large quantities of ammonium nitrate and nitric acid in the First World War.

The historic Castner-Kellner works at Weston Point, Runcorn (SJ 496814), made picric acid in the First World War, and in the 1920s turned increasingly to the manufacture of 'automotive fluids' like anti-freeze and anti-knock additives for petrol. It continued to employ electrolytic processes, and remained in the 1990s one of the largest users of electric power in Britain. Few historic buildings remained other than a range of sheds with Belfast truss roofs that may date from the First World War.

There were more extensive remains of an electrolytic plant of the early twentieth century at Bird & Hargreaves' works, Cledford Bridge, Middlewich (SJ 714648). It was established in 1899, and closed, when in the ownership of ICI, in 1928. Office blocks of 1901 and 1914 remained, together with a range of large sheds, used in the 1990s by the Ideal Standard company for the production of ceramics.

Some concrete buildings from the Second World War remained at the plant at Rock Savage, built by the government from 1938 for the production of phosgene, caustic soda and bleaching materials, and taken over by ICI in 1947. A similar government-built plant of 1941 at Burn Hall and Hillhouse was merged with the ICI plant at Lostock Hall in 1982, and electrolysis ceased there in 1993. An historic plant in Widnes, the Sullivan works that had belonged to United Alkali, built in 1916 to make chlorine and chlorine compounds, passed to Zeneca on the demerger of ICI in 1993. Its principal product was paraquat weedkiller.

The influence of the chemical industry generally, and of ICI in particular, pervades the landscape, beyond the bounds of the production plants, around Northwich, Middlewich and Runcorn. Mond House, built as the headquarters of Brunner Mond in 1899, remained in use as offices in 1999. A timber-framed recreation club and library dates from 1923. In 1873 John Brunner and Ludwig Mond bought Winnington Hall, a timber-framed house of sixteenth- or seventeenth-century date, and lived there until 1884. In 1897 it became a club for senior staff, which developed a particular culture during the inter-war period that was conducive to innovation. Unlike in other parts of ICI the atmosphere was informal. Men wore sports jackets rather than suits, and addressed each other by Christian names rather than surnames. Winnington Hall is now a listed building. Nearly 200 terraced houses built for production workers in the late nineteenth or early twentieth century remain in Solvay Road, Hemming Street and Henning Street, while Dyer Terrace consists of six rather more substantial houses for managers.[6] There are also in Northwich some remarkable timber-framed buildings of the Edwardian period that were designed to be 'liftable' with jacking points so they could be re-set or relocated if threatened by subsidence caused by brine pumping.

Teesside

The chemical industry has a long history on Teesside. In 1833 Robert Wilson of the Eaglescliffe Chemical Company began to make sulphuric acid at Urlay Nook (NZ 410150), a site still active in the 1990s.[7] Nevertheless, the region became a major centre of chemical production only in the course of the twentieth century, from the early 1920s when Brunner Mond established an ammonia plant at Billingham that was to become one of the principal plants of ICI.

During the First World War supplies of Chilean saltpetre, used as a fertiliser and as a source of sodium nitrate for explosives, had been restricted by the German U-boat blockade. Meanwhile in Germany, production of ammonia had been transformed from 1913 by the Haber–Bosch process, developed by the BASF (Badische Anilin und Soda Fabrik) company. Water gas was blended with producer gas and steam under pressure in a chromium steel vessel in the presence of a catalyst, the gases having to be carefully purified. The perfection of the process, with the need to maintain constant temperatures and pressures, was one of the principal feats of chemical engineering of the early twentieth century. In 1919 a group of chemists and engineers from Brunner Mond went to examine the BASF plant at Oppau to try to comprehend the Haber–Bosch process as a prelude to establishing plants for the synthesis of ammonia in Britain.

Armed with notes and sketches, they undertook laboratory research and built a pilot plant (No. 1) at the Castner-Kellner works in Runcorn (*see above*) where hydrogen was available as a by-product of the manufacture of caustic soda. The challenges of handling gases at high pressures and temperatures having been overcome, small quantities of ammonia were produced there by 1922.[8] Brunner Mond then took over land at Billingham (NZ 4722) in order to establish a full-scale production plant. The 266-acre site had been bought in 1918 by the Ministry of Munitions with the vague intention of building a plant for the creation of ammonium nitrate by the Haber–Bosch process, although little was understood at that stage of the technology. The site was close to a power station, nearing completion, that could provide 20,000kW, and offered good transport links. Supplies of coal, water and structural steel were to hand. The Ministry had spent over £1 million on the site by the time that Brunner Mond took it over and started building work in 1919. Workers' houses had to be provided, since the site was isolated from Stockton. A spacious and well-equipped laboratory was built, and the Billingham production unit (No. 2) first produced ammonia on Christmas Eve 1923. It was extended to have a capacity of 50 tonnes of ammonia per day in 1925, and a third unit started up in 1928.[9]

An amazing feature of the establishment of the Billingham plant is that Brunner Mond was, apparently, initially unaware of its greatest natural resource, a deep bed of anhydrite (rhombic calcium sulphate) directly underneath the site. A shaft was sunk in 1927 in the north-east corner of the complex to a depth of 600–800 feet (180–240m), and anhydrite was worked by the pillar-and-stall method from 1928 until 1971. Supplies of anhydrite permitted the economical manufacture of ammonium sulphate and hence 'nitro-chalk' without having to import sulphur.[10] The formation of ICI in 1926 enabled the investment of £20 million at Billingham, primarily for the production of fertilisers, using the locally extracted anhydrite as a raw material. This new investment, agreed in the autumn of 1927, resulted in the erection of units Nos 4 and 5 and a trebling of the plant's ammonia capacity. The new units contained about twenty 'second-generation' converters, in the form of vertically mounted cylinders made of forged steel and weighing 100 tonnes each, housed in steel-framed sheds. The high-pressure reciprocating compressors continued in use until the mid-1970s, when they were proudly maintained as operational 'museum pieces'.

Diversification led to the development of a huge integrated chemical complex at Billingham. Long cylindrical rotary kilns were erected for making cement and sulphuric acid, processes which also used anhydrite. A second unit was added in 1935, along with a pioneering compound fertiliser installation based on nitrogen and phosphate. The manufacture of Nitro-Chalk, a highly successful fertiliser, commenced in 1927. A power station was completed in 1928 and modernistic parabolic concrete silos were erected for the storage of products, one housing 100,000 tonnes of ammonium sulphate. By 1930 Billingham had developed into an integrated operation in which most by-products were used in other processes to minimise waste. Billingham became a dense rectangular complex bounded by roads and railways and subdivided by further routeways and a central spine of pipelines. Half was taken up by ammonia plant housed largely in high steel-framed sheds, and flanked by the boiler plant, workshops and stores. On the other side of the central pipeline spine two sulphate plants were erected with long process buildings and a huge silo. A water gas plant was completed for generating the gases for ammonia synthesis, with adjoining coke ovens. Next to them was the first sulphate plant. A rail network took out wagonloads of fertiliser and other chemicals. No sooner was this £20 million investment programme under way than fears of over-capacity were generated by the economic crash in the United States and the increased competition in Europe. The fertiliser plant was partly shut down over 1929–30.[11]

Once the worst effects of the Depression were over, there were major new investments in Billingham during the 1930s, which turned 'a fertilizer factory, with industrial side-lines, into an industrial chemical factory, with a small fertilizer interest'.[12] In 1931 work began at the southern end of the complex on a plant producing caustic soda and chlorine, and hence metallic sodium and sodium cyanide, using salt pumped as brine from boreholes at Port Clarence. This initiative enabled the closure of two old and inefficient works at Wallsend and Glasgow which had belonged to United Alkali, evidence of the retreat of the chemical industry from two of its heartlands of the Industrial Revolution period on Tyneside and Clydeside.[13]

The organic sector of the chemical industry depended on coal, on the products of coke ovens, the by-products of the coalgas industry, and on molasses. ICI bravely took Billingham into the world of heavy organic chemicals. Methanol was the first organic chemical to be produced, from 1928, at Billingham, but it was a slump in demand for fertilisers that encouraged the research which led to the erection of plant for the hydrogenation of coal and creosote into petrol. The plant consisted of a maze of stills, tanks and pipes, and a huge hammerhead crane, employed to lift the major vessels for servicing. Its technology drew on the experience gained from the fertiliser plant of manufacturing hydrogen and operating high-pressure chemical plant. In January 1934, 10,400 workers were committed to the project. Officially opened on 15 October 1935, the plant had important implications for national security and provided a new market for coal and for the hydrogen produced on site. It resulted also in the manufacture of a series of by-products, such as methane, which in turn promoted experiments in methane–steam re-forming that were to reach fruition in the early 1960s with petroleum rather than coal. In the changing circumstances of the 1950s it became less economic to produce petrol from coal, and production ceased in 1956, but from 1951 the plant had been adapted to produce phenol and isopropanol for use

in plastics, and later to produce detergent alcohols used in washing-up liquids and fabric conditioners. The plant closed on 19 February 1994, but extensive documentary, photographic and video records are held by ICI, and some key artefacts were deposited in the Science Museum, London, and in museums at Sheffield, Leeds and Doncaster.[14]

During the Second World War Billingham's petrol and ammonia plants were augmented by isooctane and victane units in 1940 and 1944 respectively, but Teesside was considered to be vulnerable to bombing raids. ICI agreed to construct a series of 'external factories', rather akin to shadow factories. Ammonia plants were opened at Mossend, Lanarkshire, in 1939 and at Dowlais in South Wales in 1942, and a nitric acid plant at the Bishopton Royal Ordnance Factory in Scotland. New ammonium nitrate plants works were created, at Huddersfield in 1939, at Heysham in 1940 and at Pembrey in South Wales, the latter close to another Royal Ordnance Factory. ICI collaborated with Shell in 1939–41 in building an hydrogenation plant for making aviation fuel at Heysham. A catalyst factory was developed at Clitheroe, Lancashire, from 1940 and an ammonium sulphate works at Prudhoe on the Tyne from 1942. Measures were also taken to avoid major dislocations should Billingham come under attack. The main offices were transferred to Norton Hall and the factory control system rehoused in a deep dug-out. The worst fears were unfulfilled, for Billingham never did suffer a major bombing attack.[15]

After the war ICI decided to utilise the hydrogen, ammonia, methanol and nitric acid available at Billingham in a polymer plant to supply materials for British Nylon Spinners' factory at Pontypool (see Chapter 2). A less successful venture was the construction in 1949–50 of a large new factory at Cargenbridge (NY 9474), west of Dumfries, for the production of Ardil, a synthetic substitute for wool, developed by researchers at Ardeer, which was dependent for its raw materials on groundnuts from Africa. The production of Ardil ceased in 1957 and plant was subsequently adapted to produce plastic films.[16]

ICI also made a bold commitment in the mid-1940s to establish a second integrated chemical complex on Teesside. It was anticipated that several divisions of the company could be accommodated, with good access to supplies of salt and process water, on a site of 3,500 acres (1,400ha) at Wilton (NZ 5722), on the south of the river. Wilton marked the recognition by ICI that the future organic chemical industry would be reliant on oil. In 1950 many British chemical works still had rows of coke ovens or used wood pulp and molasses. Only 6 per cent of production depended on oil, and many firms claimed to be too stretched to replace plant from the 1920s or 1930s. ICI was the exception, and made a major investment in its own cracking plant rather than allow itself to be dependent on supplies from oil companies. The first ethylene cracker came on stream in 1951. By the late 1960s Wilton had five crackers, primarily for making ethylene, capacity being more than doubled in 1966, and again in 1968, to reach 780,000 tonnes a year. The line of tall cylindrical crackers became the most distinctive feature of the Wilton skyline. Olefine Cracker V was described as 'the biggest single-stream naphtha cracker in the world'. Plants for producing nylon and Terylene were established at Wilton, and the latter was spun into fibre within the complex.[17]

The use of coal also ceased at Billingham in 1962 when the steam re-forming process was introduced for ammonia synthesis. Light petroleum was mixed with steam at high pressure and passed over a catalyst to produce a stream of mixed gas, from which ammonia could be derived. Three new ammonia plants were erected in an area that became nicknamed 'Ammonia Avenue'. A methanol plant was added in 1966. New plant was increasingly fabricated as factory-built modules. Vessels might be erected on their sides and hoisted into place by 2,000-ton cranes.[18]

Billingham and Wilton marked a high point in British confidence in high technology and large-scale industry. They were frequently described in the 1960s and 1970s as Europe's biggest petro-chemical complex. Pride was expressed in Wilton's layout and growth, and the administrative offices fronted by a formal lake were grand enough to be nicknamed 'the Wilton Hilton'. Billingham boasted laboratories, engineering workshops and a power station, 40 miles of internal railway, and the Synthonia Recreation Club with a membership of over 12,000 in the 1970s. Billingham, as the headquarters of ICI's Agricultural Division, employed around 17,000 people in 1958, and

about 10,000 in the mid-1970s, when Wilton, as headquarters of the Petrochemicals Division, had around 13,000 employees.

Wilton demonstrated also the value of pipelines in linking dispersed chemical complexes. A 138-mile pipeline was laid to carry ethylene to Runcorn and Hillhouse (*see above*), while another 155-mile line linked Olefine Cracker VI, completed around 1978, to the BP plant at Grangemouth on the Firth of Forth. Two tunnels under the Tees were bored to accommodate pipelines carrying raw materials and products to and from Billingham.

6.3
The oil refinery at Grangemouth on the River Forth.

(Crown copyright. Royal Commission on the Ancient and Historical Monuments of Scotland)

6.4
The ethanol plant at BP's Chemicals Works, alongside the oil refinery at Grangemouth.

(Crown copyright. Royal Commission on the Ancient and Historical Monuments of Scotland)

Oil had become the key raw material for the chemicals industry. Three oil refineries were completed on Teesside in the four years 1965–8, two being jointly operated by ICI and Phillips Petroleum at the North Tees Works, south of Greatham Creek (NZ 5325, NZ 5223). Naphtha from the refinery was used as feedstock for the aromatics plant and the crackers at Wilton. Shell built the third refinery at Teesport on the south bank of the estuary (NZ 5423). These refineries in turn encouraged further investments by the chemical industry. ICI erected two aromatic plants on the north side of the Tees in the late 1960s to produce cyclohexane, benzene, toluene and xylenes to be fed to Billingham and Wilton. Soon after, natural gas from the North Sea became available and was used for the production of ammonia, methane and hydrogen. A 220-mile pipeline from Phillips Petroleum's Ekofisk Field in the Norwegian sector of the North Sea was completed around 1980, terminating in an oil and gas reception and treatment plant at Seal Sands (NZ 5425) on the north bank of the Tees.[19]

In 1998 about 11,000 people were employed directly in Teesside's chemical industries, a number reflecting the continued diversification of interrelated activities. The British Oxygen Company responded to demands for nitrogen and oxygen by opening two plants in 1957, a third oxygen plant for supplying the steel industry in 1958, and by further expanding capacity in the 1960s and early 1970s. An oxygen pipeline was bolted on to the Transporter Bridge at Middlesbrough to link the north and south banks of the Tees. Three new plants for synthetic fibres were opened around 1970: a texturising factory at Thornaby by a subsidiary of British Enkalon; a plant for making acrylonitrile on the north bank of the river by Monsanto; and a nearby plant for acrylate monomer by Lennig Chemicals.[20] In 1999 BASF was operating a works at Seal Sands making chemical intermediates for fibres and plastics. Zeneca was based at Billingham, producing biodegradable plastics. The role of Teesside as a leading source of fertilisers was reinforced by the development from 1969 of a huge potash mine. Cleveland Potash Ltd, partly owned by ICI, created a deep mine at Boulby to the east of Teesside. This mine, with its huge metal-clad surface buildings and rail link, forms a distinctive feature along the coast between Skinningrove and Staithes. At Billingham the chemical complex has been rationalised, but the nine-storey rectangular office block and much of the original road system, pipe bridges, drains and perimeter fencing remain, while Wilton also retains its later and more lavishly designed administrative complex.[21]

6.5

The east elevation of the washing plant at the ICI coal-to-oil plant, Billingham.

(Crown copyright. NMR)

Dyestuffs and explosives

Another field of the chemical industry, the manufacture of dyestuffs, was the first to develop organic chemicals derived from coal tar. Aniline dyes were first produced in England in 1856 by Sir William Perkin

(1838–1907), but German manufacturers took the lead in producing synthetic dyestuffs on a large scale and in subsequent technological development. There were, reputedly, eleven factories producing dyestuffs from coal tar Britain in 1913. The three most important were Levinstein Ltd of Blackley (SD 850029), Manchester, the British Alizarine Company Ltd of Silvertown, London, and Read Holliday & Sons Ltd, founded 1830 in Huddersfield as tar distillers producing naphtha using waste tar from local gasworks, the largest of several firms serving woollen manufacturers in the Huddersfield area. Levinstein's plant at Blackley was notorious in the years before the First World War for squalid working conditions and for the noxious fumes which it released into the atmosphere, giving the locality the nickname of 'the Place of Eleven Stinks'. Two important companies from continental Europe established dyestuffs plants in Britain in the early twentieth century. The Swiss firm Ciba bought the Clayton Aniline Company of Manchester in 1911, and the German company Hoechst set up a works, owned by a subsidiary company, Meister Lucius & Brüning, for making drugs as well as dyestuffs at Ellesmere Port, Cheshire.[22]

The dyestuffs industry underwent a revolution during the First World War. First, it was necessary vastly to increase production of dyes for military uniforms. Second, as users of coal-tar dyestuffs, manufacturers had the expertise to develop the large-scale production of explosives. At Levinstein's Blackley plant new facilities were constructed for producing black and khaki dyes, as well as a large multi-purpose facility named the 'Lonsdale shed' after the company chairman, a mustard-gas plant, a still for producing nitrotoluol and a laboratory. Levinstein's grew rapidly and took over the Hoechst plant at Ellesmere Port, but the company's shares were progressively bought up by the Nobel explosives company from Ardeer during the latter part of the war.[23]

The British Alizarine plant at Silvertown was expanded in 1916, but suffered major damage in January 1917 when the neighbouring works of Brunner Mond exploded. The Silvertown works was rebuilt, but there was no space for expansion and in July 1919 the company leased a 23-acre (9ha) site at Trafford Park, transferring production to Manchester in 1921.[24]

The government encouraged the amalgamation of the principal companies and prompted the establishment of a new company, British Dyes, which from July 1915 incorporated Read Holliday. British Dyes built a new works entrance in Andrews Road, Huddersfield (SE 152170), which remained in the 1990s. The existing Huddersfield plant was expanded and largely turned over to the making of explosives, while from January 1916 a new dyestuffs plant was built at Dalton (SE 165150) on the edge of the town. The 450-acre (180ha) site, approached from Ashgrove Road, was laid out with an open geometric plan defined by roadways and rail links and designed to allow for expansion and rebuilding. Most of the buildings constructed before 1920 were traditional sheds built with bricks, cast iron and timber.

Another important wartime development in this sector of the chemicals industry was Solway Dyes Company's establishment of a works in 1918 on an 80-acre (32ha) site at Grangemouth (NT 9481), on the Firth of Forth, that was to be the nucleus of a chemical complex of major importance.

The merger that created ICI in 1926 brought together most of the British dyestuffs industry. The Dyestuffs Division of the company, which at first was in the shadow of the large-scale inorganic plants in Cheshire and the innovative developments on Teesside, assumed an increasingly important role as the focus of the chemical industry began to shift from bulk products to specialised organic materials. Most of the historic dyestuffs works taken over by ICI in 1926 were still operating in the 1990s under various ownerships, following the demerger of ICI and Zeneca in 1993 and subsequent mergers and take-overs. The works at Blackley, Grangemouth, Trafford Park, Ellesmere Port and Huddersfield were concerned with chemicals for agricultural use, and with polyurethane products, bactericides, materials for paint and paper manufacture, and medicines. Some processes and products changed with bewildering rapidity, and such a process of change will doubtless continue. What is most significant for the archaeologist is the continuity in the use of sites, showing the industry's dependence on costly infrastructures, and on its established labour force.

6.6
The vast extent of Shell's oil refinery at Stanlow, Cheshire.

(Crown copyright. NMR)

6.7
A cracker at the Stanlow oil refinery.

(Crown copyright. NMR)

Other chemical works

The example of ICI in focusing on products derived from oil was followed by other companies in the second half of the twentieth century, and most chemical plants are now grouped around the major refineries at Fawley, at Baglan Bay near Swansea, in the vicinity of Stanlow, at Grangemouth and on Humberside. The plant at Carrington, west of Manchester (SJ 7392), operated by Shell Chemicals in the 1990s, originated as Petrochemicals Ltd, and is claimed to have been the first petrochemical plant in Britain. It drew feedstock from the Stanlow refinery from 1961. Some oil companies are heavily involved in the manufacture of chemicals, and it is difficult to place a clear dividing line between the oil and chemical industries.

Nevertheless, in the late 1990s there were still several large and long-established chemical plants, some of them more than a century old, which were not directly related to oil refineries. The historic Albright & Wilson plant at Oldbury (SJ 992886) alongside the M5 motorway in the heart of the Black Country was originally set up in the 1830s to produce phosphorus for matches, but in the second half of the twentieth century produced a variety of compounds with many applications, using phosphorus from a plant at Buckingham, Quebec, purchased early in the century.[25] The Monsanto plant near Wrexham, well known to industrial archaeologists because it overlooks the Pontcysyllte aqueduct and occupies the site of the Plas Kynaston ironworks where the trough of the aqueduct was cast, is almost as old. It originated in 1867 as a shale oil works. By 1870 it was making phenol, production of which was much expanded during the First World War, when picric acid was also made on the site. The plant was acquired by Monsanto in 1928, and from 1936 concentrated on the production of plasticisers.[26] In Suffolk several fertiliser manufacturers established in the nineteenth century had been brought together as Fisons Ltd by the early 1930s in a series of take-overs and constructed a new plant at Cliff Quay, Ipswich, for producing granular fertilisers, and subsequently for the manufacture of nitrates.[27] Several other types of plant which might be considered as parts of the chemical industry are considered elsewhere in the book – synthetic fibres in Chapter 2 and coal derivatives plants in Chapter 3.

Industrial archaeologists have given relatively little attention to the pharmaceuticals industry, except for the adulation given to the Boots factory at Beeston (*see Chapter 10*), yet this was generally considered to be one of the most successful of British industries in the late twentieth century. As with other branches of chemicals, some plants are well over a century old. Wellcome's factory on Dartford Creek (TQ 546747) in Kent was a very large plant when it was built by Burroughs Wellcome & Co. in 1889. It still retained some of its older buildings in 1999.[28] May & Baker's plant at Dagenham opened in 1933 and was particularly important in the 1940s for the manufacture of penicillin. It is best known for the extension to the manufacturing facilities and the laboratory, built in 1948 to the design of E. M. Mills, with a single-span reinforced concrete shell membrane roof measuring 144ft x 64ft (44m x 20m). Another notable pharmaceuticals factory of the same era is at Welwyn Garden City, designed for Roche Products by O. R. Salvisbert and G. S. Brown.[29] Other plants, at Sandwich, Macclesfield, Greenford, Ware, the Wrexham Industrial Estate and elsewhere, await investigation.

Radio and telecommunications

Telecommunications is another a science-based industry. A starting-point for archaeological study is Porthcurno in Cornwall, landing-point of the submarine telegraph cable to India from 1870. It was the site of the experiments by Guglielmo Marconi (1874–1937) in trans-atlantic radio communication in 1901. Cable communications were vital during the two world wars when the establishment was heavily fortified, and in the Second World War parts of it were located in underground bunkers. The cable station closed in 1970, but some of its structures and many of its artefacts were by the late 1990s displayed to visitors by the Trevithick Trust.[30]

Chelmsford was the starting-point for the radio manufacturing industry. The Wireless Telegraphy & Signals Co., subsequently

Marconi's Wireless Telegraph Company Ltd, established a radio factory in 1899 in a 5-year-old building designed as a furniture warehouse at the junction of Hall Street and Mildmay Road (TL 709064). A second factory was constructed in New Street (TL 708074) in 1912, and Marconi subsequently took over a third factory in Writtle Road (TL 697060). The electronics industry was still important in Chelmsford in 1999, and took pride in its buildings and collections of artefacts.[31] Other important plants were the Strowger Works of the Automatic Telephone & Electric Co., established in Liverpool in 1912 and later part of Plessey, and Ericsson Telephones at Beeston in Nottinghamshire.

Broadcasting House in Portland Place, completed in 1931 to the design of Val Myers and Watson Hart, is pre-eminent among the buildings associated with broadcasting. From the early years of radio there remain a house and some other structures on Borough Hill, Daventry (SP 5862), one of the most historic transmission sites, together with some equipment in Daventry's museum. The aerial-capped tower block in Paradise Street, Birmingham, centre for independent television in the midlands, replaced the ornate entrance to the coal wharves of Birmingham Canal Navigation. A series of high television masts,

6.9
The image of late-twentieth-century communications: an aerial tower at Swaffham, Norfolk.

(Crown copyright. NMR)

artefacts of the industry are displayed in the National Museum of Photography, Film and Television at Bradford, but there has been scarcely any study of the buildings associated with the industry. As early as 1894 a trade journal commented:

> Very few photographers have the slightest idea of the work performed and the extent of the machinery and labour employed. It is a big industry and one entitled to rank amongst the mills of Yorkshire or the factories of Birmingham.[32]

George Eastman (1854–1932), the American pioneer of photogaphic technology, who registered the trademark 'Kodak' when he began to market a mass-produced box camera in 1888, began selling his products in Soho Square, London, in 1885, and in 1889 a British company was formed to handle the business outside the Americas. Eastman bought a 7-acre (3ha) site at Harrow, where production commenced the following year. The Harrow plant was extensively rebuilt in the late 1990s but no archaeological analysis has been published. Some historic photographic works are wholly unheroic. Some of the best cameras made in Britain were produced by the works of Thornton Pickard in Atlantic Street, Altrincham, between 1891 and 1939. The single-storey factory, which once carried the company's name in white brick, still stood, virtually unrecognised, in the late 1990s, when it was occupied by a printing company. A photographic firm that lasted through the century in spite of fluctuations in scale was founded in Balsall Heath, Birmingham, in 1895 by fire-bellows makers Harry Glanvill and his wife Florence. They began to manufacture bellows for cameras and enlargers, and expanded in the inter-war period when many popular cameras had bellows, producing over 1 million sets for Kodak Brownie cameras in the 1930s. The manufacture of bellows needs a pattern room, a cutting-and-assembly area and facilities for despatching finished products, requirements easily met either in adapted buildings or in a unit factory. The company in 1998 was part of a conglomerate, and operated with about a dozen people from a factory unit in Balsall Heath, making bellows for professional cameras, enlargers and for surgical and dental equipment.[33]

including those at Lichfield, Sutton Coldfield, Wenvoe and Holme Moss, trace the progress of television transmissions into the provinces in the 1950s.

The telegraph pole, with its crossbars carrying ceramic insulators, was one of the principal features of the British roadside in the first half of the twentieth century. The concrete telecommunications towers in big cities like London and Birmingham, and intermediate towers like that at Napton, Warwickshire (SP 458614), are evidence of technological change in the third quarter of the century, just as numerous small, aerial-carrying towers exemplify the proliferation of mobile phones and other services in the 1990s.

Scientific imaging

Another science-based industry of great importance in the twentieth century was the manufacture of photographic equipment and materials, and the processing of images. The

Computers

The computer was one of the characteristic artefacts of the 1990s. Its origins could be studied in the displays in the Science Museum, London, of calculating machines designed by Charles Babbage (1791–1871) or at the wartime code-deciphering establishment at Bletchley Park, Buckinghamshire, where a Colossus computer, developed at the Post Office research establishment at Dollis Hill, was installed in December 1943 and was operational from the following January. The experiments which produced MADM (Manchester Automatic Digital Machine) are duly commemorated at the University of Manchester.

Much less is currently recorded of the manufacture of computers and their components. In some respects this is closely linked with the history of earlier machines. IBM in the United States was already a large company whose success was based on punched-card systems of the 1880s when it began to produce its first computers in 1951–52. In the same way, British companies that manufactured earlier generations of machines involving electrical connections have turned to making computers. National Cash Register's factory at Kingsway West, Dundee (NO 370326), is in some ways comparable with the ICI plant at Billingham – it is a manufacturing facility that has provided the infrastructure for a succession of changes in technology. It was built in 1946 to manufacture cash registers, and the company reached a peak of activity in the region in 1971 when it was employing 6,000 people at seven manufacturing sites in and around Dundee. In the late 1970s it began to produce Automated Teller Machines – the 'holes in the wall' from which money can be obtained from banks by the use of plastic cards. The first machine, known as 'the 1780', was unsuccessful but the firm recovered its prosperity after the launch of a third-generation machine, the 5070, in 1984. A similar pattern can be observed in the history of the Timex factory at Dundee, built in the 1930s for the manufacture of watches. After the Second World War it mass-produced Polaroid cameras for amateurs (those for professional use were made elsewhere), and was later adapted to produce Sinclair computers.[34]

Many other computer manufacturing plants remain to be investigated. Some are purpose-built factories constructed by multinational companies. Some are notable for their lack of fenestration and their external piping, evidence of the need to create sterile conditions. Others, like those in Dundee, are older buildings which have seen diverse earlier uses. One of the most notable of the new plants is the Inmos plant at Newport, Monmouthshire, designed by Lord (Richard) Rogers and completed in 1982. It was intended for the manufacture of a new type of microchip, but production was transferred to France, and the building has seen little use.

Conclusions

We have come to appreciate in this study the boundaries between industrial archaeology and the history of science or technology, and the different time-scales that apply in the disciplines. The practical significance of much basic scientific research of the twentieth century, like the discovery of DNA, was only just emerging in 1990s. The importance of the concrete tanks at Holton Heath – the beginnings of biotechnology – can be acknowledged, but it is an acknowledgement for the future. Yet in many science-based industries there was a marked degree of stability in the twentieth century. While processes changed as a consequence of research, infrastructures might remain constant. A plant designed to produce explosives could be adapted to make plasticisers, insecticides or quick-drying paints. A factory making watches or cameras could readily turn, in wartime, to the making of air-speed indicators or radar sets and, in the latter part of the century, personal computers or automated cash-handling machines. A study of artefacts, of structures, sites and even, in the case of very large plants like Winnington, Stanlow, Carrington or Billingham, of landscapes, can raise our understanding of the 'Age of Science'.

Notes and references

1   F. A. Kirk, 'Twentieth Century Industry: Obsolescence and Change. A Case Study: The ICI Coal to Oil Plant and Its Varied Uses', *Industrial Archaeology Review*, 1998, vol. 20, pp. 83–90.

2   P. Pagnamenta and R. Overy, *All Our Working Lives*, London: BBC Books, 1984, pp. 163–7.

3   W. J. Reader, *Imperial Chemical Industries: A History*, vol. I: *The Forerunners 1879–1926*, Oxford: Oxford University Press, 1970.

4   W. J. Reader, *Imperial Chemical Industries: A History*, vol. II: *The First Quarter-Century 1926–52*, Oxford: Oxford University Press, 1975, pp. 1–70.

5   The account of the Cheshire plants that follows draws chiefly from R. Kinchin-Smith, 'A Survey of Sites in Cheshire and Merseyside Relating to the Alkali Industry', Ironbridge Institute assignment, 1993.

6   O. Ashmore, *The Industrial Archaeology of North-West England and Where to Find It*, Manchester: Manchester University Press, 1982, pp. 50–2.

7   P. W. B. Semmens, 'The Chemical Industry', in J. C. Dewdney (ed.) *Durham County and City with Teesside*, Durham: British Association, 1970, pp. 331–2.

8   T. L. Williams, *The Chemical Industry Past and Present*, Harmondsworth: Penguin, 1953, p. 79.

9   Reader, op. cit., vol. II, pp. 352–65.

10 Ibid., p. 367.

11 Semmens, op. cit., p. 332; Reader, op. cit., vol. II, pp. 98–118.

12 Reader, ibid., p. 160.

13 Reader, ibid., p. 70

14 Reader, ibid., pp. 128, 180, 318; Kirk, op. cit., pp. 83–90.

15 Reader, op. cit., vol. II, p. 366.

16 Reader, ibid., pp. 378–9; J. A. Mackay, *A Pictorial History of Dumfries*, Alloway: Darrel, 1990, p. 94; D. Carroll, *Scotland in Old Photographs: Dumfries*, Stroud: Alan Sutton, 1996, pp. 47, 50–1.

17 Reader, op. cit., pp. 392–4; Semmens, op. cit., pp. 335–6.

18 Semmens, ibid., p. 337.

19 Ibid., p. 339.

20 Ibid., pp. 337–40; Teesside TEC, *Teesside Business Yearbook*, Middlesbrough: Teesside TEC, 1998.

21 Semmens, op. cit., p. 339.

22 Reader, op. cit., vol. I, pp. 260–3; vol. II, pp. 183–6; M. R. Fox, *Dye-Makers of Great Britain 1856–1976*, Manchester: ICI Commercial Advertising Service, 1987, pp. 40–1, 139–43.

23 Fox, op. cit., p. 48; Reader, op. cit., vol. I, p. 277.

24 Fox, op. cit., p. 121.

25 R. E. Threlfall, *The Story of 100 Years of Phosphorus Making*, Oldbury: Albright & Wilson, 1951.

26 I. Edwards, 'The History of the Monsanto Chemical Works Site, Cefn Mawr, Wrexham: A Study in Industrial Archaeology', *Transactions of the Denbighshire Historical Society*, 1967, vol. 16, pp. 128–48.

27 D. Alderton and J. Booker, *The Batsford Guide to the Industrial Archaeology of East Anglia*, London: Batsford, 1980, p. 33.

28 D. Eve, *A Guide to the Industrial Archaeology of Kent*, Telford: Association for Industrial Archaeology, p. 56.

29 E. M. Mills, *The Modern Factory*, London: Architectural Press, 1951, pp. 141, 154.

30 Trevithick Trust, *The Museum of Submarine Telegraphy: The Porthcurno Story*, Camborne: Trevithick Trust, nd.

31 Alderton and Booker, op. cit., pp. 82–3.

32 *Photographic Review of Reviews*, July 1894.

33 We are grateful to Ian Grant and Clifford Morris for information on the Pickard and Glanvill companies.

34 NCR, *Cash Advance: The Story of NCR in Scotland 1946–96*, Dundee: NCR, 1996.

Chapter seven

The century of total war

Only a few survivors of the Somme and Passchendaele will experience the twenty-first century, and most memories of the thousands whose names are inscribed on the Menin Gate at Ypres (Ieper) are now hearsay reminiscences of grandfathers or great-uncles. In the year 2000 Battle of Britain pilots are in their 70s and 80s, and no one under 60 can recall the shock of evacuation in 1939, or the thump of Luftwaffe bombs. Yet the two world wars remain points of conversational and scholarly reference, compulsively fascinating to students of all ages in diverse disciplines. An industrial archaeological analysis of the impact of the wars powerfully illuminates many questions.

Historians have approached the study of war from many directions. Arthur Marwick, from whose book this chapter borrows its title, has attempted to define the ways in which war shapes society in the long term.[1] War can be seen as a test for a community, a challenge to the bonds which bind a nation together. Conflict can create an 'inspection effect', as the need to maximise economic effort leads the governing class, of whatever kind, to gain acquaintance with the living conditions of its subjects. In the Second World War, L. T. C. Rolt (1910–74), the future biographer of the engineers of the Industrial Revolution, was actually a government inspector employed by the Board of Trade to check on the practices of engineering firms, in which capacity he observed such bizarre spectacles as the use of a horse-operated plateway in the assembly of barges for the Normandy landings.[2] War artists were employed to record not just dogfights between Supermarine Spitfires and Messerschmitt 109s but historic Britain, particularly perhaps historic England, prior to its anticipated destruction by the bombers, which would always get through. Wartime 'inspection' by painters, film-makers and social scientists is a prime source of industrial archaeological evidence.

A war compels a governing class to enhance expectations of subsequent peacetime benefits. A 'participation bargain' is struck between government – making promises about future peacetime living conditions – and subjects, forced to accept the drudgery, dangers and deprivations inevitable in armed conflicts. Wars come to have not just manifest aims, like the defeat of the German army, the liberation of

Belgium or an independent Poland, but latent objectives, like better housing, full employment, a more open education system or free access to health-care facilities. When opening Birmingham's 40,000th council house in 1933, Neville Chamberlain (1869–1940) referred to 'the hopes which inspired us during the War – the hope for improved and better housing conditions'.[3] Infantrymen of the Royal Warwickshire Regiment may not have considered that they were creating the future Weoley Castle estate as they charged across the Flanders mud towards German machine-gun emplacements, but patterns of housing (the subject of Chapter 8) were changed utterly after the First World War, and there was an element of truth in Chamberlain's statement.

War certainly accelerates the rate of technological change. The beginnings of biotechnology in the First World War and the development of radar and atomic power in the Second World War would not have happened so quickly without the stimulus of conflict. Plastics, aircraft construction, hydraulic engineering and synthetic fibres developed in similar ways. Collections of artefacts, of unsuccessful products like the Fairey Battle fighter, the Whitley bomber, the Covenanter tank and the Daimler Dingo scout car, as well as the Supermarine Spitfire and the Jeep, are also archaeological evidence of war.

The impact of war on society is paradoxical. It can be demonstrated that during the the two world wars thousands of people rapidly learned new skills – piloting or navigating aircraft, installing and operating radios, driving road vehicles or manipulating machine tools – and that these skills brought post-war economic benefits. It can be argued that the relative inactivity of many British troops during the period 1943–45 led to a revival of interest in classical music, literature and current affairs. By contrast, schools and universities were severely disrupted, and the raising of the school-leaving age was postponed – and in the First World War effectively lowered. Yet Acts of Parliament making higher levels of education accessible to a greater proportion of the population were the consequence of both wars.

War changes also the industrial landscape, and the structures and sites within it, in ways that powerfully influence subsequent economic and social developments. The sites and structures created during the exigencies of conflict are some of the more measurable economic consequences of war. The structures destroyed in wartime can be studied only through documents and images. It is the purpose of this chapter to examine the influence of the two wars on the contemporary British landscape, to re-animate some features of that landscape and to make connections between field and artefactual evidence.

The nature of the two world wars

Governments and military leaders tend, understandably, to be in a state of preparation more suited to previous than to potential conflicts. A war, at the time it begins, is rarely fought in the manner planned by either side. Most wars are times of social and economic improvisation as governments attempt to match industrial production to the demands of the military, and to rationalise the distribution of manpower between the fighting forces and manufacturing industry. The strategy and tactics of both world wars remain topics of debate among military historians, and this book makes no claim to participate in such discussions; it is, however, necessary, in considering the wars' archaeological legacies, to be aware of the contrasting nature of the campaigns.

Within a few months of the outbreak in August 1914 of the First World War, British and French troops faced the German army along a front which extended from the Belgian coast to the Swiss border. An attritional conflict developed, fought by artillerymen and infantry, demanding heavy guns, shells, rifles and machine guns. The economy was re-organised to deliver men and munitions to the Western Front. The capital ships of the Royal Navy, expected to play a significant part in the war, saw little action, but blockades enforced by smaller vessels affected both Britain and Germany. Motor vehicles and aircraft were extensively deployed by 1918. The Eastern Front, the war in the Middle East, the role of Italy, the late intervention of the United States and the Gallipoli campaign were highly significant factors in the war, but had relatively little effect on the organisation of the British wartime economy.

In the Second World War much of the British army was based in Britain between the retreat from Dunkirk (May–June 1940) and D-Day (6 June 1944) – which is not to minimise the significance of the Eastern Front, nor of the campaign in North Africa, nor that of the struggle in the Far East against Japan. The armed forces at the time of Dunkirk numbered 2.212 million, a total which had risen to 3.483 million within a year. The threat of invasion in 1940 was lifted by the German attack on the USSR in June 1941. The Japanese raid on Pearl Harbor in December 1941 brought the United States into the war. The British and US governments agreed that the European theatre should have priority, and during 1942 Operation Bolero was launched, providing accommodation for American soldiers and airforce personnel in Britain, prior to an invasion of mainland Europe. As predicted in the 1930s, air power dominated the war, but the opposing bombing campaigns proved less effective than had been anticipated. The Battle of the Atlantic – the German submarine-enforced blockade of shipping lanes – was effectively won by midsummer 1943, when losses to the U-boat fleet brought about by the use of air power and radar led to the withdrawal of the U-boats to their bases.

The First World War

The first eight months of the First World War was a period of boom in such consumer goods as pianos, gramophones, motorcycles and restaurant meals, a time of 'business as usual' that was brought to an end by the battles of Neuve Chapelle during the early summer of 1915, which effectively destroyed the regular army. The failure of the early stages of the campaign was blamed by the press on shortages of shells. A political crisis ensued, as a result of which a coalition government was formed, in which David Lloyd George (1863–1945) directed a Ministry of Munitions empowered to regulate the distribution of raw materials, and to develop 'National Factories'. 'Nobody', commented the historian of ICI, 'had ever seen anything like the Ministry of

Munitions before ... and it is difficult to exaggerate its effect upon the later development of British industry.'[4]

The economy during the First World War was directed to the supply, through the Channel ports, of the army on the Western Front. Depots for accumulating supplies were established in north and west London, where many of their sites are marked by the industrial estates of the 1920s. Some impressive monuments to the supply chain remain at Richborough (TR 3361) at the mouth of the Kentish Stour, adjacent to the fifth-century fort of the Saxon Shore. The War Office acquired about 4,000 acres (1,600ha) for the accommodation of IWT (Inland Water Transport) and a section of the Royal Engineers established to take supplies by barge across the Channel and directly on to the French waterways system. Slipways for building barges were built, together with a power station and railway sidings that could accommodate over 3,000 wagons and provided employment for thirty-five shunting locomotives. Shipments to France began in December 1916, and 155 barges were in service by the end of 1917. In February 1918 a ferry service was established conveying railway wagons to Calais and Dunkirk. It was supplemented by another, between Southampton and Dieppe, later in the year. A huge camp was established, which was accommodating nearly 16,000 personnel in September 1918. Most of its buildings were Winget huts, constructed from slabs made on the site from Winget concrete-mixers. There was little use for the base once the bulk of the British army had returned from the Continent. The ferry-train installations were removed to Harwich when a freight-wagon ferry service to Zeebrugge began in 1924, utilising the three ferry vessels constructed during the war. Two were subsequently sunk in the Second World War – the third survived until the 1950s. From the early months of 1939 part of the camp was used for the accommodation of refugees from the Nazis, and was subsequently a Royal Navy base, HMS *Robertson*. Part of the Mulberry Harbour used in the Normandy landings was assembled at Richborough. The north jetty of the ferry birth, the barge basin and a slipway for the construction of barges are among the monuments to the activities of the First World War that remained in 1999.[5]

Most of the storage depots around London became centres of dynamic industrial development in the 1920s and 1930s. Peter Hall showed in 1962 that an almost continuous zone occupied by manufacturing industry extends from Colindale and Hendon through Wembley, Willesden and Park Royal to Acton, then westwards along Western Avenue, the Great Western Main Line towards Reading and the Great West Road.[6] Some large manufacturing concerns existed in the area before 1914, British Thomson-Houston's electrical works and the McVitie & Price biscuit factory at Willesden for example, but the main points of growth were around the wartime munitions and aircraft factories at the Hyde (TQ 2188) and Colindale (TQ 2189), which passed into other uses from 1920, and the munitions works at Park Royal (TQ 1982), which became derelict after 1919. A company that used the site for sorting scrap began, in 1929, to construct small factories, and discovered a substantial demand among manufacturers. By 1952 the 335-acre (136ha) Park Royal estate provided accommodation for 302 firms, which gave employment to over 30,000 people. Park Royal remains a lively manufacturing centre and retains many buildings that reflect its origins in the 1930s – for the most part small factories with not especially pretentious office blocks fronting simple sheds to the rear, and engaged in a variety of manufactures, including yeast, bodywork for vehicles, and printing.

Further west, at Slough (SU 9581), a 668-acre (270ha) farm was acquired by government in 1918 as a base for a planned motor-borne offensive on the Western Front in 1919. The thousands of vehicles on the site, and others retrieved from France and Flanders, were sold off by a company already experienced in the motor trade. By the autumn of 1920s its directors recognised the demand for manufacturing accommodation and leased several plots for industrial use as the Slough Trading Estate. The last military vehicles were sold in 1925, and the site was divided into plots for industrial purposes. From 1927 the Trading Estate's company began to build factories in advance of requirements, but most large firms, like Citroën, which in 1925 opened what was claimed to be 'the largest factory under one roof in Britain', designed their own premises. Some buildings constructed by the military remain at Slough, including an office block on Buckingham Avenue which became the first office of the Trading Estate, and now accommodates a crèche. The landscape of the early years of the company is best preserved on Ipswich Road, where there remain lines of single-storey buildings of low-cost red brickwork, with buttresses topped by blue engineering bricks, lit by large (fifty-pane) metal-framed windows with concrete lintels and, originally, roofed with corrugated asbestos.[7]

In 1914 the only government-owned sources of munitions for the army were the ancient Ordnance works at Woolwich (TQ 4479), Enfield (TQ 3698) and Waltham Abbey (TL 3701). The Munitions of War Act, of May 1915, gave authority for the establishment of National Factories, and some 240 had been constructed by 1918. The Ministry built more than twenty filling factories, in places as far apart as Paisley, Bristol, Southwark and Gainsborough. No. 1 Filling Factory, reputedly the largest, was at Barnbow (SE 3834), Leeds, where construction

7.1 (left)
A factory on Buckingham Avenue on the Slough Trading Estate, where a new administration block appears to have been built on the front of an older shed-like building, although fifty-pane windows are evident on the ground floor.

7.2 (right)
Workshops on Bedford Avenue on the Slough Trading Estate with the fifty-pane windows characteristic of many early buildings on the estate.

(Photos: Barrie Trinder)

commenced in mid-1915; a year later, 6,000 shells a day were being completed. Four National Factories made cartridges, fifteen were 'projectile factories' making shells, and others made guns and aircraft. The Ministry's factories were innovative in their use of machine tools powered by individual electric motors – and in their welfare facilities. A summary of current information about the filling factories appears in Table A1 in the Appendix.

One of the best archaeological monuments of the munitions industry of the First World War is No. 9 Filling Factory at Banbury (SP 476407), established in 1916. Many of its earthworks, mounds which once protected wooden huts used for filling shells, and the remnants of 3.5 miles of standard-gauge railway sidings, lie to the east of the town in Northamptonshire, and were little disturbed until the building of the M40 in the early 1990s. Much can still be seen on the eastern side of the motorway. There are remains from the First World War also of the factories at Birtley, Pembrey and Hereford, which were re-activated in the 1930s. Sixteen blocks of No. 10 National Filling Factory of 1915–16 at Swallow Road, Whitmore Park, Coventry (SP 3582),[8] were used for the assembly of Swallow (subsequently Jaguar) cars between 1928 and 1951, and then by Daimler aviation. Part of No. 5 Factory at Quedgeley, Gloucestershire, remains as an RAF store, while the rest is a trading estate. In all the investigations of the explosives industry by the Royal Commissions, the only timber filling sheds remaining from the First World War appear to be those at the Royal Navy works at Priddy's Hard, Gosport (SU 6201).

In terms of the history of science, one of the most important developments of the war took place at the Royal Naval Cordite Factory at Holton Heath, Dorset (SY 9591), where reinforced concrete fermentation vessels of 1916, for the manufacture of acetone from maize, still stood in 1999. This process, one of the first significant applications of biotechnology, had been devised by Chaim Weizmann (1874–1952), an industrial chemist who was subsequently President of Israel. An experimental plant had operated at Three Mills (TQ 384828) in east London.[9]

7.3
Concrete tanks at Holton Heath, Dorset, used in the First World War for the manufacture of acetone from maize using the process devised by Chaim Weizmann, photographed in 1994.

(Crown copyright. NMR)

The most architecturally impressive of the First World War plants is the National Machine Gun Factory on the eastern side of Burton upon Trent, in 1999 the Supply and Transport Store, Branston (SK 235213), where most of the original buildings appear to remain. The plant was complete but not in production when the war ended. The most prominent building is the Neo-Baroque 21-bay three-storey administrative block, in brick with stone dressings, including a heavy stone cornice between the first and second floors, with an imposing central clock tower. To the east of the main block is a range of brick sheds, some with ventilators, while to the west stands a range with clerestory roofs. North of the administrative block are two ranges of 26-bay north-lit sheds. Rolling mills were built in 1916 at Woolston near Southampton for rolling brass and cupro-nickel strip for use in small arms ammunition. The frontage building is ornamented with a colossal cornice and four pairs of giant pilasters. Equally impressive is the administrative building of the National Explosives Factory at Avonmouth, built in 1915, now the headquarters of Rhône Poulenc (ST 5583). In Birmingham the most imposing factory of the period was that in Drews Lane, Washwood Heath, built by the Electrical & Ordnance Accessories Co. Ltd, where fuses and Stellite light cars were produced during the First World War. It later produced Wolseley cars and Leyland DAF vans. The office block is a two-storey structure, 400ft (120m) long, designed by the Birmingham architect J. J. Hackett. Buildings of this kind provide an archaeological pers-pective on the Great War quite distinct from that which can be gained from documentary studies. Their lavish detailing contrasts with the chaste and undemonstrative office blocks of the Royal Ordnance Factories of the Second World War. In 1999 a variety of small structures remained of the National Factory at Sandycroft, between the railway from Chester to Holyhead and the shore of the Dee, just east of the imposing pre-war buildings of the Queensferry Engineering Co. (SJ 326680), which are constructed in dark brick, with buttress-like piers. To the south is the National Factory's housing estate at Mancot Royal, designed by Raymond Unwin.[10]

The largest of the government's explosives factories was established at Gretna in June 1915 and produced its first propellant in August 1916. It extended about 1.5 miles from north to south, and the production flow extended almost 9 miles from Dornock in Scotland in the west through new settlements at Eastriggs (NY 247664) and Gretna to Mossband and across the border to storage depots at Longtown (NY 365684). The plant included installations for the manufacture of nitric acid and sulphuric acid, a refinery for glycerine, distilleries for ether and alcohol, and storage buildings for raw cotton. Nitroglycerine and gun cotton were blended to produce cordite, known in Gretna as the devil's porridge. The main railway lines from Carlisle to Glasgow and Edinburgh passed through the site. At its peak Gretna gave employment to about 20,000 workers, most of them female. Complaints about the high wages paid and the propensity of the workers to spend them on alcohol led to the nationalisation of public houses and the brewing industry in the Carlisle region; they remained nationalised until the 1970s. Most of the site was cleared after a sale in July 1924, but storage depots were established in the area just before the Second World War, and parts remain in military occupation. The sheep-grazed fields sloping gently from the A721 towards the Solway Firth are strewn with mounds and ruins, and the chimney of the ether plant still stands near Mossband (NY 343675). The village of Gretna lies clustered around the former Institute, a two-storey building with a 19-bay north elevation and pediments over the three bays at either end and the central bay, with stone surrounds to Venetian windows. Only the rather soft, over-burnt bricks suggest that the Institute was built in the straitened circumstances of wartime. Gretna and Eastriggs are haphazard settlements, houses of many styles and date having replaced the 600 or so wooden huts that housed most of the wartime munitions workers, but the permanent houses designed by Raymond Unwin (1873–1940) retain marks of style and quality, with integral porches, porthole windows, hipped roofs and arcades linking semi-detached pairs (*see Table A4 in the Appendix; see also Chapter 8*). The 'tunnel' giving access to the backs of one terrace, Nos 4, 6, 8 and 10 Annan Road, at Gretna has a Baroque surround, while the date 1917 is displayed beneath a pediment on a terrace in Canberra Road. Central Avenue (NY 318673) runs from south to north at the heart of the village, with two churches, terraces of shops and a cinema, but no traces remain of the railway which once ran along it. The former staff club, the most elegant building in Gretna, is now the Hunters' Lodge Hotel. At Eastriggs eight hostels designed by Unwin to be readily convertible to family dwellings can be recognised in Melbourne Road, and cul-de-sacs off Pretoria Road and Dunedin Road are reminiscent of those he built at New Earswick. One wooden hut, 65 Pretoria Road, Eastriggs, retains its original external appearance, but others may survive under modern cladding.[11]

Many of the explosives used during the war were produced by private companies. Existing explosives works were enlarged and plants engaged in making related chemicals, like plastics, rubber, synthetic dyestuffs and fertilisers, were adapted to manufacture the constituents of explosives. One of the oldest centres of explosives manufacture was Faversham (TQ 999643), where there were long-established gunpowder works. The isolation of the estuary marshes was equally conducive to the manufacture of high explosives, and by 1914 the works of the Cotton Powder Company extended over 500 acres (200ha) at Uplees, alongside the rather smaller works of the Explosives Loading Company, established only in 1912. There was an explosion at the latter factory on Sunday 2 April 1916 which shook houses in Norwich, 140 miles (224 km) to the north, and caused over 100 deaths. In November 1918 all explosives manufacture in the area was taken over by Explosives Trades Ltd, which was renamed Nobel Industries Ltd in 1920 and became one of the founding constituents of ICI (Imperial Chemical Industries) in 1926. Just one small works remained on Faversham Creek in

7.4
No. 65 Pretoria Road, Eastriggs, near Gretna, a wooden hut built to house munitions workers during the First World War, and still occupied in 1996.

(Crown copyright. Royal Commission on the Ancient and Historical Monuments of Scotland)

7.5
The ICI, formerly Nobel, explosives works at Ardeer on the west coast of Scotland. In the foreground are nitroglycerine hills.

(Crown copyright. Royal Commission on the Ancient and Historical Monuments of Scotland)

1998, but there is a mass grave in the parish churchyard of sixty-nine victims of the great explosion, and the causeway across the Uplees marshes over which the victims were carried now leads to a few upstanding blast walls, some concrete hut bases and a nature reserve. Another explosion, at Silvertown (TQ 4080), east London, on 19 January 1917, at a factory adapted by Brunner Mond to produce TNT, killed 69 people, 53 of them outside the works, and set alight a gasholder at East Greenwich on the other side of the Thames.[12]

The largest explosives factory was Britain's first dynamite works, established by Alfred Nobel at Ardeer (NS 2941) in Ayrshire in 1871, which by 1902 consisted of 450 buildings, employed 1,200 people, and had its own power station and acid plants. It was considerably extended for the manufacture of cordite during the First World War. The company also built a 239-acre (97ha) plant at nearby Irvine that was just coming into production at the time of the Armistice, and ceased work in February 1919.[13]

The ad hoc nature of munitions production is well illustrated by the factories in Liverpool, where prior to 1914 there had been a considerable surplus of female labour. A National Shell Factory at Edge Lane produced blanks which were machined at four other factories, including one operated by Cunard in Rimrose Road. The company added to an existing building, which it appears to

7.6

A group of workers
from the Coalbrookdale
ironworks, Shropshire,
photographed during
the First World War.
The shells are inscribed
'A present for the
Kaiser', 'To Berlin' and
'A pill for Fritz'.

*(Ironbridge Gorge
Museum Trust)*

have acquired for use as an engineering
workshop but never used, a large two-storey
timber-framed shed with a Belfast truss roof.
There were two hydraulic presses which shaped
the domed heads of shells. Over 1,000 people
were employed, more than 70 per cent of them
women. Once the shells had been machined,
they were taken to No. 2 National Filling
Factory at Aintree.[14]

About 20 per cent of the guns supplied to
British forces in 1914 came from private firms.
Vickers originally operated a rolling mill in
Sheffield, where it built open-hearth furnaces for
steelmaking in 1871–72, and began to make guns
and armour plate for Royal Naval ships in 1888.
In 1897 the company acquired the naval
shipyard at Barrow-in-Furness, where it
subsequently constructed Dreadnoughts, and
the Maxim Nordenfelt company, which had
works in Kent, making Maxim guns at Crayford,
machine-guns at Erith and shells at the North
Kent Ironworks. All the Vickers factories –
Sheffield, Barrow, Erith and Crayford – were
expanded during the First World War. The
company employed 300 workers at Erith in
1914, but 14,500 at the time of the Armistice.
Vickers was also involved with the manufacture
of the torpedo, a weapon developed by a Briton,
Robert Whitehead (1823–1905), at Fiume
(Rijeka), the Adriatic base of the fleet of the
Habsburg Empire. At the request of the British
Admiralty Whitehead set up a factory at
Weymouth, which was taken over by Vickers
in 1906. The Royal Navy established its own

torpedo works at Greenock, but in 1915–16
Vickers adapted a derelict railway wagon
works at Caton (SD 5364), near Lancaster,
to manufacture torpedoes. Vickers produced
its first monoplane at Erith in 1911, and during
the First World War the Crayford factory, with
auxiliary works at Dartford and Bexleyheath,
became one of the principal sources of military
aircraft, while a new aircraft factory was
established in the former Itala Automobile
Company's factory at Brooklands, Weybridge,
and airship technology was developed at
Barrow.[15]

The Armstrong-Whitworth Company
resulted from the coming together in 1897 of
the concerns established by two of the leading
mechanical engineers of the nineteenth century,
the factory of Sir Joseph Whitworth (1903–87),
at Openshaw, Manchester, and the works at
Elswick, Newcastle, of Sir William Armstrong
(1810–1900). Both were extended to produce
60-pounder guns during the First World
War. Elsewhere in Newcastle, Armstrong-
Whitworth's Baroque-style offices at the Low
Walker shipyard of 1915 reflect the expansion of
shipbuilding activity during the war. The third
large manufacturer of armaments in the private
sector in 1914 was the Coventry Ordnance
Company, established in Red Lane in 1905,
which in the course of the war manufactured
large quantities of ammunition, as well as 710
aircraft, 111 tanks and 92 anti-aircraft guns.[16]

The motorcar factory of Sir Herbert Austin
(1886–1941), at Longbridge (SP 0177) on the
western fringe of Birmingham, was transformed during the First World War. The labour
force consisted of 2,638 people in August 1914,
and had expanded to over 20,000 by the time of
the Armistice. Of the 313 planning applications
relating to buildings on the site made between
1906 and 1959, 155 or 48 per cent were made in
the decade that included the First World War.
The ranges of buildings subsequently called
'the north works' and 'the west works' were
constructed, at government expense, from
February 1916. The former, built in six months,
and designed for the production of shells,
consisted of a machine shop, 850ft x 270ft
(260m x 82m) of lightweight steel construction,
with a forge, mess rooms accommodating
4,000 people, a power plant and offices. The
machines were powered by 386 electric motors.
The main building was used for making

transmissions after the war, then for engine manufacture from 1928 until the early 1990s. The west works was capable of producing over 100,000 18-pounder shells per week, and consisted of a 23-bay (660ft x 330ft or 201 x 101m) machine shop, containing 1,000 machine tools each powered by its own electric motor, together with administration buildings. Substantial extensions were made to the original core of the motorcar plant, the south works, chief among them the construction of an aeroplane shop where about 2,000 aircraft were made in the closing phases of the war. In the early 1990s over half the capacity of Britain's largest car-manufacturing plant was the result of government investment during the First World War.[17]

The First World War stimulated the production of aircraft. The Royal Aircraft Factory at Farnborough (SU 869545), Hampshire, had been established in 1894 to make balloons, but from 1912 took responsibility for airships and aeroplanes. Several buildings from the early years of the twentieth century, including an iron-framed balloon house originally erected at Aldershot, remained in the 1990s. Farnborough was of importance chiefly for its research work. It is estimated that there were less than 5,000 aircraft in the world in 1914, but about 200,000 had been built by 1918. Factories built during the war by private firms, but with capital supplied by the government, included buildings for Vickers at Brooklands, Blériot at Addlestone, Airco at Hendon, Fairey at Hayes and Hamble Point, Avro in Manchester and at Hamble, Handley Page at Cricklewood and at Chadderton near Oldham, Sopwith at Kingston upon Thames, and Armstrong Siddeley at Parkside (Coventry). Three National Aircraft Factories were commissioned by the Ministry of Munitions in 1917, at Waddon (Croydon), Aintree (Liverpool) and Heaton Chapel (Stockport). Some of the new works were very large – there were 58 separate buildings and a 720ft x 150ft (220m x 46m) erecting shop at Waddon, while at Cricklewood there were 24 bays of A-framed sheds, fronted by offices. In Coventry 1,600 aircraft were built in a factory at Canley, erected by the Standard Motor Company in 1916, while Daimler built a factory on the airfield at Radford which was turning out eighty aircraft a month by November 1918. The first portion of the Blériot factory in Station Road, Addlestone, a 15-bay

range of two-storey north-lit sheds costing £75,000, provided by the government, was begun in June 1915, and over 900 aircraft were completed there between February 1916 and the end of 1918. Its owners, trading as ANEC, made cars and a few aircraft in the 1920s but went bankrupt in 1929. The works was subsequently used by Weymann Motor Bodies, which from 1932 specialised in bus bodies. The factory employed 15,000 people in 1949, but after a period of decline in the 1950s it closed in 1966 and, after refurbishment, was taken over the following year by Plessey Radar, becoming part of the Marconi division of GEC, but was empty and awaiting re-development in 1999.[18]

The most imposing structures relating to air-power in the First World War are the airship hangars at Cardington (TL 081468), Bedfordshire, the first of which dates from 1916–17. Airship construction was divided between the government and the armaments company Vickers, which built several aircraft for the Admiralty in the closing stages of the First World War at Barrow-in-Furness. In 1926 their principal structural engineer, Barnes Wallis, moved with his team to a new factory at Howden (SE 7327), Yorkshire, where the company's 700ft R100, constructed for the government, flew for the first time in December 1929, prior to a successful return flight to Montreal in the summer of 1930. Meanwhile government engineers at Cardington had developed an alternative design, the R101, which crashed near Beauvais in France on an unwisely hurried flight to India on 5 October 1930. This brought to an end airship development in Britain, for which the Cardington hangars are almost the only monument.[19]

Iron- and steelmaking capacity was extended during the First World War, but many of the new installations were only coming on stream at the time of the Armistice, and were the cause of over-capacity in the industry in subsequent decades. At Rotherham Steel, Peech & Tozer erected the 440-yard Templeborough melting shop (SK 4595), housing fourteen 80-ton open-hearth furnaces in 1917. The Glengarnock (NS 3513) works in southern Scotland, with seven blast furnaces less than 20 years old, and both Bessemer and open-hearth steel plants, was standing idle in 1914, but was re-opened from 1915. A new melting shop came into production in 1918. The works subsequently had a chequered history. The Bessemer plant closed in 1920, and closure of the whole site was recommended a decade later. In the event, only the blast furnaces ceased work, and the steel plant and rolling mill operated until 1978. The open-hearth plant was proposed as a museum of steelmaking, but was demolished in 1981.[20]

The establishment of large factories in areas unaccustomed to industry made it essential to provide dwellings for workers, and, due largely to the influence of Sir Raymond Unwin, who from July 1915 was Chief Housing Architect for the Explosives Department of the Ministry of Munitions, high standards of accommodation were achieved in villages planned with imagination and flair under the most austere conditions. Gretna, described above, was the most important, and other significant developments are detailed in Chapter 8. Nevertheless, the archaeological evidence provides a misleading record, for many munitions workers exiled from home lived in wooden huts, one of the largest concentrations of which comprised Elisabethville, a settlement accommodating 5,000 Belgian refugees employed at the National Projectile Factory at Birtley (NZ 266588) in Co Durham. In the 1920s the huts were replaced by rows of council houses, some of them named after such Socialist heroes as George Lansbury and Keir Hardie.[21]

Most of the National Factories and military depots constructed since 1914 had few potential uses after the Armistice of November 1918. Some of the filling and explosives plants, like Banbury and most of the Gretna site, were cleared of anything that had scrap value and reverted to pasture, where sheep could graze, if not always safely. Others, like Quedgeley, on the southern edge of Gloucester, and the National Machine Gun Factory at Burton upon Trent, became military storage depots. The army depots at Didcot (SU 516910) remained until the 1960s a feature of the lineside view from Great Western's trains between Paddington and Bristol. The ammunition works at Birtley, Pembrey and Hereford were retained by the government on a care-and-maintenance basis. The majority of munitions factories and military depots were adapted to civilian use.

The Second World War: the Royal Ordnance Factories

In 1933 Adolf Hitler and the Nazi Party gained power in Germany, and it became evident that German grievances following the Treaty of Versailles of 1919 would reappear on the diplomatic agenda, and that it would be necessary for government in Britain to be mindful of the threat of renewed conflict in Europe. Government thinking became obsessed by the prospect of aerial bombing, which threatened the three state-owned armaments factories, at Woolwich, Enfield and Waltham Abbey, in the Thames Estuary and the Lee Valley. It was decided in 1935–36 to relocate the filling facilities at Woolwich to a new Royal Ordnance Factory at Chorley in Lancashire, and to move other parts of the arsenal to a new army base at Donnington (SJ 7012), Shropshire (now in Telford). Construction at Donnington began in 1938, the first stores were delivered the following year and the move was completed in 1943.[22]

When war was declared in 1939 a programme of munitions-factory construction had already been instituted. Royal Ordnance Factories employed 54,200 people in December 1939, of whom nearly half were at Woolwich, but by the end of 1940 twenty-five factories were operating, employing 112,268 people. By March 1942 there were forty, with a total workforce of 311,932. There were between forty and fifty Royal Ordnance Factories, but there is no definitive list, and it is impossible to quote a precise figure – the Bishopton site in Scotland was nominally three distinct factories; some were satellites of others, like Brackla of Bridgend and Walsall of Swynnerton; several were not completed as planned; and for certain periods other factories, including the chocolate works of Cadburys at Bournville, where anti-aircraft rockets were filled, were regarded as Royal Ordnance Factories. The engineering factories included the Bridgwater foundry at Patricroft, west of Manchester, which had been established in the 1830s by James Nasmyth, inventor of the steam hammer, and the shipbuilding yard of William Beardmore at Dalmuir, Clydebank.

In the long term the most economically significant of the Royal Ordnance Factories were those (listed, with grid references, in Table A2 in the Appendix) concerned with making

explosives and filling projectiles. Such establishments needed to be at a distance from towns and airfields, to be secure from mining subsidence, and to have water and electricity supplies and rail connections. Government policy was to locate factories in the north and the west, where they would be less vulnerable to bombing. Most were on land of low agricultural value, some of which was subject to flooding. The filling factories covered vast areas – Chorley extended over 1,000 acres (400ha), consisted of more than 1,500 buildings, and, like Bridgend, employed around 30,000 people at its peak. Construction often involved severe engineering problems. The administration buildings were of chaste design, not unlike that of the contemporary shadow factories. Remote locations brought problems with labour supply, but high wage rates drew in workers from other industries, often travelling long distances daily by train or bus. Production at most of the explosives and filling factories declined before the end of the war since the rate of consumption of artillery shells never reached that of the First World War, except for episodes of intensive bombardment of the German lines, like that prior to the battle of El Alamein or that which preceded the crossing of the Rhine. Dumps of shells on roadside verges were a feature of the English countryside in 1944 and 1945, and were still the subject of complaints in Shropshire in July 1946.

As in the First World War, munitions factories drew in workers, many of them women, from all over the country. At Chorley a new railway station was constructed on the Bolton–Preston line, and workers at the factory endured lengthy daily rail journeys from as far away as Burnley. At Swynnerton a 2-mile branch line was constructed from the Norton Bridge–Stone line to convey workers from the Potteries conurbation to a new four-platform terminal station. Three-shift, all-round-the-clock working was introduced at some factories, and some employees worked more than seventy hours per week. Forty-eight hostels were built at Royal Ordnance Factories, the most extensive accommodation being provided at Chorley, Glascoed, Hereford and Swynnerton, and some developed a vigorous social life. Complaints about working conditions led to the provision of more canteens and social facilities from February 1941, when attempts were made also to improve internal transport. Archaeological indications that many women were employed at filling and explosives factories are provided by the existence of separate changing rooms and dining rooms and, at Waltham Abbey, a women's hospital. Since the sites dealing with explosives were so dispersed, many workers were faced with lengthy walks from the – necessarily few – entrance gates to their places of work. As late as 1972 a War Department diesel locomotive with a single coach could be seen at Radway Green Station waiting to take commuters from Crewe and Stoke to their places of work in the Ordnance Factory. Few artefacts from Royal Ordnance Factories have been consciously preserved, but the National Waterways Museum in Gloucester holds a four-wheeled railway wagon, built in 1943 to an old-fashioned North Eastern Railway design by Charles Roberts & Co. of Wakefield, and used for traffic from the factories in South Wales.

By September 1945 the Royal Ordnance Factories employed only 94,600 people, less than one-third of the total three years previously, and of those 12,000 were at Woolwich. The wholesale disposal of sites which had followed the First World War was not repeated; indeed, nine of the factories of the Second World War (Birtley, Bishopton, Blackburn, Bridgwater, Chorley, Featherstone, Glascoed, Radway Green, Summerfield) remained in use in 1999 as part of the Royal Ordnance section of British Aerospace. The factories served varied functions in the late 1940s. At Woolwich railway wagons were

7.8
Modest brick-piered buildings, constructed during the Second World War, forming the Ridley Wood Industrial Complex on the Wrexham Industrial Estate that occupies the site of the wartime Royal Ordnance Factory. In the background is the gigantic Kelloggs breakfast cereal plant.

7.9
A large building constructed during the Second World War as part of the RAF training depot at Stanmore, Bridgnorth, that has been converted to new uses as part of the industrial estate now occupying the site.

(Photos: Barrie Trinder)

constructed, and the sections of Anderson shelters were re-rolled to make usable billets of steel. Concrete panels for Airey houses (*see Chapter 8*) were made at Bridgwater, Chorley and Glascoed, and military uniforms at Chorley and Swynnerton, while redundant ammunition was destroyed at Pembrey. Aycliffe, Bridgend, Wrexham and Kirkby were quickly developed as industrial estates, and most of the sites that have passed out of Royal Ordnance use now serve a similar purpose.

Some Second World War Royal Ordnance Factories have disappeared, leaving almost no traces. At Queniborough, between Loughborough and Melton Mowbray, the East Goscote Industrial Estate is situated, typically for an Ordnance Factory, on low-lying land, but neither the estate nor the adjacent housing, planned on a Radburn lay-out typical of the 1960s, betrays any signs of its wartime origins. In 1998 only an almost unfenestrated building, within the premises of a fencing contractor (SK 643132), appeared to date from wartime. This estate at Queniborough is on a small scale, including engineering machine shops, firms making paint and textile accessories, workshops for plumbers and an exhibition

contractor. The site of the explosives plant at Wrexham bears many traces of its wartime past, in the form of single-storey brick buildings of piered construction, some of which have clerestories, and a few wooden huts, all adapted to new uses. It had become by the 1990s one of the principal economic growth-points in North Wales, and includes the transmissions plant of JCB, the makers of earthmoving equipment, a Kelloggs cereal factory, the plant of Rexham Image Products, whose large-scale exterior plumbing no doubt secures a sterile interior, a Duracell battery works and a Dalgetty feed mill. The vast site of the Bridgend Ordnance Factory was likewise a centre of economic growth in South Wales, an industrial estate occupied by international companies like Bayer and Sony, as well as by local concerns. A few concrete bases were the remnants of wartime buildings.

The site of No. 4 Filling Factory at Hereford was of equal economic significance within its region. It was purchased by Herefordshire County Council in 1973 and is now known as the Rotherwas Industrial Estate, situated on either side of the B4399, where 120 companies employ more than 2,200 people. The largest factory is that of Thorn Electric, the head-quarters building of which appears to have been constructed as part of the factory built on the site during the First World War. The site retains much of archaeological interest. A shell store still stands, measuring 377ft x 123ft (115m x 37.5m), with a lattice steel roof, and from its doors extend tarmac pathways along which materials were pushed in wooden-wheeled trolleys to wooden filling sheds, which have been removed, protected by earthen banks, which remain. Many wartime buildings have been adapted as factories and workshops, and in parts of the site restored as pasture the picric acid stores of the First World War have been adapted as stables. On the southern extremity there remain some explosives stores, wooden buildings once served by railway sidings whose courses can readily be traced, which now provide safe custody for fireworks.[23] At Featherstone, north of Wolverhampton, part of the site of No. 17 Filling Factory is occupied by British Aerospace's Royal Ordnance Speciality Metals, part is a penal establishment, while the ruins on the remainder of the site include buildings where it is possible to see hatches at the sides of doors, where boxes of fuses were

7.10

The interior of a building at the Royal Ordnance Factory, Featherstone, near Wolverhampton, photographed in 1996. Detonators being carried through the factory would be placed in the hatch when the person carrying them approached a doorway, and then were picked up from the other side so that there was no danger of a collision which could lead to the detonators being dropped.

(Crown copyright. NMR)

placed while their carriers passed through the adjacent doors.[24] The site of No. 8 Filling Factory at Thorp Arch, alongside the River Wharfe between York and Wetherby, has been put to even more diverse use. The factory was composed of over 3,000 buildings, with 25 miles of railway track and 9 miles of road, and employed at its peak over 10,000 workers. It ceased production in April 1958. Part is occupied by the Lending Division of the British Library, now a distinguished modern concrete building with slit windows, not unlike those of several university libraries of the 1960s. Part is a household-waste site. Another part is occupied by the heavily secured Wealstun Prison, which appears to include a few huts of wartime origin. An industrial estate includes two large modern factories making telecommunications equipment and another making fixtures, together with an

extensive road distribution depot. Numerous single-storey brick buildings of piered construction with corrugated asbestos roofs, and of wartime date (*see Figure 7.12*), are used as warehouses, some of them protected by earth banks, with their railway sidings still in situ. The most bizarre part of the site is the retailing area, where shops selling furniture are protected by earth banks, and a children's play area includes a replica galleon (adjacent to Trafalgar Windows), a Bren-Gun carrier and a Sherman tank.[25]

Thorp Arch affords perhaps the best opportunity in the north of England to gain some understanding of the archaeology of a filling factory of the Second World War, and without trespassing. In the south the most accessible site is that of No. 16 Filling Factory at Elstow, south of Bedford, the setting for H. E. Bates's story 'The Tinkers of Elstow'. The site lies between the A6, where it is fronted by the Seasons Garden Centre, and the B530, from which entrance can be gained to the Wilstead Industrial Park, which utilises some wartime buildings, and includes the premises of a large-scale butchery business, an importer of Spanish tiles, numerous furniture makers and restorers, as well as a road-haulage company and a firm that auctions scrap motor vehicles. At least ten hangars, numerous brick buildings and large areas of earth banks which once protected wooden filling sheds, together with several stretches of abandoned railway track, were still visible in 1999.

In Staffordshire the site of No. 5 Filling Factory at Swynnerton, near Stone, which closed in May 1958, was put to diverse use. Part, in 1999, was a military training area, and part occupied by the Drake Hall Women's Prison. The railway passenger terminus was a Department of Transport testing depot, while the earthworks of the circular railway that

7.11

The buildings of the Royal Ordnance Factory, Thorp Arch, Yorkshire, when still in production in the early 1950s.

(Crown copyright. NMR)

about a mile from the factory site in Hereford, and in the middle of Alsager, at some distance from the Radway Green Factory, but clustered around the Radway Green Social Club. Both flat-roofed houses and buildings which appear to have been hostels remain at Caerwent. The largest concentration of Second World War housing is at Donnington, Telford, where some 844 houses, most of them flat-roofed, line Turreff Avenue, Baldwin Webb Avenue and adjacent roads. They were built between 1941 and 1945, and, after a period in 1945–46 when possession was contested by squatters, are now in normal civilian use. The H-block accommodation hostels of the Radway Green Factory became the halls of residence of Alsager College of Education, and two remain, although not in residential use, as part of the Alsager campus of Manchester Metropolitan University.

7.12

Some of the workers at the Royal Ordnance Factory, Thorp Arch, Yorkshire, photographed in the early 1950s. The building, of brick-piered construction, with metal-framed windows and a roof that appears to be of corrugated asbestos, is typical of those found in Royal Ordnance Factories. As the sign shows, the factory specialised in the production of small arms ammunition (SAA).

(Crown copyright. NMR)

carried raw materials and finished products remained alongside the West Coast Main Line. An area near to Swynnerton village had been used for modern housing, while other substantial areas were occupied by a British Telecom training centre and two industrial estates, each of which included adapted buildings of wartime origin.

Five Royal Ordnance Factory sites have been used by the nuclear industry: Burghfield and Cardiff (Llanishen), where atomic weapons are or were made; Risley, where the Atomic Energy Authority has its engineering workshops; Drigg, which is a dumping ground for nuclear waste; and the notorious Sellafield, once Windscale, once Calder Hall, manufactory of plutonium for British bombs, power station, and reprocessing plant. The huge site of No. 6 Filling Factory at Risley, just east of the M6 and south of the M62, is occupied by numerous other industrial concerns and by a notorious penal establishment.

The most distinctive houses built in association with Royal Ordnance Factories were box-like, flat-roofed structures in pairs and short terraces, examples of which remain at Thorp Arch, in East Road at Featherstone, where sloping tiled roofs have been placed on flat-roofed bungalows and houses, in Belmont Avenue and Springfield Avenue (SO 505390),

Shadow factories: the private sector

Government-assisted expansion of private manufacturing facilities for the Second World War began three years prior to the outbreak of hostilities. During the summer of 1936 the government initiated discussions with industrialists which led to the inauguration of the 'shadow factory programme', headed by Sir Herbert Austin. Capital for new plants was provided by government on the understanding that upon the outbreak of hostilities they would be available for munitions production. The scheme continued after the outbreak of war, and by 1945 there were 159 shadow or agency factories under the control of the Ministry of Supply, 87 under the Ministry of Aircraft Production and 19 under the direction of the Admiralty, which continued to manufacture many of its own munitions.[26]

Since its formation in 1926 ICI had dominated the supply of explosives in Britain, and most of its activities had been concentrated at Ardeer (NS 2941), where its factory in 1935 extended over 2,000 acres (800ha) and employed 13,000 people. Its staff restaurant during the Second World War was the South African pavilion from the Glasgow Exhibition of 1938, modelled on the guest house at the company's plant at Modderfontein in Cape Province. Most of the new explosives factories in the private sector were built by ICI. The company constructed eighteen new plants between the beginning of 1937 and the end of 1939, and seven more by the end of war.[27]

The best-known shadow factories were concerned with the production of aircraft. The preferred locations for new factories, in order both to lessen the dangers of bombing and to absorb surplus labour, were in the north and the west, but the principal concentration of shadow factories was nevertheless, for historically determined reasons, in the west midlands. The long engineering traditions of Coventry and the accustomed skills of metal craftsmen in Birmingham were sufficient to outweigh the openness to aerial bombing of those cities and their low rates of unemployment in the late 1930s. By August 1943, five of the six shadow factories in Coventry were employing nearly 25,000 people. The shadow factories followed a characteristic plan. Production was located in sheds, in some cases extending more than 800m, with either north-lit or ridge-and-furrow roofs, while administration was housed in chaste but well-proportioned office blocks, usually facing main roads. The shadow factory has proved to be a form of building adaptable to diverse manufacturing techniques, and many of the buildings of the late 1930s and the early 1940s were still of importance in west midlands industry in 1999. The characteristic form of the shadow factory was used in other wartime industrial buildings, as in the British Timken roller-bearing factory at Duston, Northampton (SP 726623), which housed the company's Birmingham operations when they were relocated in 1943.

Austin's motor works at Longbridge was enlarged by a new building sometimes called 'the Coften Hackett shadow factory', and sometimes 'the east works'. It was planned in 1936 and completed by the outbreak of war. Little building took place at Longbridge during the years of conflict. The new factory was linked by tunnels to the rest of the site. In the course of the war the factory produced over 1,000 Fairey Battles, over 300 Hawker Hurricanes, 620 Short Stirlings and over 300 Avro Lancasters. The fighters made in the early part of the war flew from the Coften Hackett airfield, but

final assembly of the bombers took place at Marston Green (SP 170852), whence they were towed along a concrete road across the Birmingham–Coventry rail line to Elmdon airport. The bridge they crossed was demolished when the railway was electrified in the 1960s, but its abutments could still be seen in 1999.[28]

Construction of a shadow factory for the production of the Wellington twin-engined bomber began in November 1937, on land previously used by the RAF as a relief landing area at the suburban fringe of Chester (SJ 3464), but just over the Welsh border. In the course of the war 5,540 Wellingtons were assembled on the site. It subsequently passed into RAF use, but part was used for housing, and part for the construction of aluminium prefabs (*see Chapter 8*) in 1945, and aircraft manufacture was revived when De Havilland took over part of the site in 1948. Part is now used by British Aerospace for the manufacture of wings for the European Airbus, and part by a firm making executive jet aircraft. The flying field remains operational for private purposes.[29]

Shadow factories were responsible for the manufacture of most of the British aircraft of the Second World War. A second assembly plant for Wellingtons at Squires Gate, Blackpool (SP 3232), was approved in December 1939 and was making sixty aircraft a month by the end of 1942. Most of the buildings used for assembling aircraft still stood in 1999, and the flying field remained in use as Blackpool airport. A factory at Castle Bromwich, Birmingham (SK 136905), planned by Nuffield but managed by Vickers, was the principal source of Spitfires. Jaguar cars are now produced there. A factory at Old Mixon, Weston-super-Mare (ST 3359), was the principal source of Bristol Beaufighters. A factory managed by Rootes Securities at Speke, Liverpool, made Blenheims and Halifaxes. Blenheims and Beaufighters were made also by a shadow factory at Stoke-on-Trent, also managed by Rootes Securities. Rolls-Royce were responsible for a factory at Hillingdon, Glasgow, that produced Merlin engines, while Ford's aero-engine factory at Trafford Park employed 8,411 workers at its peak, and produced 34,000 Rolls-Royce Merlin engines. A shadow factory at South Marston, Swindon, was built for Phillips & Powis to make Miles Master trainers, but was later taken over by Vickers Supermarine to produce Spitfires.[30] Not all shadow factories are well documented. At Newtown, Powys, the Lion Industrial Estate is centred around a characteristic shadow-factory building, documented in none of the principal accounts of the aircraft industry, that research shows to have been a shadow factory operated by Tube Investments, the principal wartime products of which were gun turrets for Barracuda naval bombers. At Llanfoist (SO 293136) near Abergavenny the nucleus of a factory occupied in 1999 by Cooper's Filters, and distinguished by a 1961 building with a parabolic roof, was a shadow factory that from October 1943 to October 1945 produced radiators for Spitfires, and was managed by the Lang Pen Company.[31]

The diffuse and paradoxical impact of two world wars on the industrial landscape is illustrated by the manufacturing complex that bestrides the boundary between the parishes of Brockworth and Hucclecote on the south-eastern edge of Gloucester (SO 8816). The factory originated in 1915 when a grass runway was laid out and several buildings constructed for the final assembly and acceptance by the Royal Flying Corps of aircraft made at Sunningend, Cheltenham, by H. H. Martyn, which before 1914 had been specialist woodworkers. The firm was incorporated in 1917 into the Gloucestershire (from 1926, the Gloster) Aircraft Company, which between 1925 and 1929 concentrated its activities at Brockworth. In 1934 the company became part of the Hawker Siddeley Group. Shortage of orders in the early 1930s led to diversification into the production of car bodies, roll-down shutters for shops, fish-and-chip frying ranges and even mushroom cultivation, but from 1937 capacity was enlarged by roofing over the spaces between existing buildings, and by the construction of a 450-yard-long assembly shop, and a shadow factory with 24 acres (10ha) of floor space was constructed alongside for a subsidiary company, A. W. Hawkesley. A concrete runway with an associated control tower was built in 1941–42. The factory built the Gloster Gladiator, the RAF's last biplane fighter, in the late 1930s, but its principal wartime activity was the construction of 2,750 Hawker Hurricanes between 1939 and 1942, and 3,300 Typhoons between 1941 and 1945, while Armstrong Whitworth Albemarles were made in the Hawkesley part of the complex. In 1944, 14,000 people were employed, and work

was contracted-out to unlikely locations dispersed all over Gloucestershire. The outstanding technological development at Brockworth was the construction of the first allied jet-powered aircraft, the E28/39. Building of the aircraft began at Brockworth, though most of the assembly work took place at Regent Motors, Cheltenham; but it was returned to the factory for its first flight, of no more than 150 yards at an altitude of about 6ft, on 8 April 1941. The aircraft was further developed at Cranwell, where the first official flight took place on 15 May 1941. The E28/39 became the Gloster Meteor, which came into production at Brockworth in 1944 and continued to be built until 1955. It was succeeded by the delta-winged Gloster Javelin, which first flew in 1951. Prefabricated houses were manufactured at the A. W. Hawkesley buildings in the immediate post-war period, before it was adapted to produce aircraft engines, notably the Armstrong Siddeley Sapphire. The prosperity of the aircraft industry in Gloucester in the 1950s was reflected in the building of almost 700 houses for those employed at the factory, some on the site of wartime air-raid shelters; but that prosperity was short-lived. In 1959 the shadow factory was taken over by British Nylon Spinners to produce synthetic fibres; the company was employing 1,250 people on the site in 1960. The plant still operates, in the ownership of Du Pont. Aircraft production at Brockworth ended with the completion of the last Gloster Javelin in 1960, and in 1964 the original part of the site was developed as a trading estate, which initially utilised most of the production buildings as they had existed in the Second World War, including seven storage hangars (built by German prisoners of war in the First World War) which had been incorporated in other buildings, as well as two hangars with Belfast truss roofs, also from the First World War, an office block of 1936–38 and the assembly shop of 1937–38, together with a jet-engine testing facility of 1943. RCHME made an archaeological record of the trading estate site in 1994, prior to a redevelopment that has destroyed most of the original structures. The shadow factory remains, although disguised by modern cladding, and a plaque commemorates the first flight of the E28/39, the aircraft itself being displayed in the Science Museum, London.[32]

While the production figures for the largest wartime aircraft factories seem large, they were modest by international standards, and some aircraft were made on a cottage industry basis which was perhaps designed to bolster civilian morale as much as to provide munitions. An example is provided by the 100 or so of a total of more than 7,000 Lancaster bombers that were assembled at Sywell airfield (SP 8267), Northampton, from parts made in shoe factories, bus garages and other unlikely locations throughout Northamptonshire.[33]

Every manufacturing plant was transformed by the demands of the war. The typical market-town engineering works of Taskers of Andover (SU 3243) had begun to build light steam road engines in 1902, and subsequently specialised in the trailers they pulled. At the time of the Munich crisis trailer manufacturers were asked by the Air Ministry to make plans for producing vehicles which could carry aircraft. Within a week Taskers produced what became known as the Queen Mary Trailer, with its well-remembered wartime warning on the rear: 'Caution. 60 ft long'. It was actually 55ft in length, was of welded construction, made on a turnover gig, and had a patent suspension system. Nearly 4,000 were produced at Andover in the course of the war.[34] In Liverpool employees of Littlewoods Pools made the floors for Handley Page Halifax bombers. Pharmaceutical companies concentrated on products most necessary in wartime. ICI in Manchester produced Paludrine, the anti-malarial drug, on a large scale after the beginning of the war in the Far East in 1941. Ceramics firms made stoneware food jars, porcelain insulators and drinking-water filters for use in the field, as well as tableware for factory and military canteens. The furniture company Henry Stone & Son of Banbury was given over entirely to aircraft production by the end of 1940. When air raids on Birmingham and Coventry destroyed sources of specialist tooling, it was supplied from a workshop situated in two cottages in Banbury that had previously made milk-bottle seals. Stone's most significant wartime products were the tail-ends for Horsa gliders, stringers and emergency doors for Wellington bombers and rudders for Mosquitoes.[35] The desperate wartime need for rare metals led to the opening up of modest resources in the upland regions. At Hemerdon Mine, Sparkwell (SX 572586), in Devon are the remnants of an open-cast working for tungsten, operated in 1917–19 and again in 1943–44, from which period there survives the concrete skeleton of the dressing mill.[36]

The former works of the Express Lift Company in Northampton (SP 743606), on the point of demolition in 1999, provided a particularly apt commentary on the influence of the two world wars on the engineering industry. The original Abbey Works, constructed on a greenfield site in 1910 by Smith, Major & Stevens Ltd, consisted of a 7-bay steel-framed shed with walls of carefully patterned brickwork and a detached office block. A large extension was added to the shed at the expense of the Ministry of Munitions in 1917–18. The internal steel frame, with lattice-work uprights, was almost identical to that of the original building, except that the inscription of the Dorman Long Company appeared in a different form, and a few rolled-steel joists from the Shelton works in Staffordshire and the Lanarkshire Steel Company were included. The walls are of good-quality but plain brickwork. A canteen, a single-storey building in which the original locations of the kitchen and the restaurant are revealed by differences in fenestration and in ventilation grills, is made of similar bricks and appears, like many such institutions, to have been built during the First World War. The company again went over to making munitions, including 7.2in. shells for the Royal Navy, during the Second World War, and further extensive shops were constructed in 1940–41 of poor-quality Fletton bricks, clumsily laid, with concrete lintels above metal-framed windows. The internal steel construction was of a different pattern, with uprights consisting of single RSJs. A few square-mouthed Tannoy loudspeakers of the kind used to broadcast 'Music While You Work' hung from the steelwork. The single-storey building used as an entrance lodge was of wartime construction, and originally housed the Air Raid Precautions headquarters, a medical centre and a decontamination unit. The factory included some extensions from the 1950s, but a high proportion of its working space had been constructed in wartime, and it merited analysis as a munitions works as much as a part of the lift industry.[37]

Military depots

The term *depot* may suggest a passive function, but such bases were industrial installations concerned with the support of military operations, the testing of weapons and the customising and maintenance of vehicles. Most of the storage depots constructed during the First World War were adapted for other purposes during the 1920s. The authorities in the 1930s realised that even larger bases would be needed if war again broke out, and some were already under construction in 1939. After Dunkirk it was necessary to find accommodation in Britain for most of the increasingly mechanised British Army as well as for an expanding Royal Air Force, which required weapons, ammunition, vehicles, fuel, tools, clothing, food and medical supplies.

The most extensive of the new storage depots was at Bicester, Oxfordshire, where construction began, in the month after Dunkirk, of 'the most ambitious single project ever attempted for military purposes in the United Kingdom',[38] which cost £5 million. The site lies between two low hills which gave protection from low-level bombing. Royal Engineers laid the roads and railways, while civilians built the storehouses. There were severe problems with flooding during construction. The first troop trains ran into the depot in 1942, and just before D-Day in 1944 some 24,000 troops were accommodated there. A 47-mile railway system included 6 halts, and employed 90 staff. Each Sunday evening a 12-coach 'leave train' departed from Euston, 6 coaches proceeding to Arncott and Piddington, and the other 6 to Graven Hill and Ambrosden. Recreational trains to Oxford were hauled by Dean Goods 0-6-0s and an Adams LSWR Jubilee 0-4-2 No. 625. The Bicester depot is still used by the British Army. It extends in a south-easterly direction over about 4 miles from the Oxford–Bletchley rail line. Some Nissen huts and other buildings from the 1940s remain, and a few wartime buildings stand isolated in fields which have been returned to the plough or to pasture. The depot railway, which retains semaphore signalling, extends around Graven Hill and Arncott as far as Piddington (SP 640173). The village of Ambrosden (SP 605195) has been swollen by military housing, and an amenities centre for the garrison adjoins its northern side.

The depot announces its presence to travellers on the A41 by a stack of containers. The ancient village of Upper Arncott is engulfed by the depot. Her Majesty's Prison, Bullingdon, stands alongside the B4011 (SP 626174), and some parcels of land elsewhere have passed into industrial use.

More than twenty other large-scale depots were under construction by 1939, and many more followed in the next five years. One of the largest storage depots was at Bramley (SU 6558), Berkshire. It had been built as an explosives factory between 1916 and 1920, partly by German prisoners of war, and in the Second World War was used for the storage of explosives, being served by 30 miles of standard-gauge railway track. Underground storage facilities were constructed for the Royal Navy at Dean Hill, Hampshire, and at Fishguard, Pembrokeshire, and for the army at Corsham, Wiltshire. The RAF's storage units at Hartlebury, south of Kidderminster, which now comprise several industrial estates, were constructed between June 1937 and December 1939. At Dunham on the Hill in Cheshire (SJ 467727) several large buildings remain visible from the M56 of a storage depot, with rail access from the ex-LNWR route from Chester to Warrington, which came into operation during 1942 and was used by the military until 1964. The military depot at Kineton (SP 3752), Warwickshire, which occupies much of the site where the Battle of Edgehill was fought, included 252 storehouses for explosives and 64 miles of railway track, some of which is now used for the secure storage of out-of-use railway carriages. Between March 1941 and June 1944 an army depot with more than 200 storehouses was constructed in the low, damp fields north of Shrewsbury alongside the Shropshire and Montgomeryshire Light Railway, the lines of which were operated by the military. Many of the earthen banks that protected the storehouses remain in pastures now grazed by sheep, while part of the area remains a military camp and training ground, and part is the Pentre Industrial Estate. A new training facility for the Royal Engineers, the Melbourne Military Railway, operated from 1939, and was subsequently used for training US railway operating troops in European conditions, and for the assembly of US Army railway vehicles. A prison and a scrapyard occupy parts of the site of the 155-acre (63ha) Royal Engineers storage depot at Long Marston, Warwickshire, where there were once 45 miles of rail track. One of the most astonishing choices of site for a base was the decision of the Admiralty to establish a storage depot of 550 acres (220ha) with more than 200 buildings around the terminus of the light railway from Cleobury Mortimer to Ditton Priors in south Shropshire. Water and sewage works had to be constructed, together with a 10-mile power line linking the depot to the National Grid, and all of this a long way from the sea and accessible only by a single line of lightly laid rail track. The site is now occupied by an industrial estate, which includes a fireworks factory. While the mark of the Second World War is indelible at Ditton Priors and at other rural locations, few traces remain of the war or of earlier periods at the Royal Victoria Dock in east London, which, as the principal storage depot for Operation Overlord, the invasion of Normandy, was one of the most animated sites in Britain in the first half of 1944.

The United States entered the war in late 1941, when planning had already begun for Operation Bolero, under which bases, airfields and hospitals were to be built in Britain to accommodate 1 million US personnel.[39] The first GIs to arrive disembarked at Belfast on 26 January 1942. Plans were changed many times. During the autumn of 1942 Bolero was disrupted by the decision to embark on Operation Torch, the invasion of North Africa, which involved both British and American troops. Bolero raised many problems. American service personnel were accustomed to higher standards of comfort and hygiene than were British troops, and their engineers were accustomed to working in wood, rather than the brick, tile, plasterboard and corrugated iron that were the usual materials for British military bases. There were differences in electrical standards, and in plumbing practices – the standard British grease trap could not deal with the level of fat in American rations. American military engineers were unaccustomed to British conditions and wasted much hardcore in trying to establish foundations for runways and roads. The Bolero programme was costed at £50 million, and actually cost £49.9 million, much of the work being done by the Royal Engineers and the Royal Pioneer Corps.

Construction of the prototype storage base for the US forces began at Wem in Shropshire (SJ 526295) on 14 December 1942 and was completed on 30 June 1943. There were 450,240 sq. ft of covered accommodation and 1.375 million sq. ft of open storage, with a camp for 1,250 men, and 11 miles of railway. Some of the land has been returned to agricultural use, while some is occupied by a caravan site. The railway embankment linking the depot network to the line from Shrewsbury to Crewe can still be recognised. The line was worked in wartime by three outside-cylinder 0-6-0 tank locomotives built by H. K. Porter Inc., Pittsburgh, and delivered during 1943. The core of the site is now an industrial estate, with six ranks of corrugated asbestos huts with corrugated iron end walls in which are located doors sufficiently large to admit vehicles. Each hut has four ventilators in the roof, twenty-four skylights and two concrete pipes, doubtless the flues for coke stoves. All had telephones, and swan-necked lamp standards for external lighting. The only other buildings remaining from the military period are small brick structures, such as toilet blocks and emergency water-supply installations. Users in 1999 included a manufacturer of timber-framed buildings, a tyre recycling concern, a theatre-scenery hire business, a micro-brewery, a stone and granite cutting company, a plant hire depot, a double-glazing workshop, a refrigerated distributing company and a florist. Among the depots which followed the Wem prototype were those at Honeybourne, Worcestershire (SP 0945), Boughton, near Ollerton, Nottinghamshire (SK 6867), both built by British labour, and Histon, Cambridgeshire (TZ 4362), and Lockerley, Hampshire (SU 2925), which were built by American forces.

7.13
Hangars with Belfast truss roofs built during the First World War for the airfield at Monkmoor, Shrewsbury. In the inter-war period the buildings were put to other uses, including as a sports centre. They were re-occupied in the Second World War by an RAF unit that recovered crashed aircraft, the runways having been covered with houses. Since the war the hangars have been in industrial and commercial use.

(Photo: Barrie Trinder)

Airfields

In 1939 the RAF was operating 158 airfields, most of which still had grass runways (*see Table 7.1*). The need, first, to create fighter bases from which to repel the raids of the Luftwaffe and, second, to build concrete or tarmac runways from which four-engined bombers could attack Germany dictated a massive programme of airfield construction, which was accelerated with the entry into the war of the United States at the end of 1941. Between the end of 1939 and the end of 1944, 465 flying fields were constructed for the two air forces. This was a colossal task, a twentieth-century equivalent to the construction of the first generation of main-line railways between 1830 and 1851. A chain of airfields was also constructed across the northern rim of the Atlantic, which enabled thousands of B-24 Liberators and B-17 Flying Fortresses to be ferried to Europe. Transatlantic flights, just commercially feasible in 1939, became commonplace.

Many wartime bases became redundant at the conclusion of hostilities, and the needs of the RAF further diminished with the conclusion of the Cold War in the early 1990s. The airfield building programme of the Second World War has nevertheless had a profound influence on the English landscape.[40] Some airfields have been restored to agricultural use, although in many cases, as at Harrington (SP 7679), Northamptonshire, a few huts, hard standings and concrete ruins remain as evidence of past conflict – in the case of Harrington, of buildings used by the 'Carpetbaggers', the 801st/492nd bombardment group of the USAAF whose black-painted B-24 Liberators and C-47 Dakotas supported resistance movements in continental Europe, and of Thor missile installations of the late 1950s which were intended to despatch nuclear bombs to East Germany and Poland. Of the sixteen airfields in present-day Northamptonshire, seven have been returned largely to agricultural uses; one retains a private flying facility, although most of it is used for farming; another is used both for farming and gliding; three are occupied by military radio masts; one has been open-casted for iron ore; one, at Silverstone (SP 6742), is a Grand Prix motor-racing circuit; another, at Chipping Warden (SP 4949), is an industrial estate; while that at Sywell combines private flying with industry. In Wales industrial estates now occupy the sites of the airfields at Llandow (SS 9473) near Cowbridge, and Bodorgan (SH 3867) on Anglesey, while the base at Beaumaris (SH 6076), where Catalina flying-boats flown in from the United States were adapted for RAF use, was used in 1999 for the manufacture of lifting gear for wheely-bins.[41] Many other airfield sites have contributed substantially to the growth of rural manufacturing and service activities in the second half of the century. Some case studies illustrate the process.

Construction of the airfield at Wellesbourne Mountford, Warwickshire (SP 271549), commenced in the summer of 1940, and the first unit began training in April 1941. The total of personnel rose to 2,500. The base was used primarily for training although it contributed Wellingtons to the 1,000-bomber raid on Cologne on 30 April–1 May 1942. Wellesbourne Mountford ceased to be operational in 1964, when most of the land reverted to its original owners. The runways remain in use for private flying, but most of the concrete from the

	RAF airfields	USAAF airfields	Totals
1939	158		158
1940	229		229
1941	353		353
1942	421	75	496
1943	476	119	595
1944	490	133	623

Table 7.1
Airfields used and constructed during the Second World War.

Source:
C. M. Kohan, *The History of the Second World War: Works and Buildings* (London: HMSO–Longman, 1952)

dispersal bays went as hardcore to the Warwick By-pass. The motor transport workshops are used by the Warwickshire County Surveyor's Department. The technical area became an industrial estate, now called the M40 Distribution Park, and includes a characteristic mix of activities for such an estate: computer companies, two substantial logistics concerns, an hydraulics company, and several plastics manufacturers. Five hangars remain and are used for the storage and preparation of new motorcars, of which there may be as many as 2,500 on the site at a time. Some RAF houses passed to the local authority, and some into private ownership, while new houses have been built in recent years on the site of the RAF accommodation blocks.[42]

Land at Hixon (SJ 9926), Staffordshire, was acquired for an airfield in May 1941, and the first RAF personnel arrived a year later. Nearly 3,000 personnel were involved in flying Wellingtons, which, as at Wellesbourne, were used chiefly for training but occasionally for bombing raids. Military vehicles were stored on the airfield between 1946 and 1948. It ceased to be operational in 1957, and was returned to the control of its original owners in 1962. Some buildings were used for a short time in the mid-1950s by English Electric Ltd for the manufacture of its Digital Electronic Universal Computing Engine (DEUCE), and the company's successors have used hangars at Hixon for heavy storage. Other hangars were used for grain storage in 1998, and the wall of the shooting butts supported an implement store. One runway was an excavator park for a civil engineering contractor, and police drivers trained on the dispersal area. A 35-acre (14ha) industrial estate, on which many RAF buildings remained in use, was occupied by more than forty companies, making plastics, timber roof trusses, motor body panels, concrete reinforcing, domestic showers and motorcar exhausts.[43]

A Royal Flying Corps training camp established during the First World War at Ford in Sussex (TQ 003027) was decommissioned in 1920, but ten years later two of its hangars were renovated by a private aviation company. Like the other First World War airfields, it was re-occupied by the RAF at considerable cost in 1937. After passing out of military use in 1957, the main camp became an open prison in 1961.

The large Coastal Command Base at Silloth (NY 125540) in Cumberland is now an industrial estate on which many pre-war hangars remain in use, the principal company being a manufacturer of automotive controls, and part appears to have become a holiday camp.

At the satellite landing ground at Barnsley Park, Gloucestershire (SP 075975), used between 1941 and 1945, the headquarters and guardroom were designed to look like an ordinary bungalow, and remained in use in 1999 for precisely that purpose.

The role of the Ministry of Works

Government control of the economy during the Second World War was expressed in many non-military structures.[44] More than 150 standard stores were built for the Ministry of Food between April 1941 and December 1942, for the most part with rail access. They were lightweight steel-framed structures, 214ft x 120ft (65m x 36m) in plan. Nearly fifty cold storage depots for food were built for the same ministry, almost unfenestrated Cubist structures, constructed of low-cost Fletton-type bricks, around insulated steel frames. Many remain in use as refrigerated stores, and during the writing of this book we have noted examples at Banbury (SP 642218), at Warwick (SP 309663), at Broughton (SP 737653), north of Northampton, at Wigston (SP 594904), south of Leicester, at Harlescott (SJ 510159), north of Shrewsbury, and at Llandudno Junction (SH 806777). All were once rail-connected. Sixteen grain silos were built during the early stages of the war. Each consisted of a brick, steel-framed, tower, 80ft (24m) high and 30ft (9m) square, flanked by 2 wings, each composed of 6 pairs of 62ft reinforced concrete storage bins. Extensive underground stores were built for both civilian and military use, and were usually rail-connected. Examples are a store at Farley Dingle (SJ 632018), Shropshire, in a former limestone quarry, now a slurry processing plant, and at Bramhall (SJ 900843), Goostrey (SJ 782695) and Mollington (SJ 392710) in Cheshire.

Many hostels were constructed for workers living away from home, in addition to those at

Royal Ordnance Factories mentioned above. There were forty-five hostels at aircraft factories with a total capacity of 35,000 beds. Some of the larger examples, like that at Smiths Industries, Cheltenham, were run by Billy Butlin, the holiday-camp entrepreneur. By the spring of 1943 there were approximately 970 agricultural hostels, 299 of which had been built in 1941 for the Women's Land Army Volunteers. Some were, in the event, used for Italian prisoners of war. Some new factory developments necessitated new housing. Glasgow Corporation built 1,500 houses for workers from the Rolls-Royce shadow factory at Hillingdon, and the Meadoway Estate at Cheltenham was built to accommodate workers from the Smiths Industries factory at Bishop's Cleeve (SO 955261), which had moved from Cricklewood in north London, and provided more than 6.5 million air-speed indicators in the course of the war. Opponents of the factory in 1939 had forecast that it would 'bring all the riff-raff to work and live in working-class houses'. There were also more ephemeral structures that may no longer stand but which will have left archaeological traces – in almost every town there were street shelters, in brick with concrete roofs, and open-air raised reservoirs, most of which were removed before the conclusion of hostilities, as well as steel Anderson shelters, and shelters of concrete sections that were installed in many cellars and gardens.

Railways

Railways formed the veins and arteries of inland transport in both conflicts. In the First World War the system was taken over by government and adapted to supply troops on the Western Front, which involved intensive operation of some hitherto little-used lines in southern England. Steam coal was carried from South Wales to the fleet based at Scapa Flow, in Orkney, in such quantities that trains were routed along such previously quiet by-ways as the Mid-Wales line from Three Cocks Junction near Brecon to Caersws. Considerable numbers of British locomotives were sent to France. The standard freight locomotive of the First World

War was the rugged 2-8-0 designed by J. G. Robinson (1856–1943) in 1911 for the Great Central Railway, which had built 130 by 1914. Government funded the construction by the GCR works at Gorton, Manchester, and by private contractors of a further 521 examples. The Great Western Railway bought fifty, a few were purchased by the London & North Western and the South East & Chatham Railways, and after the grouping of 1923 the LNER purchased 273, some of them new locomotives which had never been used, at very low prices. At the end of the war 100 sets of parts for the 'N' class 2-6-0 locomotive designed by R. L. Maunsell for the South East & Chatham Railway were built at Woolwich Arsenal. The Southern Railway bought fifty sets, which were assembled at Ashford in 1924–25, and twenty-six were converted to the 5ft 3in. gauge and worked in Ireland. One example of a Robinson 2-8-0 and one of an 'N' class 2-6-0 are preserved. They are evidence of a widespread assumption after 1918 that government would continue to control the railways in peacetime as it had done during the war, and that it would be able to impose standardisation.

The railways played a different role in the Second World War. Between Dunkirk and D-Day the British forces were effectively mechanised, as was the US Army which began to assemble in Britain during 1942. The allied armies travelled and moved their supplies in such vehicles as Jeeps, US International M5 half-tracks, General Motors CCKW-353 2.5-ton trucks and Bedford QL 3-ton trucks. Nevertheless, behind the front, food, ammunition, petrol, guns and replacement parts for vehicles moved around Britain (and later across France, Belgium and occupied Germany) by rail.

The archaeology of the railway system reflects the pressures of wartime. While the system was hard pressed to handle the heavy traffic of the First World War, its infrastructure was scarcely changed by wartime demands, apart from the installation of sidings at munitions factories. Only four new connections were constructed on the main lines: links from the Tottenham & Hampstead line to the Great Northern and Midland Main Lines at Harringay (TQ 314881) and Gospel Oak (TQ 285855) in north London; a junction between the Great Northern and Midland Lines at Peterborough; and a curve from the Great Central Main Line at

Whetstone (SP 558981), south of Leicester, to the LNWR route from Nuneaton, which was never actually used. During the Second World War the capacity of the system was increased by the construction of junctions, loops and marshalling yards, by the doubling of some single lines, and by the quadrupling of tracks on some heavily used routes.[45]

One of the main preoccupations of railway managers was traffic originating in the north and the midlands consigned for southern England, which included coal, imports from Merseyside and Clydeside, and supplies for troops – in particular, from 1942, the US Army which was assembling in anticipation of the invasion of continental Europe.[46] As much as possible of this traffic was diverted away from London and the threat of bombing. Much of it was conveyed along the Great Western Main Line from Banbury through Oxford, having been passed from the LMSR at Bordesley Junction (SP 088857), Birmingham, or from the Great Central Section of the LNER at Banbury North Junction (SP 462426). Traffic could be transferred to the Eastern and Central Sections of the Southern Railway at Reading, and to the Western Section by the line from Reading to Basingstoke or that from Didcot to Winchester. Many trains from the Channel ports carrying troops evacuated from Dunkirk had used the old junction at Reading in May and June 1940. The junction at Oxford with the LMSR route to Bletchley and Cambridge offered alternative connections to and from the north-west of England. In 1940 the line from Banbury to Didcot was one of the most congested parts of the railway system, particularly during October and November, when the marshalling yards in Birmingham were bombed on twelve occasions,

and it again came under pressure with the build-up of traffic for American forces in 1942. The schemes designed to improve traffic flows on these routes are shown in Table 7.2.

Railways in South Wales also came under pressure. The mines in the Valleys were a principal source of coal for southern and western England, and the coal-exporting ports, depressed and under-used in the 1930s, came back to life handling imports from the USA and Canada. The threat of bombing made it essential that such imports should be rapidly and efficiently dispersed. The railway improvements carried out to improve traffic flows from the South Wales ports are shown in Table 7.3.

Railway managers were also concerned with the southward movement of coal from mines in Northumberland and Durham which had previously travelled by coastal shipping. The East Coast Main Line was the only outlet to the south between the Pennines and the Cleveland Hills, and the capacity of the lines from Northallerton to Leeds and York, and southwards to Doncaster, was much increased (*see Table 7.4*).

Many other improvements were made to the system. Numerous loops and sidings were constructed in the Southampton area, and in Devon and Cornwall, to aid the assembly of troops for the D-Day invasion. The line from Ayr to Stranraer was improved to speed the handling of imports from Cairnryan. Even some of the most remote and little-used parts of the system were affected. Sidings at Wrexham

7.14 (*left*)
The railway marshalling yard at Banbury *c*. 1960. The former LNWR 0-8-0 locomotive has worked in with a coal train from the Warwickshire coalfield, although it is equipped with a tender cab for the line between Abergavenny and Merthyr in South Wales. The sidings to the right are part of the marshalling yard built by the GWR in 1931, and beyond them is a cold-storage depot built during the Second World War.

(*Photo: Barrie Trinder*)

7.15 (*right*)
Chepstow and the River Wye in December 1941. Brunel's celebrated bridge still carried the railway from Gloucester to Newport across the Wye (it was replaced in the 1950s). Between the railway and the river is an area that was used for shipbuilding in both world wars. In 1942 it was being used for the assembly of landing craft and similar vessels.

(*Crown copyright/MOD*)

Location and nature of work	Railway company	Cost (£1,000s)	Dates
Great Central Main Line: marshalling yard extensions at Woodford Halse and Annesley, loops at Charwelton, Rugby, Ashby Magna, Swithland, Loughborough, Ruddington, Hucknall	LNER	158	June 1940–March 1942
Banbury: new sidings in marshalling yard	GWR	170	Dec. 1940–Feb. 1941
Banbury: extension to locomotive depot	GWR	41	April 1943
Oxford: loops at Kenning, Radley, Didcot	GWR	68	Dec. 1939–Dec. 1940
Oxford: loops to Wolvercote Junction and Kennington Junction	GWR	128	June 1942–Oct.1942
Oxford: Yarnton exchange sidings	GWR/LMSR	25	May 1941
Oxford: Hinksey marshalling yard	GWR	127	August 1942
Oxford: new junction between GWR and LMSR route to Bletchley	GWR/LMSR	10	November 1940
Sandy: chord linking East Coast Main Line to LMSR Cambridge–Oxford route	LNER/LMSR	19	June 1940
Calvert: chord linking Great Central line of LNER to LMSR Cambridge–Oxford route	LNER/LMSR	18	July 1940
Didcot: loops to Appleford Junction and Milton	GWR	73	Mar. 1941–Mar. 1942
Didcot: Moreton Cutting, extension of marshalling yard	GWR	54	July 1943
Didcot–Newbury: doubling of single line	GWR	248	April 1943
Newbury–Winchester: new loops and new junction with Southern Railway	GWR	122	Jan. 1943–May 1943
Shawford–Eastleigh: new loop and sidings	SR	90	March 1943
Reading: new junction between GWR and Southern Railway route to Guildford and London	GWR/SR	91	February 1941
Reading–Tonbridge line: extension to marshalling yard at Tonbridge, loops at Wokingham, North Camp, Shalford, Gomshall	SR	86	Aug. 1941–Nov. 1941

Table 7.2
Some wartime improvements to railways between the midlands and southern England.

Source:
C. I. Savage, *The History of the Second World War: Inland Transport* (London, HMSO–Longman, 1957)

Location and nature of work	Railway company	Cost (£1,000s)	Dates
Cardiff, Newport, Barry, Swansea: sidings at docks	GWR	117	July 1940–January 1941
Quadrupling of route from Newport (Monmouth) to Severn Tunnel Junction	GWR	257	November 1941
Quadrupling of route from Gloucester to Cheltenham	GWR/LMSR	500	August 1942

Table 7.3
Some wartime improvements to rail lines in and leading from the South Wales ports.

(Source: as above)

Location and nature of work	Railway company	Cost (£1,000s)	Dates
Northallerton–Leeds route, eight loops	LNER	76	April 1942–Sep. 1942
Quadrupling of route from Pilmoor to Thirsk	LNER	374	Aug. 1942–May 1943
York: new reception sidings in marshalling yard	LNER	82	December 1942
Doncaster: extension to Decoy marshalling yard	LNER	59	February 1943

Table 7.4
Some wartime improvements to railways in Yorkshire.

(Source: as above)

Exchange Station were enlarged in the spring of 1943 to cope with traffic to and from the Wrexham Royal Ordnance Factory. In September 1942 a new junction was constructed at Broome Junction (SP 084533) in Warwickshire, where the previously lightly trafficked Ashchurch–Barnt Green loop of the one-time Midland Railway was joined by the route of the former Stratford & Midland Junction Railway.

The impact of wartime railway construction remains in the landscape. The weed-strewn remains of the marshalling yards at Moreton Cutting (SU 545895) and New Hinksey (SU 513046) can still be seen on a journey from Reading to Oxford, while the site of the wartime sidings at Banbury (SP 461418) is now a roadstone terminal. The wartime marshalling yard on the western side of the Great Northern Main Line on the edges of the Fens at Conington (TL 200861) has disappeared from the landscape, except for a part used as a ballast dump. Most loops and refuge sidings, wartime and otherwise, have been taken up, but their traces can still be seen.

The need to handle imports carried across the Atlantic stimulated the construction of three new ports during the Second World War. Marchwood (SZ 406105) on Southampton Water remained in use in 1999 as a military port, while Faslane (NS 2489) on the Clyde was an operational Royal Navy base. Cairnryan (NX 072672) in Galloway became a ferry port for road vehicles crossing the North Channel to and from Northern Ireland.

British locomotives were again sent abroad – 138 were abandoned in France in 1940, and in the autumn of 1941 the government ordered the despatch of 151 2-8-0s to Persia. For most of the war the system was operated with just under 20,000 locomotives, a total that rose to a peak of 20,824 in July 1944. Some locomotives were built by the four railway companies during the war, including the innovative Pacifics designed by Oliver Bullied for the Southern Railway, but many locomotives, already life-expired in 1939, were kept at work, wheezing and clanking their way with wartime supplies in unbraked wagons, from marshalling yard to marshalling yard, from loop to loop, simmering for hours in queues at approaches to junctions. In 1943–44 British locomotives were supplemented by 398 American 2-8-0s, which were sent to the Continent soon after D-Day. LMS-type 8F 2-8-0

locomotives were built by the three other companies, at Swindon, Brighton and Doncaster, and from early 1943 deliveries began of standard freight locomotives, 935 'Austerity' 2-8-0s, and 150 2-10-0s, which worked on the lines of all four companies, and passed into the service of British Railways after nationalisation of the railways in 1948. A standard 0-6-0 saddle-tank locomotive was built for the War Department from 1943 by the Hunslet Locomotive Company and extensively employed at Ordnance Factories and military depots. After the war 75 of the 485 produced were acquired by the LNER and passed into the service of British Railways, while many were used by industrial concerns. All the American 2-8-0s were taken to the Continent in the months after D-Day, but four were brought back to Britain and preserved. British Railways operated 748 of the Austerity locomotives, but they were not regarded with especial favour by their crews, nor did they inspire the imagination of preservationists. None was saved from scrapping, but Gordon, a 2-10-0 that had remained in army service, plus two other 2-10-0s repatriated from Greece and a 2-8-0 from Sweden, are now on preserved railways, together with more than seventy of the WD saddle-tank design.[47]

Plans, statistics, timetables and even photographs give an inadequate impression of the nature of railway work in wartime, though that work has been to some extent been captured by the reminiscences of those who worked for, travelled on and observed trains at the time. Enormous trains were operated throughout the war. The 'up' Flying Scotsman on Easter Tuesday 1940 consisted of twenty-one coaches weighing 720 tonnes when it changed locomotives at Grantham. George Behrend, a student at Oxford in 1940, recalled the anxiety felt in the city as, nightly, bombers droned northwards towards Coventry and Birmingham, but also the reassuring procession, each morning after, of southbound freight trains, hauled by dirty locomotives, displaying the stencilled codes for their home depots to the north – OXleY (Wolverhampton), TYSeley (Birmingham) and BANbury. Harold Gasson was a fireman based at Didcot, and recalled long, somnolent days in 1942 tending locomotives employed in laying the second track on the line to Newbury, a busy week of shunting in the depot the US

Army had established on Newbury Racecourse, and plodding, much-delayed journeys on ill-maintained locomotives, hauling war supplies southwards. George Bushell, a fireman based at Willesden, remembered an autumn night in 1940 when bombs caused his Fowler 3MT 2-6-2T locomotive No. 4 to bounce on its springs as it waited at Willesden No. 6 Box, while Park Royal to the west was in flames. He experienced 20-hour return trips from London to Crewe, and a 23-hour shift during which he took a freight train only as far as Northampton. Harry Aland (1906–66), who worked at Welford & Kilworth Station (SP 624835) on the line from Peterborough to Rugby, recalled difficulties in persuading soldiers and airmen to pay fares, and the sombre task of loading the coffins, one to a van, of eight airmen killed when a Lancaster crashed on a training flight at nearby Bruntingthorpe.[48]

Benjamin Brookshank spent the afternoon and evening of 1 August 1944 recording trains at Ashchurch (SO 926332), near Tewkesbury, on the Birmingham–Bristol LMSR Main Line, junction for the branch line to Malvern and for the loop through Evesham to Barnt Green, and for the large War Department depot established in 1942. During 6.5 hours of observation he recorded 53 workings, many of which were typical of wartime operation. There were 4 workings into or out of the army depot; 5 troop trains passed through Ashchurch, 4 southbound and 1 northbound. A hospital train carrying casualties from Normandy, headed by two 0-6-0 locomotives, lumbered across the junction towards a military hospital at Malvern. An almost new Stanier 2-8-0 locomotive passed southwards with a load of armoured vehicles, while a train of new American bogie wagons destined for use on the Continent passed through northbound. One locomotive, now preserved, the pioneer Midland Compound 4-4-0 1000, then 39 years old, worked the 15.05 express from Bristol to Sheffield.[49] Re-enactments of wartime operations have become popular on preserved railways, and the survival of individual locomotives and other vehicles makes it possible to appreciate some aspects of the period, but the sense of working under pressure for long shifts, with inadequate equipment and little knowledge of what was happening elsewhere, is impossible to re-capture.

Conclusions

The world wars of the twentieth century have left a massive if incomplete archaeological record. The number of National Factories built during the First World War, and of shadow factories built during the Second, the sheer size of the Royal Ordance Factories, the many oil depots and refrigerated stores are evidence of the response of British society to the challenge of war. The contrast between the flamboyant Baroque style of some of the First World War factories, lurking, scarcely recognised, in the industrial landscapes of Avonmouth or Burton upon Trent, and the cheap and chaste functionality of those of the Second World War, gives ground for reflection.

The legacy of images of the two wars, many of them officially sponsored, like Stanhope Forbes's 1918 painting *The Munitions Girls Forging 4.5in. Shells at Kilnhurst* (Rotherham), and Humphrey Jennings's footage of miners and railwaymen working, and of service personnel celebrating Christmas in decorated but spartan huts, miles from their homes,[50] is evidence of the 'inspection effect' created by the need to re-organise the economy. The quality of the housing at Gretna and Mancot Royal, the quantity of that erected at Donnington, the proliferation of hostels and canteens, all demonstrate the working of the 'participation bargain' during the two wars, just as the 'homes fit for heroes' built under the Addison Act, and the prefabs, council houses and new towns of the late 1940s, are evidence of its continuing momentum in peacetime. Many artefacts are preserved both in public collections and privately – about 250 Spitfires remain worldwide, together with more than a dozen Lancasters, two of them airworthy, while Douglas C-47s (or DC3s, in civilian parlance) continue to fly in many parts of the world. The effects of the acceleration of research in wartime pervade our everyday lives – electricity generated by nuclear power, jet aircraft and air-traffic-control systems, polythene buckets, earth-moving machines and welded ships. The everyday artefacts that came to characterise the war – ration books, packet of dried eggs, tins of powdered milk, nylon stockings, American Cheddar cheese, Spam, spearmint gum, US Army soft leather boots, Chesterfield cigarettes,

Hershey chocolate-bars, Jack Frost sugar cubes and Dinky Toy models of Flying Fortress bombers and Sunderland flying-boats – are evidence both of the order that government attempted to impose on wartime society and of the cultural impact of the presence of large numbers of American personnel. Above all, the two wars have moulded the industrial landscape. The location of manufacturing and distribution in north and west London has been shaped largely by the munitions depots of the First World War. Most of the shadow factories of the Second World War remain in industrial use. The assembly of Rover cars at Longbridge, of Jaguar cars at Tyburn Road, of Airbus wings at Chester, takes place in buildings which resulted from wartime investment. Numerous earthworks are monuments to improvised attempts to increase the capacity of the railways during the Second World War. The Royal Ordnance Factories and the airfields have become industrial estates, which are at the heart of the economy of the 1990s, whether on a grand scale, as at Slough, Park Royal, Wrexham or Bridgend, or in microcosm, as at Ditton Priors or Wellesbourne Mountford. If this chapter has demonstrated the potential of archaeological methodology to raise questions and present evidence about the impact of war on twentieth-century society, it will have achieved its purpose.

Notes and references

1 A. W. Marwick, *The Deluge*, London: Bodley Head, 1965; *Britain in the Century of Total War*, London: Bodley Head, 1968.

2 L. T. C. Rolt, *Landscape with Canals*, London: Allen Lane, 1977, pp. 54–6.

3 Speech at the opening of Birmingham's 40,000th council house at Weoley Castle, 23 October 1933, reported in the *Birmingham Post*, 24 October 1933.

4 W. J. Reader, *A History of ICI*, vol. I: *The Forerunners 1870–1926*, Oxford: Oxford University Press, 1970, p. 249.

5 J. A. B. Hamilton, *Britain's Railways in Wartime*, London: Allen & Unwin, 1967; H. Best, *The Mystery Port of Richborough*, London: Concrete Institute (subsequently the Institute of Structural Engineering), 1929; War Office, *Account of the Construction and Working of the Port of Richborough*, London: War Office, 1920.

6 P. Hall, *The Industries of London*, London: Hutchinson, 1962, pp. 124–45.

7 The information on munitions factories is drawn from Hall, ibid.; G. J. DeGroot, *Blighty: British Society in the Era of the Great War*, London: Longman, 1996, p. 83; M. Cassell, *Long Lease: The Story of Slough Estates 1920–1991*, London: Pencorp, 1991.

8 P. Collins and M. Stratton, *British Car Factories from 1896*, Godmanstone: Veloce, 1993, pp. 219–20.

9 Survey information in National Monuments Record, Swindon. We are grateful for information on this site to Dr Robert Bud of the Science Museum and Wayne Cocroft of English Heritage.

10 W. Cocroft, *Dangerous Energy: The Archaeology of Gunpowder and Military Explosives Manufacture*, Swindon: English Heritage, 2000 (forthcoming); Collins and Stratton, op. cit., pp. 196–7; P. Moore, *A Guide to the Industrial Archaeology of Hampshire and the Isle of Wight*, Southampton: Southampton University Industrial Archaeology Group, 1984, p. 29.

11 M. Miller, *Raymond Unwin: Garden Cities and Town Planning*, Leicester: Leicester University Press, 1992, pp. 49–68; M. Swenarton, *Homes Fit for Heroes: The Politics and Architecture of Early State Houses in Britain*, London: Heinemann, 1981, pp. 50–62. We are grateful for information from Dr Miles Oglethorpe.

12 Percival, 'The Great Explosion at Faversham, 2 April 1916', *Archaeologia Cantiana*, 1985, vol. 100, pp. 425–63; Reader, op. cit., p. 286. We are grateful for information from David Eve of Kent County Council.

13 J. E. Dolan and M. K. Oglethorpe, *Explosives in the Service of Man: Ardeer and the Nobel Heritage*, Edinburgh: RCAHMS, 1996.

14 W. D. Cocroft and I. Leith, 'Cunard's Shellworks, Liverpool', *Archive*, 1996, vol. 11, pp. 53–64.

15 J. D. Scott, *Vickers: A History*, London: Weidenfeld & Nicolson, 1963.

16 K. Richardson, *Twentieth Century Coventry*, Coventry: City of Coventry, 1972; B. Lancaster and T. Mason, *Life and Labour in a Twentieth Century City: The Experience of Coventry*, Coventry: Cryfield Press, 1987. Information from the National Monuments Record Centre, Swindon.

17 Collins and Stratton, op. cit., pp. 180–91.

18 M. Stratton, 'Skating Rinks to Shadow Factories: The Evolution of British Aircraft Manufacturing Complexes', *Industrial Archaeology Review*, 1996, vol. 18, pp. 230–33. For information on the Addlestone factory, we are grateful to Dr Derek Merfield.

19 Scott, op. cit., pp. 69–73, 169–74.

20 D. Charman, *Glengarnock*, Aalst-Walre:
    de Archaeologische Pers, 1981.

21 Collins and Stratton, op. cit., pp. 172–4.

22 The account of the Royal Ordnance Factories is
    drawn from fieldwork and from: C. M. Kohan, *The
    History of the Second Word War: Works and Buildings*,
    London: HMSO–Longman, 1952; W. Hornby, *History
    of the Second World War: Factories and Plant*, London,
    HMSO–Longman, 1958, pp. 83–106; and I. Hay, *ROF
    – the Story of the Royal Ordnance Factories 1939–48*,
    London: HMSO. We are grateful for information
    also from Dr Wayne Cocroft of English Heritage.

23 We are indebted to John Edmunds for information
    on the Hereford factory.

24 Information on Featherstone is drawn from NMRC,
    Swindon.

25 M. Christensen, 'ROF Thorp Arch', *Archive*, 1999,
    no. 22, pp. 15–20; no. 23, 1999, pp. 14–25.

26 M. Stratton and B. Trinder, *Industrial England*,
    London: Batsford, 1997, pp. 113–14; Collins
    and Stratton, op. cit., pp. 50–2; Kohan, op. cit.,
    pp. 218–41.

27 W. J. Reader, *Imperial Chemical Industries: A History*,
    vol. II: *The First Quarter-Century 1926–52*, Oxford:
    Oxford University Press, 1975, pp. 218–50; Dolan
    and Oglethorpe, op. cit.

28 Collins and Stratton, op. cit., pp. 180–91; G. Negus
    and J. Stoddon, *Aviation in Birmingham*, Earl Shilton:
    Midland Counties Publications, 1984, p. 45.

29 We are grateful to Medwyn Parry of RCAHMW
    for information on the Hawarden factory.

30 Kohan, op. cit., pp. 195–278; Hornby, op. cit.,
    pp. 395–49. We are grateful to Julian Temple of
    Brooklands Museum for information in this
    paragraph.

31 We are grateful to Brian Malaws of RCAHMW
    for information on the Newtown and Llanfoist
    factories.

32 The account of Brockworth is drawn from a survey
    in NMRC Swindon.

33 M. L. Gibson, *Aviation in Northamptonshire*,
    Northampton: Northamptonshire Libraries, 1982,
    pp. 340–51.

34 L. T. C. Rolt, *Waterloo Ironworks: A History of Taskers
    of Andover 1809–1968*, Newton Abbot: David &
    Charles, 1969, pp. 120–9; A. W. Marwick, *Britain in
    the Century of Total War*, London: Bodley Head, 1968,
    pp. 265–93.

35 W. McCanna, 'The War Effort at Henry Stone's',
    Cake & Cockhorse, 1999, vol. 14, pp. 122–7.

36 M. Bone and P. Stanier, *A Guide to the Industrial
    Archaeology of Devon*, Telford: Association for
    Industrial Archaeology, 1998, p. 32.

37 We are grateful to Ian Soden of Northamptonshire
    Archaeology for his expert observations on the
    Express Lifts factory. Albums of photographs of the
    factory during the two world wars are in the
    Express Lifts Collection in the Northamptonshire
    Record Office.

38 Kohan, op. cit., p. 257.

39 Ibid., pp. 303–58. We are also grateful to Patrick
    MacDermott for his expert observations on the
    surviving buildings.

40 R. Blake, 'The Impact of Airfields on the British
    Landscape', *Geographical Journal*, 1969, vol. 135,
    pp. 502–28; R. Blake, M. Hodgson and B. Taylor,
    The Airfields of Lincolnshire since 1912, Earl Shilton:
    Midland Counties Publications, 1984; R. Blake,
    'The Changing Distribution of Military Airfields in
    the East Midlands, 1914–1980', *The East Midlands
    Geographer*, 1981, vol. 7, pp. 286–302.

41 We are grateful to Medwyn Parry of RCAHMW
    for information on Welsh sites.

42 The account of Wellesbourne Mountford is based
    on research by Dr Michael Harrison.

43 The account of Hixon is based on research by
    Tony Parkes.

44 Kohan, op. cit., pp. 251–3.

45 J. A. B. Hamilton, *Britain's Railways in the First World
    War*, London: Allen & Unwin, 1967, pp. 102–4.

46 L. Savage, *History of the Second World War: Inland
    Transport*, London: Longman, 1957, pp. 202–62,
    402–29, 571, 648–60.

47 P. Ransome-Wallis, *The Last Steam Locomotives of
    British Railways*, London: Ian Allan, 1966, pp. 118–20;
    B. Haresnape, *Maunsell Locomotives: A Pictorial
    History*, London: Ian Allan, 1977, pp. 24–7, 116;
    P. Fox and P. Hall, *Preserved Locomotives of British
    Railways*, 9th edn, Sheffield: Platform 5, 1995,
    pp. 16, 19, 50, 57–61.

48 G. Behrend, *Gone with Regret*, Sidcup: Lambarde,
    1964, pp. 92–4; H. Gasson, *Firing Days: Reminiscences
    of a Great Western Fireman*, Oxford: Oxford
    Publishing Company, 1973, pp. 57–84; G. Bushell,
    LMS Locoman: Willesden Footplate Memories, Truro:
    Bradford Barton, nd, pp. 12–19; H. Aland,
    Recollections of Country Station Life, Blaby: Anderson,
    1980, pp. 56–67.

49 W. L. Brookshank, *Train Watchers No. 1*,
    Burton upon Trent: Pearson, 1982, pp. 24–7.

50 In Jennings's film *Diary for Timothy*.

Constructing dwellings was one of the
characteristic activities of twentieth-
century Britain, but not one in which it was
customary to take pride.[1] Building houses on
land once used for agriculture was seen as the
'destruction' of the romantic fantasy known as
the countryside, and the new creations of the
century – curving verge-and-tree-lined avenues
of semi-detached houses, the New Towns of the
post-Second World War era, the tower blocks
of the 1960s – were rarely praised. Scunthorpe,
an attractive steel-working town built in
the Garden City style, and Milton Keynes,
which includes some of the most imaginative
housing of the second half of the century,
were unthinkingly regarded with derision by
the metropolitan media. Conventional wisdom
asserted that suburbia is monotonous.

> One road or one suburb is to the eye of a stranger
> identical with another road or another suburb....
> Ruislip is indistinguishable from Cowley;
> Mapperley might just as well be in Bristol as in
> Nottingham.

Even council houses are not, as George Orwell
claimed, just 'row upon row of little red houses,
all much liker than two peas'.[2] It is our
contention that archaeological study reveals,
on the contrary, significant evidence of the
idiosyncrasies of local builders, architects and
councils, and that the landscape of twentieth-
century suburbia reflects changing aesthetic
and social aspirations, the fluctuations of the
economy, the development of many species of
technology and the rhythms of political fashion.
The landscape of housing is one of the richest
sources of evidence of twentieth-century British
history. Just as a walk across ridge-and-furrow,
past the house platforms of a deserted village,
to some medieval church (wherein stands the
gaudy tomb of the landowner who enclosed
the fields and cleared the village) encapsulates
much of the social history of the sixteenth
century, so a walk through the suburbs of
any sizeable town or city can richly illuminate
the twentieth century.

Chapter eight

The great rebuildings

Starting-points

The pace of building was at a low ebb in the period before the First World War (*see Table A3 in the Appendix*). The highest annual rate of building in the early part of the century was recorded in 1903, when 156,900 houses were constructed. The highest total in any of the five years before the First World War was in 1910, when only 86,000 houses were built. Most of the new dwellings of this period were built for private landlords for letting to working- and middle-class tenants, and followed the patterns of by-law housing established in most towns in the 1850s, terraces of tunnel-back cottages in what appear at first sight to be long terraces but which on closer examination prove to be groups of not more than six houses abutting on to each other. The front doors open either directly on to the pavement or into tiny front gardens, the stubby walls of which often bear evidence of iron railings removed for scrap in the Second World War. This kind of landscape is exemplified by parts of Selly Oak in Birmingham, or Kingsthorpe in Northampton. Some regional characteristics were maintained. Firewalls extending through roof spaces were a feature of terraced housing in London, where they were imposed by fire regulations, and spread to Luton, Northampton and Oxford. The Tyneside two-storey flat was easily adapted to by-law regulation and to the architectural fashions of the Edwardian period. In Leeds the construction of back-to-back housing continued well into the twentieth century. Houses built in the Edwardian period are more likely than those of earlier decades to be constructed of hard, shiny, red bricks of the kind for which the works of Accrington and Ruabon were celebrated, to have front parlours lit by bow windows, and to be ornamented with terracotta, stained-glass panels and, particularly in Cardiff and Crewe, decorative tiles.

Much of the housing occupied at the turn of the century was of execrable quality. In Leeds the first generations of back-to-back housing constructed in the 1780s and 1790s remained in use, while in east London many families lived in houses of the early nineteenth century, the walls of which, as Sir Arthur Elton demonstrated in the 1935 film *Housing Problems*, could be brought down by the not-very-energetic push of a demolition worker's not-especially-muscular forearm. In most small towns, insanitary rows and rookeries accommodated the poor in close proximity to timber-framed or Classically styled houses of distinction. Legislation enabled local authorities to clear slums, but many remained. The Housing of the Working Classes Act of 1890 authorised borough and district councils to construct houses for letting, but outside London the obligation to charge economic rents meant that houses of an appreciably higher standard than those built by private landlords were difficult to let. In Northampton three-bedroom council houses built in Bective Road in 1913–14 with baths and cellars proved difficult to let at seven shillings a week, and construction of further houses was abandoned, while there was enthusiastic demand for two-bedroom houses without baths and cellars in Naseby Street which let at five shillings per week. Neither group of houses is significantly different from contemporary privately built dwellings in adjacent streets. The private landlord was the principal provider of housing in the Edwardian period. Only about 10 per cent of occupiers owned their own homes, and less than 1 per cent of the total housing stock was owned by local authorities.[3] Outside London the role of local government in providing accommodation was insignificant.

In the capital the London County Council, established in 1888, and some of the twenty-nine boroughs created in 1899, continued the tradition – established by voluntary philanthropic societies in the late 1840s – of building multi-storey blocks of apartments in central areas. The Boundary Street Estate in Bethnal Green, with its radial lay-out and buildings designed by different members of the LCC architects' department, was completed about 1900, while the most notable multi-storey development after the turn of the century was the Bourne Estate, between Clerkenwell Road and Portpool Lane, designed by Rowland Plumbe. The LCC also continued philanthropic society practice in building 'cottage estates' in the outer suburbs. The Artisans', Labourers' and General Dwellings Company, one of the many charities with which the seventh Earl of Shaftesbury was connected, had built estates at Shaftesbury Park near Clapham Junction, Queen's Park in Kilburn, and Noel Park at

Wood Green. In the years before the First World War the LCC built similar estates at Totterdown Fields, Tooting, Norbury, White Hart Lane and Old Oak, the last of these, clustered around East Acton Station on the Central Line, introducing into local authority housing the design principles of the Garden City movement, with sinuous roads, plentiful trees and gables in great variety.[4]

Many innovations in house building in the first two-thirds of the twentieth century were derived from the tradition of the Garden City, inspired by three company villages: Port Sunlight (SJ 3384) in the Wirral, Merseyside, laid out by W. H. Lever from 1888; Bournville (SP 0481), on the western side of Birmingham, built by George Cadbury from 1893; and New Earswick (SE 6055), on the northern edge of York. All three had open lay-outs in which houses, faintly following historical styles, were surrounded by broad grass verges and large private gardens. Port Sunlight had about it an element of ostentation, but Cadbury and his architect, W. Alexander Harvey, had broader ambitions and practised restraint in their designs, hoping that Bournville would be an example for others. This intent was taken further by Joseph Rowntree, the York chocolate manufacturer, who from 1900 built New Earswick with the object of providing houses 'artistic in appearance, sanitary and thoroughly well-built, yet within the means of working men earning about 25s a week'. Rowntree acknowledged in 1904 that 'Villages like ours ... are watched with great interest by social workers throughout the country ... we want at Earswick to do something towards the housing problem'. New Earswick was designed by cousins Raymond Unwin and Barry Parker, an engineer and an architect, who had been partners in professional practice since 1896 and had published *The Art of Building a House* in 1901. Their ideas were closely aligned to those of Ebenezer Howard (1850–1928), who in 1898 published *Tomorrow: A Peaceful Path to Real Reform*, the visionary ideas of which are better indicated in the title it assumed from 1902, *Garden Cities of Tomorrow*.[5]

The origins of many of the industrial landscapes of the first two-thirds of the twentieth century are best observed at Letchworth (TL 2132), the first Garden City, established in 1903.[6] Unwin and Parker planned Letchworth by adapting to the demands of the local topography the diagrams that appeared in Ebenezer Howard's prophecies. Houses and factories were built in separate zones. Some archetypal twentieth-century products have been manufactured in the main industrial belt to the east of the town centre – Phoenix motorcars, Idris mineral waters, Shelvoke refuse-collection vehicles, Ewart geysers and Everyman books. On the other side of the town centre stands Letchworth's most noteworthy industrial building, Spirella's corset factory, built – in brick and glass around a concrete frame – in three stages between 1912 and 1920 for William Wallace Kincaid, the founder of the company. The Spirella corset, with coiled metal springs instead of whalebone, was sold by lady representatives whose affiliation to the company would be discreetly indicated on most housing estates in Britain between 1920 and 1970.

Letchworth displays the possibilities for new methods of constructing houses in the early years of the century. The Cheap Cottages Exhibition of 1905 challenged competitors to construct a dwelling for no more than £150, less the cost of land. Most of the 121 entries still stand between the railway station and Norton Common. No. 158 Wilbury Road was designed by J. Brodie, City Engineer of Liverpool, and is made of interlocking prefabricated panels, cast from concrete in which clinker ash from the city incinerator formed the aggregate. Potter & Co. built 15, 17 and 19 Cross Street, with lightweight steel frames, supporting steel meshes covered

8.1
Letchworth: 158 Wilbury Road, constructed of large concrete panels to the design of J. Brodie, the City Engineer of Liverpool.

(Photo: Barrie Trinder)

with rendering. No. 241 Icknield Way, built by the Fireproof Partition & Spandrel Wall Co., has a brick outer skin reinforced by rolled-steel joists, with a lining of composition board. Gilbert Fraser, of the Concrete Machinery Company in Liverpool, designed 4 Cross Street, the concrete blocks of which were cast on site. The Stone House in Nevells Road, by local architects Bennett & Bidwell, is also constructed from concrete blocks, in this case designed to look like stone. No. 216 Nevells Road was built to a system of prefabrication, designed by W. Moss Settle, in which concrete panels were fitted into grooved oak posts, but the house leaked and has been substantially altered. By contrast, 8 The Quadrant, designed by Lionel Crane, has a timber frame clad with traditional Hertfordshire weather-boarding, and survives in its original state. No. 222 Nevells Road was designed by Wheeler & Son, utilising panels of British Uralite (*see Chapter 2*). The tradition from which Letchworth sprang is represented by 206 and 208 Nevells Road and by 6 The Quadrant, designed by W. Alexander Harvey of the Bournville Village Trust. The winning entry, 217 Icknield Way, a modest cottage of traditional construction with rendered walls, was designed by Percy Houfton, architect of many miners' houses in Yorkshire (*see Chapter 3*). A second display, the Urban Cottages Exhibition, took place in 1907, and most of the houses built for it remain, the majority of them in Lytton Avenue, of which Nos 10, 12, 14 and 16 were designed by Percy Houfton.

Many of these innovatory forms of construction recurred in the history of twentieth-century housing, but most housing has followed conventional methods, similar to those employed in Parker and Unwin's houses in Letchworth. Unwin believed that housing should break away from the constraints of Victorian by-laws, and that every room of every house should be accessible to sunlight, thus necessitating informal, open lay-outs. He disliked the 'unsightly rear extension' of the tunnel-back house, the most popular form of urban dwelling between 1850 and 1914, and designed houses in which coal stores, lavatories and other features usually found in the back yard were incorporated under the main roof. The lay-outs of Parker and Unwin's houses, whether the mock timber-framed dwellings around the 'village green' at Westholm Green or the short neat terraces with large gardens in Ridge Avenue, were widely copied.

Raymond Unwin planned Hampstead Garden Suburb (TQ 2588) also, established by Dame Henrietta Barnett and inaugurated in 1907, although it marked a break with Ebenezer Howard's view that new housing should be constructed in self-sufficient towns, separated by green belts. In the years before the First World War co-operatives built garden suburbs in most of Britain's large cities. A lecture in Manchester by Ebenezer Howard in 1908 prompted clerks from the Co-operative Wholesale Society offices to develop the 136-dwelling garden suburb of Burnage (SJ 8693), designed by J. Horner Hargreaves. Houses copying designs used at Letchworth were built in Thorneycroft Lane in the Fallings Park Garden Suburb (SJ 9200) in Wolverhampton, where the first home was handed over to its tenant by the Bishop of Lichfield in February 1908. Raymond Unwin designed lay-outs for garden suburbs at Brentham in Ealing, Humberstone (SK 6105) in Leicester, Wavertree (SJ 3790) in Liverpool, Garscube in Glasgow and Rhiwbina (ST 1681) in Cardiff.[7]

By 1914 the Garden City style was well established in the voluntary sector, and faintly, at Old Oak Common, in the sphere of local authority provision. It came to be accepted also by government. Before 1914 the government had accepted the principle that its employees should be accommodated according to the standards set by the Garden City movement

8.2
Letchworth: 222 Nevells Road, constructed of panels of British Uralite, most of which have been replaced.

(Photo: Barrie Trinder)

The great rebuildings

in new housing provided at the naval bases at Rosyth and Crombie on the north bank of the Forth, and at Farnborough in Surrey at the Royal Aircraft Factory. The exigencies of wartime dictated an even closer involvement with housing. The Ministry of Munitions, for whose Explosives Department Raymond Unwin was Chief Housing Architect from July 1915, spent over £4 million on housing in the course of the war: 10,000 permanent houses were built at some thirty-eight different locations (*see Table A4 in the Appendix*), for the most part on Garden City lines.[8]

The qualities and limitations of wartime house building are revealed by fieldwork. The landscape of Gretna and Eastriggs is discussed in Chapter 7. Perhaps the most significant evidence is that of the Well Hall estate (TQ 4275), where the average cost of dwellings was £622. Frank Baines designed dwellings of four types, including two-storey flats. His houses are constructed with varied materials in a picturesque style, with gables and dormers, and the street names have associations with the Woolwich Arsenal, for whose swollen wartime labour force the estate was designed. An outstanding example of private provision during the First World War is the estate built by Sir Herbert Austin (1866–1941) for workers at his Longbridge plant, constructed between November 1916 and 1917. It consisted of 199 Readi-Cut bungalows, prefabricated from cedar by the Aladdin Company of Bay City, Michigan, together with twenty-five semi-detached pairs of

conventional construction, intended as fire-breaks. The houses lining Hawkesley Crescent, Hawkesley Drive and Cypress Way give to that quarter of suburban Birmingham (SP 020782) an unmistakably North American ambience.[9]

The council house

The housing of the period following the First World War is wholly different from the generality of that built prior to 1914. After 1918 the patterns of housing favoured by Unwin became the norm, if often in a bowdlerised form, throughout most of Britain. The two-storey cottages, in semi-detached pairs, or in terraces of not more than six, with large gardens, along avenues lined by grass verges punctuated with chestnut or cherry trees, or laid out around greens or in cul-de-sacs, built both by private developers and by local authorities, can be seen throughout England and Wales. In some towns it is possible archaeologically to locate the point of transition. The western end of St David's Avenue in Northampton (SP 755629) consists of the tightly grouped Edwardian terraces typical of the town's shoemaking boom, but there is a dramatic change at the point where the corporation began, about 1919, to build 'homes fit for heroes'.[10] In Copthorne Drive, Shrewsbury (SJ 490127), two pairs of post-war houses, with broad gables and tree-lined gardens, are distinctive from the rather grim pre-war dwellings in Accrington-style brick.

After the First World War the provision of housing became one of the principal activities of local authorities. The coalition government headed by David Lloyd George, which had taken office in 1916, won a hastily arranged election in December 1918, when one of its principal promises was the provision of homes fit to accommodate the heroes of the war. Wartime deprivation had brought revolution to Russia and to parts of Germany, and there were genuine fears of severe social unrest in Britain. House building was seen both as a means of absorbing demobilised labour and as visible proof that the promises made by government in wartime were being met.[11]

8.3
Austin Village, Birmingham: a prefabricated wooden house provided by the Aladdin Company of Bay City, Michigan, one of 199 erected by Sir Herbert Austin in 1916–17.

(Photo: Barrie Trinder)

The government's intentions were encapsulated in the Housing Act of 1919, carried through by Christopher Addison, which provided generous subsidies to local authorities for the construction of new houses. The form of the houses was determined largely by the Tudor Walters Report, published in October 1918, and by the Housing and Town Planning Act of 1919 with its accompanying design manual, which were the work largely of Raymond Unwin. The Ministry of Health tended to favour Georgian designs, regarding the Moulescombe estate (TQ 3306) at Brighton, designed by S. D. Adshead, particularly highly, but its handbook published in 1920 included numerous designs with dormer windows, gables and broken eaves lines, particularly intended for use in the south, where the clay tiles traditionally used for roofing were more porous than the Welsh slate used elsewhere. The housing built under Addison's Act varies in detail from town to town, and from rural district to rural district. All of it has an air of solidity, a sense that it was built with good intentions with the best available materials, and in spacious settings. The Tang Hall estate in York (SE 6252) or the houses built by Derby City Corporation on Victory and Stenson Roads (SK 3333) at an average cost of £788 each are characteristic examples.

Lloyd George's coalition was replaced by a Conservative government in 1921, and housing policy abruptly changed. The threat of revolution had diminished, and the model houses with generous amenities built under Addison's Act were abandoned in favour of the cheapest houses which would effectively accommodate the poor, although for several years schemes already sanctioned under the 1919 legislation were still being completed. Nevertheless, it was acknowledged that the role of local authorities in providing housing with financial support from central government, perceived in 1919 as a temporary expedient to deal with the post-war shortage of accommodation, would continue. Further changes in policy were brought about by Neville Chamberlain's Housing Act of 1923, and by John Wheatley's Act of 1924. In the 1930s most local authorities could gain government assistance in the provision of housing only through slum-clearance schemes. Between 1919 and 1939 over 1.111 million houses were built by local authorities, 170,000 under the Addison Act,

75,300 under the Chamberlain Act, 504,500 under the Wheatley Act and 289,100 under slum-clearance and overcrowding legislation.[12]

The nature of council housing after 1921 varies from authority to authority and indeed within particular authorities. In many the quality of building deteriorated from the standards set in 1919–21, and some of the slum-clearance housing of the 1930s, built of low-quality brick, remains instantly recognisable. Some local authorities began in the 1920s to build very large estates remote from city centres, often without social facilities and not always well placed for workers. Kingstanding (SP 0894), 5 miles north of the centre of Birmingham, with which it was linked by the slow Nos 29 and 29A bus routes, had a population of over 30,000 by the early 1930s, but only one church and one public hall. Its Odeon cinema, whose ceramic fins tower above the adjacent shopping parade, was not built until 1935.[13] Manchester City Corporation put much of its housing energies into the building of Wythenshawe (SJ 8288), linked with the city centre by Princess Road and Kingsway, broad and straight highways with reserved tram tracks. Most of its communal buildings were not constructed until after the Second World War.[14] In London the LCC completed eight 'cottage estates' in the inter-war period and had begun seven more by 1939, constructing over 60,000 dwellings in all. They included Watling (TQ 2091), off the Edgware Road, 4,021 dwellings built between 1926 and 1930, and subsequently the subject of a pioneering social survey, and St Helier, on either side of the Sutton By-pass, where 9,068 dwellings were built between 1926 and 1934, the last LCC estate to have building materials distributed by a light railway.[15] The largest such estate was Becontree (TQ 4885), where construction of houses under the terms of the Addison Act started in 1920. By 1939, 116,000 people were living there in 25,769 houses. Most people had to travel along the District Line to work in central London, or in East Ham or West Ham. Becontree was transformed in 1931 when the Ford Motor Company and its principal suppliers moved to Dagenham from Manchester, but skilled migrant workers were ineligible for LCC housing, and their needs were met by a private estate at Rylands Farm built by Costains in 1931–34.[16] Some prosperous authorities persisted in building housing of a high standard. This was particularly so in Birmingham, where the spacious boulevards of the Weoley Castle estate of 1931–34 (SP 0282), and the streamlined houses designed by Sir Herbert Manzoni in areas like Umberslade Road in Stirchley (SP 0581), eclipse the standards of all but the best of comparably priced private-sector building.

Slum-clearance programmes in the 1930s created the elegant if unhistoric character of some of the most admired English towns. In 1961 council house tenants formed 35 per cent of the population of Stamford, 'the most perfect Georgian town in England' and setting for the television series *Middlemarch*, the result of the demolition in the 1920s and 1930s of courtyard and alley housing in the town centre, and the re-housing of the inhabitants on council estates on the outskirts. 'It takes an effort of the imagination', remarked a commentator in 1965, 'to realise that many of the open spaces and car parks in the centre of the town were once overcrowded tenements'. The town's first council houses were built in 1921 on Melbourne Road and New Cross Road under the Addison Act, and in the 1930s the Northumberland Avenue estate was built to permit the demolition of the slums in the centre. In Market Harborough the council's house-building programme in the 1930s, particularly its Welland Park estate, had the specific objective of clearing the yards and rows in the town centre where, between 1933 and 1938, 67 houses were demolished and another 32 closed.[17]

The majority of the 4 million houses built between the two world wars were of conventional construction, 'cottages', detached or in pairs or short terraces, with brick load-bearing walls. The long-established tradition of building apartments for working-class tenants in central London was continued by the LCC, but none exceeded six storeys and most were of conventional construction. In a few instances non-traditional methods were used in the construction of 'cottages', usually by local authorities. The houses at Dormanstown (NZ 5823) built in 1918 (*see Chapter 7*) had steel frames and walls of rendered panels. John Laing & Son, based at Carlisle in the 1920s, built some 5,500 'Easiform' houses, many under the terms of the Addison Act. The first had 8-inch solid concrete walls, cast on site within wooden shuttering, but when the name was patented

in 1924 'Easiform' houses had cavity walls and were built using steel shuttering. Easiforms were constructed for local authorities, including Tottenham, Woolwich, Croydon, Hereford, Exeter, Brighton, Wrexham and Carlisle, and the Great Western Railway used them to accommodate staff at Hayes and Plymouth.[18] A works in rural Shropshire, at the railway terminus at Ditton Priors (SO 613894), made concrete blocks used for the construction of estates in north London and Wolverhampton in the early 1920s.[19] Cambridge Corporation in 1927 built two-storey houses with walls that were completely pre-cast using a Dutch technology. They were the first large concrete-panel houses to be built in Britain after those designed by Brodie at Letchworth in 1905. Northampton Borough Council built fifty-eight houses from concrete blocks in Warren Road (SP 740615) in 1922, in only one of which could the original form of building still be readily recognised in 1999.[20] Walsall Corporation built concrete-block houses in the Leamore area (SJ 9900) in the 1930s. On its Watling estate in north London in the late 1920s the LCC built 1,331 houses with concrete external walls, 252 with steel frames on the same principle as those at Dormanstown, and 464 with timber frames. Derby Corporation about 1927 built 500 'Thorncliffe' cast-iron houses, supplied by Newton Chambers. At Clydebank nearly 600 'Atholl' houses, with steel frames clad with steel panels, were fabricated in the locomotive shops of William Beardmore in 1925 and 1926. One, a bungalow, stands by the former entrance to the works, but many more remain in the nearby Whitecrook area (NS 5069), and others were sold to local authorities elsewhere in Scotland.[21]

The most notable example of non-conventional housing in the inter-war period was Quarry Hill flats (SE 307338) in Leeds, built close to the city centre on a 67-acre (27ha) site previously occupied by 2,790 houses, most of them the back-to-back terraces for which the city was notorious, and fifty-three pubs. Most of the previous inhabitants had been moved to allow demolition of the houses before 1930. The project reflected tension between the Revd Charles Jenkinson, vicar of Leeds and a councillor from 1930, and R. J. Livett, Director of the Housing Department from 1929, the former seeing the flats as a stage for people on their way from the slums to a cottage, the latter conceiving the project as the creation of a balanced and permanent inner-urban community. The inspiration for the flats came from the schemes built in Vienna in the 1920s, of which the Karl Marxhof is the most celebrated. The scheme followed Austrian practice and used the Mopin system of construction, in which a light steel frame was encased in pre-cast units and filled with poured concrete. The contractor was Robert Tarran of Hull, a traditional builder unaccustomed to the exacting demands of concrete construction, and much of the steelwork was allowed to corrode during construction. The scheme provided 938 dwellings of various sizes in blocks up to six storeys high, served by 88 passenger lifts. The perimeter blocks formed a wall, pierced by arched entrances following Viennese precedents, enclosing green swards. The lavish plans for communal facilities, intended to make Quarry Hill a village within the city, were never wholly implemented, but the communal laundry proved popular. The first stage was opened on 30 March 1938. There were some serious design faults, particularly the ineffective rubbish chutes. The worst disadvantage was perhaps to live in a place that was a continuing source of political controversy and media attention. Nevertheless, surveys show that tenants generally thought well of Quarry Hill, and were dismayed when, on account of structural faults caused by the corrosion of the steel frame during construction, the council decided in November 1973 to demolish the blocks.[22]

The private sector

Almost half (49.1 per cent) of the new houses built between 1919 and 1939 were intended for owner occupation, while 31.5 per cent were built by local authorities and 19.4 per cent for private landlords. The suburbs built by developers attracted much hostility. John Betjeman wrote of a battle, fought with red bricks, between town and university in Oxford.[23] The extravagant language of those who marketed houses in the London suburbs merits derision. Advertisements in 1935 for Morrell's

'Wondervalue Homes De Luxe' drew attention both to their supposedly unspoilt country surroundings and to 'Morrell's Gigantic Scale Methods'. The same kind of estate, with sinuous roads, grass verges, sometimes tree-lined, and houses that usually became more expensive as they incorporated more Tudor features, distinguishing them from 'Georgian' local authority dwellings, can be seen not just in the suburbs of London but in most towns. They appear, for example, in the steelmaking community of Scunthorpe, where 6,835 houses were built between 1919 and 1939, over 80 per cent of them for owner occupation.[24] Fieldwork shows that estates of the 1920s and 1930s are far from uniform. While houses were usually built according to a limited range of basic plans, they often show much variation in detail. The rhythms of the building process are illustrated by the uses of batches of particular items: 'porthole' windows, stained-glass heraldic shields in front doors, or quarry tiles in porches. There were local idiosyncrasies: corkscrew columns made up of clay tiles in the porches of houses in Northampton, or the small, smooth concrete quoins used in Abergavenny. A change in attitude to inter-war housing was brought about by Oliver, Davis and Bentley in 1981, who argued that whatever its failings, the housing had many merits, concluding that 'many suburbs deserve respect and careful examination'.[25] The most effective examination is archaeological.

The 400-acre (160ha) Petts Wood estate (TQ 4467) is one of the archetypal London suburban communities of the inter-war period.[26] It was developed from 1928 by Basil Scuby & Co. Two years later several hundred dwellings were occupied, and more than forty firms were building houses, mostly priced between £1,000 and £1,500. Developers stressed to purchasers the rural context of Petts Wood, in that part of Kent south of Elmstead Tunnel, where

cottage gardens are at their brightest and best ... roses that climb and roses less ambitious, of hollyhocks tall as guardsmen, Sweet Williams growing the more luxuriously for not being fussed over ... in the orchards, the plum trees weighed down with growing fruit.

Potential buyers were offered the prospect of motoring in the nearby countryside, and of reaching the coast within an hour. Petts Wood also had the advantages of the metropolis: 'London stores' delivered there, and banks and chain stores were opening branches in the 'well-designed, half-timbered rows of shops, sparkling clean shops, all live and active' that, with 'the Estate Office with its Old World garden', faced the station across a green. Suburban thoroughfares, consciously called ways, drives and avenues, were lined by

> houses of distinctive design, pleasant half-timbering, overhanging bays, sweeping gables, timbered porches, all set well away from the road, bright and sunning in their white dress ... no fences but little low crazy stone walls, where iris and rock plants grow, crazy paths, flower-laden beds, and bright green lawns, while at the back nod the health-laden pines.

Petts Wood is a characteristic Southern Electric suburb (*see Chapter 9*). It lies 2 miles north of Orpington on the route of the South Eastern Railway from Charing Cross to the coast. In 1899 South Eastern merged with the London, Chatham & Dover company, and in 1902 their two main lines had been linked by a complex series of junctions (TQ 4368) a mile north of Petts Wood, enabling trains from the Orpington direction to travel to Victoria, London Bridge, Charing Cross, Blackfriars or Holborn Viaduct. All the routes were electrified in 1925–26, and by 1930 developers could promise potential residents the prospect of 210 daily trains to central London. The estate office has become the Trencherman's Brasserie, an annexe of the roadhouse-style public house that occupied the green in 1935 and was named the Daylight Inn, after daylight saving, the invention of William Willetts, a Petts Wood resident. Semi-detached houses in 1999 cost in the region of £200,000, and detached villas about £300,000. On the north side of Petts Wood Road it is evident that a succession of semi-detached pairs had been built to the same plan, and all have large rectangular windows lighting the stairs, but there are innumerable variations in detail – in the form of rendering, in the style of timber-framing, in the arrangement of dormers and bow windows, in the application of hanging tiles, stained glass and weather-boarding. Larger houses in Birchwood Road, completed by 1930, have integral garages, unlike their

semi-detached neighbours. Some houses have a low wall at the end of the front garden made of overburnt waster bricks, similar to those to be seen around the former brickyards of the Medway valley. The detached houses at the eastern end of Kingsway are rendered, painted white, stand amid spacious lawns, and have the appearance of expensive dolls' houses in the summer sun. An eccentric feature of many of them is a semi-circular arch of considerable span forming the entrance to the front porch. Near to the station is a succession of closes, conventionally named after the maple, acacia, ash and hawthorn trees. These had not been built by 1930, and display the curving brickwork and every form of window characteristic of the decade that followed. Fieldwork in Petts Wood reveals differences in detail, confirming that many builders constructed portions of the estate. It raises queries about when garages became the norm in the homes of the middle class, and about the origins of the overburnt bricks. It confirms, too, the soundness of the developers' judgement: they may have used weasel words to disguise their destruction of the countryside but nevertheless created an environment that is still cherished, and is probably more ecologically diverse than when it was farmed.

While most private building followed conventional Tudor models, it is possible to find in most towns isolated houses in the Modernist style, some of them designed by leading architects. Thus 508 Wellingborough Road, Northampton, was designed by Peter Behrens in 1925, and incorporated a room from a preceding house designed by Charles Rennie Mackintosh. Shub's Wood, at Chalfont St Peter, was designed in 1933–35 by Mendelsohn & Chermayeff for a manager at the Aspro plant at Slough, and six notable Modernist houses line Windsor Road, Gerrards Cross. In Rugby 116 Dunchurch Road was built in 1934 to the design of Serge Chermayeff. Others are by local, or sometimes unknown, architects. In Scunthorpe, 10 Vicarage Gardens is a reinforced concrete house of 1936, with a flat roof, curving staircase tower and steel-framed windows, by J. H. Johnson of Doncaster. Similar houses include 59 and 59a Park Road, Abergavenny, 57 Marine Drive, Rhos-on-Sea, and 33 Woodfield Road, Shrewsbury. The Scottish partnership Gordon & Scrymgeour built Ingle Neuk at Arbroath and

45 Forfar Avenue, Dundee, both in the Modernist style. Another house in the same idiom was built in 1936 by Sir James Millar amid the bungalows of Old Kirk Road in Corstorphine. There were a few, usually rather half-hearted, attempts by developers to use an openly Modernist style, the Howard estate of 1934 at West Molesey being one example, but by the late 1930s developers were offering 'Sunshine Homes', which had wide, usually metal-framed, windows, rendered walls and overhanging eaves, having forsaken Elizabethan detailing without fully embracing the Bauhaus.

During the 1930s, as the pace of building for owner occupation increased and council housing in many towns came to be concerned principally with slum clearance, antagonisms between the two increased. The most notable instance was at Cutteslowe (SP 507101), on the northern edge of Oxford, where the City Corporation began a programme to construct 298 houses on a 34-acre (14ha) estate in 1931. Two years later OCC sold a further 22 acres to a private developer for the construction of 208 semi-detached houses, to be sold at the relatively low price of £650 each. The developer claimed that OCC had given an assurance that no slum-cleared families would be settled in the Cutteslowe council houses, but in the event twenty-eight such families did move there. During 1934, as building progressed, there were disputes over the naming of the streets, and walls were built separating the two parts of the estate. On 11 May 1935 a demonstration was organised to demand the removal of the walls, but a public inquiry failed to meet its wishes. On 7 June 1938 OCC demolished the walls with steamrollers but a court ordered their re-building; in 1943 they were again knocked down, this time by a tank, and once more re-built, this time at the expense of the War Office. They were finally demolished on 9 May 1959. Aldrich Road, the thoroughfare leading eastwards off Banbury Road, still becomes Wentworth Road as it enters the area built by the city corporation. This is the only trace that now remains of one of the most contentious housing *causes célèbres* of the twentieth century.[27]

The word *bungalow* originally meant a peasant hut in rural Bengal, and came to be applied to a house in India intended for Europeans.[28] The first single-storey buildings in Britain to be called bungalows were built at Birchington, Kent, in 1869. The term came to mean a speculatively built holiday home at the seaside, often a prefabricated building. In the 1920s and 1930s bungalows of conventional construction were built in large numbers on low-cost land and often as part of ribbon development along the radial routes out of towns. To the east of London there were large estates at Upminster and Hornchurch, and to the west an estate at Colnbrook (TQ 0277) which particularly offended aesthetic sensibilities. Anthony King's study of this type of dwelling identifies bungalow colonies near other cities, Moreton in the Wirral (SJ 2690) on Merseyside, Whitesand Bay (SX 4051) near Plymouth, and Withernsea (TA 3427) near Hull. Bungalows were the characteristic means by which the just-comfortably retired colonised the coastline, and large numbers were built at Clacton, Worthing, Bexhill and Herne Bay. The bungalow provoked violent language. Ramsey Macdonald in 1929 said that 'every day ... some offensive bungalow ... destroys not only the immediate spot where it is placed, but the whole sweep of the countryside'. Sir Thomas Sharp, the town planner, expressed his annoyance in 1932:

> Every little owner of every little bungalow in every roadside ribbon thinks he is living in Merrie England because he has those 'roses round the door' and because he has Sweet Williams and Michaelmas Daisies in his front garden.... [The] bungalow now stands for all that is vile and contemptible.

One of the attractions of Petts Wood was the developers' promise that no terraces or bungalows would be built there. Conversely the bungalow was popular, and was lauded in the words of a Henry Hall song: 'Three little things are all I desire, dear ... a bungalow, a piccolo and you'. A concentration of inter-war bungalows raises many questions about how the land became available for building, whether the bungalows were constructed by a builder to standard designs or by the purchasers, and about building materials.

Since the mid-eighteenth century some employers had provided housing for their workers, and this tradition continued through the inter-war period, and even into the 1950s. Stewartby and Silver End are considered in this chapter because they accommodated the workers who made building materials. There were other examples in southern England: the village in Surrey (TQ 0962) built from 1917 by William Whiteley, the department-store entrepreneur who styled himself 'the universal provider', for his company pensioners; Kemsley in Kent, built in 1925–26 by Bowaters for workers at their paper mills; and Woodbridge Hill, Guildford, where Dennis Brothers Ltd built 223 houses for their motor workers. East Tilbury (TQ 6879) on the Essex marshes is an astonishing company village. It was built from 1933 to the designs of the Slovak architects Vladimir Karfik and Frantizek Cahura for the company established by the footwear manufacturer Tomas Bata from Zlin in Slovakia. All the building materials except for bricks and mortar were imported from Czechoslovakia. At Stratford-upon-Avon a terrace of houses for workers at Flowers' brewery was built on Birmingham Road (SP 198553) in 1938 to the design of the Modernist architect F. R. S. Yorke. William Beardmore, the Clydebank shipbuilder, built 59 tenements and 12 semi-detached villas for his workers between 1904 and 1914, and a further 71 tenements during the First World War. The most significant company villages of the twentieth century accommodated coal miners (*see Chapter 3*), and the National Coal Board was still providing houses for its employees in the 1950s, as was the Stanton Iron Company, which built 560 houses for its workers at Kirk Hallam (SK 4540).

Plotland settlement

The plotland was the antithesis of the neatly planned council estate, the idyllic half-timbered private development and the company village. It was the twentieth-century continuation of the centuries-old English tradition of squatting on land unused by its owners. Sir Thomas Sharp commented in 1948 when discussing Catshill on the fringe of Birmingham: 'Round most of the great cities of England there are extensive districts whose disordered appearance expresses in a physical form the conflict that has existed during the last few decades between the competing uses to which land may be put.'[29]

Plotland settlement was stimulated by low agricultural land values – it was difficult to make a living in the 1920s and 1930s by farming on unfavourably situated land of indifferent quality. By the 1920s intending plotland settlers had access to a wealth of twentieth-century building materials: asbestos sheets and tiles, redundant military huts, bus bodies and, particularly, railway carriages. *Railway Magazine* in 1922 published an article explaining that an individual could purchase a five-compartment carriage body from the carriage sidings of the LSWR at Micheldever, Hampshire (SU 519435), for £20. The company would take it to the works at Eastleigh, where the bolts securing the body to the frame would be loosened, and then deliver it to any of its stations, where the body could be rolled on to a lorry or cart to be delivered to a site prepared with a few brick piers. The writer pointed out that larger dwellings could be created by using several carriage bodies, perhaps ranging them in parallel and roofing over the space between, or by adding verandahs. He concluded:

> A home in an old coach is not to everyone's taste, of course, but it has many good points, not the least of which is that its owner can be more or less independent. Given an ingenious man and an old railway coach, there is no limit to the comfortable, useful and inexpensive dwellings which may be planned.[30]

Hardy and Ward showed in 1983 that plotland settlements were widespread on many parts of the south and east coasts, in the Thames and Lea Valleys around London, in the Severn Valley between Stourport and Bridgnorth, and on Kinver Edge (SO 8383) in the west midlands. They also flourished around Marple, Mottram and the Macclesfield Canal in the north-west, in locations like Pickmere, Rudyard Lake, Hazel Grove and Ludworth Moor. The landscape of the plotlands of the 1930s can be observed along a trail at Dunton Hills. In the north-east unemployed miners' families, dispossessed of their homes, lived in sheds and pigeon crees on allotments, while George Orwell noted a settlement of old single-decker buses along the canal in Wigan.[31] The density of plotland settlements created by people from the East End of London around Laindon and Pitsea was the reason for the designation of the area as the

New Town of Basildon in 1949. Hardy and Ward argued convincingly in *Arcadia for All* that plotlands were important expressions of libertarian ideals, that they provided fulfilling experiences for townspeople, and that they foreshadowed the rapid spread of owner occupation and regular holidays in the second half of the twentieth century.

Plotlands were anathema to post-Second World War planners, and after 1947 it became almost impossible to establish new settlements. Most of those on the coast were cleared under the wartime Defence of the Realm Act, and most were never rebuilt. Nevertheless, many traces of plotlands can be found. Plotland settlements which evolved in various ways in the second half of the twentieth century can be recognised in many places between Dungeness and Hastings, and further west between Bexhill and Eastbourne. In many places haphazardly created homesteads of the inter-war period have been replaced by factory-made portable buildings, and many settlements on the coast or in river valleys have evolved into caravan sites. Many settlements that originated as plotlands can be observed from the Severn Valley Railway, including a well-preserved hut close to the station at Highley (SO 749830).

Building materials

The housing boom depended on the large-scale production of cheap bricks. In 1881 brickmakers at Fletton near Peterborough discovered that the 10 per cent content of oil in the Oxford Clay enabled bricks fashioned from it to be fired with very little additional fuel. Brickworks similarly situated on the Oxford Clay became the chief source of bricks in southern England. The industry prospered, using large Hoffman kilns, and, from 1901, mechanical clay excavators. During the 1920s many of the smaller firms in the region were taken over by the London Brick Company, established at Fletton by John Cathless Hill in 1889, and incorporated in 1900. The company's *Phorpres* (i.e. four press) brick was introduced in 1901. By 1923 LBC controlled all the major brickworks in the Peterborough area, and was operating a total of twenty-seven separate works in the late 1930s. The company's chairman in the early twentieth century was Halley Stewart, who with his son P. Malcolm Stewart established a model village from 1927 adjacent to the LBC brickworks at Wootton Pillinge in Bedfordshire. The name of the spacious, well-ordered village was changed to Stewartby (TL 0242) in 1936, when the company was employing 2,000 people to produce 500 million bricks a year. The brickworks at Bletchley (SP 8532), in the angle between the railways to Euston and Oxford, was established in the 1890s by Thomas George Read. At first hand-made bricks were manufactured but the works was taken over by LBC in 1905, and Fletton-style bricks were being produced by the 1920s. The works at Calvert (SP 6823) alongside the Great Central Railway was built in 1905 by Arthur Itter, and taken over by LBC in 1937. He is commemorated by Itters Terrace, twelve cottages built in 1904–5. The road between Lidlington and Marston Moretaine, below the Greensand Ridge, is lined with monuments to the Marston Valley Brick Company Ltd, another of the providers of bricks for the great rebuilding of rural England in the inter-war period and for the housing boom of the 1950s. The company's two-storey 7-bay headquarters building (SP 9939), with its name imposingly carved above the entrance, remains amid a landscape of deserted clay pits, some of them flooded, that supplied the Lidlington brickworks, which flourished between 1929 and 1977. The road is lined by company houses with steeply pitched clay-tile roofs, while near Millbrook railway station stands the Marston Valley Social Club, in a faintly Modernist style with metal-framed windows.[32]

The folklore relating to Calvert and Bletchley in the 1930s revolves around out-and-back-in-a-day journeys to building sites around London and along the south coast, a much-repeated, and possibly apocryphal, incident being the discovery by the transport manager of drivers playing cricket in the early afternoon following the completion of their deliveries while their vehicles were parked in a lay-by at Runnymede. Through the 1920s and 1930s bricks were moved by hand at almost every stage of manufacture, but the nature of the work was transformed from 1947–48 with the introduction of fork-lift trucks. Stewartby remains in operation, but Calvert and Bletchley closed in 1991. The pits at Calvert were used in 1999 for the disposal of refuse from London and Bristol delivered by container train.[33]

The other great concentration of brickworks lay south of Peterborough, extending about 3 miles south from Fletton High Street (A605) to the village of Yaxley, bounded on the east by the B1091 road, and bisected by the A15 and the Great Northern Railway Main Line to London. Two brickworks remain in operation: Beebys works, with a single chimney, alongside the railway in Yaxley (TL 192938), and the Orton Works, with three chimneys, west of the A15 (TL 168936). Some quarries remain as lakes, some are landfill sites, others, already filled, have been adapted to form picturesque settings for superstores and telemarketing centres, with such names as Serpentine Way and Cygnet Park. Contractors' roads across the sites of future warehouses are surfaced with crushed bricks. The buildings of one former brickworks form a depot for a haulage concern. The ribbon-developed housing clusters around the northern and eastern sides of the clay pits. It reflects the growth of brickmaking from the 1880s until the 1960s, terraces from the late nineteenth century, shorter terraces and semi-detached pairs from the inter-war period, and a spacious development in Yaxley of the 1950s. Two substantial buildings remain as evidence of brickmaking's prosperous past: the rather pompous three-storey Phorpres House (TL 197967), now called Phorpres Court and divided into apartments, and the Phorpres Social Club, a two-storey five-bay structure, with metal-framed windows and a concrete porch, which stands alongside the A15 against a western backdrop of land cleared for redevelopment.

Portland cement, the invention of Joseph Aspdin in the 1820s, gained acceptance slowly, but by 1900 it was rapidly displacing lime in the building trade, and cement manufacture was one of the keys to the two house-building booms of the twentieth century. The main concentrations of works were in the Medway Valley, in Essex, and in the Rugby area. Cement production peaked at 7.7 million tonnes in 1938, but the growing use of concrete ensured that this figure was comfortably exceeded soon after the conclusion of the Second World War, and the post-war peak of production was 19.7 million tonnes in 1973. The technology of the industry

changed during the twentieth century and there are few remains of obsolete plant, not least because large rotary kilns are of steel construction and have a high scrap value. A considerable number of works stood derelict in the 1990s, long after they had ceased production, at Pitstone (SP 9315), Bletchingdon (SP 4817) and Harbury (SP 3958), for example. Production was concentrated in very large plants like those at Barrington near Cambridge (TL 3950), Westbury in Wiltshire (ST 8852), Clitheroe (SD 7543), Ketton (SK 9805) and Penyfford (SJ 2962). Chalk slurry is conveyed from the Chilterns to the modern works at Rugby (SP 4976) by a pipeline, opened in 1965, replacing the trains which rattled along the West Coast Main Line, on dry days trailing clouds of white dust, whether loaded or empty.[34]

Metal-framed windows were used in an increasing proportion of the houses built in the 1920s and 1930s. They were vigorously promoted and became one of the symbols of the inter-war housing boom. One manufacturer claimed in 1939 that they had 'grown up with the English tradition of building', that they had been used in 'every English-speaking country ... and some others as well', and that they pleased women by providing an abundance of light, and because their modern appearance fitted in with schemes for curtains and furnishings, and were easy to clean. Dimensions were standardised in 1919. Typical forms were the curved 'turret' at the corner of a bow window installation, the window that extended round the corner of a house, the 'porthole' and the window whose underside reflected the pattern of a staircase. Steel-framed windows could be fitted with leaded lights, or arranged in bays with wooden surrounds. The windows provided by Henry Hope Ltd for an estate of 100 modest three-bedroomed semis in Cambridge in 1939 cost £10 13s per house.

The two most significant suppliers of such windows were Crittall and Henry Hope. Crittall Ltd, a company conscious of its modern and progressive image, sprang from a nineteenth-century ironmongery business at 27 Bank Street, Braintree (TL 757231), which was taken over by Francis Barrington Crittall in 1849.[35] His son Francis Henry (1860–1934) began to manufacture windows in 1884, and formed the Crittall Manufacturing Company in 1889, opening a new factory in Manor Street,

Braintree, five years later. The company supplied windows for Ford car factories in Detroit in the first decade of the century, and in 1909 began to make windows from steel in a form that could be rolled only in Germany or Belgium. The factory was involved in munitions work during the First World War, when F. H. Crittall was impressed by the notion of mass production. He opened new factories at Witham (TL 822155), in 1919, and at Heybridge, Maldon (TL 858078), in 1922, and by 1926 his labour force exceeded 1,600. Some sixty-five houses for employees were built at Clockhouse Way, Braintree (TL 722230), from 1919. They were Modernist in design, with concrete and steel construction, flat roofs, steel-framed windows of standard sizes, doors of pressed steel, with metal staircases and built-in furnishings. A fourth factory, specialising in small window fittings made by automatic and semi-automatic machines and transferred to other works by lorries, was built on a 220-acre (90ha) estate at Silver End (TL 809197), purchased in 1925. Around the Silver End factory Crittall created a model village of just under 500 houses. It is best known for the thirty-two houses in the International Modern style (but of brick construction, rendered over) designed by Frederick McManus, and for houses in the same idiom designed for members of the Crittall family by Sir Thomas Tait, but about two-thirds of the houses in the village are in a Garden City Georgian style. In 1989 the activities of the Crittall company were concentrated in a factory at Braintree, and the works at Witham and Braintree were demolished. The Silver End factory is now occupied by a subsidiary company, but the village remains as archaeological evidence of many characteristic features of British industry in the 1920s and 1930s: the chance location of large industries in small towns where entrepreneurs happened to have prospered; the survival into the twentieth century of a tradition of entrepreneurial philanthropy exemplified in earlier generations by Robert Owen, Sir Titus Salt and George Cadbury; the role of factories in the provision of increasing numbers of houses; the hygienic, streamlined, progressive image associated with the housing industry, expressed in the Modernist dwellings; and also, through the Georgian-style houses, the industry's hankering after tradition.

8.4
The factory of Henry Hope Ltd, makers of metal window frames, at Halfords Lane, Smethwick, photographed in 1939.

Henry Hope of Smethwick, the other principal manufacturer, arose from the most traditional of roots – the metal trades.[36] The company was established in Lionel Street, Birmingham, in 1818, and through the nineteenth century was known for fabricating non-ferrous metals, including the bronze windows for the Houses of Parliament, supplied in 1845–57, and for horticultural work, including the frames for the hot-houses at Osborne. A catalogue specifically devoted to metal windows was published as early as 1887, and in 1905 the first stage of a new works, on a 17-acre (7ha) site in fields, was constructed along the west side of Halfords Lane (SK 023895) on the northern edge of Smethwick. By 1939 the factory consisted of six main blocks, an administrative building with a landscaped entrance off Halfords Lane, the south works used for making casement windows from steel and aluminium, and a range of single-storey brick sheds fronted on the corner of Halfords Lane and Dartmouth Road by a two-storey streamlined range. To the west of the administrative building stood a brass shop, while to the north were a pressed-metal department, a lantern light department, and the north works, where specialist windows were made and steel bars received. Only a few of the single-storey sheds now remain alongside Halfords Lane. The corner site is occupied by a vehicle-hire concern with a new building; a six-storey office block has replaced the administrative building; and most of the site is managed as The Hawthorns, an industrial park taking its name from the nearby football ground for whose spectators it provides match-day parking.

Housing was changed by many other new twentieth-century materials. Concrete tiles, far less expensive than clay tiles or slates, came into widespread use in the mid-1920s. Slabbed concrete fireplaces faced with tiles were mass-produced in the 1930s by companies such as Bells of Northampton. Stained glass was mass-produced for use in doors and porthole windows. Millboard, made from woodpulp, was invented by D. M. Sutherland in 1898 and first made in a factory at Sunbury on Thames. Plasterboard, a sandwich of gypsum plaster between two layers of thick paper, was patented in the United States in 1894. Manufacture in Britain began at Wallasey with the establishment of British Plaster Board Ltd in 1917. By the 1930s the company had a works at Erith, supplied with gypsum from its own quarries at Robertsbridge. Plasterboard was extensively used in the 1930s, and was much employed in the construction of military and other accommodation during the Second World War. Particle board, in which shredded wood is mixed with urea formaldehyde, was first widely used after 1945. The clinker block came into widespread use during the Second World War, and was subsequently the most commonly used material for internal partitions.[37] Plastics were increasingly used in the 1960s, polystyrene for insulation and polythene for pipes. A knowledge of building materials provides a foundation for the understanding of the housing of the twentieth century, as of any other period. It is also important for archaeologists to comprehend the sources of materials, to recognise that they do not fit readily into categories like 'the brick industry' or 'the lime and cement industry', and to identify the relevant sites.

The post-war period

The rate of house building recovered slowly after the Second World War, constrained by shortages of materials and by wartime distortions of the labour market. An increasingly significant factor was the impact of the planning legislation of 1946 and 1947. The need for 'planning' in the post-war world had been asserted in the many propaganda media of the closing months of the war. Many of the assumptions of the Garden City movement were now codified in statutes: green belts, the zoning of housing and manufacturing, overspill programmes and the creation of New Towns by unelected development corporations. The government felt uneasy about housing, not least because the austere standards of accommodation in wartime hostels were demonstrably better than those to which many working-class people were accustomed, and because ex-service families had shown impatience with unused military housing and camps and, following a centuries-old tradition, begun to squat in them.

The symbol of the housing programme in the immediate post-war period was the *prefab*, a term which, like *spiv*, *snoek*, *nutty slack*, and other features of the age of austerity, gained a pejorative meaning. Nevertheless, oral evidence suggests that prefabricated housing was widely welcomed. The United Kingdom Temporary Housing Programme was established in 1944, provided over 156,000 temporary bungalows in England, Scotland and Wales by March 1949, and was wound up almost unnoticed in 1956.[38] The houses provided under the programme had been widely publicised. An example of the prototype, the Portal Bungalow, named after the Minister of Works, was shown in the Tate Gallery from May 1944, and others were exhibited in Scotland, and in Cairo, for the attention of the British troops who remained in Egypt. The prototype was not put into production but was intended to indicate to manufacturers the intentions of the government.

The houses built under the programme were bungalows of four principal types. The Arcon, designed by the firm of architects responsible for the Transport Pavilion at the Festival of Britain in 1951, incorporated an innovative roof of steel tubing, a steel frame, sheet cladding by Turner Asbestos, windows by Crittalls and service cores made by Fisher & Ludlow, manufacturers of motorcar bodies, and resin glues, of the kind used in the Mosquito aircraft. Nearly 40,000 Arcons were constructed by Taylor Woodrow, some on very large estates

at Shrublands in Great Yarmouth, at Newport (Gwent) and at Kirkconnel, Dumfriesshire (NS 7312). The Uni-Seco prefab was manufactured by the Selection Engineering Company, mass-producers of timber huts for the military during the Second World War. It had a timber frame clad with asbestos sheets and a timber roof of shallow pitch, with a plasterboard ceiling beneath. The Tarran prefab was produced by the company owned by Robert G. Tarran, builder of Quarry Hill Flats (*see above*). He had supplied huts also to the military, and his prefab was constructed with panels of Lignocrete, concrete made with Portland cement and chemically treated (and thus inert) sawdust aggregate. The most widely built prefab was the Aluminium Temporary Bungalow, the prototype of which was exhibited at Selfridges in the summer of 1945. Nearly 55,000 were built in four years. It was the work of aircraft designers, and was built at five wartime aircraft factories: the Vickers works at Blackpool and Chester; the Bristol factory at Weston-super-Mare; Blackburn Aircraft at Dumbarton; and A. W. Hawksley of Gloucester (*see Chapter 7*). The bungalow was prefabricated in four sections, and could be lifted on to a prepared site by a 5-ton crane. It had four sections, and is recognisable by the cover strips over the joints between them. The frame and roof were of extruded aluminium, the cladding of aluminium sheet, the window frames of rolled aluminium and the floor of tongue-and-groove boarding.

8.5
An example of the Modernist houses of the inter-war period that can be found in most parts of Britain: Bungalow A at Whipsnade, designed by Berthold Lubetkin.

(Crown copyright. NMR)

8.6
An estate of prefabs of the late 1940s at Bridgemary, alongside the railway between Fareham and Gosport in Hampshire.

(Collection of Brian Malaws)

The first three bungalow types had a design life of up to 15 years, and the Aluminium Temporary Bungalow was designed to last 40 years. In the event over 67,000 remained in occupation in 1964, and in some areas many survived to be purchased by tenants under the Housing Act of 1980. The archaeological trace of many prefab estates is the existence of an enclave of local authority or housing association dwellings built at any time in the last four decades of the century, surrounded by the rather more solid permanent housing of the immediate post-war period. The difference in brickwork is usually striking. The later houses indicate that prefabs once occupied the site. In some cases aluminium or asbestos panels re-used in outbuildings, or concrete slabs used in boundary walls, are indicative of the prefabs that earlier had stood there. Some prefabs are still in occupation, and appear likely to remain so, in Dolce Road in Northampton (SP 723618), in Wolverhampton, in Stafford (SJ 935221), in Bristol and in Ludlow (SO 523752). The future of the 647 prefabs remaining in Newport, Monmouthshire, was the subject of debate in 1999. The largest concentration in London in 1999 was the Downham estate in Catford, where 185 remained in occupation, many of them heavily customised. Others have been adapted as garages or outhouses. The best-known surviving prefab is the Arcon V, displayed at the Avoncroft Museum of Buildings (SO 951683), demolished at Yardley, Birmingham, in the summer of 1981 and re-erected a year later. Prefabs are displayed also at Duxford and St Fagan's, Cardiff, and several in Wake Green Road, Birmingham, have been listed.

Prefabrication was used also in the building of two-storied and permanent houses. In 1943 the Ministry of Works bought a 6.5-acre (2.6ha) site on Edward Road, Northolt (TQ 114833), where in the following year thirteen pairs of experimental semi-detached houses of several different types were constructed of non-traditional materials, including concrete slabs and non-fines concrete (*see below*), cast in situ, as well as a pair of control houses of conventional brick construction. The Department of Health built a similar group of demonstration houses in the 1940s at Sighthill, Edinburgh, while the Building Research Station constructed experi-mental semi-detached dwellings in Bucknall's Close, Abbot's Langley, Hertfordshire.

8.7
A British Iron & Steel
Federation house at
Crowmore Road,
Shrewsbury.

(Photo: Barrie Trinder)

Two of the semi-detached pairs built at Northolt comprised British Iron & Steel Federation (BISF) houses, designed by Sir Frederick Gibberd (1908–84), with steel frames and partial steel cladding, and a design life of up to sixty years.[39] More than 30,000 BISF houses were built – Cubitts constructed 502 on the LCC's estate at Oxhey in 1946–48, Derby Corporation built 150, and some of the 390 constructed in Coventry can be observed from the railway between Tile Hill (SP 2877) and Canley. They are likely to remain in occupation well beyond their intended three score years.

The Airey House, designed as early as 1925 by the Leeds builder Sir Edwin Airey (1878–1955), consisted of single-storey 4in. x 2.25in. concrete posts positioned at intervals around the perimeter, clad with 3ft x 1ft reinforced concrete blocks, each weighing 35 pounds, which were cast in vibrating aluminium moulds. Prototypes were built at Seacroft, Leeds. Airey Houses were manufactured in the late 1940s at nine sites, including the Royal Ordnance Factories at Chorley, Glascoed and Bridgwater, and Airey's own works at York. The components for a pair of houses could be loaded on to five lorries, and erection could be completed within two weeks. The Airey House was said to resemble the traditional American frame house made familiar to the British public in Hollywood films.[40] There were both pitched-roof and flat-roofed examples and they were built in pairs or in four-dwelling terraces. About 20,000 Airey Houses were built, many of them in rural areas. Examples have been noted on the west side of the A483 at Ruabon (SJ 306440), at Clee Rise, Ludlow (SO 523752), and at Sawtry (TL 170835). In the last two decades of the century many Airey Houses lost their distinctive appearance when the discovery of corrosion in an example damaged by fire in Bradford in 1981 led to a programme of rebuilding.

A third type of prefabricated house of the late 1940s and early 1950s was the Cornish Unit house, developed by the English China Clay Company, with walls constructed from units made of concrete in which the aggregate was fine sand, the waste material from china clay pits, and roofs of dark, reddish-brown, concrete tiles.[41] The first of the type was a bungalow erected at Bugle in 1945. A subsequent two-storey pair at Menage Villas, St Austell, favourably impressed Aneurin Bevan, the Minister of Health. Standard designs were finalised in 1946 and more than 40,000 Cornish Unit dwellings were built by local authorities in the following decade. Characteristic two-storey pairs with Mansard roofs can be seen in many towns, and on some estates, as in Hereford (SO 498388), there are three-storey apartment blocks. Cornish Unit houses can be recognised in many towns, although many are now clad. Examples have been noted at Nant-y-Bwlch north of Tredegar (SO 130108), at Clipstone (SK 596635), at Banbury (SP 444406) and at Hereford (SP 499388).

John Laing & Co. improved the design of the Easiform house of the 1920s (*see above*), which used standardised shutters for the erection of poured-concrete cavity walls, and in the first ten years after the end of the Second World War constructed 47,000 for local authorities.[42] Well

8.8
Cornish Unit houses
at Bilsthorpe in the
Dukeries coalfield,
Nottinghamshire.

(Photo: Barrie Trinder)

over 100,000 Easiform houses had been built
before the system was withdrawn in 1971.
In 1951–52 Easiform houses were being built
in Cambridge, Carlisle, Plymouth, Swindon,
Bristol, Leicester and Bradford. Variants on
standard forms included three- and four-
storey flats, bungalows for elderly persons,
and parades of shops surmounted by flats.
Many of those employed to construct Easiform
houses were Polish ex-refugees.

Several other types of prefabricated house
were constructed in considerable numbers.
Glasgow Corporation had a factory which
produced 10ft x 8ft 8in. x 6in. panels which
were used in the construction of many flat-
roofed houses in the late 1940s. Derby
Corporation was proud that a pair of the 100
Trusteel Houses it built were constructed within
twenty-one days. The No-Fines House, built by
pouring concrete made without sand or other
fine aggregate (hence, no fines), was designed
by Wimpey. Prototypes were erected at Northolt
(*see above*) and in Field End Road, Eastcote,
Middlesex, in 1945. Many No-Fines Houses
have brick fronts, and are difficult to distinguish
from conventional buildings. Wimpey built
more than 6,000 No-Fines for Coventry
Corporation before 1958, and in the mid-1960s
contracts included the Rivers Estate at Walsall,
and 1,052 dwellings on the Trowbridge Road
estate in Cardiff. About 30,000 No-Fines were
built by Wates. There were many in Cwmbran
New Town, where they were cast on site from
huge concrete mixers, and in Derby and
Walsall.[43] The Hill House had a lightweight
steel frame clad in coloured concrete blocks or
bricks. Cranwell Houses also had steel frames,

fabricated at the Lea Bridge Steelworks in
Leyton. The Stent House was constructed
from concrete slabs made by the Stent Precast
Concrete works at Dagenham Dock. Orlit
Houses, built to a pier-and-panel system using
concrete slabs attached to reinforced-concrete
frame members, could have either flat roofs
or pitched roofs, and were built for the LCC
at Headstone Lane and at Chingford, for Poplar
Borough Council on the Glengall Grove estate
on the Isle of Dogs, and at Dudley Fields,
Walsall.[44] The Reema House, made of hollow
pre-cast concrete panels, designed by the
architects Reed & Malik, was introduced in
1948. Over 20,000 were built by 1962, together
with more than 300 village halls using the
same constructional techniques.

Other types of prefabricated house were
developed and built in Scotland. The Weir
House was a steel-clad bungalow erected
on dwarf concrete walls, but production was
abandoned after the construction of prototypes
in Glasgow and Edinburgh and a batch of
about 100 dwellings. Many more examples
were built of the Weir 'Quality' House, a two-
storey dwelling, also of steel construction. Some
1,500 were built in Scotland, the first 1,000 with
flat roofs, the remainder with pitched and tiled
roofs. The Cruden House designed in 1946 had
a steel frame clad with 2-inch-thick concrete
slabs. Some 3,000 were built for Scottish local
authorities at a factory at Coatbridge. Over
17,000 Orlit Houses (*see above*) were built in
Scotland by the Scottish Orlit Company, whose
factory was at Sighthill, Edinburgh. The firm
of R. G. Tarran, builders of the Tarran prefab
in England, adapted the former dyeworks of
Pullars of Perth to produce the Dorran House,
a single-storey dwelling, the external walls of
which were storey-high concrete slabs. Some
2,500 had been built by 1962.

It was widely assumed that prefabrication
was an emergency expedient, that once
the post-war housing crisis had passed
conventional construction would once more
become the norm. As early as the autumn of
1948 a commentator on LCC cottage estates
remarked: 'Apart from these prefabricated
structures there is a growing number of
traditional types which will eventually acquire
predominance.' During the 1950s interest in the
prefabrication of conventionally grouped semi-
detached houses and short terraces diminished.

Most conventionally constructed council houses of the immediate post-war period are spacious and well provided with garden space, if rather rugged in appearance, and constructed from bricks of indifferent quality. Modestly priced private houses of the same period are not strikingly different from those of 1939. In Banbury, construction of the estate centred on Grimsbury Square (SP 465415) was abandoned in 1939 and recommenced after the war. The post-war houses are uniformly of London Brick Company combed bricks, while pre-war houses have side and back walls of Flettons, and front elevations of better-quality bricks, with some hanging tiles, which appear not to have been used on the later houses. Concrete canopies over the front doors, and windows of much simpler design than those of the 1930s are other features of the post-war houses, but the differences have to be sought in the detail. During the 1950s conventionally built council houses and modestly priced dwellings built for owner occupation came to have much in common. Many were built in what has been called the 'Anglo-Scandinavian' style, with simply designed front elevations, with large areas of glass and either hanging tiles or cedar matchboarding.[45] The boyhood home of Sir Paul McCartney, 20 Forthlin Road, Allerton, Liverpool, opened to the public by the National Trust in 1998, is a good example of a simple council house of the 1950s.

The planning ideals of the post-war period can best be studied in the twenty-eight New Towns[46] constructed under Lord Silkin's New Towns Act of 1946. New Towns were contentious, and the contentiousness often crossed party political lines. The development corporations that created them were appointed by government, not elected, and their powers over-rode those of local councils, and challenged the authority of big city corporations. New Towns were offensive to the prevailing political outlook of the 1980s and 1990s, and none of the development corporations has survived into the twenty-first century. Most of the first generation, designed after the 1946 Act, were logical successors to Letchworth, modest-sized and economically balanced communities, mostly near London, with factories zoned away from housing, much of which had Garden City features. Peterlee, Washington and Newton Aycliffe were designed to counter the decline

of coal mining in the north-east. The designation of Corby was intended to relieve the area's dependence on the steel industry. Most of the second generation of New Towns in the 1960s were intended to accelerate economic growth free from the bureaucratic ties of existing authorities. Milton Keynes fitted neatly into the M1 corridor between London and Birmingham, and in Northampton, Peterborough, Warrington and Runcorn development corporations were established with some success in towns that were already sizeable. New Towns have great archaeological value. What seemed to be the most enlightened views about housing and society in the immediate post-war period can be observed in Sir Frederick Gibberd's housing at Harlow. Telford reflects the changing opinions of the 1960s and 1970s, its first estates at Sutton Hill and Woodside designed on the Radburn principle, intended to separate people from cars, their successors with curvaceous thoroughfares designed to minimise vehicle speeds, and idiosyncratic Postmodernist tower houses built around 1980. The later New Towns must be investigated resolutely, and on foot, if they are to be understood, since their main road systems are likely to be tree-lined 'parkways', making observation from a vehicle of housing or factories almost impossible. Milton Keynes in particular repays exploration.[47] Some of its housing, like the terrace of 1974–77 which follows the curve of the Grand Junction Canal at Pear Tree Bridge, and the timber-framed, aluminium- and plastic-clad terraces of Netherfield, are highly imaginative, and the industrial zones are the source of many characteristic products of the early twenty-first century, including WD40, animal vaccines and palm-top computers.

8.9
Characteristic New Town housing of the immediate post-Second World War period, at Peterlee, Co Durham.

(Crown copyright. NMR)

Tower blocks

Architects came to be excited in the early 1950s by the prospects of using prefabrication in the erection of multi-storey dwellings. In the principal cities of Scotland multi-storey apartment blocks had long been the characteristic dwellings of many middle-class as well as of the majority of working-class people. Multi-storey living had also been a feature of working-class life in central London since about 1850 – one of the pioneering apartment blocks of that period, designed by Henry Roberts, remains in occupation in Streatham Street near the British Museum. The practice of constructing multi-storey blocks was continued by several charities in the second half of the nineteenth century, most notably by the trust founded in 1862 by Henry Peabody, and was taken up by the LCC upon its establishment in 1898. While the LCC built suburban cottage estates in the 1920s and 1930s, it continued to provide multi-storey blocks in central areas, as did some of the London boroughs. The most notable LCC examples were Chamberlain House, Walker House and Levita House, five- and six-storey blocks containing in all 310 dwellings, constructed as part of the Ossulton estate near St Pancras in 1929–34. Most blocks of this kind were of traditional construction, with load-bearing walls, and rarely exceeded six storeys in height. One of the few Modernist blocks was John Scurr House, built for the Borough of Stepney, at the junction of Branch Road and Rose Lane, a six-storey structure with a steel frame, Truscon floors and prominent reinforced concrete balconies, and designed by the architects Adshead & Ramsey. It has been demolished. Kensal House in Ladbroke Grove, a four- and five-storey block designed by the Modernist architect Maxwell Fry, and completed in 1936, was a flagship of philanthropic development. It was financed by the Gas Light & Coke Co., owners of the adjacent gasworks, included a nursery school, a social club and a profusion of gas appliances, and featured as an example of enlightened practice in Sir Arthur Elton's film *Housing Problems*. In structural terms the most innovative pre-war tower blocks in London were in the private sector, Highpoint 1 and Highpoint 2 at Highgate, eight-storey buildings, designed by the Tecton practice,

which included Berthold Lubetkin, that had concrete box frames, stood on piloti, and were erected in a parkland setting among old trees.[48]

In the post-war period steel, and later concrete, frames offered new possibilities, and the construction of tower blocks came to be fashionable.[49] Such buildings depended on techniques for sinking piles for foundations and on tower cranes, the first of which appeared in Great Britain about 1950. Over 200 had been supplied by 1954, and whole projects came to be focused on the capability of a crane. Abelson & Co. of Sheldon, Birmingham, supplied Buildmaster cranes specifically for multi-storey construction. Before 1948 approvals were given in the United Kingdom for the construction of 81 blocks of public housing with six or more storeys, most of them in London. Gradually the number of approvals increased, reaching its peak in the five-year period 1963–67, diminishing rapidly after 1968 and through the 1970s, and ending with the virtual cessation of local authority house building during the Thatcher regime of the 1980s. In the course of this period over 6,500 blocks of local authority housing of six or more storeys were constructed, some 42 per cent of them in London, 13 per cent in Scotland and 7 per cent in Birmingham, but in the boom of tower-block construction they appeared in many parts of Britain, in county towns of modest size like Bedford, and, most grotesquely, in South Wales at Hirwaun (SO 955055), where building land can never have been expensive, being at a high altitude and exposed to westerly winds.

At first multi-storey dwellings appeared in 'point blocks', high towers within new estates that were principally of low-rise housing seen as conforming to an English tradition of housing in landscaped gardens, surrounded by trees. The first consciously designed point block was the ten-storey Mark Hall (TL 4610) at Harlow, designed by Sir Frederick Gibberd and built in 1950, but the most celebrated were the eleven-storey towers on the much-applauded LCC estate at Roehampton (TQ 2174).

From the late 1950s local authorities turned increasingly to 'slab blocks', large multi-storey towers that did not form parts of low-rise estates. The technological development of steel-and-concrete framing increased the potential height of buildings, but political circumstances and architectural fashions were also favourable

Pre-1948	81
1948–52	324
1953–57	694
1958–62	1,309
1963–67	2,935
1968–72	1,037
Post-1972	155
Total	6,535 [50]

Table 8.1
Construction of tower blocks by five-year periods.

Source:
M. Glendinning and S. Muthesius, *Tower Block: Modern Public Housing in England, Scotland, Wales and Northern Ireland*, London: Yale University Press, 1994

to tower-block construction. For local politicians in proud cities like Birmingham and Glasgow tower blocks offered an opportunity to house citizens within existing authority boundaries, avoiding government directions to reduce population by overspill schemes. Alderman Harry Watton asserted in 1959: 'Birmingham people are entitled to remain in Birmingham if they wish, and Birmingham industry has a right to remain in the city it has done so much to make great.' Some architects and planners came to reject the ideals of the Garden City movement and the achievements in the New Towns, and to argue that the sense of community in old neighbourhoods, identified most notably in Young and Willmott's 1957 book *Family and Kinship in East London*, and evidently lacking on suburban cottage estates, could be re-created in large blocks designed for both maximum privacy and maximum contacts, with 'bridges' linking the blocks, elaborate walkways at ground level or just above, and deck access. The apogee of this form of thinking was Park Hill, Sheffield, the first part completed in 1959 and the second (often called Hyde Park) in 1966. One of the councillors responsible for approving the design, which included a 19-storey block containing 678 dwellings, said that the development 'would create something of the picturesque fascination of Italian hill towns'. Contemporary architectural fashions reflected in tower blocks included 'Brutalism', the use of rough concrete surfaces commended in Rayner Banham's book of 1966,[51] to be seen in numerous developments of the period, and the exposure of the technology of buildings, expressed most typically in tower blocks by the provision of detached lift towers, like that in the highest block of council flats in London, the 99-metre-high, 31-storey Trellick Tower in north Kensington, designed by Ernö Goldfinger for the GLC, built in 1968–72, derided in the 1970s and fashionable in the 1990s.

The proliferation of tower blocks in the 1960s was dependent on the establishment by the principal contractors of factories for the prefabrication of the concrete frames of which most were constructed. Some were well-established factories. The Bison Company had been producing concrete floors since 1919, and began to produce pre-stressed building components in 1954, when it had factories in Green Lane, Ashford, Middlesex, at Stourton,

Leeds, at Dovehouse Fields, Lichfield, at Etna Road, Falkirk, and on the Sighthill Industrial Estate in Edinburgh. Girlings Ferroconcrete Ltd had works at Feltham, Middlesex, at Rothwell near Leeds and at Kirkintilloch near Glasgow. As early as 1948 the Liverpool Artificial Stone Company was offering to supply structural members for frame buildings from works at Wavertree, Rotherhithe and Trafford Park. Cementation Ltd had a factory at Bentley, on the northern side of Doncaster, and Tarmac Ltd at Ettingshall, Wolverhampton. John Laing & Co. had works at Andover, for the supply of projects in London, Heywood Junction near Manchester and Livingston in central Scotland. The Scottish company Cruden built a factory in Longhaugh Quarry, Dundee, adjacent to the huge development at Whitfield, from which it supplied parts for two 16-storey slab blocks and a high honeycomb-shaped range of 6-storey dwellings between 1968 and 1972. Other such factories remain to be identified. All the main developers had their own systems, some developed within the companies concerned, others used on licence, usually from foreign engineers. The most commonly used was the Bison wall-frame, used by Concrete Ltd. Once facilities for making concrete frames were established, it became imperative to build more tower blocks. The senior engineer of Glasgow Corporation, appointed in 1965, remarked: 'I had five large-panel firms situated round Glasgow – all sitting on my doorstep demanding a chance to build flats.'

Tower-block construction in the 1960s was influenced by individual officials and councillors, particularly chairs of housing committees. In some authorities there was tension between engineers, anxious to build large numbers of dwellings, and architects, who considered that tower blocks should be designed as part of an urban environment rather than ordered off-the-peg on design-and-build contracts from building companies. Councillors like David Gibson in Glasgow, Harry Watton in Birmingham and T. Dan Smith in Newcastle were influential, and to a large extent their actions were the result of popular pressure for new local authority housing. From all parts of the country, in large towns and small, it is evident that councillors were subject to pressure from people seeking rehousing for whom built-in cupboards, bathrooms, inside lavatories and

8.10
The tower blocks of
the Red Road estate,
Glasgow, photographed
in 1988.

*(Crown copyright.
Royal Commission on the
Ancient and Historical
Monuments of Scotland)*

plentiful electric power sockets, giving potential for the use of a variety of domestic appliances, were as attractive in a tower block as elsewhere. There was remarkable political unanimity concerning the desirability of building large numbers of dwellings. Building was encouraged by the Conservatives – from 1956 special government subsidies were made available for multi-storey developments, and Sir Keith Joseph at the Party Conference of 1963 suggested a target of 400,000 dwellings a year – but was carried out largely by Labour-controlled councils.

Outside of London the fastest rate of tower-block construction was in Glasgow, where blocks were built throughout the city wherever land was available. A series of ten 20-storey slab blocks was built by Cruden in 1963–69 on the waste tips of one of the city's principal manufactories of the Industrial Revolution period, the bleach works of Charles Tennant Ltd. One of the most chaotic schemes was the Red Road development, designed by the ambitious private architect Sam Bunton, a vivacious proponent of multi-storey building, who was ambitious to build the highest blocks in Europe. The first dwellings in the colossal 26- and 31-storey blocks were completed in 1966, after many troubles with the city's direct labour organisation, and pilferage on an enormous scale.

From 1968 the tide of tower-block construction turned. The most obvious cause was the partial collapse in that year of Ronan Point, one of nine 23-storey blocks at Mortlake Road (TQ 405812) in West Ham, built for the borough by Taylor Woodrow. Four people were

killed in the accident. There were other factors. The demand for new housing was easing. Some blocks had obvious and serious faults – condensation, malfunctioning lifts and rubbish chutes that were perpetually blocked. Others deteriorated through inadequate systems of management. Many Conservative councillors, elected in the years of the Labour government's unpopularity in 1967–69, regarded tower blocks as 'Socialist architecture' and sought to halt their construction. Among architects there was more interest in refurbishing existing housing, and a sense that much of value had been destroyed, along with virtually all the worst and unim-provable housing of the nineteenth century and earlier. Some tower blocks have been demolished, some with much publicity, including eight blocks at Kersal Vale, Manchester, in 1990; the towers of the Trowbridge estate in north London, one of which remained for a time as 'the leaning tower of Hackney'; two 15-storey blocks at Niddrie Marischall, Edinburgh, in 1991; and the Hutchesontown C Blocks in Glasgow, designed by Sir Basil Spence, which killed one bystander and injured four others when the blocks were felled in 1993. Some tower blocks in Dudley, a principal landmark of the Black Country, were demolished in the summer of 1999.

Glendinning and Muthesius visited all the remaining local-authority tower blocks as part of their survey of the subject in the mid-1990s, and concluded that most were in good condition and well managed. They pondered whether the degradation of some estates was the result of a betrayal of tenants by providers or of providers by tenants, or simply of bad management. Lord Hattersley, once involved as a Sheffield councillor with the provision of tower blocks, has justified them as a temporary expedient, an effective means of solving the slum problem quickly. There were many indications that skilful management was revitalising tower blocks in the late 1990s.[52] For the archaeologist the existence of some short-lived towers is indicated only by 'fossils', by the boundaries of the new housing which has replaced them. The majority remain, however, potent evidence of the power over housing exercised by local councils between the end of the Great War and the 1980s, and also of the way in which a speedy if flawed solution to the problem of urban slums was found in the 1960s.

With the demise of the tower block and the enforced retreat of local authorities from the management of housing in the 1980s, the provision of accommodation for the poor became the concern largely of housing associations, and the accommodation provided, though often imaginatively designed, resembles Victorian terraces rather than garden suburbs. Private housing became ever more bizarre as the post-war restraints on gables, timber framing and excessive ornamentation were abandoned in the 1980s in favour of houses constructed, in the Jacobethan style, of low-maintenance materials.[53]

Conclusions

There were two periods of particularly intensive building activity in twentieth-century Britain: the years between the General Strike and the outbreak of the Second World War, and the two decades that followed the coronation of Elizabeth II. Both periods had their successes and their failures. The majority of the homes built in the twentieth century still stand, and provide one of the best sources for the social history of the period, in particular of the assumptions of those who provided the housing, and of the lives of their occupants. Study of the archaeology of housing poses many questions. How is 'success' to be judged? Is it the popularity of the Trellick Tower in the late 1990s, the gentle dispersal along the bifurcating, tree-lined pedestrian ways of mothers taking home children from a New Town infant school, contented or perhaps discontented old age in a bungalow at Herne Bay, or the shimmering white but fortress-like villas of Petts Wood? The archaeology of housing is also the contemplation of paradox. It requires imagination and reflection rather than quick judgements. George Orwell remarked, after walking through the slums of Manchester in the 1930s: 'you think that nothing is needed except to tear down these abominations and build decent houses in their place. But the trouble is that in destroying the slum you destroy other things as well.'[54] Archaeology may help to identify the 'other things'.

Notes and references

1   Annual figures for house building are listed in Table A3 in the Appendix.
2   A. M. Edwards, *The Design of Suburbia*, London: Pembridge, 1981, p. 134; G. Orwell, *The Road to Wigan Pier*, Harmondsworth: Penguin, 1962, pp. 15–16.
3   C. Brown, *Northampton 1835–1985: Shoe Town, New Town*, Chichester: Phillimore, 1990, p. 116.
4   Edwards, op. cit., p. 91.
5   B. Trinder, *The Making of the Industrial Landscape*, London: Orion, 1997, pp. 248–52.
6   M. Miller, *Letchworth: The First Garden City*, Chichester: Phillimore, 1993; M. Miller, *Raymond Unwin*, Leicester: Leicester University Press, 1992, pp. 60–74. The section on Letchworth also draws on interpretive materials published by the First Garden City Museum.
7   Miller, op. cit., pp. 101–14.
8   M. Swenarton, *Homes Fit for Heroes: The Politics and Architecture of Early State Housing in Britain*, London: Heinemann, pp. 44–67.
9   D. Arrand, *The Austin Village*, Birmingham: Northfield Society, 1990.
10 Brown, op. cit. , pp. 141–2.
11 Swenarton, op. cit., pp. 85–99.
12 Ibid., pp. 135–40; C. L. Mowat, *Britain between the Wars 1918–1940*, London: Methuen, pp. 43–5.
13 A. Briggs, *A History of Birmingham*, Oxford: Oxford University Press, 1952, vol. 2, pp. 228, 235, 238, 306–8.
14 B. Rodgers, 'Manchester: Metropolitan Planning by Collaboration and Consent; or Civic Hope Frustrated?', in G. Gordon (ed.) *Regional Cities in the UK 1890–1980*, London: Harper & Row, 1986, pp. 44–6, 50–1.
15 R. Durant, *Watling: A Survey of Social Life on a New Housing Estate*, quoted in C. L. Mowat, *Britain between the Wars*, London: Methuen, 1955, pp. 230–1.
16 Mowat, op. cit., p. 230; Swenarton, op. cit., p. 161.
17 A. Rogers, *The Making of Stamford*, Leicester: Leicester University Press, 1965, p. 100; S. Mullins and M. Glasson, *Hidden Harborough: The Making of the Townscape of Market Harborough*, Leicester: Leicester University Press, 1985.
18 We are grateful to John McGuinness for access to pamphlets produced by John Laing & Co.
19 W. Smith and K. Beddoes, *The Cleobury Mortimer and Ditton Priors Light Railway*, Oxford: Oxford Publishing Company, 1980, pp. 39, 53.
20 Brown, op. cit., p. 142.
21 E. J. Burrows, *Derby*, Cheltenham: E. J. Burrows, 1951; I. Johnson, *Beardmore Built: The Rise and Fall of a Clydeside Shipyard*, Clydebank: Clydebank Libraries

22 A. Ravetz, *Model Estate: Planned Housing at Quarry Hill Flats, Leeds*, London: Croom Helm, 1974.

23 J. Betjeman, *John Betjeman's Oxford*, Oxford: Oxford University Press, 1990, p. 32.

24 M. E. Armstrong, *An Industrial Island: A History of Scunthorpe*, Scunthorpe: Scunthorpe Borough Museum & Art Gallery, 1981, pp. 138–48.

25 P. Oliver, I. Davis and I. Bentley, *Dunroamin: The Suburban Semi and Its Enemies*, London: Barrie & Jenkins, 1981, pp. 9–10, 23–5, 200–4.

26 C. Dendy Marshall, *A History of the Southern Railway*, London: Southern Railway, 1936, p. 484; A. Jackson, *Semi-Detached London: Suburban Development, Life and Transport, 1900–39*, London: Allen & Unwin, 1973, pp. 206–8. The account of Petts Wood is based also on fieldwork, and on pamphlets published by Basil Scuby & Co. and other firms, kindly loaned by Norman Nelson.

27 P. Collinson, *The Cutteslowe Walls: A Study in Social Class*, Oxford: Oxford University Press, 1963.

28 A. D. King, *The Bungalow: The Production of a Global Culture*, London: Routledge & Kegan Paul, 1984.

29 D. Hardy and C. Ward, *Arcadia for All: The Legacy of a Makeshift Landscape*, London: Mansell, 1983. Sharp's comment appears in *West Midlands Group, Conurbation: A Planning Survey of Birmingham and the Black Country*, London: Architectural Press, 1948, pp. 242–9.

30 *Railway Magazine*, 1922, vol. 43, pp. 366–9.

31 W. H. Shercliff, *Nature's Joys Are Free for All: A History of Countryside Recreation in North-East Cheshire*, Stockport, privately published, 1987, pp. 85–8; Orwell, op. cit., pp. 15–16.

32 A. Cox, *Survey of Bedfordshire Brickmaking: A History and Gazetteer*, Bedford: Bedfordshire County Council (with RCHME), 1979; F. E. Towndrow, 'Brickmaking', *DUC*, December 1936, pp. 40–4.

33 R. Cook, *Bucks Bricks: A History of the Bletchley and Calvert Brickworks and the London Brick Company*, Whittlebury: Baron Borch, 1997, p. 17.

34 Monuments Protection Programme, *Lime, Cement and Plaster*, London: English Heritage, 1997. We are grateful to David Eve of Kent County Council and to Chris Barney for advice on the cement industry.

35 A. Crosby, 'The Silver End Model Village for Crittall Manufacturing Co. Ltd', *Industrial Archaeology Review*, 1998, vol. 20, pp. 69–82.

36 The account of Henry Hope Ltd is drawn from pamphlets published by the firm, now in the library of the Ironbridge Gorge Museum. We are grateful to John Powell for bringing them to our attention.

37 K. Hudson, *Food, Clothes and Shelter*, London: John Baker, 1978, pp. 105–16.

38 B. Vale, *Prefabs: A History of the UK Temporary Housing Programme*, London: Spon, 1995.

39 Vale, op. cit., pp. 107–8.

40 I. Hay, *ROF – the Story of the Royal Ordnance Factories 1939–48*, London: HMSO, 1949, pp. 71–2; *The Builder*, 14 December 1945.

41 Hudson, op. cit., p. 105.

42 We are grateful to John McGuinness for access to pamphlet material relating to John Laing & Co., and for general advice on housing in the post-war period.

43 *The Builder*, 31 August 1945; P. Riden, *Rebuilding a Valley: A History of Cwmbran Development Corporation*, Cwmbran: Cwmbran Development Corporation, 1988, pp. 50–9.

44 *The Builder*, 18 September 1945.

45 Edwards, op. cit., p. 162.

46 Basildon (designated 1949), Bracknell (1949), Central Lancashire (1970), Corby (1950), Crawley (1947), Cumbernauld (195), Cwmbran (1949), East Kilbride (1947), Glenrothes (1948), Harlow (1947), Hatfield (1948), Hemel Hempstead (1947), Irvine (1966), Livingston (1962), Milton Keynes (1967), Newton Aycliffe (1947), Newtown and Mid-Wales (1967), Northampton (1968), Peterborough (1967), Peterlee (1948), Redditch (1964), Runcorn (1964), Skelmersdale (1961), Stevenage (1946), Telford (1963/1968), Warrington (1968), Washington (1964), Welwyn Garden City (1948).

47 N. Pevsner and E. Williamson, *The Buildings of England: Buckinghamshire*, 2nd edn, London: Penguin, 1994, pp. 498–570.

48 N. Pevsner, *The Buildings of England: London except the Cities of London and Westminster*, Harmondsworth: Penguin, 1952, pp. 314, 378–9; *Architectural Design & Construction*, September 1935 and April 1938.

49 The section which follows is based on M. Glendinning and S. Muthesius, *Tower Block: Modern Public Housing in England, Scotland, Wales and Northern Ireland*, London: Yale University Press, 1994. See also P. Wright, *A Journey through Ruins: The Last Days of London*, London: Radius, 1991, pp. 68–96; A. Sutcliffe (ed.) *Multi-Storey Living: The British Working-Class Experience*, London: Croom Helm, 1974.

50 Figures from Table 2 in Glendinning and Muthesius, op. cit., in which there is a slight discrepancy, the total figure appearing as 6,544.

51 R. Banham, *The New Brutalism*, London: Architectural Press, 1966.

52 *Guardian*, 6 January 1999, 8 February 1999, 11 February 1999.

53 H. Barrett and J. Phillips, *Suburban Style – the British Home 1840–1960*, London: MacDonald Orbis, 1987.

54 Orwell, op. cit., p. 62.

Chapter nine

Changes in transport transformed people's perspectives during the twentieth century. Journey times to overseas destinations were dramatically reduced by the development of airliners. North America, more than a five-day journey from Britain in 1900, could be reached within seven hours in 1999, or in half that time, though at great expense, by Concorde. Australia, six weeks away by sea in the first decade of the century, could be reached in about twenty-four hours in the 1990s. Within Britain, the reduction in city-to-city journey times was less dramatic, but motorways brought about a substantial reduction in journey times, while train services – of a frequency unimagined in 1900 – steadily changed people's social horizons from the 1920s onwards. The object of this chapter is to define the crucial moments of change in various forms of transport, and to highlight the archaeological record of transport in the twentieth century.

Changing horizons

the archaeology

of transport

Ships at sea

Many Britains in 1900 went in ships to the sea, not just to pass leisurely weekends but to do business across great waters. Britain's mercantile marine as well as the Royal Navy ruled the waves from coaling stations all along the international shipping lanes.

Most of the principal British ports of the nineteenth century had developed around wet docks, sheets of enclosed water entered by locks where ships could float at any state of the tide.[1] In the first generation of such docks goods were handled in multi-storey warehouses. The coming of railways and steam ships led to the development of facilities for bunkering ships with coal and the replacement of the earlier pattern of warehouses by transit sheds, although multi-storey buildings, like C. F. Lyster's twelve-storey tobacco warehouse at the Stanley Dock, Liverpool, with its 36 acres (15ha) of floor space, continued to be built for special purposes. Most ports by 1900 used hydraulic power to operate lock gates, lifting bridges, cranes, hoists and capstans for moving railway wagons. Most of the elements of this kind of dock system can be observed at the Albert Dock in Liverpool.

9.1
Nineteenth-century methods of working a port, photographed at Gloucester in the mid-1920s.

(Crown copyright. NMR)

Wet dock systems continued to be extended in the twentieth century. One of the most ambitious developments was the Great Central Railway's new port of Immingham on the Humber, with a 45-acre (18ha) wet dock set in a dock estate of 1,000 acres (400ha). The company's chairman, Sir Sam Fay, was knighted on the spot by King George V at the formal opening on 22 July 1912. At Liverpool a fifteen-year programme of expansion, during which many dock entrances were widened and concrete transit sheds constructed in the Sandon Dock, was completed in 1907, and the 54-acre (22ha) Gladstone Dock was first used in 1927. The Port of London Authority, whose grandiose offices dominate Tower Hill, came into existence in 1909 following the recommendations of a royal commission, and began to extend the royal group of docks, completing the King George V Dock in 1921. Other docks named after the King were opened in Hull in 1914 and in Glasgow in 1931. The Corporation of Bristol had created a new port in 1877 at Avonmouth, where the Royal Edward Dock was opened in 1907, and there were further extensions in 1928. The opening of the Manchester Ship Canal in 1894 created a new seaport at Manchester, which after many difficulties became by 1914 the fourth British port in terms of the value of cargoes handled.

Many specialist handling facilities were installed in the early twentieth century. Tobacco warehouses were built at Bristol, as well as Liverpool, and one now houses the city's archives. Grain elevators were installed at Millwall in London, Manchester and Avonmouth, and by the 1920s overhead rail conveyors were taking meat directly from refrigerated holds to cold stores in the Royal Victoria Dock in London. Jetties for handling oil were constructed, one of the first being that at Saltend, Hull, built in 1906. Concrete silos for grain were constructed at Avonmouth and at Hull. Specialist facilities were also constructed for handling fish, the most notable being the vast concrete building completed by the LNER at Grimsby in 1934.[2]

Ports specialising in the export of coal were still being extended in the early years of the twentieth century. The only staithes that remain on the River Tyne – at Dunston – had been erected by the North Eastern Railway in 1893. The 52-acre (21ha) Queen Alexandra Dock in Cardiff was opened in 1907, and the Alexandra Dock in nearby Newport extended in 1907 and 1914. There was much investment in coal-shipping facilities in Scotland, with new docks at Burntisland in 1901, Leith in 1902, Grangemouth in 1906 and Methil in 1913. The 20-acre (8ha) Rothesay Dock at Clydebank, opened in 1907, was supposedly the first to be equipped with electric hoists for the export of coal and the import of iron ore.[3]

The symbol of sea transport in 1900, and for much of the century, was the ocean liner, a ship designed primarily to carry passengers at high speeds between continents, and to accommodate some passengers in great comfort.[4] The economic basis of the transatlantic liner trade before the First World War was the carriage of emigrants to North America. Between 1900 and 1914 some 12 million Europeans travelled in steerage and third class to the United States and Canada. The two principal British shipping lines, Cunard and White Star, faced competition from French and Dutch companies, and particularly from the German Hamburg–Amerika line. The most up-to-date ship on the North Atlantic in 1900 was White Star's 17,200-ton *Oceanic*, but the size of the largest ships increased rapidly in the years that followed. Cunard took delivery in 1907 of the 32,000-ton *Lusitania* and, in 1913, of the 45,600-ton

Aquitania. In 1911 White Star began to operate the 46,500-ton *Olympic*. It is tragically ironic that such a high proportion of the sparse archaeological record of the early-twentieth-century liner trade should be centred around the *Olympic*'s sister ship *Titanic*, which collided with an iceberg on her maiden voyage on 14 April 1912, with the loss of about 1,500 of the 2,200 people on board. The disaster has been analysed many times, in print and on film and television. The wreck has been explored, artefacts retrieved, testimonies of survivors collected from all over the world, and exhibitions have been staged in museums on both sides of the Atlantic. The disaster illustrates the extent of competition between shipping companies: one of the accepted reasons for the large number of lives lost was White Star's decision to reduce the number of lifeboats on the grounds that too many spoiled the appearance of the ship. What happened was also symbolic of the British class system: officers prevented steerage passengers from escaping through first-class areas, so that most of those who perished were emigrants. The loss of the *Titanic* has often been interpreted as a token of British decline, of the ill-founded arrogance which led the owners, though not the builders, to proclaim the ship unsinkable. The irony of the incident was aptly summarised by Thomas Hardy:

> Over the mirrors meant
> To glass the opulent
> The sea-worm crawls – grotesque,
> Slimed, dumb, indifferent.[5]

The legacy of buildings associated with the early-twentieth-century liner trade is more substantial, particularly on the waterfront at Liverpool. White Star's building, designed by Richard Norman Shaw (1831–1912), outside which crowds awaited news of the *Titanic*, was built on the eve of the twentieth century in 1895–98, but the three dominant buildings at the Pierhead were all built just after 1900. The Mersey Docks & Harbour Board's office of 1907 was designed by Arnold Thornley, with a Baroque dome on a steel frame provided by Dorman Long. The Royal Liver Insurance Company's building of 1908–11, designed by W. Aubrey Thomas, was of Hennebique concrete construction, and clad in grey stone. Cunard's building of 1915 has stone elevations in a Greek style on a Truscon concrete frame. The three

buildings show the importance of shipping lines, the harbour authorities and insurance companies. A further element in the pattern of liner travel, the railway, is missing. Riverside Station, whose first passengers, bound for Cunard's *Germania*, alighted on 12 June 1895, handled its last train on 25 February 1971, and most traces of it have now gone.[6]

The increasing size of ships threatened the future of Liverpool as a passenger port. Very large passenger ships were more easily handled at jetties than in enclosed docks, and they needed dry docks in which they could be maintained. The operation of Southampton, a port blessed with four high tides every 24 hours, had been taken over by the LSWR in the 1890s. The railway company constructed new deep-water quays, and in 1905 brought into operation the Trafalgar Dry Dock, which provided repair facilities for ships of greater size than could be accommodated in London or Liverpool. The White Star Line began to transfer its operations to Southampton in 1907, and a new Ocean Dock was first used by its new liner *Oceanic* in 1911, and by her sister ship *Titanic* the following year. Cunard began sailings from Southampton in 1919 and the United States line in 1921. In 1934, New Dock, actually a quay, was opened, providing berths for up to nine liners, and in 1933 an even larger maintenance facility, another King George V Dock, was commissioned. In the inter-war period Southampton was the principal port for transatlantic liners and for many of the services linking Britain with her empire overseas.[7]

The commissioning of the *Mauritania* and *Lusitania* in 1907 reduced the time taken for a transatlantic crossing to less than five days, but there were still pressures from wealthy passengers to reduce the New York–London time. Southampton-bound liners or those bound for Continental ports could discharge passengers by tenders at Plymouth, for which the LSWR had landing facilities at Stonehouse Pool and the GWR at Millbay Docks. The railway companies competed to rush them to London, and it was on a boat train that the GWR locomotive *City of Truro*, part of the collection at the National Railway Museum, possibly exceeded 100 mph on 9 May 1904; another crashed at excessive speed at Salisbury on the LSWR on 30 June 1906 with the loss of twenty-eight lives. Evidence of the importance of this kind of traffic is provided by the artificial harbour at Fishguard (SM 951389), with its innovative concrete sea-wall, built by the GWR and opened in 1906. The *Mauritania* was the first transatlantic liner to call there, on 30 August 1909; but as the shipping lines transferred to Southampton, Fishguard's potential as a stopping-point for liners proved disappointing, although it prospered as a ferry port for southern Ireland. Traffic from Plymouth continued until the early 1960s. The best evidence for its latter decades is provided by the eight luxurious special saloon coaches named after members of the royal family constructed by the GWR in 1931, five of which are preserved at Didcot and in Devon.[8]

Travel to continental Europe, Ireland, the Channel Islands and the Isle of Man in 1900 was by boat train and channel packet. Ferry ports rose and declined in the course of the twentieth century. In the first decade of the century on the west coast the GWR ran boat trains for passengers to Ireland to Birkenhead and, from 1906, to Fishguard, the LNWR to Holyhead and Liverpool, the Midland Railway to Heysham, where a new pier for the Belfast ferries opened in 1906, and the North British Railway to Silloth. A network of competing services linked Glasgow with steamers for Ireland, and also for Arran, Bute and the Mull of Kintyre. In the 1990s ferries connecting with electric trains remained a feature of the life of that part of Scotland, where the two outstanding legacies of earlier periods of operation were the spectacular railway station at Wemyss Bay (NS 194685), designed for the Caledonian Railway by James Miller in 1905, with an overall glass roof and a covered way to the ferry boats, and the 693-ton paddle steamer *Waverley* of 1946–47, which sailed on the Clyde each summer.

In England most railway links with ferries to continental Europe were focused on London. At various times in the twentieth century ferry ships sailed to France from Plymouth, Poole, Southampton, Portsmouth, Newhaven, Folkestone, Dover and Ramsgate, and to the Low Countries, Germany and Scandinavia from Queenborough, Sheerness, Tilbury, Harwich, Felixstowe, Great Yarmouth, Immingham, Hull and Newcastle. Dover remained the principal Channel port throughout the century. Large-scale improvements to the harbour were carried out by the Admiralty between 1897 and 1909, as part of which the SECR built Dover Marine Station (TR 321401) in the western docks, which was completed in January 1915, but not used for the purposes for which it was intended until after the First World War. Boat trains to Dover were distinguished by the inclusion of Pullman cars (*see below*), and by connecting trains from Calais direct to the Riviera. In 1922 a first-class passenger could leave Victoria at 11.00 and arrive in Paris at 18.35, or, after a night in a sleeping car, at Nice at 11.30 the following day. From 1929 this service was designated the 'Golden Arrow', and its passengers crossed the sea in *Canterbury*, the steamer dedicated to that service. After the financial crisis of 1931 the Golden Arrow carried non-Pullman passengers. The outstanding innovation of the inter-war period at Dover was the inauguration, on 4 October 1936, of direct sleeping car services between London and Paris using the train ferry to Dunkirk. One of the vehicles built for the service by the international sleeping car company CIWL is preserved at the National Railway Museum, which also shows a short film entitled *Night Ferry*. A ferry service for freight wagons between Harwich and Zeebrugge began in 1924 (*see Chapter 7*).[9]

The nature of intercontinental travel changed in the inter-war period. The restriction of immigration into the United States from 1924 led the shipping lines' marketeers to target Americans of modest wealth, and 'steerage' became 'tourist class'. New liners were oil-fired, and older vessels like *Aquitania*, *Mauritania* and *Majestic* were converted to burn oil rather than coal. The ocean liner was one of the icons of the period. That Cunard and White Star sailed to North America, Union Castle to South Africa, and P&O to India and Australia, was common knowledge among children reared as subjects of the British empire, even though in peacetime most could have had few expectations of travelling on such services. A more realistic prospect might have been to spend time at the LMSR holiday camp at Prestatyn (*see Chapter 10*), the structures of which were modelled on those of a liner.

One project came to symbolise many aspects of the period. In 1930 Cunard ordered a new vessel, job number 534, from John Brown's shipyard at Clydebank, but the recession forced the abandonment of construction in December 1931, by which time the hull was towering over a landscape of unemployment on the north shore of the Clyde. In April 1934 the government provided funds which enabled work to continue, contingent upon the merger of the rival Cunard and White Star Lines. The ship was named *Queen Mary* and launched in September 1934, and the 80,750-ton liner made her maiden voyage in May 1936. The *Queen Mary* became part of the English language, the point of comparison with Britain's most prominent power station (*see Chapter 3*) and the name of the 60ft trailer used for transporting aircraft in the Second World War (*see Chapter 7*). When Esavian in 1946 wished to draw attention to the door installed in the hangar for the Bristol Brabazon aircraft at Filton, the company described it as 25ft longer than the *Queen Mary*. Two popular board games of the late 1930s were '*Queen Mary* Ahoy' and '*Queen Mary* Steering Round Great Britain'. The ship was conservative in design. There was little use of welding, and Cunard took pride in her millions of rivets. The interiors were comfortable rather than stylishly Modernist. She achieved the first transatlantic crossing in less than four days in August 1936. During the Second World War *Queen Mary*, like other liners, was painted grey and zig-zagged across the oceans, visiting such ports as Cape Town, Singapore and Sydney, carrying thousands of soldiers on each voyage, rotating the use of bunks with continuous service of

9.2
The *Queen Mary* under construction at Clydebank.

(*Crown copyright. NMR*)

meals in the dining rooms. On one journey in July 1943 she carried 16,683 troops from New York to Gourock. On 2 October 1942 she sliced through the cruiser *Curacoa* off the north coast of Ireland with the loss of 338 lives. For the first two years of peacetime she ferried GI brides to the United States, with the swimming pool used to dry nappies. *Queen Mary*'s first post-war voyage from Southampton to New York took place on 31 July 1947, and her last, in the return direction, on 22 October 1967. She remains at Long Beach, California, in use as a hotel, a symbol of many aspects of mid-twentieth-century Britain. Her slightly larger sister ship *Queen Elizabeth* was all but complete at the outbreak of the Second World War, and did not make her maiden civilian voyage, from Southampton to New York, until October 1946.[10]

After the Second World War sea travel seems to have returned to normality. A congregation of four or five liners at Southampton was awe-inspiring. A voyage from central London to Greenwich, or a walk along Waterloo Road and Regent Road from the Pier Head to the Gladstone Dock in Liverpool, revealed multitudes of cargo ships and, except during industrial disputes, intense waterside activity. Many of these ships were, for a generation, the 7,176-ton Liberty ships, of which 2,710 were built in Britain, Canada and the United States during the Second World War, based on a design by Joseph L. Thompson & Son, Sunderland, which involved much welding and prefabrication. Two Liberty ships are preserved in the United States.

At Southampton a new Ocean Terminal was opened on 31 July 1950, a 1,297-ft-long (395m) structure, with two storeys linked by 21 lifts and 4 escalators, housing reception and customs facilities on the first floor and platforms for two boat trains at ground level. In 1957 the Port of London Authority opened a similar facility at Tilbury for passengers on P&O and Orient Line sailings. A new 842ft (257m) quay was built on the site of jetties built for PLUTO (*see Chapter 3*) during the Second World War. The building had a distinctive series of shell roofs, five on each side of a central viewing gallery. Tilbury was important for both outward and inward migration. Many thousands of Britons in the early 1950s left on P&O's older ships, like the *Ranchi*, on assisted passages to Australia, while in 1948 it was the arrival point of the *Empire*

9.3
The Ocean Terminal
at Southampton,
opened in 1950.

(Crown copyright. NMR)

9.4
Liners, including
the *Queen Mary*,
at Southampton,
photographed in 1966.

*(Southampton City
Council, Cultural Services)*

Railway responded by introducing a car ferry, the *Autocarrier*, in 1931. Townsend's service was revived after the Second World War, in 1950. Subsequently British Railways opened a car-ferry terminal in 1953, offering a service to Boulogne, the only French port equipped at that date with the necessary facilities. The development of ramps to enable the rapid loading and unloading of vehicles owed much to the systems used on landing craft in the Second World War. During the 1950s and 1960s roll-on, roll-off methods were extended to freight traffic. In 1956 British Transport's ships carried 500 lorries over the channel – by 1972 the total had increased to 80,000. The roll-on, roll-off installations for trucks at Felixstowe began operation in 1965. The ports were orientated away from rail and towards road traffic, and in 1999 ferries carrying trucks were sailing from almost every significant east coast and south coast port.[12]

The railways to Folkestone and Dover were electrified in 1959 and 1962, and, as wealthier passengers were attracted to the airlines, the special character of boat trains was lost. Ordinary coaches replaced the second-class Pullmans on the Golden Arrow in 1965, and the train ran for the last time on 30 September 1972. The Night Ferry ceased operation in 1980.

Another far-reaching change was the substitution for traditional screw-propelled motor ships of faster unconventional vessels. On the Boulogne–Dover crossing ferries were supplemented from 1968 by hovercraft which required wide concrete landing 'beaches', while jetfoils began to operate alongside ferries to and from Ostend. On longer routes, like those between Holyhead and Ireland and Harwich and the Hook of Holland, where there were overnight sailings on which it was possible to book sleeping cabins, the advent of faster vessels, High Speed Ships (HSS) or SeaCats (i.e. catamarans) in the 1990s completely changed established patterns of operation.

The greatest change of the century in communications with continental Europe was the opening of the Channel Tunnel in 1994. Eurostar trains linking a new Waterloo, designed by Nicholas Grimshaw, with Paris and Brussels brought a standard of comfort to such routes that had been lacking since the withdrawal of the Golden Arrow and the Night Ferry, while the shuttle trains through the Tunnel attracted many cars and lorries from the ferries.

Windrush, bringing to Britain the first party of 492 immigrants from the Caribbean.[11]

Likewise there seemed to be a return to normality on routes to continental Europe. The Golden Arrow Pullman service recommenced in October 1946, when a new vessel, the *Invicta*, began to carry its passengers across the Channel. The Night Ferry was revived from December 1947. The 'mail boats', *Cambria* and *Hibernia*, with the appearance of miniature Cunarders, from 1954 carried passengers on alternate nights from Holyhead to Dun Laoghaire. Nevertheless, the nature of short-distance sea travel began to change radically in 1953.

Services for carrying motorcars over the Channel were inaugurated from Dover in 1928 by the Townsend Ferry Service. The Southern

Between 1958 and about 1972 the nature of trans-oceanic travel changed completely. In the summer of 1957 Cunard alone was operating twelve liners on the North Atlantic. In October 1958 Boeing 707 airliners began direct flights between New York and London. Within six months the airlines had secured 65 per cent of transatlantic passenger traffic, a proportion which increased to 95 per cent by 1965. The last England cricket team to travel to Australia by sea left in the autumn of 1958. The government was operating twenty-one troopships in 1951, but ceased in 1960 to carry soldiers by sea in peacetime in its own vessels, and in chartered ships in 1962. The shipping companies sooner or later withdrew from the liner trade, Canadian Pacific in 1971, Union Castle in 1977. New large passenger ships, like *Queen Elizabeth II*, delivered in 1969 after many difficulties during trials, were designed for cruising, a trade which had its origins in the 1930s when Canadian Pacific, which could not operate services up the St Lawrence in winter when the river was frozen, used the 42,350-ton *Empress of Britain* for round-the-world cruises. Cunard's 34,100-ton *Caronia* of 1948 was specifically designed for winter cruises in warm waters. The largest cruise liners of the 1990s eclipsed the size of the Cunard 'Queens' of the 1930s. The sight of the new 70,000-ton, German-built *Oriana* at Southampton in 1995 was impressive, but cruising is an international, not a British, industry, and is based principally in the Caribbean.[13]

The closure of the Suez Canal following the war of 1956 led to an increase in the size of oil tankers, and of bulk carriers – the ships that move grain, iron ore and coal between continents. Such traffics had always required specialist facilities, but the larger vessels could call only at deep-water facilities like those for tankers at Milford Haven, Fawley, and Finnart on the Clyde, the facilities for iron ore at Port Talbot, Immingham, Teesside and Hunterston, or the grain terminal at Seaforth Dock, Liverpool.

The handling of general cargo was transformed during the 1960s. The use of pallets that could be handled by fork-lift trucks began in the 1950s, and was particularly important in the timber trade. Fork-lift trucks required smooth dockside surfaces rather than the traditional setts. Containers had been employed on railways in Britain from the 1920s, and there were earlier precedents. Tarred crates to contain deck cargoes had been used by the US forces in the Second World War. The container revolution in shipping began in the late 1960s, one of its indications being the inauguration of a short-haul service from Tilbury to Continental ports. New types of ship were built, like the Encounter Bay class and the Liverpool Bay class, which were reaching the ends of their useful lives only in the late 1990s. Standard sizes of container for sea trade were agreed in 1970, the year in which containers came to be used for trade between Europe and Australia by Ocean Containers Ltd (OCL), a consortium of companies that had previously operated traditional cargo vessels on the route. Container vessels from the beginning could spend 80 per cent of their time at sea, while traditional cargo liners spent about 40 per cent of their time in ports.[14] The principal ports were transformed as facilities for large container ships were constructed. The dock at Tilbury, east of London, originally dating from 1886, was extended, and ships ceased to use the upstream enclosed docks, which soon closed – St Katharine's in 1968, the London group in 1969, the Surrey Commercial Docks in 1970, and the West India, Millwall and Royal groups in 1978. Cargo handling on the Clyde moved from Glasgow to Greenock. Felixstowe, a harbour of no particular eminence when it was bought by the grain factor H. G. Parker in 1951, opened its container terminal in 1968, and expanded to become Britain's busiest container port. The ports of Glasgow, Manchester, Gloucester and Preston ceased to operate. Some ports which had previously been commercially insignificant, like Ramsgate, Portsmouth, Shoreham, Poole and Watchett, found new and expansive roles, while others, like Goole, where the import of motorcars replaced the export of coal, were successfully adapted to new functions.

9.5
The hub of London's overseas trade in the late twentieth century: the port of Tilbury, photographed in 1994.

(Crown copyright. NMR)

The archaeological record of ways of working ships is uneven. Many features of past landscapes remain. The Liverpool waterfront is one of Britain's architectural treasures. Many wet docks form features of new post-industrial landscapes like Canary Wharf and Salford Quays. Warehouses in most major ports have been converted to apartments or offices. The emphasis on conservation in ports has naturally been on buildings and structures of the nineteenth century and earlier rather than those of the twentieth century. The Ocean Terminal at Southampton has been demolished. Dover Marine station was no longer used in 1999, and boat trains had ceased to traverse the steeply graded line from Folkestone Junction to Folkestone Harbour (TR 234457).

9.6
The industrial landscape of the port of Avonmouth, photographed in 1986.

(Crown copyright. NMR)

Nor have all the changes been to the modes of operation of the first half of the twentieth century. Container-handling facilities installed at Avonmouth, Manchester and Holyhead in the 1960s and early 1970s have disappeared. While some aspects of the container revolution, like the Liverpool Bay ships, proved long-lived, some have proved transitory. The preservation of large ocean-going ships is expensive, and the only twentieth-century examples in Britain are warships. Fortunately the models of ships made for owners and builders provide a comprehensive record of twentieth-century shipping that can be admired at the National Maritime Museum, Greenwich, the Merseyside Maritime Museum, and the museums at Glasgow and Newcastle.

Road

In 1900 England was criss-crossed by white roads from whose unbonded surfaces clouds of dust were set in motion by the first generation of motorcars. In March 1904 there were 8,000 private cars in Great Britain, 5,000 buses and 4,000 goods vehicles, all of which were obliged by the Motor Car Act of 1903 to carry number plates, with combinations of letters relating to towns and counties which are still current. The first great change of the twentieth century came in most counties before 1914 when county surveyors directed the bonding of surfaces, and the white roads of England became black. In Kent Sir Henry Maybury (1864–1943), County Surveyor from 1904, began tar spraying on main roads in 1906, and introduced tarred macadam in 1910. By 1914 the road system was being used by over 100,000 cars. The first motor omnibus had begun to work in London just before the century began, in 1899.

Large-scale road improvements in the years before the First World War were confined largely to urban areas. In London several schemes combined the construction of new thoroughfares with the elimination of insanitary houses. The best known was the building of Kingsway, completed in 1905, but Sir Algernon Osborn directed a large-scale scheme round Cobb Street in Spitalfields in 1899–1904. The principal road bridges of the early twentieth century were the transporter bridges, across the Mersey at Runcorn (SJ 510835), completed in 1905, over the Tees at Middlesbrough (NZ 501213), completed in 1911, and at Newport (Monmouth), over the mouth of the Usk (ST 318862) in 1906. Significantly, two of the other principal bridge projects of the period, the Queen Alexandra Bridge in Sunderland (NZ 396574), of 1909, and the crossing of the Trent at Keadby (SE 840105), completed in 1916, carried rail tracks as well as roads. The construction of special buildings for selling and servicing motorcars had already begun. Some showrooms were parts of the principal motorcar factories built in the Edwardian period (*see Chapter 5*) but some, like Mitchell Motors in Wardour Street, London, which had a lift for cars, and Darracque's Showrooms of 1914 in New Bond Street, were independent operations. The most significant pre-war building providing services for motorcars was that of the Michelin Tyre Company in Fulham Road, opened in 1905.[15]

Roads in Britain changed dramatically in the inter-war period. Main roads were classified by number, many with A- and B-prefixes, which were still in use at the end of the 1990s. Signposts displaying the new road numbers, and the signs and huts erected by the Automobile Association (AA) and the Royal Automobile Club (RAC), proliferated. The number of licensed private cars increased from 110,000 in 1919, to 474,000 in 1924, 981,000 in 1929, 1,308,000 in 1934 and 1,944,000 in 1938. A substantial proportion of the new roads built in the period were in the conurbations, designed to ease traffic flows in central areas, like the Headrow in Leeds, built between 1926 and 1932, or to enhance links with suburbs, like the highways connecting Manchester with Wythenshawe (see Chapter 8) or Queen's Drive in Liverpool, the 6.5-mile (10.4-km) peripheral boulevard from Sefton Park (SJ 379867) to Walton (SJ 358949). The most ambitious urban scheme was the construction in 1934 of Silvertown Way and the Silvertown By-pass in east London. The former incorporated what is thought to be the first road traffic flyover to be constructed in Britain (TQ 397811). Silvertown Way was incorporated in a new pattern of dockland roads in the 1990s but the Silvertown By-pass was demolished in 1995. The North Circular Road, an arc of 26.9 miles (43.2 km) around London, north of the Thames, between the A4 to Bath and the A13 to Southend, at a radius of about 7 miles from Charing Cross, was officially opened in July 1934 when much of its route was lined with fields that the road made ripe for development. By the 1990s it linked many sites which exemplified twentieth-century culture: Wembley Stadium, the Brent Cross shopping centre, many supermarkets, the Walthamstow greyhound racing track, the streamlined Ace Café built in the late 1930s and base in the 1950s for dare-devil bikers riding Triumphs and Nortons, and the statue of John Lennon over the entrance to a nightclub in Bounds Green.[16]

The characteristic road of the 1920s and 1930s was the by-pass. The pressures of motorcar traffic from London to the coast had by 1930 already resulted in the construction of by-passes around Eltham, Dartford, Bexleyheath and Sidcup. To the west of

London, the Brentford By-pass, completed in 1925 and better known as the Great West Road, became a focus for industrial growth, as did Western Avenue, while the construction of the Sutton By-pass in the early 1930s enabled the LCC to develop the St Helier estate (see Chapter 8). Colchester, Winchester, Coventry, Oxford and Shrewsbury were among the historic towns from which traffic was diverted via by-passes. Osbert Lancaster characterised the Tudor-revival style of domestic building as 'by-pass variegated', and many of the by-passes of the 1920s and 1930s all too easily stimulated residential developments that diminished their effectiveness as through routes. In some cases service roads were built parallel to the main highways, but in others, as on parts of the Shrewsbury By-pass, drives from many domestic garages run directly on to the trunk road.

Other new roads had a wider regional significance. The East Lancashire Road (the present A580), built in the early 1930s, was just part of what was intended as a network of dual-carriageway roads linking the principal towns in Lancashire. Its completion was inhibited by disputes between local authorities, and several dual-carriageways built in Manchester in the 1930s end at the boundaries of councils which refused to co-operate with the city corporation. In the west midlands the outstanding road of the 1930s was the 'Wolverhampton New Road', the dual-carriageway (now the A4123) running from a junction with the Hagley Road in Birmingham (SP 012853) almost to Wolverhampton (SO 921965). Optimistic post-war planners forecast that it might become 'one of the finest parkways in England'. A road that perhaps does deserve that title is the A423 between Bix (SU 725853) and Henley-on-Thames, built by Oxfordshire County Council in the late 1930s.

9.7
The Ace Café on the North Circular Road, an Art Deco building of 1938, famous as the resort of motorcyclists in the 1960s. It closed in 1969 and became a tyre warehouse, but such was its fame that motor-cyclists still resort there on occasion, and there are proposals to re-open it.

(Crown copyright. NMR)

9.8
The Scherzer-style road-and-rail bridge over the River Trent at Keadby, Lincolnshire, opened by the Great Central Railway in 1916.

(Photo: Barrie Trinder)

9.9
The transporter bridge across the River Tees at Middlesbrough, completed in 1911.

(Photo: Barrie Trinder)

Some major road bridges were completed in the 1920s and 1930s. Two important steel bridges in the north-east were the New Tyne Bridge (NZ 253637) of 1925–28, linking Newcastle with Gateshead, and the Wearmouth Bridge (NZ 396574) of 1929, which replaced Rowland Burdon's iron bridge of 1796. Some major crossings were achieved with concrete structures, including that which carries the Farningham By-pass over the River Darent (TQ 548672) on the A20, the four-arched Royal Tweed Bridge at Berwick, designed by L. G. Mouchel and completed in 1928, and the bowstring bridge at Ballast Hill, South Shields (NZ 360675). One of the 'flagship' road-building projects of the period was the Mersey Tunnel, begun 1925 and opened in 1934, which from the beginning was electrically lit and had ventilation towers with something of the look of New York skyscrapers.

Few of the first-generation wayside facilities remain along the by-passes of the inter-war period. The most enduring monuments are roadhouse inns. J. B. Priestley commented:

> Some of them are admirably designed and built, others have been inspired by the idea of Merrie England popular in the neighbourhood of Los Angeles ... some have bowling greens, some advertised their food, others their music.

9.10
The Tyne Bridge in Newcastle, completed in 1928.

(Crown copyright. NMR)

9.11
The Bluebird Garage,
330–340 King's Road,
London, built in 1924
for the Bluebird Motor
Company to the design
of Robert Sharp.

(Crown copyright. NMR)

Many, by the 1990s, had been demolished or adapted to new purposes. An outstanding survivor is the Black Horse on the Bristol Road in Northfield, Birmingham (SP 020795), completed in 1929 to the design of Francis Goldbrough. It has the appearance of a rambling, timber-framed, Tudor mansion. The Modernist Nautical William (SO 771833), on the Bridgnorth–Kidderminster road in Shropshire, built in 1937 for Derick Burcher, a 'live wire' in the motor industry, and intended to look like the superstructure of an ocean liner, was a 'postmodernised' nursing home in 1999.[17]

Motorcar showrooms and garages catering for wealthy motorists were the focus of much interest in big cities. They reflected a period when motoring was to a large extent an exclusive activity, and provided facilities akin to those of first-class travel by rail or sea. Almost all such buildings have now been put to other uses. The Bluebird Garage at 330–340 King's Road in London, designed by Robert Sharp (1881–1950) and completed in 1924, had capacity for 300 cars, and segregated lounges for ladies, gentlemen drivers and chauffeurs. It later became an ambulance station. The Daimler Car Hire Garage in Herbrand Street, near the Russell Hotel, was designed by Wallis Gilbert & Partners and opened in 1931. It could accommodate about 500 vehicles, ramps giving access to the upper floors. In 1999 the building

was a terminus for tourist coaches. The Olympia Garage in Kensington, designed by Joseph Emberton and opened in 1937, was even larger, with eleven mezzanine floors, providing space for about 1,000 cars. Perhaps the best example of a filling station of the period was Golly's Garage in Earl's Court Road, opened about 1935, magnificently adorned in decorative tiles, with an elaborate canopy to protect the staff from the elements.[18] Buildings of this kind were found less frequently in the provinces. One example was the showroom of Morris Garages in St Aldates, Oxford (SP 515057), in the Classical style but with much plate glass, and curving ramps to enable cars to reach the first floor. In 1999 it was part of a magistrates' court.

Roadside amenities for the less-well-off motorist of the 1930s had a very different appearance. Remnants of the untidy, disorganised, raucous world of inter-war road travel had almost totally disappeared by the 1990s, kept alive only by sporadic mobile snack bars in converted vans or buses plying their trade in lay-bys. That world, brought to an end by the planning legislation of the late 1940s, is captured in the photographs collected in the late 1920s and early 1930s by the Council for the Preservation of Rural England, which show café buildings heavy with advertisements, 'Michelin men' lodged in the branches of wayside trees and filling stations, unmercifully forced into historic buildings in towns. 'To many people', declared the Design and Industries Association, 'the petrol pump is the symbol of ugliness'. Ironically, the CPRE collection includes also examples of good practice in Amsterdam and Düsseldorf, submitted by Frank Pick (*see below*). In just a few places, particularly at strategic crossroads and above and below steep hills, it is possible to see traces of the disordered landscape of inter-war road travel. Prees Heath, Shropshire (SJ 555380), for example, at the junction of the A41 and A49, on land which was historically common, where a military camp had been built in the First World War, was developed to service road transport in the inter-war period. Its surviving buildings in 1999 included a mock-timber-framed wayside inn, a cottage tearoom, a Modernist building which now serves as a truck stop, and a former lido, now used for car auctions, together with a measure of bungaloid sprawl.[19]

9.12

Symbols of the 1920s:
a filling station and a
cinema, both apparently
accommodated in older
buildings, at Lutterworth,
Leicestershire, *c.* 1929.

*(University of Reading:
Museum of English Rural
Life, CPRE collection)*

Britain's first kerbside petrol pump, the invention of the American Sylvanus F. Bowser in 1905, was supposedly installed at F. A. Legge's garage in Shrewsbury in 1914. A bulk tanker to deliver motor spirit to pumps was employed for the first time in 1919, the year in which the first purpose-built filling station was opened by the AA at Aldermaston. Most filling stations of the 1920s were corrugated iron sheds, although there were some zany exceptions – a filling station in the style of a cottage at Colyford, Devon, and the pagoda-like Park Langley Garage at Beckenham. From 1932 a joint-marketing operation by Shell-Mex and BP led to the adoption by oil companies of distinctive liveries, and increasing standardisation. Self-service pumps were introduced in 1963, but their number increased rapidly in the 1970s, making the canopy, protecting the customer from rain, an essential feature of the filling station.[20] New features controlling traffic appeared in British streets throughout the twentieth century: bus stops in 1913, white lines in roads at Ashford, Kent, in 1914; automatic traffic lights in Princes Square, Wolverhampton, in 1927; Belisha beacons in 1934; zebra crossings in 1951; yellow roadside lines prohibiting parking at Slough, in 1955.

The new roads were used by public transport as well as by private motorists. Over 100 new tramway systems were constructed in the larger towns in the first decade of the twentieth century, and most existing systems, previously worked by horses, steam or cable haulage, were electrified. London's first electric trams began to run in 1901, and a new tramway was opened in 1903 to serve LCC's Totterdown estate at Tooting. The systems in Cardiff, West Bromwich and Rochdale were electrified in 1902, those in Darlington and Derby in 1904. More than 300 tramway systems were operating in 1914. The first trolley bus services in Leeds and Bradford were introduced on 20 June 1911, and after the First World War trolley buses took over many tramway routes. Trams also faced competition from motor buses. Tramway patronage reached its peak in 1927–28, but the number of undertakings was already declining – 34 systems closed in the 1920s, 81 in the 1930s, 23 in the 1940s and 20 in the 1950s. Nevertheless, in London, Leeds, Manchester, Sheffield and Birmingham, the tramway system was developed in the inter-war period, with lines on reserved tracks running out to the suburbs. The almost complete demise of the tramways came in the 1950s. Trams ceased to run in Birmingham in 1953, in Edinburgh in 1956, in Leeds and Liverpool in 1957, and in Glasgow in 1962. The last London services, in 1952, were poignantly commemorated by the film *The Elephant Will Never Forget*. Trolley bus operation ceased in London in the early 1970s. For the century's remaining decades the only flourishing urban tramway was that from Squires Gate, along the front at Blackpool, to Fleetwood. Tramways revived in the 1990s, in Manchester in 1992, in Sheffield two years later, and between Birmingham and Wolverhampton and at Croydon in 1999. The vehicles used on the older tramways, many of them actually built in the nineteenth century, and magnificently restored, work in a former quarry at Crich (SK 346548) in Derbyshire, while trolley buses perform, rather less frequently, at Sandtoft near Doncaster (SE 148081). Remnants of tramway shelters remain in some towns, Northampton and Dover for example, and some tramway depots survive, most of them having been converted to bus garages. The outstanding building of this type is the bus depot at Stockwell in south London, a concrete structure with a huge area of unsupported roof, built to the design of Adie, Button & Partners in 1951–52.[21]

The network of country buses expanded rapidly in the 1920s and 1930s, stimulated initially by the availability of low-cost ex-military vehicles from Slough. Some country carriers bought buses and continued their traditional trades of taking parcels and passengers between town and village. Small concerns tended to be taken over by larger companies like Thames Valley, Scottish Motor Traction and Crossville. Some were able to use purpose-built bus stations like that in Durham, which has since been removed to Beamish, or the combined garage and bus station built by Maidstone & District Traction at Hawkhurst (TQ 764305). In most towns facilities for bus passengers were of an ad hoc nature: loading bays marked out by kerbstones in a market place, as at Gloucester Green in Oxford, or a makeshift shelter in front of a town hall, as at Banbury. In Brecon (SO 048283) the focus of road-passenger transport until after the Second World War was a coal wharf alongside the canal. A coal merchant who used it was the first operator of buses in the town. In the early

1990s the wharf was still ringed with collapsing temporary buildings, by then of considerable age. One had been the Old Oak Tearooms, one an ice-cream parlour, and another a base for the repair in the winter months of the steamrollers used by the contractor who maintained the county's roads. An adjacent building on the main road, the Watton, was a fish-and-chip shop in the inter-war period, profiting from the trade of bus passengers.[22]

Long-distance motorcoach services originated in 1905 when open-top double-deckers began to work between London and Brighton. There were few services before the First World War, but they developed rapidly afterwards, and 300,000 people went to Blackpool by coach on August Bank Holiday in 1919. Coach companies were able to pick up passengers in the suburbs of big cities, which was particularly advantageous in their competition with the railways for seaside traffic. By 1930 there were scheduled daily services from London to most cities, the longest journey being to Glasgow. The low cost of coach travel opened up the seaside to people previously unable to afford the journey. In the east midlands companies like Trent and Lincolnshire Road Car linked Nottingham with such resorts as Skegness, Mablethorpe and Great Yarmouth. J. B. Priestley experienced a guilty pleasure travelling in coaches, finding them 'voluptuous, sybaritic, of doubtful morality.... They offer luxury to all but the most poverty-stricken. They have annihilated the old distinction between rich and poor travellers.' From 1927 Black & White, which worked services to London from Cheltenham, began to co-operate with other firms, among them Greyhound Motors, based in Bristol, Midland Red from Birmingham, Red & White from South Wales, United Counties from Northampton and Royal Blue from Bournemouth, in offering connections at Cheltenham. The partnership was formalised in 1934 as Associated Motorways. A purpose-built coach station, from which it was possible to travel to most parts of Britain by departures just after midday, was opened by Black & White in 1932. In the same year the Victoria Coach Station, designed by Wallis, Gilbert & Partners, was opened in London. Long-distance coach services were effectively nationalised after the Second World War, but privatised and de-regulated in the 1980s. Their subsequent demise is evidenced most clearly in

9.13 *(top)*
The Barton Transport Company bus and coach depot in Nottingham, faced with terracotta by Hathern.

(Ironbridge Gorge Museum: Hathern collection)

9.14 *(bottom)*
A filling station forced into an older building at Theale, Berkshire, *c*. 1929.

(University of Reading: Museum of English Rural Life, CPRE collection)

the demolition of Cheltenham's coach station. The fast services from London to towns within a radius of about 30 miles, branded as Green Line, were commenced by the London General Omnibus Company in 1930, and passed to the LPTB three years later. There were few comparable services from provincial cities. Archaeological evidence of Green Line's operation includes the coach station at Windsor, designed by Wallis, Gilbert & Partners, which opened in 1933 with space for sixty vehicles, and the garage-cum-terminus at Amersham, designed by the same architects and completed in 1935.[23]

Road freight transport grew steadily in the inter-war period. Its growth had been stimulated in the 1920s by the availability of second-hand ex-military vehicles. Gradually an infrastructure of fuelling and servicing facilities was developed that enabled long-distance operations, like that of milk tankers in competition with the railways between Wiltshire and London, or the distribution of bricks from Buckinghamshire and Bedfordshire (*see Chapter 8*). Through the 1920s and the early 1930s many transport companies chose to operate steam rather than motorised lorries, and the vehicles built by companies like Foden in Sandbach and Sentinel in Shrewsbury were capable of operation over considerable distances. Never-theless, the building of steam road vehicles was drawing to a close by the end of the 1930s.

Many steam lorries, motor lorries, buses and coaches are preserved by private individuals and by institutions like the Science Museum, the Museum of British Road Transport at Coventry and the London Transport Museum, and such vehicles congregate from time to time at rallies, as do steamrollers, which are sometimes accompanied by road-building equipment and the caravans that accommodated their crews. Amberley Museum (TQ 028120) in Sussex includes a village garage, a bus depot, road-making equipment and vehicles from the 1920s and 1930s, and is probably the best place at which to appreciate the context of inter-war road transport, although a garage of 1938 is now displayed at the National Motor Museum, Beaulieu.

Road transport grew prodigiously in the second half of the twentieth century. At the end of 1997 more than 27 million vehicles were licensed, and road transport carried more than 80 per cent of freight if measured by tonnage, or 67 per cent if reckoned in terms of tonnes per kilometre.

Traffic in towns, the title of Sir Colin Buchanan's noteworthy report of 1963, became an increasing problem. In London the flyovers at Chiswick and Hammersmith were completed, respectively, in 1959 and 1961.[24] Birmingham City Corporation built a prefabricated flyover at the intersection of the Coventry and Stratford roads at Camp Hill in 1961, and a succession of permanent flyovers at major intersections on radial routes followed through the 1960s. Birmingham was also the first city to adopt parking meters, in 1962, and part of the Bull Ring development of the early 1960s was a unique multi-storey car park at which motorists handed over their vehicles to attendants, who took them away on lifts. It was never popular, was quickly abandoned, and after many years of dereliction was demolished in 1999.[25]

The most profound change was the construction between 1959 and 1999 of 2,020 miles (3,250 km) of motorways. The network

9.15
The M1 motorway under construction between Dunstable and Luton in the late 1950s.

(Crown copyright. NMR)

Changing horizons:

9.16 *(left)*
The bridge carrying the lane between Hanslope and Salcey Forest over the M1 on the borders of Northamptonshire and Buckinghamshire. The mushroom-topped concrete columns are characteristic of the designs of Sir Owen Williams, and can be observed also in the factory he built for Boots at Beeston.

(Crown copyright. NMR)

9.17 *(right)*
One of the most celebrated features of the motorway system of the late 1960s was the Gravelly Hill interchange on the eastern side of Birmingham, junction 6 on the M6, which became known as Spaghetti Junction and was sufficiently famous to be the subject of a 750-piece jigsaw.

(Collection of Tony Herbert)

was conceived under the Special Roads Act of 1949. A motorway is officially defined as a 'limited access dual-carriageway road with grade separations, completely fenced in, normally with hard shoulders ... for the exclusive use of prescribed classes of motor vehicles'. The first was the 8-mile Preston By-pass, now part of the M6, opened on 5 December 1958, but temporarily closed due to frost damage forty-six days later. The first 70-mile section of the M1, north of London, opened on 2 November 1959 and the network expanded steadily through the ensuing decades. The M1 finally reached Leeds in 1977. The M40, completed in 1991, offered a route between London and Birmingham alternative to that provided by the M1. The construction of the M3 through Twyford Down (SU 4827), near Winchester, led to the abandonment of the 1930s by-pass as a feature of road communication. The motorway system includes some notable river crossings, including the Barton High-Level Bridge over the Irwell and the Manchester Ship Canal of 1960, the Thelwall Viaduct over the Mersey of 1963, the crossing of the Medway west of Chatham of 1963, the Forth road bridge of 1964, the first Severn crossing of 1966 and the second of 1997, the Tinsley Viaduct, Sheffield, of 1968, the Avonmouth crossing of 1974, the Ouse Bridge near Goole of 1976, and the 1963 Dartford Tunnel, under the Thames. The first motorway service areas (MSAs), at Newport Pagnell (SP 860435) and Watford Gap (SP 600680) on the M1, opened in 1960. The character of such areas changed considerably after 1981, when private contractors were allowed to invest in them and franchised catering operations were permitted, but the principle of separating truckdrivers

from private motorists has continued. The motorways revolutionised freight transport by road; indeed, most of the companies involved in the 1990s saw themselves as providing logistical services, including warehousing and the breaking down of loads en route. Such companies commonly have depots on industrial estates, like that at Wellesbourne Mountford (*see Chapter 6*) or, on a much larger scale, the Wakefield Freight Interchange, in the vicinity of motorway junctions. *The Times* commented, as early as 1972, that 'Industrial estates are drawn to motorways these days like pins to a magnet', and the steel-clad, steel-framed, warehouses near to motorway junctions and alongside trunk roads were among the largest buildings being constructed in the 1990s.[26]

Rail

For more than half the twentieth century the railway system was the backbone of inland transport in Britain, and a reduced system performs essential social and economic roles in the twenty-first century. The first main-line railway – that is, one carrying passengers, open to public traffic, subject to public control, and with reserved track and mechanical traction – was that between Liverpool and Manchester, opened in 1830. By 1851 most towns of consequence were linked by a network of 6,000 route miles, which had grown to nearly 19,000 miles by 1900, and exceeded 20,000 miles by 1911. Some of the growth was at the extremities. The LSWR had reached Bude in 1898 and Padstow in 1899. The Highland Railway began to work trains from Wick to Lybster in 1903. Tenterden became a railway terminus in the same year, Ditton Priors in 1908, Aberaeron in 1911 and Thaxted in 1913. Other new lines shortened routes between large towns. The LBSCR inaugurated the Quarry Line on 1 April 1900, enabling expresses between London and Brighton to avoid Redhill. The Great Western Railway on 1 October 1900 opened its avoiding line around Westbury, one of a series of new works between Reading and Taunton which from 1906 enabled trains between London and Exeter to use a route 20 miles shorter than the original main line through Bristol. In 1903 the company's Badminton line similarly improved journey times for trains from London to South Wales. A new route from Birmingham through Stratford on Avon to Cheltenham was opened in 1908, and in 1910 the line from Ashendon in Buckinghamshire to Aynho near Banbury reduced the company's route from London to Birmingham by 19 miles.

The most paradoxical line of this type was the extension of the Manchester, Sheffield & Lincoln Railway, subsequently known as the Great Central, from Annesley (SK 517536), north of Nottingham, 95 miles south through Nottingham and Leicester, to Quainton Road (SP 737190) near Aylesbury, whence it used the tracks of the Metropolitan Railway to Canfield Place near Finchley Road, before burrowing under Lord's Cricket Ground to a new terminus at Marylebone. The extension fulfilled in part an ambition of Sir Edward Watkin (1819–1901), one of the most visionary of Victorian railway entrepreneurs, to run trains from the industrial towns of northern England to the projected Channel Tunnel. While Eurostar trains since 1994 have run to Brussels and Paris from Nicholas Grimshaw's spectacular new station at Waterloo, which symbolises late-twentieth-century railways as Marylebone represents those of the late nineteenth century, it was still not possible in 1999 to reach continental Europe by direct train from Manchester or Sheffield. Marylebone is busy with little trains that travel no further than Aylesbury on former Great Central tracks, although they reach Birmingham on former Great Western metals, and the cuttings, embankments and logically planned island platform stations of the Great Central Main Line have since 1969 formed a feature of

linear dereliction across the shires of midland England. It was a line of two generations. The local historian of Eydon, Northamptonshire, saw gaps being cut in hedges to make way for the London extension in 1895, and lived to miss the familiar sound of the train which had passed at his bedtime after the line closed in 1966.[27] The hotel built by the GCR at its Marylebone terminus became the headquarters of the LNER, and subsequently of the nationalised railway system.

Notable engineering structures were still being added to the railway system in 1900. The line to Ballachulish crossed the steel cantilevered Connel Ferry bridge, which now carries road traffic. The route to Mallaig included the twenty-one-arch Glenfinnan Viaduct, one of the first large-scale concrete structures in Britain. The North Eastern Railway opened the steel lattice King Edward Bridge over the Tyne between Newcastle and Gateshead in 1906. The Caledonian Railway built a steel roof with a 140ft (42.67m) span over the platforms of Glasgow Central Station between 1901 and 1906. The Great Central Railway opened a new road and rail lifting bridge on the Scherzer principle, which originated in Chicago, over the Trent at Keadby (SE 840105) in Lincolnshire on 21 May 1916.

Elsewhere some tiny towns and larger villages were linked to the railway network by lines constructed under the Light Railways Act of 1896. Few lasted for more than a generation, particularly those built to narrow gauges. The (1ft 11.5in.-gauge) Lynton & Barnstaple Railway, which had opened in 1898, closed in 1935, and the (2ft 6in.-gauge) Leek & Manifold Railway, opened in 1904, lasted only until 1934. Already by 1900 the railways were failing to find customers at the margins of the network. Passenger trains between Towcester and Olney, inaugurated in December 1892, continued only until March 1893.

The railway system in 1900 was owned by more than 100 companies, ranging from some of the country's largest commercial organisations, like the Great Western, the London & North Western and the North Eastern, through lines like the Taff Vale with limited mileage but high profits, and those like the Highland or the Cambrian with extensive networks but modest traffic potential, to local concerns in rural areas, like the Stratford & Midland Junction, or the

East Suffolk. During the First World War the system was managed by the government, and it was confidently expected after the Armistice that it would be nationalised (*see Chapter 7*). Instead the companies were formed into four groups – the London Midland & Scottish, the London & North Eastern, the Great Western and the Southern Railways – which took responsibility for their sections of the network from 1 January 1923. During the 1920s and 1930s the railways faced competition in certain aspects of their business, yet were still constrained by the legislation imposed when they had a monopoly. The 'big four' railway companies developed some effective initiatives, but many aspects of their operations were constrained by loss-making practices, excessive supervision, and inflexibility in responding to customer demand, deeply ingrained in what had become rigidly hierarchical organisations. After the Second World War the whole transport system was nationalised with effect from 1 January 1948, but in many respects little changed. A modernisation plan published in 1955 proposed the continuation of many practices that were already the cause of financial haemorrhage, and many of its assumptions were reversed when, after several years of excessive loss, Dr Richard Beeching (1913–85), a director of ICI, was appointed in 1961 to chair the British Railways Board, a position he held until 1965. Route mileage was drastically cut as branch lines, secondary routes and even some main lines were closed. The use of steam locomotives on normal services ceased during the summer of 1968, while many of the diesel locomotives, hurriedly supplied by a variety of British manufacturers under the 1955 modernisation plan, proved unfit for their purpose. The network totalled just over 19,500 route miles at the time of nationalisation, but by 1972 this had been reduced to 11,500 miles. Freight traffic dwindled, but some new developments in passenger services proved socially significant – the use of High-Speed Trains on services from Paddington stimulated the economic growth of the middle Thames Valley, while access to central Glasgow was transformed by the electrification of almost all the routes into the city and the revitalisation of some that ran through it. The railways were privatised in the early 1990s, and it is some measure of their continuing significance in certain aspects of life

at the beginning of the twenty-first century that the shortcomings of the new companies provoke bitter, and usually justified, complaints. Perhaps one of the most significant developments of the post-privatisation era was the import on a large scale in the late 1990s of freight locomotives, built in North America by General Motors, more than a generation after the same company transferred its effective technology to other European countries.

Main-line services around 1900 were falling into a pattern that was to last for more than fifty years. On the longest routes from London – to Plymouth, Glasgow and Edinburgh – there were only a few daytime through trains, one of them a 'flagship' service, often named, that departed mid-morning. Standards of comfort on such services had improved markedly in the closing years of the nineteenth century, and it was assumed that a high proportion of passengers would take meals en route. Night trains with sleeping-cars operated on most long-distance routes. In 1907 the North British Railway drew the attention of Scots customers to its through services from Edinburgh to St Pancras and King's Cross, where passengers were offered corridors, lavatories, meals in restaurant cars, and sleeping saloons on overnight services. Ironically the occasion was a promotion for the sixth Motor Exhibition at Olympia. The evidence most evocative of this kind of travel is the twelve-wheeled restaurant-car built at Derby in 1913 for the daytime service between St Pancras in London and St Enoch in Glasgow worked jointly by the Midland Railway and the Glasgow and South Western. Passengers on this service, leaving London at 09.30, could visit the restaurant-car for morning coffee, lunch and afternoon tea before arriving at Glasgow at 18.35. On shorter routes from London services were naturally more frequent. The highest levels of comfort were to be found in the Pullman cars which ran on at least some of the trains between London and the principal resorts in Kent and Sussex. The company that managed the Pullman brand-name in Britain established a carriage works at Brighton in 1906. The Pullman car was part of upper-middle-class culture in south-eastern England. John Betjeman identified 'the sort of boy'

Whose parents go by Pullman once a month
To do a show in town.[28]

9.18

The 'Golden Arrow'
hauled by British
Railways standard-class
7MT 4-6-2 No. 70014
'Iron Duke' passing
Folkestone junction on
a July evening in 1957.
The sidings to the right
enabled boat trains to
reverse to go down a
steep gradient to
Folkestone harbour. The
second vehicle in the
train conveys containers
of mail, and those
behind it are Pullman
cars.

(Photo: Barrie Trinder)

There is a copious archaeological record of
Pullman travel – about 100 carriages survive in
Britain, ranging from the immaculate 1914 *Topaz*,
in the National Railway Museum, to examples
used as dining saloons in country pubs far from
any line on which Pullmans ever worked.

Facilities for travelling to the seaside were
being improved around 1900. In the 1890s the
Great Western had begun to provide through
carriages to Barmouth, and by 1922 was running
through carriages to Kingsbridge, Newquay,
Minehead, Ilfracombe and Falmouth in the
west of England. In 1900 the LSWR carried
passengers by various trains leaving Waterloo
around 11.00 to such distant destinations as
Padstow, Torrington and Bude, as well as to
Ilfracombe and Plymouth. In 1907 the Great
Eastern Railway began to work its Norfolk
Coast Express non-stop from Liverpool Street
to North Walsham, conveying through carriages
for Cromer, Sheringham, Mundesley and
Overstrand. In 1900 the Great Central Railway
opened a branch of its London extension from
Woodford (SP 5452) in Northamptonshire to the
Great Western at Banbury (SP 462424), along
which, by 1914, it had developed services
linking Manchester, Bradford, Newcastle and
Hull with Swansea, Cardiff, Bournemouth,
Bristol, Exeter and Ilfracombe. The company
was following the example of its partner, the
Great Western, which in the 1890s had begun

through services from Birkenhead and
Manchester to resorts on the south and south-
east coasts. In 1904 the LNWR and LBSCR co-
operated in the provision of through coaches
between Lancashire and the Sussex coast
and the following year inaugurated a through
train, the Sunny South Express, which linked
Liverpool and Manchester with Brighton and
Eastbourne. The archaeological record of the
Edwardian excursion to the seaside is rich and
varied. Posters were designed to attract visitors
to many resorts, displaying the early-twentieth-
century ambitions of places like New Brighton,
Withernsea and Mundesley. The National
Railway Museum displays a coach built for this
kind of traffic by the LSWR in 1903. It carries
a destination board for Torrington, and there
are lavatories attached to each compartment,
indicating something of the demand for long-
distance through services from people perhaps
unused to rail travel, who would be carrying
heavy luggage. There are compartments for
first-, second- and third-class passengers,
showing that railways mirrored the class
structure. Some monuments in the landscape
recall complex past journeys to the coast: the
earthworks of the triangular junction at Firsby
(TF 456635), which enabled trains from the north
to reach Skegness; the remnants at Kingham
(SP 255230) of the abutments of the bridge by
which the Ports-to-Ports Express from the north-
east to South Wales crossed the line from Oxford
to Worcester; and the earthworks near Ellesmere
(SJ 383350) of a curve by which Great Central
trains from Leicester, Sheffield and Manchester
could, having travelled a devious route, gain
access to the tracks of the Cambrian Railway
and thus reach Aberystwyth.

Locomotive technology of the first years
of the century is best illustrated by the Great
Western Railway's 4-6-0 *Lode Star* and its near
contemporary, the 2-8-0 freight locomotive
No. 2818, displayed in the National Railway
Museum. Both resulted from policies of
scientific testing by the GWR's Chief Mechanical
Engineer, G. J. Churchward (1857–1933), who
purchased three locomotives designed by the
French engineer Alfred de Glehn (1848–1936),
and built a locomotive testing plant at Swindon
in 1900–4. A similar policy of basing design on
scientific observation rather than established
practice was pursued by J. G. Robinson (1856–
1943) of the Great Central Railway, two of

whose designs, the express locomotive *Butler Henderson* and the 2-8-0 freight locomotive No. 63601, form part of the national collection. Several experiments were carried out in the inter-war period with innovative forms of steam propulsion, but none had any long-term influence on locomotive design. The locomotives of the post-war period, with their exposed motions, self-cleaning smoke boxes and enclosed cabs, provide evidence of the difficulties experienced by the railways in recruiting labour and of the exhausting drudgery involved in operating steam locomotives. The traditional system of the slow promotion of footplate staff did not encourage experimentation.

The most far-reaching experiments, both in management and technology, were those which related to suburban services. The 'last word in steam-operated suburban train services' was inaugurated on 2 July 1920 by the Great Eastern Railway, linking Liverpool Street with Hertford, Chingford and Enfield. Its pattern of operation had been devised by the company's American General Manager, Henry Thornton, and its Superintendent of Operations, Frederick Russell. Ingeniously designed trackwork at Liverpool Street enabled locomotives to back on to incoming trains, and return to the suburbs with little delay. More circulation space for pedestrians was provided at Liverpool Street. Trains ran every ten minutes to Chingford and Enfield, and 848 seats were provided on rush-hour services. The whole operation cost only £80,000, compared with £3 million, which was the estimated cost of electrification. Apart from the replacement of smaller locomotives by 0-6-2T locomotives of the N7 class, and the introduction of articulated carriages after the formation of the LNER in 1923, the service was little altered until electrification in November 1960. An N7 class locomotive is preserved at the East Anglian Railway Museum, and a set of articulated coaches on the North Norfolk Railway.[29]

The future appeared to be electric traction, and the American entrepreneur George Westinghouse (1846–1914) opened his works at Trafford Park (*see Chapter 4*) in 1902 in the expectation that he would be able to supply electric rolling stock to railways throughout Europe. He achieved some initial success, but the progress of electrification was slow. In London the first of the deep 'tube' lines, from Monument to Stockwell, was opened in 1890, but abandoned in 1900 when a new line was constructed, which by the following year extended from Clapham Common to the Angel. One of the locomotives used on the line is in the collection of the London Transport Museum. The Central Line opened in 1900, the Waterloo & City in 1898 – acquired by the LSWR in 1907 – the Great Northern & City in 1904, the Bakerloo in 1906. The subsurface lines of the District Railway and the Metropolitan Railway were electrified in 1905. In 1903 the Mersey Railway began to operate electric trains, supplied by Westinghouse, through the tunnel connecting Liverpool and Birkenhead. The Lancashire & Yorkshire Railway began to run electric trains from Liverpool to Southport in 1904 and from Manchester to Bury in 1916, and the first electric trains on Tyneside began to run in 1904. The Midland Railway opened an experimental electrified system linking Lancaster with Heysham in 1908. In 1909 the London, Brighton & South Coast Railway electrified its South London line. The first of the London & North Western Railway's lines in London to be electrified, between Willesden and Earls Court, was completed in 1914, and by 1922 the system extended from Watford to Euston and from Broad Street to Richmond.

In the long term the most significant line to be electrified was that of the London & South Western Railway between Waterloo and Wimbledon through East Putney, where work was completed in 1915. Its trains were driven by equipment supplied by Westinghouse. In the 1920s and 1930s this pattern of third rail operation (providing current at 600 volts DC) was adopted by the Southern Railway, managed by Sir Herbert Walker, and extended over much of south-east England.[30] The maze of lines south of London that had resulted from inter-company competition in the nineteenth century was electrified in 1925 to provide a means of transport which stimulated suburban development on a massive scale (*see Chapter 7*). On 1 January 1933 electric trains began to run from Victoria to Brighton, and by 1939 all the coastal resorts between Hastings and Portsmouth were similarly served, as were all the significant towns in an arc extending from the Medway towns to Reading. In many respects this was an unheroic development. New and rebuilt stations looked like cinemas constructed by small companies in small towns, and few matched in style those built by London Transport. The station at Surbiton, with its square clock-tower ornamented by horizontal fins and its streamlined platform buildings, was perhaps the most fashionable Southern Electric building. Most stations, like those along the main line to the west at New Malden, Berrylands, Esher and Hersham, were characterised by bleak simplicity, with extended platforms carried on concrete frames. There were also economies with rolling stock. Old coach bodies with slam doors were mounted on new underframes and bogies, and fitted with electric motors. Some Pullman cars were used on coastal services, most notably on the Brighton Belle, an all-Pullman train which shuttled several times a day between the capital and the coast from 1934 until 1972. Fourteen of its vehicles are preserved, some in unlikely locations. Two non-Pullman Southern Railway electric multiple units form part of the national collection, but the greatest memorial to the work of Sir Herbert Walker is the continuing role in the life of south-east England of the network he created. To stand around 08.30 at the southern end of the platform at London Bridge or at the eastern end of Clapham Junction at 17.30 and to see the non-stop processions of trains into and out of the capital is to sense the scale of Walker's achievement.

The other principal development of electric railways was also centred on London, but has left a more distinguished archaeological legacy, better interpreted as part of a uniquely effective public transport system than as railway archaeology. The Metropolitan District Railway was expanding rapidly in the years before the First World War under the management of Albert Stanley, later Lord Ashfield (1874–1948). It took over the London General Omnibus Company in 1912 and the various 'tube' railways in 1913. In 1906 Frank Pick (1878–1941), son of a Spalding draper and a statistician working for the North Eastern Railway, was recruited by the District Railway, and by 1912 was Commercial Manager. He was responsible for the first escalator in London at the new station at Paddington, for the design of a new alphabet for the company by Edward Johnson in 1913–16, for the red disque 'UndergrounD' logo, and for many imaginative posters. In 1933 the District, the Metropolitan

9.19
The Northern Line station at Edgware c. 1929, described as 'simple, tidy and effective' by the member of the CPRE who photographed it.

(University of Reading: Museum of English Rural Life, CPRE collection)

and various bus and tramway companies were brought together at the London Passenger Transport Board, of which Pick was Vice-Chairman and Chief Executive Officer. Throughout the inter-war period Pick profoundly influenced the expansion of the District Railway's activities, and later those of the LPTB. He introduced destination blinds on buses, concrete bus-stop posts with panels for the display of timetables, bifurcation signs directing pedestrians coming off staircases or escalators, free-standing seats bearing station names, and station signs on platform walls. He introduced automatic machines operated by ticket clerks in 1926, and automatic coin-operated machines giving change in 1928. He commissioned much work by the architect Charles Holden (1875–1960), including the new Piccadilly Circus Station in 1928, and the company headquarters at 55 Broadway in 1929. In 1930 he toured The Netherlands and Sweden with Holden, and thereafter new stations were inspired by the work of the Dutch architect Willem Marinus Dudok (1884–1974). Holden's work remains at stations like Hangar Lane (TQ 184827), Arnos Grove (TQ 294926) and Boston Manor (TQ 163787), the best-preserved detailing of the 1930s surviving at Southgate (TQ 296942). Pick died in 1941 after organising the evacuation of children from London at the outbreak of the Second World War. Passenger transport in London underwent many changes during the period after his death, but much of what Pick did can still be seen in the city's streets, at underground stations and in the London Transport Museum.[31]

The place of the railways in the popular imagination was most clearly indicated in the

Changing horizons:

short-lived 'streamline era' of the late 1930s. 'Streamlined', a word favoured by advertisers, was applied to semi-detached houses, motorcycles and toothbrushes, but was most familiarly applied to four train services on the LNER. Three ran on the East Coast Main Line and were hauled by the wedge-fronted, air-smoothed, Pacific locomotives of the A4 class introduced by Sir Nigel Gresley (1876–1941) in 1935. The first, the 'Silver Jubilee', with its newly designed coaches and locomotive in silver-grey, began to run between Newcastle and King's Cross on 30 September 1935. In July 1937 the blue-liveried 'Coronation' linked King's Cross and Edinburgh, while from October 1937 Leeds and Bradford were served by the 'West Riding Limited', and two 4-6-0 locomotives were fitted with streamlined casings to work the 'East Anglian', between Liverpool Street and Norwich. The 'Coronation' trains were distinguished by observation cars with sloping rear windows in Perspex, both of which still survived in 1999. The LMS responded to the 'Coronation' by running the 'Coronation Scot', between Euston and Glasgow, but it lacked the panache of the LNER's service, which gained added glory when the locomotive *Mallard* gained the world speed record for steam railway traction on 3 July 1938 when running down Stoke Bank between Grantham and Peterborough. The Great Western Railway rather clumsily followed fashion by putting curved facings on to two of its locomotives. The thirty-eight streamlined diesel cars built by the company between 1934 and 1942, of which two survive, were aesthetically more pleasing. London Transport introduced three trains with streamlined ends on the Piccadilly Line in 1935. The 'streamline era' ended with the outbreak of the Second World War, and one of the most memorable images created by the war artists was that of a filthy Stanier streamlined Pacific locomotive, of the kind used on the Coronation Scot, being cleaned by a group of young women in smart blue overalls with radiant golden hair.[32]

Freight traffic in 1900 had in many respects settled into a pattern that was scarcely altered until it was lost to the roads. In every great city there had long been vast freight depots, interchanges between road and rail, sometimes with canal facilities in addition. Their

components included sheds for handling small consignments, open sidings where cranes could operate, cattle docks, wagon repair facilities, and stables to accommodate the motive power which drew delivery carts through the streets. In 1935 the LMSR filmed operations at its Camden depot (TQ 285838), showing the rapid, if dangerous, progress of wagons through the sheds which could be achieved by hydraulically operated turntables, capstans and traversers. Operations were labour-intensive, loaders being watched by a hierarchy of overlookers and supervisors, while checkers shuffled papers recording the passage of consignments, most of which were delivered from horse-drawn flat-bed road wagons with tarpaulin tops, although a few Karrier mechanical horses had just been introduced. Most such depots were well established by 1900 and saw few changes before they were closed in the 1960s. Thorne, Duckworth and Jones found that the King's Cross goods yard (TQ 300835) lived after 1900 on its nineteenth-century inheritance of buildings and facilities. A survey of the depot at Bricklayer's Arms (TQ 337785) in south-east London revealed only two entirely twentieth-century structures, and they were built in 1902 and 1903.[33] The New Bridge Street depot in Newcastle of 1903 was constructed by Mouchel-Hennebique with 52ft concrete girders supporting an upper floor, and there were also substantial concrete additions to the Great Western Railway's depot at Canons Marsh, Bristol. There were some other changes in railway freight handling. More through trains of brake-fitted wagons were introduced between some principal depots. The V2 class locomotive *Green Arrow*, now in the national collection, was built in 1936, and took its name from a premium service of this kind offered by the LNER. The railway companies introduced container services in the 1920s, and the LMSR film of 1935 shows, rather whimsically, how a container, the 'suitcase of commerce', could be used when a family moved house. Road distribution of consignments by lorry became universal after the Second World War, and some mechanical handling facilities were introduced by British Railways. Railway depots have left substantial imprints in the big cities. The sites of some, like Bishopsgate (TQ 335822) on the edge of the City of London, and Canons Marsh in Bristol, remained undeveloped in 1999. Others have been re-used. The Somers Town depot of the Midland Railway is now occupied by the British Library, while the sheds and sidings of the Liverpool Road depot in Manchester are occupied by the Museum of Science and Industry. In market towns and country stations freight was handled on a smaller scale, but depots had the same basic components. Many sheds designed for transferring sundry traffic between railway wagons and road vehicles have been adapted to new uses, and some yards are now industrial estates.

Coal remained a basic railway traffic throughout the twentieth century. When the Midland Railway opened its own route into London in 1869 it constructed sidings at Toton (SK 4835), near Nottingham, where traffic was collected from coal mines in the Erewash Valley and worked to Wellingborough (SP 905686), Northamptonshire, a day's task for a crew who would lodge overnight in a hostel and return with a train of empties the next day. There were extensive sidings at Wellingborough, and a large locomotive depot from which coal wagons were worked south to be sorted for London destinations at Cricklewood (TQ 235865), where, in similar fashion, crews would lodge and work back with empties the next day. In 1900 most such trains were hauled by pairs of 0-6-0 locomotives, and most were still so worked until the late 1930s. George Bushell, a teenage fireman at Wellingborough in 1936, recalled that, while staying overnight on his first working trip to London, he saw the glow from the burning Crystal Palace.[34] From the late 1920s some such trains began to be worked by thirty-three articulated Beyer-Garratt locomotives, but operation by single locomotives became the norm only in the late 1930s, with the introduction of Sir William Stanier's 8F 2-8-0 locomotives and their multiplication during the Second World War. Other classic coal movements involving the use of two, and sometimes more, locomotives on trains were from the south Yorkshire and the Nottinghamshire coalfields through the Woodhead Tunnel (SE 156022, SK 114999) to Lancashire, and from South Wales through the Severn Tunnel to Bristol and south-west England. Most coal moved in wooden-framed, wooden-bodied, unbraked wagons with grease axle boxes, owned by colliery companies or coal merchants, which required complicated sorting.

9.20
A train bound for South Wales loaded with iron ore from Irthlingborough, Northamptonshire, passing through Verney junction, Buckinghamshire, on a June afternoon in 1961. The sidings to the right were used for the storage of passenger carriages, which were used only during the summer holiday traffic peak.

(Photo: Barrie Trinder)

All were brought into common use during the Second World War; they continued to be so used after nationalisation, when they were steadily replaced by steel-bodied 16-ton wagons without continuous brakes, which were considered unacceptable at collieries. Coal carrying by rail diminished sharply after 1960 (see Chapter 3), when 5,031 depots remained nominally in use, although 1,172 had handled no traffic in 1960. In the early 1960s a new method of operating coal trains was developed by the Eastern Region of British Railways. Permanently coupled trains of 26-ton hopper wagons, with galvanised bodywork, air-braked and hauled by locomotives adapted for slow-speed running, were filled with coal from overhead bunkers at collieries, their cargo being discharged as the wagons moved across under-floor bunkers at power stations.[35] 'Merry-go-round' trains of this sort continued in use in 1999, although the closure of most collieries in Britain had re-shaped patterns of coal movement. The archaeological record of coal movement by rail is far from complete. Few locomotives designed for this kind of traffic and used before the Second World War are preserved. One of the locomotive roundhouses at Wellingborough is now a warehouse, while a forest grows on the sidings to the north. The most eloquent record is the operation of 'Windcutter' trains by the preserved railway based at Loughborough. These are shortened representations of the freight trains which from 1947 worked on a timetabled basis on the Great Central London extension between Annesley and Woodford. In management terms this was a successful innovation, but the unbraked wagons are evidence of the retarded technology characteristic of much twentieth-century freight operation.

Unlike the railway freight depot, the marshalling yard was to a large extent a twentieth-century creation.[36] There were large groups of sidings in the nineteenth century, connected chiefly with coal traffic, but it is generally accepted that the gently inclined sidings at Edge Hill, Liverpool, laid out by the LNWR about 1900 and known as 'the gridiron', represented an innovation. A similar yard was constructed by the same company at Basford Hall, Crewe, in 1901. Midland Railway in 1901 constructed a 'hump' yard at Toton in which rakes of wagons were pushed up a gentle incline so that, once over the summit, their own momentum and a steeper gradient would take them down into a fan of reception sidings. In 1907 Great Central Railway opened a hump yard at Wath (SE 4301), south Yorkshire, in which wagons were slowed down by mechanical retarders, and by 1910 had four other gravity yards. North Eastern Railway constructed a complex yard at Newport, Teesside, in 1910. Further extensive yards were constructed in the inter-war years: at Feltham (TQ 0872), Middlesex, by the LSWR (1921–23); at Whitemoor (TL 4198), Cambridgeshire (1929 and 1933); at Mottram (SJ 9794), near Manchester (1935) and at Hull (1935), by the LNER; and at Banbury (1931), by the GWR. Most marshalling yards were extended during the Second World War, and some new, but generally modest-sized, yards were built (see Chapter 7). There were 94 hump marshalling yards at the time of nationalisation, but only 35 were still working by 1972. The modernisation plan of 1955 had proposed further large and expensive mechanised yards, but projects – at Elmbridge in Gloucestershire, Walcot in Shropshire and at Swanbourne, Buckinghamshire – were abandoned, and hump-shunting operations continued for only a few years at most of those that were built.

Most of the artefacts relating to marshalling yards have been destroyed. Powerful tank locomotives were specifically designed for hump shunting: the 99-ton 0-8-4Ts, the 'Wath Daisies' of the GCR, the 95-ton G16 4-8-0Ts of the LSWR which worked at Feltham, or the 85-ton T1 4-8-0Ts of the North Eastern Railway which worked at Hull and Newport. None has been preserved. Marshalling yards remain a feature of the British landscape. Some have been adapted to meet the different demands of modern railway operations. Some, like Banbury, have provided land for housing. Others, like Feltham and Whitemoor, have become forests of birch, buddleia and bramble, monuments to the need for the complex sorting of wagons that was intrinsic to conservative patterns of railway operation, and to the grandiose ambitions of the 1950s.

There were about 350 steam locomotive sheds or depots at the time of nationalisation, in 1947. Locomotives stood on reception lines for their smoke boxes to be emptied and their fire boxes cleared of ashes. Their tenders or bunkers would be filled with coal, and they would be topped up with water and sand. Fitters would attend to minor items of maintenance, and at most depots there were workshops where attention could be given to serious faults. A locomotive would be turned on a turntable so that it faced in the right direction for its next duty, and its fire would be either dropped or banked down. The disappearance of the sulphurous haze that permanently clouded the atmosphere around the large depots – Stewarts Lane at Battersea (TQ 290772), Newton Heath (SJ 845997) in Manchester, Holbeck (SE 923326) in Leeds and St Margaret's in Edinburgh – was one of the more fortunate consequences of the demise of steam traction. The most obvious change at the larger depots during the twentieth century was the construction of

9.21
The sulphur-laden atmosphere that surrounded a large locomotive shed: Stewarts Lane, which provided locomotives for trains from Victoria, on 30 July 1957.

(Photo: Barrie Trinder)

concrete coaling stages, on which wagons were lifted so that the coal they contained could be tipped into bunkers, from which locomotives were fuelled by gravity. The first were built by the Mitchell Engineering Group in the mid-1930s, for the LNER at Doncaster and Gorton (Manchester), and for the Southern Railway at Nine Elms (Battersea). About 100 had been built by 1946.[37] There were three at Crewe's north shed in the 1950s. Only the LMS structure at Carnforth (SD 496707) remained in 1999, but a typical example of Great Western practice, a brick-built stage to which wagons were pushed up a ramp, remains at Didcot (SU 525905). A few shed buildings were adapted for present-day railway operation, as at Bescot (SP 005962); some were re-used for different purposes, as at Peterborough (East), Wellingborough and Mirfield; while those at Carnforth, Didcot and Staveley formed parts of preservation projects, as did the much-altered building at York, which houses part of the National Railway Museum.

The very nature of railed ways changed after nationalisation, as traditional bullhead rails, held by wooden keys in cast-iron chairs carried on wooden sleepers, were replaced by flat-bottomed rails, welded together and held by Pandrol clips on steel pads mounted on concrete sleepers. Standardisation became effective only slowly in an industry where loyalties from before 1923, as well as from before nationalisation, remained strong. Many stations were rebuilt. Banbury (SP 462404) is a good example of work carried out in the early stages of the modernisation plan, and contrasts well with the next station to the north, at Leamington (SP 318662), which was the last to be rebuilt by the Great Western Railway immediately prior to the Second World War. Coventry (SP 332782), built in 1959–62, was in architectural terms the best of the modernisation plan stations, and while still new was often compared with its contemporary, Coventry Cathedral. Two of the more substantial rebuildings, which formed part of the electrification of the West Coast Main Line, were at New Street in Birmingham and at Euston, where unexciting but functional structures replaced much squalor, although the arch at Euston, symbol of the great expectations of railways in the 1830s, was needlessly destroyed. Nearly 1,000 standard steam locomotives were built in the 1950s, and before the end of the decade main-line diesel locomotives were introduced in large numbers. The Mark I Carriage, introduced in 1951, was an unspectacular vehicle that lacked style, but was tolerably comfortable, and safer than earlier vehicles at the speeds attained during the 1950s. Many remain on preserved railways.

The railway system changed utterly in the 1960s. At the beginning of 1959 nearly 16,000 steam locomotives were still employed on British Railways track. The last of that number

9.22
The changing order on the railways in the early 1960s. The station at Wells-next-the-Sea, Norfolk, in September 1960, with a new diesel multiple-unit train just arrived from Norwich, while an aged J17-class 0-6-0 locomotive built by the Great Eastern Railway is about to leave with the daily freight train. The line to Wells was closed later in the decade as part of the Beeching cuts.

(Photo: Barrie Trinder)

Changing horizons:

ceased to work in the summer of 1968. The scrapping of so many redundant machines was itself a major operation.[38] In East Anglia the changeover from steam to diesel and electric operation, chronicled by Richard Hardy, was achieved in a disciplined manner.[39] In other areas, retreat turned into rout.

The principal archaeological record of railway activity in the 1960s is of that retreat, the many miles of trackbed that, if not at the time returned to agricultural use, have served – officially or unofficially – as nature reserves or cycle-ways. Much of the contraction was clearly necessary. The demand for passenger services from Oxford to Fairford (or rather to a field at a distance from Fairford), or from Church Fenton to Wetherby, was probably never sufficient to make services viable. Other lines, with imagination, could have been regarded as potential long-term assets, rather than as the causes of short-term deficits. Several passenger services were restored in the 1990s – from Nottingham to Worksop, from Cardiff to Aberdare, and, as a modern tramway, from Birmingham by the Great Western's route to Wolverhampton. As the railway system was constrained in the 1990s by lack of capacity, the closure of the Great Central London extension, the route through the Peak from Matlock to Buxton, the Nottingham–Melton Mowbray link, and the ex-LSWR line to Padstow may, for different reasons, be regarded as regrettable.

The railways changed slowly in the 1970s and 1980s. The most imaginative experiment of the period, the tilting Advanced Passenger Train, which at Beattock achieved a speed of 162.2 mph on 20 December 1979, was abandoned and became an archaeological artefact, displayed at Crewe and York. Freight traffic steadily declined, accelerating the closure of depots and marshalling yards, and in 1987 seven Freightliner container depots of the 1960s – at Aberdeen, Dundee, Edinburgh, Longsight (Manchester), Newcastle, Nottingham and Swansea – were closed. Passenger traffic increased markedly in some areas. By 1999 the last of the main-line diesel locomotives and multiple units built under the 1955 modernisation plan were being replaced. Following privatisation the railway network was at an interesting point in its history, with many indications that it was on the point of a revival.

Air

Commercial air transport in Britain began on 25 August 1919 when a solitary passenger was flown from Hounslow Heath to Paris in a converted De Havilland 4A fighter belonging to Air Transport and Travel Ltd. Later in the day four passengers made the same journey in a De Havilland 16. Air travel in Britain in the 1920s was a minority pastime, a world of pageants and aerobatics, of grass runways and military surplus biplanes, of joyrides of the kind for which the first air ticket office, a wooden hut set up at Brooklands in 1911 and now part of the Brooklands Museum (TQ 068629), is the symbol.

There were much more serious aspects to civil aviation. The British government, like those of other European imperial powers, was anxious to use air power to maintain regular links with its possessions in Africa and Asia, and when several companies were persuaded to combine in a single national airline in 1924 it was appropriately called Imperial Airways. One of the achievements of the airline was to establish communications by journeys of many stages, and with different types of aircraft, through the Mediterranean to Egypt, and thence across the Middle East and the Empire of India to Burma, Malaya and the dominions of Australia and New Zealand, and also from Cairo to the Cape. Through services to India began in 1929, to Singapore in 1932, to Australia in 1934, and to South Africa in 1932, but until 1937 passengers had to travel by rail over the stage from Paris to the Mediterranean coast.[40]

Imperial Airways had its base at Croydon (TQ 305636), which became London's official airport on 29 March 1920, on a site adjoining

9.23
One of the two airship hangars at Cardington, Bedfordshire.

(Photo: Barrie Trinder)

flying fields established in 1915 at Wallington and Waddon, the latter having also been the site of one of the largest National Factories producing aircraft. A hotel and terminal building were constructed in 1926–28, and still stood in 1999, although much of the flying field area was taken up with houses and factories. Croydon was the focus of most international air travel in the 1920s and 1930s, with flights by continental European airlines as well as Imperial Airways. British air travel in the 1930s was symbolised by the eight Handley Page HP42 four-engined airliners introduced in 1932. Of these aircraft, four carried 32 passengers, in reasonable comfort, on short-distance routes to the Continent, and four accommodated 24 passengers on some stages of empire routes. By the end of the decade Imperial Airways' flights had become competitive with traditional rail services like the Golden Arrow.[41]

By the late 1930s the focus for long-distance services was moving from Croydon to the Imperial Airways terminal at Imperial House, Berth 109, Southampton (SU 395123), opened in 1938, where a passenger could catch one of the twenty-eight Short Empire four-engined flying-boats ordered in 1934, which offered sleeping cabins and a promenade deck. New four-engined land planes, the Armstrong Whitworth Ensign and the De Havilland Albatross, were also coming into service, and the prospect was emerging of transatlantic services, by flights in several stages. The growing self-confidence of the airline industry was marked by the construction in Buckingham Palace Road, London, of the imposing Imperial Airways terminal, designed by A. Lakeman and opened

in 1939, from which passengers were conveyed by coach to Croydon and by special train from Victoria Station to Southampton. The new services were marketed through posters which matched in style those of London Transport, emphasising the safety of four-engined aircraft and the comforts of the flying-boat. After the Second World War BOAC, the successor to Imperial Airways, operated flying-boats from the new Maritime Air Terminal at Berth 50 (SU 422106) in Southampton, built in 1948. The corporation ceased to use flying-boats two years later, but the terminal was used by Aquila Airways until 1959 when commercial flying-boat operation in Britain finally ceased. For a period of time, before, during and just after the Second World War, flying-boats were important in inter-continental travel, and it is fitting that the pre-war terminal building at Southampton remains – Imperial House is adapted as offices. The Maritime Air Terminal, after a spell as a naval reserve base, was demolished in the mid-1990s. The city's museum service holds the only civilian Short Sandringham flying-boat in Britain, although the RAF Museum and the Imperial War Museum have examples of the military version, the Sunderland.[42]

There was a very different aspect to air travel in the 1930s: services which competed not with

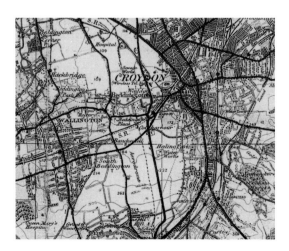

9.24 (*left*) Croydon airfield as depicted on the Ordnance Survey map of 1929.

(*Authors' collection*)

9.25 (*right*) The spiral staircase to the control tower in Airport House, Croydon, built in 1927–28.

(*Crown copyright. NMR*)

the Golden Arrow or the Union Castle line but with the motorcoach and the excursion train. Archaeological evidence throughout Britain reflects the widespread assumption that air travel would be used for relatively short distances, and that every self-respecting city would need its own airport. Some services were established by railway companies, particularly over routes, like Cardiff–Exeter, where the rail journey was circuitous. Others, like the Romford–Clacton service operated by Edward Hillman in the mid-1930s, appear to have had no credible rationale. Some 35 municipal airports were licensed between 1929 and 1937, by which time 18 other local authorities had purchased land for aerodromes. The first was at Barton, Manchester, opened in 1929, where the control tower and two hangars remain, and the runways are still used for private flying. The municipal airport at Whitchurch Down (ST 620675), Bristol, was opened in 1930, and became the base for Imperial Airways during the Second World War. The joint Leeds–Bradford airport at Yeadon (SE 2241), opened in 1931, was the site of a large aircraft factory in the Second World War, and was still used by airliners in 1999, although the original terminal buildings have disappeared. Luton's municipal airport (TL 1120), opened in 1938, was the site of the Percival aircraft factory in the Second World War, and was enlarged in the 1970s, 1980s and 1990s to accommodate charter and cut-price airline flights. Derby's municipal airport at Burnaston (SK 2930) opened in 1939 and was the base from 1949 until 1965 of the airline that in 1964 took the name British Midland. Flying ceased in 1990, and by 1999 it was the site of Toyota's car factory. Particular features of certain municipal airports were terminal buildings in a Modernist, or perhaps more accurately 'streamlined', style, with steel frames, flat roofs and curving walls that were more likely to be rendered brick than poured concrete. The 'Beehive' terminal and control tower at Gatwick (TQ 282404), built in 1936 to the design of Hoar, Marlow & Lovatt, from which passengers walked through tunnels to waiting planes, was fortunately retained when the airport was re-constructed in 1958. The terminal at Elmdon, Birmingham, designed by Norman & Dawbarn, was completed in 1939, and still stands, although it ceased to be used by passengers when a new terminal was opened in 1984. A

control tower and terminal designed by Stavers & Tiltman at the joint Brighton, Hove and Worthing airport at Shoreham (TQ 203052) was opened in 1936 and remains part of an active civilian airfield, as does a terminal designed by Graham Dawbarn at Perth. At Speke (SJ 431825), Liverpool's municipal airport, opened in 1930, a large 1939 terminal with a concave plan became redundant in 1986 but was being restored as an hotel in the late 1990s. Notable 'streamlined' airport buildings at Ramsgate and Grangemouth have been demolished. Other towns and cities which had or have municipal airports include Blackpool, Cardiff, Coventry, Exeter, Ipswich, Wolverhampton, Nottingham and Newcastle.[43]

Air transport was changed utterly by the Second World War. There were still grass runways at Croydon when it was taken over by the RAF in September 1939. By 1945 there were

9.26 *(top)*
The terminal of the airport at Gatwick, built in 1936.

(Crown copyright. NMR)

9.27 *(bottom)*
The interior of the passenger terminal of 1936 at Gatwick Airport.

(Crown copyright. NMR)

hundreds of airfields with hard runways, not just in Britain but around the rim of the North Atlantic, and along the main lines of communication to the fighting zones in all parts of the world. Thousands had learned how to pilot and navigate aircraft, and tens of thousands how to maintain airframes, engines, radios and radar. A notable figure in air transport commented in 1961:

> At the close of hostilities we found ourselves probably 50 years further ahead in air transport techniques, in aeronautical knowledge, in the development of flying equipment and devices which could be adapted to commercial use, and in public acceptance of this new means of getting about the world than we would have been if the conflict had not taken place.[44]

The US government sold more than 4,000 DC3 Dakotas in the late 1940s, and in Britain a Halifax four-engined bomber could be obtained for as little as £100.

The air transport industry was nationalised with effect from 1 August 1946, when three airlines – British Overseas Airways Corporation, successor to Imperial Airways, British European Airways, successor to British Airways, an unsuccessful company that resulted from a government-prompted merger in 1935, and British South American Airways – began to operate. The latter was taken over by BOAC in 1949 after a series of disasters to Avro Tudor airliners, and BEA and BOAC merged as British Airways in 1972. The company was privatised in 1987. There were still opportunities for private companies in the years after the war. In 1948 the Russian authorities in Germany imposed a blockade on the British, French and American zones of Berlin, and the city was supplied by an airlift which at first involved military planes, but civilian aircraft of twenty-five British carriers took part between July 1948 and May 1949. Evidence evocative of the freight carried to the German capital is provided by the coal dust in crevices of the airframe of the Avro York at Cosford Aerospace Museum. From 1950 independent airlines increasingly carried troops between Britain and bases overseas, a traffic that reached a peak in 1963–64. Diminishing commitments and the increased capacity of RAF Transport Command led to the disappearance of this traffic in the early 1970s.[45]

Flying was glamorous in the early post-war period. On 1 July 1946 BOAC inaugurated direct flights to New York via Shannon with Lockheed Constellations. Experimental aircraft of strange shapes and bright colours, like the Avro 707 and the Fairey FD2 preserved at Cosford, could be seen flitting across the skies of southern England. Schoolchildren aspired to careers as test pilots or air hostesses. By 1948 enclosures for spectators had been opened up at Northolt, then the base for BEA, and Heathrow, but even those who patronised the latter would have seen only about 80 movements of scheduled passenger aircraft every 24 hours. Several services were operated by adapted military aircraft – BOAC Yorks to Nairobi and Liberators to Montreal, and BSAA Lancastrians to Santiago – but American four-engined aircraft were used on flagship services – DC4 Skymasters by South African Airlines to Johannesburg, by KLM to Amsterdam and by Iberia to Madrid, and Lockheed Constellations by Pan American and BOAC to New York, and by BOAC to Sydney. Northolt was slightly busier in 1948, most services being worked by Douglas DC3 Dakotas, except the more prestigious BEA flights operated by Vickers Vikings. Prestwick was a refuelling stop for several transatlantic services from Amsterdam and the Scandinavian capitals as well as from London.[46]

London Heathrow is the most vibrant industrial site created in Britain in the latter part of the twentieth century. The heathland west of London was an attractive location for airfields in the inter-war period. Hounslow Heath's airfield, from which the first commercial flight to Paris was made in 1919, closed the following year and is now a recreation ground, its importance commemorated by a plaque on the Hussar public house. An airport opened at nearby Heston (TQ 118777) in 1929 was the terminus

9.28
Heathrow:
Terminal 2 from the car park at night.

(Crown copyright. NMR)

Changing horizons:

9.29
Heathrow: the prospect from the viewing platform at Terminal 2. To the left is the hangar used by British Airways, designed by Sir Owen Williams.

(Crown copyright. NMR)

of Neville Chamberlain's return flight from Germany in a Lockheed 14 on 30 September 1938 after signing the Munich agreement. The flying field at Heston has disappeared, but a concrete hangar of 1929 remains adjacent to the services on the M4. Another development of 1929 was the establishment by the aircraft manufacturer Richard Fairey of an airfield, variously called Heath Row, Harmondsworth or the Great West Aerodrome, from which his company flew new aircraft brought by road from its factory at Hayes. The development of an international civil airport on the site was due largely to Harold Balfour, Secretary of State for Air in the latter part of the Second World War. The land was purchased in 1944. Expenditure was justified on the grounds that a large base would be needed for military transport aircraft to sustain the fighting against Japan, but the war was ended by the atomic bombs dropped on Hiroshima and Nagasaki before the first runway had been completed. It is likely, however, that Heathrow was always intended for civilian use. BOAC's management still considered flying boats the likeliest means of operating the imperial routes, and envisaged a 4,000-yard x 200-yard water taxiway. Nevertheless, the first arrival after the official opening on 31 May 1946 was a land plane operating on a traditional flying-boat route, an Avro Lancastrian completing a 63-hour journey from Sydney. The first flight from the new airport, on 1 January 1946, the day on which control passed from the military to the Ministry of Civil Aviation, was a BSAA Lancastrian bound for Santiago. Most early peacetime BOAC flights were from Hurn (SZ 1197), near Bournemouth, about 100 miles

from London, and the last were transferred to Heathrow only in 1951. BEA's operations were moved from Northolt between 1950 and 1954. In its early years Heathrow consisted of runways and taxiways, of vast extent for their time, and an untidy assemblage of military huts, caravans and even tents. Its subsequent growth has been a story of dynamic and kaleidoscopic change, preserved in part by photographs and plans, but almost impossible to comprehend. The decision to establish the main terminals within the runways, with tunnel links to the outside world, was made in 1947. The main tunnel came into use on 7 October 1953, and the freight tunnel in 1968. The first of the terminals in the central area, the present Terminal 2, was first used in 1955. The Oceanic Terminal, now Terminal 3, was designed by Sir Frederick Gibberd and opened in 1961, and Terminal 1 opened in 1968. Extensive rebuilding preceded the first scheduled arrival of a Boeing 747 Jumbo Jet on 21 January 1970. Regular supersonic flights to New York by BOAC Concorde began on 22 November 1977. Terminal 4, outside the main pattern of runways, opened in 1986. There is much more to the archaeology of Heathrow than the public buildings. British Airways' maintenance is based in a cathedral-like concrete hangar designed by Sir Owen Williams. British Airways' headquarters, a building of the late 1990s, is intended to have the air of a village street.

Transport links to and from the airport have changed over time. In the post-war period passengers were conveyed there by coaches, some of them one and a half deckers, from terminals at Victoria and Cromwell Road. The Piccadilly Line reached the airport in 1977, and the fast rail link from the GWR Main Line, the Heathrow Express, in 1998. Buildings, roads and open spaces throughout the airport have been adapted and put to successive new uses.[47]

Car ferry flights to continental Europe were a passing feature of the 1950s. The best known were operated by Silver City Airways, at first from Lympne, but from 1954 from a new terminus on the site of an RAF flying field at nearby Lydd (TR 061213), on the edge of Romney Marsh. High-wing Bristol Freighters flew the short distance over the English Channel to Le Touquet. Services to France ceased in 1970, but British United Air Ferries, the result of a merger between Silver City and Channel Air Bridge in 1962, continued flights to Ostend until

1971. Channel Air Bridge flew from Southend (TQ 8689) to Strasbourg and Basle until 1970, and British United Air Ferries for a time operated services from Coventry (SP 3574) to Calais.[48]

Airports, like seaports, rose and declined in the twentieth century. Southend was the busiest airport in England apart from Heathrow in 1963. Thirty years later, its services had all but disappeared and it was threatened with closure. Blackbush (SU 8058) in Surrey, taken over from the RAF by the Ministry of Civil Aviation in 1947, was the base of trooping and charter operations by Airwork, Silver City, Danair and Eagle in the 1950s, closed in 1960, and is now a base for private flying. At Luton the municipality installed a new concrete runway in 1959. The proximity of the M1 and the proliferation of charter flights stimulated vigorous expansion. A new terminus was opened in 1960, succeeded by another in 1990, and a railway station opened in 1999. By contrast Stansted was built as a result of a tormented and protracted process by which the government decided where to locate London's 'third airport'. Lord Foster's magnificent terminal is certainly a flagship building, but one perhaps born out of collective guilt as much as self-confidence.

There is a good archaeological record of the commercial aircraft used in Britain since the Second World War. Examples of most of the significant types are in museum collections, the chief of which is that of British Airways at Cosford Aerospace Museum (SJ 7905), which includes a Boeing 707, a VC10, a De Havilland Comet I, a Vickers Viscount, a BAC 111, a De Havilland Trident and a Bristol Britannia, and is supported by models and a collection of artefacts, while in the military section of the museum a DC3, a Junkers 52, a Consolidated B24 Liberator and an Avro York also illustrate

important aspects of civil aviation. Another example of the most successful British-built airliner, the Vickers Viscount, is at Duxford (TL 4646), together with a Concorde, a Liberator, a York, a Comet IV, a Trident, a BAC 111, a Britannia and a De Havilland Dragon Rapide. The reserve collection of the Science Museum includes a Lockheed Constellation, and Brooklands Museum has examples of the Vickers Viking, the Vickers Viscount, the VC10 and the BAC 1-11.

Conclusions

Archaeological analysis of transport poses many challenges. Much can be learned from straightforward desktop studies, plotting, for example, the locations and dates of municipal airports or hump marshalling yards. Images can add much to our understanding, particularly posters that persuaded Londoners to live in Metroland, families to take holidays at Skegness or ladies rich enough to wear fur coats and to be driven in Rolls-Royces to fly to Paris in Vickers Viscounts. Artefacts can provide much evidence. The Edwardian railway carriages in the National Railway Museum were the product of a society very different from that which produced the Mark I standard coaches of the 1950s. The buses and even the tramcars of the 1990s were clearly not designed for the kinds of mass movement by gondolas of the people and double-deckers that occurred in the first half of the century when a shift finished at Westinghouse, Trafford Park, or a football match ended at St Andrews or Villa Park. Vehicles and buildings may have been put to different uses. A Great Eastern Railway non-corridor coach of the early years of the century, with sit-up-and-beg seats giving its compartments the appearance of padded cells, may have spent much of its working life in the 1920s on suburban trains between London and Chingford. It would have been regarded differently when working on a quiet East Anglian branch line, or on a 6-hour journey overcrowded with returning holidaymakers from Cromer to Birmingham on a summer Saturday in 1954. The Boeing 707 displayed at Cosford can be interpreted in terms of the

9.30
Lord (Norman) Foster's terminal at Stansted.

(Crown copyright. NMR)

history of technology as an example of a machine that transformed air travel by making possible direct flights from North America to European capitals. Its interior – identical rows of seats throughout, arranged for charter work – is evidence of another revolution, the proliferation of flights carrying holidaymakers to southern Europe. Transport archaeology, whether artefacts, images, structures sites or landscapes, should be interpreted in context. Studying transport involves at least some attempt at process recording or reconstitution. Numerous recollections give us impressions of what it was like to drive or fire a steam locomotive or manage a locomotive depot. It would be enlightening to know something of what it was like to provide meals throughout the day in the Midland Railway restaurant-car now preserved at York, or to drive a Sentinel steam wagon up the A6 from Manchester to Carlisle in 1930. A perfect record of all the structures at Heathrow would mean little without some knowledge of the purposes for which they were designed, and the ways in which they were used. Transport is activity. The first step in understanding the achievement of Sir Herbert Walker may be, as suggested above, to observe Clapham Junction or London Bridge in the rush hour. Appreciation of other aspects of transport history can be derived from time spent under the flight path to Heathrow, a distant view of trucks reduced to the scale of toys crossing the Ouse Viaduct on the M62 outside Goole, or the sight of a container ship calling at Felixstowe with little more fuss than a tram picking up and setting down at a tram stop.

Notes and references

1 The account of ports which follows is drawn from G. Jackson, *The History and Archaeology of Ports*, Tadworth: World's Work, 1983, pp. 113–67; A. Jarvis, *Liverpool Central Docks 1799–1905: An Illustrated History*, Stroud: Alan Sutton, 1991, pp. 178–221.

2 M. Stratton, 'New Materials for a New Age: Steel and Concrete Construction in the North of England, 1860–1939', *Industrial Archaeology Review*, 1999, vol. 21, pp. 16–18; *Railway Magazine*, 1934, vol. 75, p. 381.

3 Jackson, op. cit., pp. 126–32.

4 The account of the liner trade is drawn from R. McAuley, *The Liners: A Voyage of Discovery*, London: Boxtree, 1997; J. M. Brinnin and K. Galvin, *Grand Luxe: The Transatlantic Style*, London: Bloomsbury, 1988; N. T. Cairns, *North Atlantic Passenger Liners since 1900*, London: Ian Allan, 1972; C. R. V. Gibbs, *British Passenger Liners of the Five Oceans*, London: Putnam, 1963; R. Wall, *Ocean Liners*, New York: E. P. Dutton, 1977; M. H. Watson, *Flagships of the Line*, Cambridge: Patrick Stephens, 1988.

5 T. Hardy, 'The Convergence of the Twain', in *The Poems of Thomas Hardy: A New Selection*, ed. T. R. M. Creighton, London: Macmillan, 1974, pp. 216–18.

6 Stratton, op. cit., pp. 20–1.

7 C. F. Klapper, *Sir Herbert Walker's Southern Railway*, London: Ian Allan, 1973, pp. 230–5.

8 W. J. Gordon, *Our Home Railways: How They Began and How They Work*, vol. I, London: Warne, 1910, pp. 51–4; J. Simmons, *The Railway in England and Wales 1830–1914*, vol. I: *The System and Its Working*, Leicester: Leicester University Press, 1978, pp. 46, 96, 257; P. Hall and P. Fox, *Preserved Coaching Stock of British Railways*, Part Two: *Pre-Nationalisation Stock*, Sheffield: Platform 5, 1996; J. H. Russell, *A Pictorial Record of Great Western Coaches 1903–1948*, Sparkford: Haynes, 1990, pp. 174–8.

9 R. Bucknall, *Boat Trains and Channel Packets: The English Short Sea Routes*, London: Vincent Stuart, 1957, pp. 8–31, 142–4; G. Behrend and G. Buchanan, *Night Ferry*, Jersey: Jersey Artists Ltd.

10 McAuley, op. cit., pp. 82–9, 98–105.

11 British Transport Commission, *Ocean Terminal: Southampton Docks*, Southampton: British Transport Commission, 1950; pamphlet in National Monuments Record, Swindon; '£1½m. Quay and Terminal Buildings at Tilbury', *Contract Journal*, 11 July 1957; *Manchester Guardian*, 23 June 1948.

12 Bucknall, op. cit., pp. 31, 158, 183; Klapper, op. cit., pp. 248–9.

13 McAuley, op. cit., pp. 111–53.

14 M. Meek, 'They That Go Down to the Sea in Ships', *RSA Journal*, 1998, no. 114, pp. 82–115.

15 Material on London filling stations is drawn from data held in the National Monuments Record, Swindon.

16 G. Gordon (ed.) *Regional Cities in the United Kingdom 1890–1980*, London: Harper & Row, 1986, pp. 47, 69, 107; *Observer*, 26 July 1998; T. Smith, 'Silvertown Way and the Silvertown By-pass', *London's Industrial Archaeology*, 1996, vol. 6, pp. 31–8.

17 J. B. Priestley, *English Journey*, London: Heinemann, 1934, pp. 77–8; R. Elwall, *Bricks and Beer: English Pub Architecture 1830–1939*, London: British Architects Library, 1983, pp. 39–45; B. Trinder, *The Industrial*

Archaeology of Shropshire, Chichester: Phillimore, 1996, p. 200.

18 A. Forsyth, *Buildings for the Age: New Building Types 1900–39*, London: RCHME, pp. 3–15.

19 Trinder, op. cit., p. 200; we are grateful to Roy Brigden of the Museum of English Rural Life, University of Reading, for his advice on the CPRE collection.

20 H. Jones, 'Buildings Designed to Advertise Fuel', *British Archaeology*, 1998, no. 38, pp. 6–7.

21 P. Collins, *The Tram Book*, London: Ian Allan; T. C. Barker and M. Robbins, *A History of London Transport*, vol. 2: *The Twentieth Century*, London: Allen & Unwin, 1974, pp. 7, 21, 91, 94; O. Green and J. Reed, *The London Transport Golden Jubilee Book*, London: Daily Telegraph, 1983, pp. 112–13.

22 J. Hibbs, *The History of British Bus Services*, Newton Abbot: David & Charles, 1968, pp. 69–107. We are grateful to David Percival of RCAHMW and Richard Hayman of the Ironbridge Gorge Museum Archaeology Unit for their co-operation in a survey of the Brecon wharf in 1995.

23 Priestley, op. cit., pp. 3–4; Hibbs, op. cit., pp. 158–77.

24 Barker and Robbins, op. cit., p. 9.

25 A. R. Sutcliffe and R. Smith, *Birmingham 1939–1970*, Oxford: Oxford University Press, 1974, pp. 409–10. We are grateful to Tony Herbert for information on the Bull Ring's car park.

26 G. Charlesworth, *A History of Britain's Motorways*, London: Thomas Telford, 1984.

27 J. Simmonds, *The Railway in England and Wales 1830–1914*, vol. I: *The System and Its Working*, Leicester: Leicester University Press, 1978, pp. 92–3 ; S. D. Tyrrell, *A Countryman's Tale*, London: Constable, 1973, pp. 12–14, 120–2.

28 J. Betjeman, 'Original Sin on the Sussex Coast' (1954), in *John Betjeman's Collected Poems*, London: John Murray, 1980.

29 C. J. Allen, *The Great Eastern Railway*, London: Ian Allan, 1955, pp. 78, 175–89.

30 C. Dendy Marshall, *A History of the Southern Railway*, London: Southern Railway, 1938; Klapper, op. cit., pp. 161–220.

31 C. Barman, *The Man Who Built London Transport: A Biography of Frank Pick*, Newton Abbot: David & Charles, 1979.

32 *Railway Magazine*, 1935, vol. 77, pp. 353–62; 1937, vol. 81, pp. 39–42, 79–81, 103, 348–51; British Railways Press Office, *British Railways in Peace and War*, London: British Railways Press Office, 1944, p. 10; *Women Cleaning LMS Locomotives, Camden Shed*, by Norman Wilkinson, in G. C. Nash, *The LMS at War*, London: LMSR, 1946, p. 83; Green and Reed, op. cit., p. 53.

33 S. Duckworth, B. Jones and R. Thorne, 'King's Cross Goods Yard', in M. Hunter and R. Thorne (eds) *Change at King's Cross*, London: Historical Publications, 1990; M. Tucker, 'Bricklayer's Arms Station', *London's Industrial Archaeology*, 1989, vol. 4, pp. 3–23; *LMS Freight 1935*, video copy by Railfilms (1995).

34 G. Bushell, *LMS Locoman: Wellingborough*, Truro: Bradford Barton, nd, p. 7.

35 R. T. Munns, *Milk Churns to Merry-Go-Round: A Century of Train Operation*, Newton Abbot: David & Charles, 1986, pp. 148–75.

36 M. Rhodes, *British Marshalling Yards*, Sparkford: Oxford Publishing Company, 1988.

37 Mitchell Engineering Group, *British Industrial and Engineering Installations*, London: Mitchell Engineering Group, 1946, pp. 159–62.

38 N. Trevenna, *Steam for Scrap*, Penryn: Atlantic Transport, 1992.

39 R. H. N. Hardy, *Steam in the Blood*, Shepperton: Ian Allan, 1973.

40 A. J. Quin-Harkin, 'Imperial Airways 1924–40', *Journal of Transport History* (first series), 1954, vol. 1, pp. 197–215.

41 B. Learmouth, J. Nash and D. Cluett, *The First Croydon Airport 1915–28*, Sutton: Sutton Libraries & Arts Service, 1977; *Croydon Airport: The Great Days 1928–39*, Sutton: Sutton Libraries & Arts Service, 1980; and *Croydon Airport and the Battle for Britain*, Sutton: Sutton Libraries & Arts Service, 1984.

42 P. Moore, *A Guide to the Industrial Archaeology of Hampshire and the Isle of Wight*, Southampton: Southampton University Industrial Archaeology Group, 1984, pp. 66–9.

43 L. Marriott, 1993, *British Airports Then and Now*, Shepperton: Ian Allan, 1993; C. Pudney, 'A Survey of the Remaining Civilian Airport Terminals', Ironbridge Institute, Master's dissertation, 1989.

44 J. A. Frederick, quoted in B. K. Humphreys, 'Nationalisation and the Independent Airlines in the UK 1945–53', *Journal of Transport History* (second series), 1976, vol. 3, pp. 265–81.

45 B. K. Humphreys, 'Trooping and the Development of the British Independent Airlines', *Journal of Transport History* (second series), 1979, vol. 5, pp. 46–59.

46 O. G. Thetford, *ABC of Airports and Airliners*, London: Ian Allan, 1948.

47 G. Hayter, *Heathrow: The Story of the World's Greatest International Airport*, London: Pan, 1979; P. Sherwood, *The History of Heathrow*, Hillingdon: Hillingdon Libraries, 1993; Marriott, op. cit.; P. W. Brooks, 'A Short History of London's Airports', *Journal of Transport History* (first series), 1957, vol. 4, pp. 12–22.

48 Marriott, op. cit.

Chapter ten

Expanding services

When monetarist economics in the early 1980s provoked a cull of manufacturing industry, Britain's future was said to lie in the provision of services. At one level this meant financial services – banking, insurance, mortgages, investment management, pensions, stockbroking. Even such desk-based activities as these leave an archaeological record: the profusion of 1960s office tower blocks in London, the largely anonymous blocks of Croydon and Romford that mark the growing middle-class interest in financial planning of the 1970s, the prestigious buildings to which financial companies were proud to put their names in new towns like Telford. Ancient traditions ensured the continued presence of financial concerns in Scotland and the construction of prestigious company headquarters in towns, like Halifax and Leek, long linked with financial services. Archaeological evidence of change in the financial services industry could be seen all over Britain in the late 1990s. Bank buildings in many small towns, some in a pompous Baroque or even a Gothic style, had been abandoned by their former owners and put to other uses. On the sites of brickworks south of Peterborough, and on a former colliery site at Wath in Yorkshire, developers were offering new building suitable for use as telephone call centres.

Two sites exemplify the change of emphasis from manufacturing to services in the final twenty years of the century. At Wednesbury (SJ 988972), in the heart of the Black Country, alongside the most congested section of the M6 motorway and within sight of the railway marshalling yard at Bescot, stood the steel foundry of F. H. Lloyd & Co., for long one of the most important British manufacturing plants. In the late 1980s it became a retail park, of which the Swedish store Ikea is the chief attraction.[1] Wearmouth Colliery in Sunderland (NZ 396575), on the north bank of the river, occupied a position of equal importance in coal mining – it included the first shafts in Co Durham to penetrate to the coal beneath the magnesian limestone. Sunk in the 1820s and 1830s, it was said in 1992 to have reserves that would last for fifty years. It was closed in 1993, and its site is now occupied by the Stadium of Light, home of Sunderland Football Club, which moved there in 1997 from Roker Park, a ground set among terraced streets named after the members of W. E. Gladstone's second cabinet of 1880–85. Nevertheless, the service industries have long histories, and the purpose of this chapter is to indicate the archaeological evidence of the ways in which these industries changed during the twentieth century.

Retailing

The oldest of the service industries, with the exception of one that has left few archaeological traces, is retailing, an activity in respect of which British accomplishments have been acknowledged since the time of Napoleon. Retailing was changing rapidly in the early years of the twentieth century as the fascias of the chainstores proliferated in the streets of all but the smallest of towns. The rich collection of photographs in Market Harborough's museum shows the colonisation of the marketplace by Boots, Woolworths, Melias and Hepworths, as well as by the regional grocery and provision chain Star Supply Stores.[2] The pace of chainstore expansion was set by traders in food (*see Chapter 4*) who sold principally low-cost eggs, bacon and dairy produce imported from Denmark, The Netherlands, northern Germany and North America, and new products like margarine, condensed milk and canned meat, in many respects establishing new markets rather than competing with traditional grocers. Beef from South America and lamb from New Zealand were sold initially from specialist shops rather than by traditional butchers.

Typically, a 'chain' would be established by a shopkeeper setting up a branch in the town where he or she was already trading.[3] The next step would be to establish other stores, within a few miles, so that a network began to operate, which, if successful, subsequently took over similar networks in other parts of the country. The most ostentatious of the new traders was Thomas Lipton, who, having started trading in Scotland in 1871, used vigorous forms of advertising – delivering giant cheeses to his shops on wagons hauled by elephants, and dropping leaflets from balloons – to draw attention to new stores. Liptons had 500

shops by 1900. J. Sainsbury started a shop specialising in dairy produce at 173 Drury Lane, London, and in 1876 opened his first branch, in Kentish Town. His shops had counters on either side with sufficient space between to accommodate prams. There was an emphasis on cleanliness, with marble-faced pillars to the windows, extensive use of tiles, and the company's name displayed on gilded panels decorated with wrought iron. By 1900 the company had 48 branches in and around London. The Home & Colonial Stores, the Maypole Dairies, Pearks Stores, Cochranes, Galbraiths, Duncans, Melias, George Masons – all operated in similar ways and grew into substantial regional or national chains. Maypole expanded from 185 shops in 1898 to 958 in 1915. Most of the food chains went into new shops in the suburbs, but they occupied existing buildings in established towns. Most continued to expand in the inter-war period – Maypole had 977 branches in 1937, Home & Colonial 798 and Lipton 449. They disappeared during the 1960s and 1970s, but not entirely without trace. A mosaic doorstep and a decorative tile panel at 15 King Street in Ludlow (SO 512745) show that for about 50 years of its 500-year history it was a branch of Maypole Dairies. A Maypole store in Mersey Road, Widnes, which had been inserted in a terraced house, retained its fixtures, glazed tiles and vitrolite fascia, and was occupied by an upholsterer.[4] In the 1920s Home & Colonial regarded its distinctive features to be its black-and-white tiled floors, its gas globes and its practice of weighing tea in shop windows. In Scotland the most distinctive shops were those of the Buttercup Dairy chain, founded in Leith in 1909 by Andrew Ewing. Each of Ewing's shops had a mosaic doorstep on which a wreath of buttercups encircled the company monogram, while on the wall of each recessed doorway was a tiled picture of a little girl in a blue sunbonnet and white pinafore offering one from a bunch of buttercups to a friendly cow.

Chainstores supplying men's clothing also grew rapidly in the first half of the twentieth century. One of the most successful companies was that of Montague Burton, the 'tailor of taste' who by 1935 had built up a network of over 500 branches. Burton's purpose-built shops were the most distinctive on provincial high streets, with bold Art Deco motifs including stylised elephants' heads, faience panels made by Hathern, bronzed metal and polished granite. Many that have long served other purposes can still be recognised. The hub of Burton's business was a vast model factory in Leeds (SE 323344), built in 1934. Other chains supplying men's clothes included Dunns, whose house style featured wood panelling and stained glass, and Greenwoods, whose fascias were adorned with green vitrolite.

Jesse Boot (1850–1931) was chief among those who brought about a revolution in the supply of medicine and cosmetics.[5] From beginnings as a traditional herbalist in Nottingham, he began to show skill in the energetic promotion of new products, and from 1884 dispensed prescriptions. By 1902 he had 252 branches, a total that by 1914 had increased to 560, and included shops in Regent Street, London, and Princes Street, Edinburgh. Boot and his American wife Florence Anne developed a distinctive ambience in their stores. After 1900 customers at many branches could borrow books from Boots Booklovers Library, and take refreshment at tasteful cafés. In many towns existing buildings on the sites purchased by Boot were replaced by shops in a Tudor-revival style designed by A. N. Bromley. Characteristic examples remain in Lichfield, Shrewsbury and Winchester. Like many chainstores, Boots established its own factory and distribution base in the inter-war period, an innovative complex at Beeston (SK 546371), the principal feature of which was the 531-ft-long (162m) wet processes building, designed by Sir Owen Williams (1890–1969) and built in 1930–32. Externally it has the appearance of a colossal greenhouse, while internally galleries supported by mushroom-headed concrete columns surround the packing area on the ground floor. It is not just the 'flagship' of a successful company, but one of the most satisfying examples of industrial architecture in Europe.

One of the largest chainstores, the newspaper, stationery and bookselling business of W. H. Smith, which once operated over 1,000 branches, restored its shop at Newtown, Powys (SO 107915), to resemble its state in 1927, when it had opened, with a tiled fascia, bow windows and interior fittings of oak bearing the shields of sixteen universities. The company had adopted a distinctive Arts and Crafts house style in 1905. A display indicates the character of the lending libraries that until 1961 flourished in many

Smith's shops. The Newtown branch was too small to have stained glass, but some panels from the store at Worcester are displayed, together with a handcart from Whitchurch (Shropshire) of the kind used by Smith's employees to collect newspapers from railway stations.

The future direction of another of the century's most influential chainstores was less certain in 1900. 'Marks and Spencer' was a partnership established in Manchester in 1894 between Michael Marks (1859–1907), who was born at Slonim in Russia, moved to Leeds by 1884, and gained his living from stalls and penny bazaars in markets, and Tom Spencer, a book-keeper with one of Marks's suppliers.[6] The partners opened their first shop in Manchester in 1894, and by 1900 had 12 shops and 24 market stalls. In 1999 the company still operated a bazaar, in Grainger Market, Newcastle (NZ 250645), which displayed its early-twentieth-century gold-on-crimson fascia, and there are good photographic records of other early branches, like that at 574 Station Road, Brixton, a penny bazaar set in a railway arch of considerable depth. By 1911 Marks & Spencer had 89 shops and stalls, and three years later acquired 26 more with the purchase of the London Penny Bazaar Company. From the early 1920s the company concentrated on the sale of clothing, while sales of food increased gradually. Expansion was through the building of large new stores, with island counters rather than counters lining the walls, and fronted from 1924 with a new green-and-gold fascia. The company had 234 stores by 1939. Some were successfully established in areas where high levels of unemployment had deterred other companies from expanding – stores were opened in 1933, for example, in Rotherham, Halifax and Rochdale. The company's flagships were in London, at Marble Arch where a steel-framed building providing 19,190 sq. ft of selling space was opened in 1930, and by 1994 extended to 174,000 sq. ft, and in Oxford Street, where a new store opened in 1938 on the site of the eighteenth-century Pantheon Pleasure Gardens, a subtle indication that by the 1930s shopping was for a proportion of the population a leisure activity as much as it was a means of acquiring the necessities of life. Between 1935 and 1942 Marks & Spencer established cafés in eighty of their larger stores.

One of the fastest-growing chainstores of the inter-war period, the American concern F. W. Woolworth & Co., had established its first shop in Britain in 1909, in Liverpool. By 1939 the presence or otherwise of a Woolworth store in a settlement was an indication of whether it was truly a town. Most Woolworth stores were new brick buildings in a pallid Georgian style on cleared town-centre sites. They were, in the words of Graves and Hodge, 'the great cheap providers of household utensils and materials ... the focus of popular life in most small towns'.[7] They provided for all classes a link with the image of daily life in the United States conveyed in Hollywood films. For many years the crew of the dustcart in Banbury regularly took their mid-morning break on red leatherette-topped buffet stools in front of the formidable chromium-plated, steam-spurting tea and coffee machine, at the back of the store that in 1933 replaced the town's historic Red Lion Hotel (SP 456405). In major towns and at the seaside (see below) the reputation of F. W. Woolworth drew shoppers to very large stores with extensive refreshment facilities. By the 1960s the style of traditional Woolworth shops was passing out of fashion, and many were closed or reduced in size, but the characteristic buildings of the 1920s and 1930s can readily be recognised, particularly in smaller towns.

Inexpensive American grain and large-scale corn mills (see Chapter 4) made possible the development of industrial-scale bakeries, some of which established chains of shops and cafés. The two best-known, at least in the south of England, were the Aerated Bread Company, set up in London in 1862, and J. Lyons & Co., celebrated for its corner houses in London, each of which provided a range of restaurants, with food at varied prices, but which had also restaurants with distinctive gold-and-white fascias in most high streets, and supplied individual fruit pies and meat pies from its headquarters at Cadby Hall in west London to railway refreshment counters throughout Britain. Most Lyons' and ABC cafés were set in existing buildings, and are now difficult to trace. They were nevertheless a distinctive feature of metropolitan and provincial life in the first sixty years of the twentieth century. Arnold Bennett took tea in the ABC shop opposite Charing Cross Station on 4 November 1914, and observed its masculine atmosphere,

noting that 'ABC shops are still for men one of the most characteristic things in London'.[8]

Other notable chains of the inter-war period included British Home Stores, principally a clothing and drapery business, established at Brixton in south London in 1928. A range of companies supplied footwear, including Freeman, Hardy & Willis and the Czech company Bata, which operated from a factory at East Tilbury (TQ 678783), some of whose workers were accommodated in a Modernist company village (see Chapter 7). The stylish shops of Macfisheries flourished in many suburban shopping parades, and competed with traditional fishmongers in many market towns. The Times Furnishing Company was the principal supplier of furniture from shops like that built at Ilford, in 1926, with a frontage of glass and faience by Hathern, which was illuminated by floodlights. One of the largest chains was that of the Singer Company, which had shops on most high streets supplying sewing machines made at its enormous factory at Clydebank (NS 499712), opened in 1884.

By 1900 there were department stores in most towns of consequence. Most had evolved from drapers' or ironmongers' shops to sell clothing for the whole family, haberdashery, fabrics, stationery, toiletries, hardware, furniture, and sometimes other goods, and many had cafés or restaurants. Stores like Elliston & Cavell in Oxford (SP 512064) were by the beginning of the century the centres of retailing activity in their localities. Some department stores, like Mathias Robinson in Stockton (now Debenhams), a steel-framed structure of three bays with much glass in the front elevation, built about 1901,[9] used innovative forms of construction, while some colonised existing buildings – part of the Richard Maddox store in Shrewsbury (SJ 452125) was located in a late-sixteenth-century townhouse. By 1900 the provincial stores were increasingly in the shadow of those in London. William Whiteley (1831–1907) prided himself on being the 'universal provider' – the description of his occupation given on the Census enumerator's return for his house at 2 Kildare Terrace, Paddington, in 1881. His store grew from a draper's shop in Westbourne Grove (TQ 268012), where he began business in 1863. It set the pattern for London's department stores. As rebuilt by Belcher & Joass in 1908–12, after Whiteley had been shot dead by Horace Rayner, it had gigantic external columns in a vaguely French style, and internal glazed courtyards. Much evidence of his activity remains – in the village at Burr Hill, Surrey (TQ 0962), built to accommodate his company's pensioners, and the warehouse alongside the West London Extension Railway near Earls Court (TQ 261771), which still displays his inscription. Most of London's principal department stores came to be concentrated in Oxford Street, where the flagship building was the store built by Gordon Selfridge (1858–1947), an American who had amassed a fortune by mail-order trading in Chicago; it opened in 1909 with 130 departments, including Britain's first ice-cream soda fountain, in a building that utilised the latest US techniques of steel-framing, as well as marketing techniques like colour co-ordination and stylish window-dressing.[10] Harrods in Knightsbridge took its present form, a Baroque-style building with an enormous terracotta dome, in 1901, and was further extended in 1911. Department stores were subjected to many changes in the last forty years of the twentieth century. Many provincial stores were taken over by larger concerns, and lost their individuality. Some closed, and their buildings, sometimes distinctive, were occupied by smaller shops. The distinctive characteristics of some, like Gamages and Biba, passed out of fashion, and the shops were closed. Others, like Selfridges and Harrods, adapted themselves to new conditions. There is a legacy of buildings that were built for one style of retailing and are now adapted for others, and also of artefacts, not just of the goods sold but of the whole apparatus of retailing: cash registers, pneumatic despatch systems, advertising placards, counters, wrapping materials and delivery vehicles.

Co-operative shops multiplied rapidly in the decades before the Second World War. The larger retail societies established individual house-styles, often using white- or cream-glazed faience in loosely Classical styles for their suburban stores. W. A. Johnson, the architect of the Co-operative Wholesale Society, justified his use of faience and other synthetic materials as an essential part of a new architecture 'in keeping with the motor car, the aeroplane and other phases of our time'.[11] The larger societies were intensely proud of their 'flagship' department stores, like that of the

10.1
A general store of the inter-war period opened by the Sheffield & Ecclesall Co-operative Society, faced with tiles by Hathern, and advertising Heinz's 57 varieties on the window.

(Ironbridge Gorge Museum: Hathern collection)

Royal Arsenal Society at Lewisham, completed in 1933, with faience by Hathern, or the Central Store of the Sheffield & Ecclesall Society, designed in 1930 by W. A. Johnson with faience by Doulton.

At the far end of the retailing scale, at some remove from the department stores, were the thousands of corner shops in working-class areas. In the first decade of the century buildings designed to be used as shops were commonly erected at the ends of working-class terraces, with modest-sized plate-glass windows, chamfered corners with entrance doors, and hefty beams built into the walls, acting as lintels for windows and anchoring-points for fascias. Some remained in use for much of the century, but their numbers declined after the Second World War. Corner shops offered opportunities for 'penny capitalism', the investment of small sums, obtained perhaps by legacies or bets, in modest enterprises that involved much family labour. A particular type of penny capitalist trade was that in fish-and-chips, which consisted almost entirely of single-family businesses.[12] George Orwell considered that fish-and-chip shops, which for sixpence provided nutritious meals for an entire family, helped to prevent violent protest in regions of high unemployment in the early 1930s.[13] The archaeology of the trade can be seen in ranges displayed at St Fagans

(ST 118772), and at the City Museum in Stoke-on-Trent (SJ 882474); a few surviving detached huts, used specifically for frying, remain in the Yorkshire coalfield, and there is a unique fish-and-chip shop, the original Harry Ramsden's at Guiseley (SE 182424), which opened in 1931 with chandeliers, carpets and music. The use of the brand name for restaurants in resorts, airports and at motorway service areas in the 1990s was evidence of Ramsden's impact.

The progress of the more prosperous chainstores in the inter-war period is illustrated by the expansion of J. Sainsbury Ltd, whose total of 123 branches in 1919 had grown to 255 within the next twenty years, primarily by opening new shops in the outer suburbs created by railway electrification around London (*see Chapter 8*) but partly by the acquisition in 1936 of the Thoroughgoods chain with shops in the Midlands and on the south coast.[14] Like Marks & Spencer, Sainsbury developed long-term links with suppliers of such commodities as butter and Scottish beef, and in 1936 opened a new factory near to its existing headquarters in Blackfriars, an innovative pre-stressed concrete structure designed by Sir Owen Williams (1890–1969), with facilities for cutting meat, preparing sausages and baking pies. Sainsbury nevertheless retained much of the character of the traditional grocery trade in the 1930s. Even in its shops in the new suburbs, single male employees were expected to live-in under the supervision of a housekeeper, and to take their meals sitting at table in hierarchical order. Shop counters followed a U-plan, with six departments – dairy, bacon and hams, poultry and game, cooked meat, fresh meat and groceries. Customers were provided with a free delivery service. Sainsbury first used motor vehicles in 1919 after the purchase of six ex-RAF Leyland lorries. Through its own property company, Cheyne Investments, Sainsbury constructed shopping parades at places like Ruislip, Haywards Heath and Amersham, which provided premises for its own stores – and for non-competing chainstores like Boots and Freeman, Hardy & Willis, as well as local retailers.

The principal in-store change in retailing in the second half of the century was the introduction of self-service, and the consequent replacement of traditional counters by check-outs, which from the late 1970s made increasing use of information technology. Self-service was commonplace in the United States in the inter-war period, and following a transatlantic visit in 1936 by Jack Cohen, creator of Tesco, was tried at a store in St Albans. Tesco installed open shelving and check-outs on a significant scale only after the Second World War, and had converted twenty shops by the end of 1950, the year in which, on 26 June, Sainsbury opened its first self-service store, at Croydon. The most vigorous growth in the 1950s and 1960s was shown by the new chains that specialised in self-service. Tesco had 150 stores by 1962 while Fine Fare had 200. Tesco expanded rapidly, establishing new stores with extensive car parks and buying up other chains of self-service stores. Sainsbury closed its original counter shop at 173 Drury Lane in 1978, and its last counter shop at 61–63 Rye Lane, Peckham, in 1982. The number of Sainsbury stores fell from 256 in 1960 to 231 in 1980, but the company's growth was prodigious as it replaced old counter shops by new large stores, which from 1969 it called 'supermarkets'. Supermarkets built prior to the mid-1970s were by the 1990s perceived to be unfashionably small and often inappropriately located, and at the end of the century many remained empty or had been adapted for re-use.

The contexts in which shops were set also changed in the second half of the century. The centres of Exeter, Plymouth, Bristol and Coventry had been severely damaged by bombing in the Second World War. In the new centres planned after the war shops were aligned along wide boulevards ornamented with beds of flowers and patterned paving, open to traffic with roundabouts at inter-sections.[15] Just a little concern was given to protecting customers from the weather. The corporation of Plymouth in 1960 was proud of 'the finest shopping centre in the west', a re-built area of 300 acres (SX 477546) where 'modern architecture makes it possible to walk by many of the sparkling windows in complete shelter'. Such centres dated rapidly, not least because Coventry developed in a different way. Pedestrians were protected from traffic in the Upper and Lower Precinct (SP 333789), the first phases of which were completed in 1955. The area's 'flagship' was Owen Owen's store in Broadgate, designed by Rolf Helbert and Maurice Harris, a six-storey building with 4 acres (1.6ha) of floor space, of concrete construction with slab floors supported by mushroom columns in the sales area, and beam and slab construction in the stock rooms. The new centre marked an end to the austerity of recovery from the trauma of wartime. In 1949 Owen Owen had promised that 'when homes have been built for the homeless and when coupons and dockets have been pasted into the scrapbook, a great new Owen Owen store will arise, like the Phoenix, from the ashes of destruction', although the company at that time envisaged a four-storey Neo-Classical building. The Precinct was the beginning of a trend which still continued through the 1990s, of separating pedestrians and traffic in central shopping areas, whether by excluding through traffic from narrow streets, or by creating large, often indoor, shopping centres. Such centres were built in many towns from the 1960s – on the sites of old town-centre inns, as in Cambridge, on land previously occupied by town-centre industries like brewing, as in Wellingborough, on plots patiently accumulated by developers over many years, or by local authorities. They can be seen as the successors to nineteenth-century arcades and markets, although the architectural banality of some would be difficult to equal. The Bull Ring Centre in Birmingham, a flagship of the city's ambitions in the early 1960s, was in 1999 awaiting demolition. In Oxford the nucleus of one such centre was Lord Holford's elephantine Woolworth building of 1956–58 (SP 513062), the initial prosperity of which was seen to symbolise the Conservative victory in the 'Never had it so good' election of 1959.

By the 1970s the faults in many town-centre shopping schemes were becoming evident, and were ruthlessly exposed in 1972 by Professor Peter Hall at a seminar in Cambridge organised by Sainsbury. Tiered car parks with lift stops between the floors were unusable by wheelchair-bound shoppers. There were restrictions as to where trolleys could be taken. Pedestrians were not protected from traffic. This was the prelude to a dramatic 'take-off' in the diffusion of hypermarkets, strictly speaking shops with floor areas in excess of 50,000 sq. ft, set amid extensive car parks, away from traditional shopping centres and the 'superstores' (with areas from 25,000 up to 50,000 sq. ft). The first hypermarket in Britain was reputedly opened by the French company Carrefour, at Caerphilly in 1972. The same

company opened a store in the New Town of Telford the following year.

The relaxation of planning restrictions by the Conservative government in the late 1980s enabled the development of larger out-of-town retailing sites. The annual report of J. Sainsbury in 1986 had noted: 'We now have more sites awaiting development than ever before.' A journey in September 1987 on the boat train from Glasgow to Harwich, including an arc through Outer London from Watford to Shenfield, revealed superstores under construction every few miles. Another feature of the last quarter of the century was the construction of huge out-of-town centres each containing at least one superstore selling food, and branches of most of the major non-food chains.[16] The first was opened in 1976 on the 52-acre (21ha) site at Brent Cross (TQ 2387), one of north London's principal traffic intersections. The MetroCentre, Gateshead (NZ 253634), which opened in 1986, included a cinema and an hotel, as well as 100 shops. Lakeside, Thurrock (TQ 5878), opened in 1990 with 250 shops and a white marble arch with glass-and-chrome lifts on either side. Subsequently Bluewater opened near Dartford and Brayhead near Glasgow. The Trafford Centre (SJ 775964), at the western end of Trafford Park, opened in 1998, with an astronomically correct indoor sky, a multiplex cinema, embalmed palm trees and the first provincial branch of Selfridges.

The growing size of stores was matched by an expansion of warehousing. Sainsbury again provides a good case study. The main focus of distribution was at Blackfriars, subject to the worst of central London's traffic congestion, until 1960 when a depot was established on the site of an Ordnance Depot (*see Chapter 7*) at Buntingford (TL 3629) on the A10 trunk road. Further warehouses were opened at Hoddesdon (TL 3709) in 1962, at Basingstoke in 1964 and at Charlton in south London (TQ 4278) in 1969. In the 1980s Sainsbury, like other major retailing concerns, began to contract-out much of its distribution to logistics firms which had grown out of road-haulage businesses (*see Chapter 9*).

The expansion of J. Sainsbury in the 1980s and 1990s involved the re-use of some interesting industrial sites and the conservation of industrial archaeological features of earlier centuries. The company's most innovative new building is its store at Camden, opened in 1988 and designed by Nicholas Grimshaw. A roof span of over 40m is supported by webbed steel cantilevers and hawsers, and the store stands on the site of an ABC bakery, built in 1936 to the design of Sir Alexander Gibb & Partners. The store at Canley, Coventry, occupies the site of a car factory, and the Apsley Mills store, Hemel Hempstead (TL 060052), that of a paper mill. In 1982 a new store in Bath incorporated the train shed of the terminus of the Somerset & Dorset Joint Railway. The store at Cromwell Road, west London (TQ 252782), occupies the ground floor of the West London Air Terminal (*see Chapter 9*) through whose mushroom columns shoppers progress from their cars to the entrance. The store at Streatham, opened in 1989, incorporates the surviving buildings of an eighteenth-century silk mill.[17]

Printing

In 1861 more than half the printers in England and Wales plied their trade in London, and the proportion remained high for much of the twentieth century – it was still over 40 per cent in 1950 – but moves to provincial centres, beginning in the 1860s and 1870s, steadily continued, and by 1999 many newspapers read in southern England were printed outside the capital. Watson & Hazell's book-printing works at Aylesbury was set up in 1867, later becoming Hazell, Watson & Viney. Its huge hot-metal presses were heavily occupied with printing the *Reader's Digest* in the 1950s. William Clowes, similarly, moved to Beccles, Suffolk, to print books in 1873, while Unwins moved its printing department to Chilworth, Surrey, in 1871. When an industrial exhibition was held in Watford in 1947, about one-third of the space was taken up by printing firms, and it was acknowledged that printing was Watford's premier industry, providing employment for 1 in 13 of its workers, in 26 factories. One of the largest was the plant of Odhams Press, built in the 1930s to the design of Sir Owen Williams (1890–1969). From the 1960s printing began to change, with the diffusion of litho processes and computerised

setting. The industry is now very dispersed, many companies producing highly specialised work in unremarkable small units on industrial estates. A particularly poignant memorial to the hot-metal book-printing industry is a group of twenty-four houses in Dunraven Avenue, Salfords, in Surrey (TQ 287463). The houses were built for workers employed by the Monotype Corporation, formed in 1897, whose plant in nearby Honeycrock Lane employed 2,500 people in 1965, when it was the largest factory in Surrey. It closed in 1974, made redundant by the first generation of computer technology, and its site has been redeveloped.

The Times set the pace in newspaper printing, installing one of the first steam presses in England in 1814, and using railways for distribution from the 1840s. The scale of newspaper printing was greatly enlarged from 1896, when Alfred Harmsworth launched the *Daily Mail*. By 1900 a pattern of printing newspapers on a large scale in Fleet Street in London was established that was not radically altered until the 1980s. Most national newspapers were based in buildings in which linotype composing took place on the top floor, with editorial and management accommodation on the middle floors, the publishing department at street level, and the presses and stores for paper in the basement. Carmelite House, designed by Herbert O. Ellis, and built in 1897–99 for the production of the *Daily Mail*, set the pattern for other buildings. Production on this scale depended on a network of trains that ran specifically to distribute newspapers. There was a boom in the construction of newspaper headquarters in 1929–33, coinciding with the Great Depression. New premises were constructed for the *News of the World*, the *Daily Telegraph* and the *Daily Express*, the latter a striking concrete-framed building designed by Sir Owen William, clad with black glass. It set the pattern for the buildings constructed for the same newspaper in Manchester and Glasgow. The principal event in the dispersal of newspaper printing from Fleet Street was the removal to Wapping of Rupert Murdoch's titles the *Sun*, *The Times* and the *News of the World* in 1986. By 1999 newspaper text was distributed electronically to a variety of printing works, rather smaller than those which once flourished in Fleet Street, and the printed papers taken to agents by truck.[18]

Cinema

The most prominent additions to the urban and suburban landscapes of the first half of the twentieth century were the cinemas.[19] By 1914 there were in Britain about 3,000 picture houses, as they were then called. Many had been established from other buildings, like corn exchanges and warehouses. The Geisha Pavilion in Scunthorpe was opened as a roller-skating rink in 1909 and converted to a cinema in 1911. The Cinematograph Act of 1909 made obligatory the provision of at least two exits from auditoria where films were shown, and of separate fireproofed projection rooms, and thereafter most cinemas were purpose-built. The best archaeological evidence of the cinema before the First World War is provided by the Electric Palace at Harwich, a purpose-built picture house of 1911 (TM 262327), restored after some years of dilapidation. It still shows films, and its original external appearance and entrance have been restored. A larger cinema of similar date is the former Picture House in Liverpool, with a nine-bay facade of which the entrance occupied the three central bays, flanked by lock-up shops on either side. It became a religious centre. Many cinemas of the period, particularly of the Coliseum chain, had white faience fascias adorned with relief laurel wreaths.

Cinema-going increased during the First World War, and filmgoers became increasingly acquainted with films made in Hollywood. The Cinematograph Film Act of 1927 attempted to impose a minimum quota of British films which all cinemas were obliged to show. Almost all the British film-making industry was located in the outer suburbs of London, at Pinewood, Ealing, Elstree, Shepperton and Denham. The last-named of these studios, built for Alexander Korda by Walter Gropius and Maxwell Fry in 1936, was replaced by the Broadwater Business Park in the 1980s, except for one building on North Orbital Road used by Rank Laboratories.[20] In 1999 it was possible for a former employee of Ealing Studios, who was aged 18 in 1943, to point out precisely how and where the set for the war film *Battle of the Atlantic* was made.

The cinema was transformed by the introduction of talking films, in which sound tracks replaced improvised musical accompaniments. The first talkie-equipped cinema in London, the Lido at Golders Green, opened on 1 October 1928, and with its car park holding 100 vehicles, its 1,959 seats, its organ and its café, it established the notion of cinemas in large towns as social centres for purposes other than just watching films. The journal *Cinema Construction* proclaimed in 1933:

> The really successful cinema is far more than a mere house of entertainment. It is part of the life of the people. It is a place where brightness takes the place of gloom and an atmosphere of hope and cheer accompanies a trip to a cloudland of romance and beauty.

Cinema construction accelerated in the 1930s, in town centres, in suburbs and, on a modest scale in the remoter industrial communities, in the prosperous new mining villages of the Dukeries (*see Chapter 3*), as well as in depressed settlements like Hirwaun (SN 956015), where the plain brick construction and concrete detailing of the Palace Cinema is very different from the Granada in Tooting or the Odeons at Woolwich and Kingstanding (SP 081944). Like fish-and-chips, the cinema was a significant means of sustenance for the unemployed in the depressed areas. George Orwell noted:

> In Wigan the favourite refuge is the pictures, which are fantastically cheap there. You can always get a seat for fourpence and at the matinées at some houses you can even get a seat for twopence. Even people on the verge of starvation will readily pay twopence to get out of the ghastly cold of a winter afternoon.[21]

By 1938 there were nearly 5,000 cinemas in Britain, attended weekly by about 40 per cent of the population. The industry was dominated by three principal chains: Associated British Cinemas (ABC), which in 1937 had 431 cinemas; Gaumont–British, which had 345; and Oscar Deutsch's Odeon (*Oscar Deutsch entertains our nation*), which had 200. Expanding companies developed a fine balance between borrowed capital and rapid construction. Many of the larger cinemas were built within six months. The auditoria with galleries were usually steel-framed, and clad with hastily laid bricks. The street frontage was often adorned with faience in the Art Deco style. Windows at first floor level might

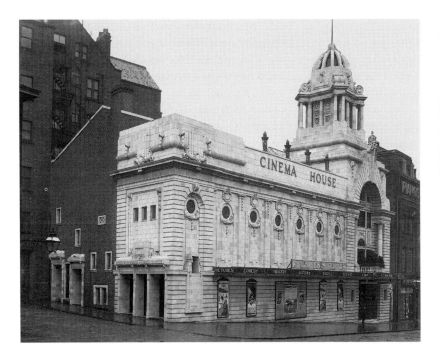

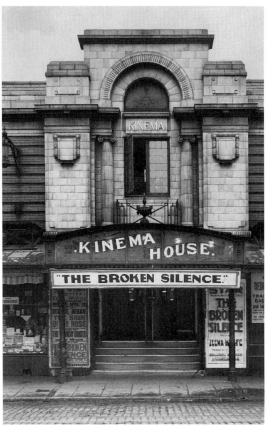

10.2 *(left)*
The Cinema House in Sheffield, faced with faience by Hathern.

(Ironbridge Gorge Museum: Hathern collection)

10.3 *(right)*
The Kinema House in Warrington, a much less grand cinema, but also faced with faience by Hathern.

(Ironbridge Gorge Museum: Hathern collection)

illuminate a café, which, with the gallery, might be linked with a ground-floor ticket hall by a chandelier-lit stairway, providing a foretaste of that descended by Scarlett O'Hara in the opening sequence of *Gone with the Wind*.[22]

Cinema going, like seaside holidays and attendance at football matches, reached a peak in the years immediately after the Second World War. It declined in the 1950s with the growth of television. In Birmingham 86 cinemas were operating in 1950. The first closure occurred in 1953; 54 remained open in 1960, and only 29 in 1968. Many cinema buildings became bingo halls in the 1960s and 1970s, but bingo, too, lost popularity in the last decade of the century, and in 1999 less than 800 of the 1,500 bingo halls operating ten years earlier were still open. Other cinemas were adapted as garages, spare-parts depots, antiques centres and low-cost food stores, while one of post-1949 date in Northampton became a Methodist church. The auditoria of some cinemas were divided up to establish multiplexes, where several films could be shown in at the same time, each with its own audience. Out-of-town multiplex cinemas proliferated in the late 1980s and 1990s, and in many places the multiplex became a focus for car-borne entertainment seekers, standing amid the bowling-alley, computerised interactive games and franchised fast-food outlets.

Sport

Spectator sports, many of them performed by professional players, comprised a major industry by 1900. In the latter part of the nineteenth century national governing organisations had been established, rules codified, and leagues and cup competitions established. In most towns there were specialist facilities for the principal sports.

Most football grounds used by professional clubs established before 1914 remained in use for much of the century.[23] The larger grounds were steadily improved. The huge 'kops', often hills of ashes in the early part of the century, became concrete terraces or stands with seats overhung by steel canopies. They are illustrated in early cinema newsreels, and in Humphrey Jennings's film *Spare Time* of 1932, in which the class identity of the spectators is signalled by their caps and hats. Most were in inner-city areas, and until the 1960s most spectators reached them by public transport. One of the few wholly new stadiums of the interwar period was that at Wembley (TQ 194854), designed by Simpson Ayrton in collaboration with Sir Owen Williams as part of the British Empire Exhibition of 1924. The twin ferroconcrete towers, which pedestrians could approach along the broad Wembley Way, became a footballing icon, but most spectators once inside the ground had to endure conditions of some discomfort, and its replacement was under way by the end of the century. The most successful club of the 1930s was Herbert Chapman's Arsenal, whose ground at Highbury (TQ 316860) retains its two-tiered east stand, designed by William Binnie in 1936, with its ornate administration and changing-room block below. The Old Trafford stadium of Manchester United, the most successful club of the closing years of the century, which stands on the edge of Trafford Park, was severely damaged during the Second World War and was enlarged in several stages in the 1990s. Disasters at Valley Parade,

Bradford's ground, in 1985, and at Hillsborough, Sheffield, in 1989 increased pressures for change, and during the 1990s a succession of major clubs moved to wholly new grounds, like the Stadium of Light at Sunderland (*see above*) and the Reebok Stadium at Bolton, which were accessible by car, provided sheltered seating for all spectators, and incorporated restaurants and other facilities to ensure regular use by their respective communities outside of match hours.

The significant buildings for other sports tended to be the national stadiums, the innovative concrete buildings erected at the All-England Croquet and Lawn Tennis Club at Wimbledon in the 1930s, the remarkable additions made to Lord's cricket ground in the 1990s, and in Cardiff the new Millennium Stadium that opened in 1999, intended primarily for rugby union. Lidos for outdoor swimming, like the Showboat Lido of 1933 at Maidenhead, proliferated in the 1930s, some of them components of roadhouse-style public houses, and pools forming part of recreation centres, became commonplace from the 1970s. The most notable swimming facilities were the Empire Pool at Wembley, of 1934, designed by Sir Owen Williams, with a concrete cantilevered roof, and the Derby Baths at Blackpool, now demolished. Other spectator sports, like greyhound racing and speedway, rose and declined in popularity, but retained some much-improved stadia at the close of the century. Ice-rinks were built from time to time throughout the century, examples including the streamlined rink of the 1930s at Kirkcaldy, and the tent-like structure of the 1980s on Oxpens Road, Oxford (SP 506067).

The seaside

On Friday 15 June 1900, the Midland Railway conveyed 11,241 people on 17 trains from Burton upon Trent to Blackpool, the most popular of the 41 trips for its employees organised by the management of the Bass brewery between 1865 and 1914.[24] Never again did so many people take advantage of the firm's generosity. The day trip to the seaside, which could be prolonged by means of an 'extension

10.4
The Arsenal FC stadium at Highbury, designed by Archibald Leitch, who designed at least twenty-eight of the grounds used by clubs in the Football League. The west stand was built in 1932 to the design of C. W. Ferrier and the east stand, with its frontage to Avenell Road, to the design of William Binnie in 1936.

(Crown copyright. NMR)

ticket' allowing a passenger to return a day or so later by normal trains, had been characteristic of the second half of the nineteenth century. Gradually the short stay at the seaside became the typical holiday taken during the first three-quarters of the twentieth century. A railway poster in 1906 proclaimed that 'Herne Bay's Industry is Healthmaking'. The seaside was indeed an industry, and its archaeological record is extensive.

> As she lay in salt water in Wonderland, Alice mused that she had been to the seaside once in her life, and had come to the general conclusions that wherever you go on the English coast you can find a number of bathing machines in the sea, some children digging in the sand with wooden spades, then a row of lodging houses and behind them a railway station.[25]

She had recognised some of the key features in the rise of the seaside holiday. Resorts have been analysed by urban historians, geographers and sociologists, who have recognised a model with five principal stages:

▮ discovery;

▮ local initiatives;

▮ the introduction of outside capital;

▮ consolidation – mass tourism and the predominance of artificial over natural attractions;

▮ stagnation or rejuvenation.[26]

The seaside holiday rose gradually in popularity in the first decades of the century, as an increasing proportion of the working population gained holidays with pay. The Holidays with Pay Act of 1938, which extended the principle to most full-time workers, was due to come into force in 1939, but its implementation was postponed until after the Second World War. The end of the war brought a widespread yearning for the seaside. The largest number of rail travellers ever to reach Blackpool on one day – 102,889 – arrived there on the first July Wakes holiday of 1945. A woman who had grown up in poverty in the Black Country in the 1930s recalled that her father amassed a little money once he gained employment during the war, and that in 1945 at the age of 15 she enjoyed her first holiday, and her first new dress, travelling by coach to Rhyl, where her party was met by youths with hand-made carts plying to carry luggage, and staying in adapted army huts that were let for £3 a week.[27] The numbers taking seaside holidays remained very high throughout the 1950s, but the spread of car ownership, the contraction of the railways and the availability of charter flights to resorts in southern Europe brought rapid changes. Some resorts which had advertised vigorously for long-stay visitors in the 1950s, like New Brighton and Herne Bay, evolved as dormitory settlements, or resorts for the elderly–retired. Others adapted themselves to different patterns: short, generally motor-borne, holidays in the more comfortable hotels, self-catering accommodation for more extended family holidays, and provision for special-interest groups like brass bands or collectors of Dinky Toys.

10.5
Nardini's café and ice-cream parlour on the seafront at Largs.

(*Crown copyright. Royal Commission on the Ancient and Historical Monuments of Scotland*)

Much of the infrastructure that lasted through the twentieth century was in place by 1914, if not by 1900. The principal seaside hotels are of Victorian origin. The Midland Hotel, built by the LMSR at Morecambe in 1933 and designed by Oliver Hill, was probably the last hotel to be constructed by a railway company in a seaside resort. Boarding houses, as Alice noticed, were an essential feature of resorts. Most of the distinctive areas made up of purpose-built boarding houses, like the bay-windowed, Accrington-brick lodging houses around the stations in Blackpool, were constructed before the First World War. In the resorts that have remained prosperous, like Blackpool, Torquay or Llandudno, such buildings have been much altered, externally by dormers lighting attic bedrooms, and internally by the insertion of en-suite toilet facilities, and extended ground-floor dining rooms. John Walton's studies of Blackpool have shown that most boarding houses were kept by women – in 1911, in the Fylde resort, lodgings were let by 4,174 householders, over 2,000 of whom were widows or spinsters.[28] The two purpose-built convalescent homes for miners, built in 1927 at Bispham (SD 310405), Blackpool, and at Skegness (TF 658574), were redundant in the late 1990s. Housing developments at resorts after the First World War were similar to those in other parts of the country (*see Chapter 8*), but many of the semi-detached villas and bungalows of that period contributed, if only marginally, to the accommodation of the huge numbers of visitors of the late 1940s and 1950s.

Many of the principal places of seaside entertainment were also flourishing by 1900. The most celebrated – Blackpool Tower – had been completed in 1894, during a decade when the resort's population increased from 22,000 to 47,000. At Great Yarmouth the Prince of Wales Theatre dates from 1883, and the principal centres of entertainment at the south end of the front – the terracotta Hippodrome, designed to accommodate a circus, the twin copper-domed Windmill of 1908, the Empire Picture Palace of 1911, the arcades of 1902 and 1904, and the

terracotta building that in 1998 bore the name Caesar's Palace – would all have been seen by the Bass employees who participated in the company's annual excursion on 25 July 1913. Most piers and cliff railways pre-date the First World War, although the concrete pier at Deal (TR 378528) was opened in 1957 and the Babbacombe Cliff Railway at Torquay (SX 925657) in 1926. The open area at the south end of the front at Blackpool, the resort of itinerant fairground showmen in the 1890s, was named the Pleasure Beach in 1905, and was successively changed throughout the century. Anthony Burgess, a regular visitor in the 1930s, recalled its Noah's Ark and its Big Dipper. There was little investment in the years after 1945, but as the tide of holidaymakers ebbed, such rides as the Log Flume of 1967 and the Space Tower of 1974 were added, and by the late 1980s it was attracting 6.5 million visitors a year, the most popular paid attraction in Britain.

The most significant new buildings designed for seaside entertainment during the century were multipurpose centres, following the examples of the Tower buildings and the Winter Gardens at Blackpool of the 1890s. The Kursaal at Southend was built between 1898 and 1901, to the design of George Sherrin and John Clark, on the site of an existing pleasure ground, and incorporated a casino, snooker and billiard rooms, a cinema and a ballroom. Spanish City (in 1998, Fast Eddie's) at Whitley Bay

10.6
Dreamland at Margate before it was rebuilt in 1934.

(Crown copyright: NMR)

10.7
The Great Wheel and the Winter Gardens at Blackpool in the early twentieth century viewed from the Tower.

(Crown copyright. NMR)

(NZ 355721), built to the design of J. T. Cackett and R. Burns Dick in 1910–11, has a 55-m-long Renaissance-style front, with a concrete dome designed by the Hennebique company, 16m in diameter and much lighter than if it had been made of any other material.[29] The Pavilion at Torquay is a florid domed structured adorned with Doulton's Cararraware, and built in 1911 to the design of H. A. Garnett, the Borough Surveyor. At Blackpool the Winter Gardens were extensively rebuilt from 1929, with white faience supplied by Shaws of Darwen. Dreamland at Margate (TR 353711), recorded in Lindsay Anderson's none-too-flattering film of the early 1950s,[30] was designed by Iles, Leathart & Grainger in 1934, a steel-and-concrete structure with a fin-like tower, incorporating a cinema, buffets and a miniature railway, as well as fairground attractions. It has been rebuilt since the time of Anderson's film. The Scottish architect James Carrick designed Cragburn at Gourock in 1936 and the Pavilion at Rothesay in 1936, both incorporating ballrooms and restaurants. Architecturally, the most distinguished of these multipurpose attractions is the pavilion at Bexhill (TQ 736072), named after Earl de la Warr, the borough's Mayor in 1935, the year of its completion. Designed by Erich Mendelsohn and Serge Chermayeff, it was the first major building in Britain with a steel frame that was welded rather than riveted. Its smooth concrete walls and curving windows were intended to create the ambience of an

ocean liner, and enclosed an auditorium that doubled as a cinema and a reading room.[31] There were few similar developments in the 1950s, but as the popularity of the seaside holiday began to ebb, some resorts built indoor centres like that at Rhyl, intended to replicate the climatic conditions of the Mediterranean coast.

In 1911 there were 2,000 shops in Blackpool, 96 of which sold fish-and-chips. Subsistence needs aside, recreational shopping is very much part of the holiday experience. A holiday provides time generally unavailable in the working week to buy clothes, books, records, household gadgets and presents. All the principal non-food chainstores built premises at the principal resorts that were much larger than their resident (wintertime) populations would have justified. The flagship of such premises was the Woolworth store at Blackpool, completed in time for the Whitsun Bank Holiday of 1938, on an awkward corner site adjacent to the Tower. The steel-framed terracotta-clad store has five storeys, a basement and a tower, and looks rather like a miniature version of a Manhattan skyscraper. Truscon provided pre-cast units for the roof and floors. The counters for retailing were laid out in the basement and on the ground floor, while the first and second floors accommodated self-service American-style dining areas, which introduced the word 'cafeteria' to the British. The walls of the cafeterias were of vitrolite, and their kitchen was distinguished by three large dishwashers. Accommodation for staff was provided on the third floor, storage for stock on the fourth, and a bakery on the fifth. The building has long ceased to be a Woolworth store, but its presence on the promenade is powerful evidence of a particular stage in the evolution of mass tourism.[32]

Prior to the Second World War plotland settlements were as important in the colonisation of the coastline as in the creation of suburbia (*see Chapter 8*). Along many stretches of the coast in the first four decades of the twentieth century military huts and old railway-carriage bodies formed clusters of family holiday homes. At Pagham Beach near Chichester (SZ 883970) the redundant carriages of the Chichester & Selsey Tramway, closed in 1935, were converted to holiday bungalows. On the clifftops at Cayton Bay (TA 068842), south of Scarborough, a member of the CPRE recorded in

10.8
The Pleasure Beach
at Blackpool.

(Crown copyright. NMR)

the late 1920s a settlement of huts and railway carriages, the most prominent of which appears to have been the bulky and doubtless heavy body of an East Coast joint-stock sleeping car, named 'Beach View', and equipped with barrels to catch rainwater from the roof. Two other carriages laid out at right angles to each other formed the Bay Café, and the settlement included at least two wooden huts and a water tank. Curiously, 94 acres (38ha) of land at Cayton Bay was purchased in 1932 by the National and Local Government Officers' Association (NALGO) for the development of a members' holiday camp; it opened in July 1933, with 124 wooden bungalows which, the advertisements insisted, were waterproof. NALGO sold the camp in 1976, and it was subsequently re-developed by its new owners. At the other extremity of England, at least one converted railway carriage can still be recognised in the settlement of plotland origins lining Polzeath Bay in north Cornwall.[33]

The best remaining landscape of coastal plotland settlement is at Dungeness, a remarkable survival on a shingle beach. A spluttering of huts litters about a mile of the route of the miniature Romney, Hythe & Dymchurch Railway between its Dungeness terminus (TR 08974) and Pilot Halt (TR 090185)

in the shadow of a lighthouse and a nuclear power station. Elliptical and segmental roofs show that many of the dwellings were once railway carriages, while steeper pitched roofs may indicate former military huts. The houses have been enlarged with asbestos sheets, weather-boarding, ready-made window frames and fretwork verandahs. Stove pipes emerge from most roofs, but some huts have free-standing brick chimneys – faintly reflecting Richard Rogers' Lloyds Building or the detached lift-shaft of Ernö Goldfinger's Trellick Tower.

Plotlands exemplified the freeborn English person's right of access to the sea, a right denied during the threat of invasion in the Second World War when the coastline from Berwick to Dorset (Brighton excepted) became territory prohibited to holidaymakers. The significance of this denial can be seen in Humphrey Jennings's film *Diary for Timothy*, released in 1945, where three separate sequences show mines and barbed wire being cleared from beaches. Most plotlanders were prevented from returning to the sites of their demolished dwellings, until the Town and Country Planning Act of 1947 gave local authorities powers to prevent new plotland developments. Settlements that survived, and those on western coasts that remained undisturbed, gradually changed as cladding enveloped the original buildings and as the common desire to settle at the seaside became focused on caravan sites. The North Wales coast between Talacre and Penmaenmawr (*see Chapter 11*) has what is probably the greatest concentration of caravans on the British coast. As John Betjeman[34] recorded in 1969:

> The green Welsh hills come steeply down
> To many a cara-circled town,
> Prestatyn, Rhyl...

The dividing line between plotlands and conventional settlement patterns is difficult to determine. At Pevensey Bay (TQ 663042), flat-roofed bow-fronted bungalows, apparently constructed of pre-cast concrete panels, line a road which runs just behind the sea defences. They form one of many small communities, stemming from the time before strict planning controls, that are neither plotland nor conventional settlement. Three relatively substantial communities further illustrate this division.

Peacehaven (TQ 0141), between Newhaven and Brighton, was developed by Charles Neville, who acquired the land over the years 1914–23. He planned to call his development 'New Anzac on Sea', but decided against it when the scale of casualties in the Dardanelles became known. A grid of streets was laid out, and plots on which purchasers could erect their own dwellings were offered for sale. On 29 September 1922 a special train with Pullman cars was provided to bring potential buyers from London, and by 1929 advertisements were promising a seaside home for £350. A high proportion of the first dwellings to be occupied were war-surplus huts from a nearby army camp, but many incorporated asbestos sheets, tiles imported from Spain, and bricks from Belgium. To the chagrin of planners like Sir Thomas Sharp, Peacehaven was promoted as 'The Garden City by the Sea'. Neville erected the Peacehaven Hotel, opened in 1922 and demolished in 1987, a 300-seat pavilion which was opened in 1923, became a cinema in 1929 and was destroyed by fire in 1940, and a power station with diesel generators in a building with a lightweight steel frame, which began generating in 1922 and was demolished in 1960. Peacehaven's most celebrated resident was the Rochdale-born singer Gracie Fields, who bought a bungalow for her father in 1927 and later a larger house called 'The Haven', which is now an orphanage.[35]

Jaywick (TM 1513) is located around a Martello tower 2 miles west of Clacton, and was the creation of Frank Stedman (1874–1963), a land surveyor from Dulwich, who bought the site in 1928. He employed contractors to build roads, and offered plots for as little as £25, promising that a house could be built for £395. One part of the estate was reserved for chalets and houses, the other for beach huts. An artificial lake was created, and in 1936 a miniature railway with an 8-foot model of a Patrick Stirling 4-2-2 locomotive began to operate. Jaywick appealed strongly to East Enders, who, particularly after the Colchester By-pass was opened in 1933, travelled there by coaches which picked up at Romford and Ilford. Entertainment in the 1930s was organised by 'Uncle Peter' and featured the 'Three Jolly Jays'. In the great east-coast flood of 1953 about 250 properties were severely damaged, and many lives were lost. The local authority, which had always been uneasy about the siting of houses on a flood-prone site, tried in 1971–74 to clear 770 dwellings, but the attempt failed, and mains drainage was installed in 1977.[36]

Canvey Island is one of the most interesting industrial archaeological sites in Britain – as the site of a substantial oil terminal of 1936, which serves the nearby refineries at Shellhaven, Coryton and Thames Haven, and as Britain's first natural gas terminal, opened in 1959, and the start of the gas pipeline network that subsequently covered the whole country (see Chapter 3). It is of great interest also as a resort. The population of the island diminished during the nineteenth century and numbered only about 300 in 1900. Several thousand acres were bought by Frederick B. Hester, who created over 1,000 plots on which purchasers were able to erect their own dwellings, and two communal buildings – the Winter Gardens (TQ 9784) and the Palace of Glass – linked to the ferry landing stage by a horse-operated monorail that was in the process of electrification when Hester was declared bankrupt in 1905. A bridge to Benfleet on the mainland was opened in 1931. The Danish pioneer of concrete construction Ove Arup, who had settled in London in 1923, designed a café and shelter at Canvey Island in 1932–33. Several hotels and a casino flourished in the 1930s, but most visitors stayed in their own holiday homes, plots for which could be obtained for as little as £6 10s. The fretwork artistry of some of the houses built on Canvey was the most ornate to be found at any plotland site in Britain. The island's funfairs were popular with East Enders, many of whom until the 1950s would cycle on day trips to the island. Canvey, like Jaywick, suffered from the flood of 31 January 1953, when fifty-eight islanders lost their lives. A holiday camp was established on a former camping site on the island in 1956. The population of Canvey Island increased rapidly, from 1,795 in 1921, to 3,532 in 1931 to 11,258 in 1951.[37]

Fieldwork suggests that some other coastal settlements had similar origins. One is the Sandy Cove Residential Estate (SH 982802) at Kimnel Bay, west of Rhyl, an area described, in about 1930, with some irony as 'the Garden City of Wales'. Small, tightly spaced bungalows, some probably of prefabricated construction, line a network of unsurfaced roads immediately east of the Golden Sands Holiday Camp (see below).

Expanding services

The appearance of Peacehaven, Jaywick and Canvey changed in the latter part of the twentieth century, as huts came to be clad with modern materials, or replaced by new buildings. Local authorities, if unwillingly, have taken over responsibility for basic services. The landscapes that remain can be interpreted as evidence of the aesthetic damage and the actual dangers that can arise from establishing settlements outside a considered planning process. They can, on the other hand, be seen more positively, as evidence of social vitality, of the determination of individuals and families to gain access to the sea by their own efforts, and to enjoy the benefits of owning property.

An officially approved, though curious, form of plotland holiday could be taken in camping coaches. In the mid-1930s all four of the major railway companies themselves adapted redundant coaches and placed them in sidings in such holiday areas as the Yorkshire Dales, the Lake District, Devon and Cornwall, to be let by the week to families. The greatest concentration appears to have been at Heysham, where the LMSR parked thirty-six coaches together. The same company had seventeen at Blackpool. The practice was extended in the 1950s, and promoted by a British Transport film, but ceased with the Beeching cuts in the following decade.[38]

The holiday camp was a twentieth-century innovation that commercialised many of the attractive features of plotlands.[39] Camping became popular in the early years of the century with the growth of the Boy Scouts movement, and the glorification of the achievements of empire pioneers. Several organised tented camps were developed before the First World War, among them a camp established at Caister, north of Yarmouth, in 1906 by the socialist J. Fletcher Dodd. Tents were soon supplemented by chalets, and Dodd was still running the camp after the Second World War. By the mid-1980s it had been taken over by a conglomerate, but still it flourished in 1999, as did other camps on the same stretch of coast. Several camps were established as family businesses in the 1920s, including two near Yarmouth, at Hopton on Sea and Hemsby (TG 4917), one at Littlestone (TR 0824) near Dungeness, and several on the North Wales coast. The Co-operative movement and various trade unions also became involved in the

provision of camps. By 1939 there were over 170 holiday camps in England and Wales, more than 50 of them tented.

Capitalist holiday camps were developed in the 1930s and reached a peak of prosperity in the 1950s, when they provided much of the accommodation demanded by the surging numbers who wished to pass a week or so of the summer on the coast. The pre-war holiday camp industry was dominated by two entrepreneurs. Harry Warner established his first camp at Hayling Island in 1931, opened three more before the Second World War, and had fourteen, all in southern England, by 1964. Billy Butlin (1899–1980) was a fairground showman who, in 1927, opened an amusement park at Skegness, introduced dodgem-cars to Britain the following year, and opened his first holiday camp at Easter 1936. He conceived a camp as offering the open air and freedom he remembered from a summer camp on Lake Ontario in his youth, and as a liberating contrast to the authoritarianism which he had suffered in a traditional seaside boarding house at Barry Island. It was an ambitious venture, since he had calculated that at least 500 campers would be needed to create the ambience that would persuade them to return and to advertise the camp by word of mouth. By September 1936 the camp could accommodate 1,200 people and the capacity was increased to 2,000 for the summer of 1937. Butlin opened a second camp at Clacton (TM 166137) on 1 June 1938. He quickly gained expertise in accommodating and catering for large numbers of people, expertise that was sought by the government during the Second World War, when Butlin was asked to advise on the provision of hostels and restaurants at Royal Ordnance Factories (see Chapter 7). The Skegness camp (TF 566617) was used by the Royal Navy, and that at Clacton by the army. A new camp, on the Yorkshire coast at Filey (TA 120775), scheduled to open in 1940, was completed at government expense, and used during the war by the RAF Regiment. Butlin built two other camps for the Royal Navy, HMS Glendower at Pwllheli (SH 370341) on the Lleyn Peninsula, and HMS Scotia at Ayr (NS 300184), and was able to buy them after the war.

Butlin was well placed to accommodate the surging demand for seaside holidays which followed the war, and his company prospered through the 1950s. As tastes in holidays changed, Butlin built three new holiday centres – at Bognor (SZ 940990) in 1960, Minehead (SS 980463) in 1962 and Barry Island (ST 120663) in 1964. Accommodation was improved and the option of self-catering was introduced. Eventually the traditional camps ceased to be viable, and Filey and Clacton were closed at the end of 1983. In 1998 the Pwllheli camp was marketed as 'Starcoast World near the Snowdonia National Park', with an emphasis on its Starsplash flume, its Boomerang roller-coaster, its Paratrooper and even its dodgems. It had become an attraction rather than a place of accommodation, and the Butlin phenomenon had returned to its fairground origins.

Other entrepreneurs profited from holiday camps, chief among them Fred Pontin, whose first venture was at Brean Sands, Somerset, a pre-war camp that had been occupied and severely damaged by the US Army. He subsequently acquired other camps, including that built by the LMSR at Prestatyn, and had the foresight to begin providing package holidays to Mediterranean resorts in 1963. Butlin, Warner and Pontin concerns had all been taken over by leisure industry conglomerates by the early 1980s.

The Welsh coastline around Rhyl illustrates well the varied history of the holiday camp. At Prestatyn, east of Rhyl, Pontin's Prestatyn Sands Camp (SS 068835) was still flourishing in 1999, though its accommodation blocks appeared to be almost entirely of 1950s construction – two-storey buildings in yellow brick and artificial stone. A short distance to the west was the Robin Hood Camp, also flourishing in 1999, which from the beginning leased chalets to private owners, and provided plots for caravans. It was established in the 1930s by a Nottingham entrepreneur, and included the Maid Marion Store and the Friar Tuck Café. Perhaps the most ambitious British holiday camp built before the Second World War was opened by the LMSR at Prestatyn (SJ 052831) in 1939. It was designed by the company's architect as a 'chalet village by the sea', with its principal buildings in white-painted concrete, giving the ambience of an ocean liner. There was an observation tower, a dining room that accommodated 1,750 at a sitting, and 600 couples could dance in the maple-floored ballroom. The camp was used by the army in the Second World War, and after nationalisation of the railways it was sold to

Pontin, who used it until the early 1980s, adding some accommodation blocks similar to those at Prestatyn Sands. In 1999 the camp stood derelict, its original single-storey chalets made uninhabitable by asbestos, the rendering falling from its communal buildings, and mallards breeding on the muddy swamp that was once the ornamental pool in the central quadrangle. The Coventry Co-operative Society opened a camp at Kimnel Bay, to the west of Rhyl, in 1930, with 6 huts, a railway-carriage body and more than 24 tents. The camp continued to provide inexpensive holidays for Coventrians until the late 1970s, when it was sold and cleared for housing. Further west, the Golden Sands Camp (SH 980800) was opened in 1933 by a local timber merchant, who provided chalets, tents and a pavilion on the beach. The camp remained in use during the Second World War, although the pavilion was used as a factory, and was still offering low-cost holidays in 1999, although much of its space was occupied by caravans.[40]

Holiday camps had passed out of the news by the late 1990s but remained a substantial niche market within the seaside holiday industry. The survivors offered either large-scale attractions, like Starcoast World, or, in the original tradition of camps, holidays that were inexpensive and simple. The smaller examples, like that at Norman's Bay, Pevensey (TQ 684055), where the entrance comprises a pair of hipped-roofed bungalows and a traditional red telephone box alongside a lifting gate, or Rye Harbour, which is grouped around a Martello tower, retain a slightly militaristic air. Holiday camps are recorded on thousands of postcards, and many of the artefacts – for which there was fierce bidding when the contents of the Clacton camp were sold in 1985 – are doubtless retained with respect. Some camps have long histories reflected by their larger buildings even if the first and second generations of accommodation have been replaced. Pontin's portfolio for 1999 reflected the history and the origins of camps, including Camber Bay, on a stretch of coast rich in plotland development; Brean Sands, Fred Pontin's first venture on a one-time US Army base; Hemsby in Norfolk, site of one of the very first camps; and Prestatyn Sands, in another classic holiday camp area. In many respects holiday-camp owners exploited their staff, who in turn exploited their customers. Yet traditional camps were innovative in that they provided holidays that were free of the constraints of the boarding house, that could be child-centred, and that could bring relief from the chores of housework. They also catered well for the disabled and provided an unthreatening environment for members of ethnic minorities. The holiday-camp holiday, between 1930 and 1960, was one of the most successful products of the twentieth-century service industries.

The boom in British seaside holidaymaking in the 1950s was largely dependent on rail transport. Some seaside stations, like Llandudno and Paignton, were enlarged in the inter-war period. British Railways stored large numbers of coaches for much of the year, some of them in the depths of the Buckinghamshire countryside at Verney Junction, that were used on only about ten Saturdays each summer. Stations that were quiet for much of the year, like Belgrave Road at Leicester, Green Park at Bath and Melton Constable in the hills of north Norfolk, were centres of frantic activity on Saturdays during the summer. The greatest strains on the system were probably around Preston, whose junctions provided the only rail access to Blackpool, and on the line between Taunton and Newton Abbot, where traffic probably reached an all-time peak on Saturday 27 July 1957 when a coach-drivers' strike coincided with the start of the holiday fortnight in the west midlands. In the space of 13 hours 80 trains arrived at Newton Abbot, on average 122 minutes behind schedule, and 32,000 passengers from more than 100 miles away alighted at the Torbay resorts. Symbolically, the site of some new carriage sidings installed in 1957 at Goodrington on that line is now a car park.[41]

By 1960 increasing numbers of people were travelling to the seaside by car, and congestion on the Exeter By-pass became newsworthy. The need to accommodate cars reduced the attractiveness of traditional terraced boarding houses in narrow streets. The car also made self-catering the more attractive option. At the same time British Railways closed many branch lines which served resorts, and its summer-holiday traffic fell away rapidly from the mid-1960s. By the 1990s holiday patterns had changed, but the attractions of the seaside remained sufficient to create peaks, if less dramatic ones, in both rail and road traffic on Saturdays in July and August.

Day trips

The day excursion was the creation of the railways, and its popularity was boosted after 1918 by the motorcoach. Excursions by car were available only to a minority before 1939, but became a mass experience in the 1950s. Destinations varied with tastes and fashions, but by the 1980s the provision of destinations for day trips had consciously developed into a distinct industry.

An impression of tastes in day excursions in the early 1930s is provided by the *Daily Mail's* reports on Whit Monday in 1931, a day of fine weather in southern England, but at a time when more than 2.5 million were unemployed, and only three months before the financial crisis that would bring down the government. Headlines proclaimed 'Whole Nation Has A Day Out.... Enormous Crowds Everywhere', and the front-page report began: 'Unparalleled crowds besieged all outdoor events yesterday.' It was reported that 50,000 had gone to the motor-racing at Brooklands, 40,000 to horse-racing at Hurst Park, 63,675 to the Crystal Palace at Sydenham, 20,000 to watch Middlesex play Sussex at Lord's Cricket Ground, 30,000 to athletics at Stamford Bridge and 45,000 to speedway at West Ham. It was claimed, rather improbably, that approximately 350,000 visited Hampton Court, though eyewitness reports stated that the paths in the grounds were solid with people. Huge crowds travelled by car to such resorts as Hastings, Eastbourne and Felixstowe, but the impression that this was a national experience shared by all social classes was dimmed by the *Daily Mail's* observation: 'Women in light summer frocks ... stood in crowds near the obelisk at Lewisham SE watching the cars returning from the coast resorts'.[42]

The new attraction of Whit Monday 1931 was the London Zoological Society's open-air zoo at Whipsnade on Dunstable Downs, which was visited by 28,000 people, while 68,000 went to the zoo in Regent's Park. Zoos were some of the most popular destinations for excursions in the inter-war period, and their archaeology reflects the thinking of the time. The Russian-born Modernist architect Berthold Lubetkin (1901–90) designed the concrete house for the gorillas at London Zoo which was opened on

28 April 1933, and the penguin pools, completed in 1934. At Whipsnade he was responsible for the entrance buildings and the giraffe house of 1934, the elephant house of 1935, and the restaurant, which was tastefully added to an existing farmhouse. Lubetkin also designed and built the zoo in the grounds of the castle at Dudley in the west midlands, which was opened on 5 May 1937, only eighteenth months after the project was launched. His bear ravine, polar bear pit, elephant house, penguin pool and reptiliary can still be admired.[43]

In the immediate aftermath of the Second World War the seaside and sporting events remained the principal destinations for day excursions, but the agenda gradually changed. Some historic houses were opened to visitors on a commercial basis, and the principal objective of the National Trust came to be perceived as the preservation and interpretation of such houses. Quite suddenly, in the mid-1960s, parts of the industrial heritage became destinations for excursions. The principal open-air museums in England were established within a few years of each other, in the mid-1960s – Ironbridge, Beamish, Avoncroft, the Black Country Museum and the Weald & Downland Museum – all of them having greater or lesser industrial components. At much the same time, the first major standard-gauge railway preservation schemes were emerging as successful concerns, for example the Severn Valley Railway, the Bluebell Railway, the Keighley & Worth Valley Railway and the Great Western Society at Didcot. In many respects the Ironbridge Gorge Museum was the flagship of such ventures. The importance of destinations for excursions was indicated by a proliferation of awards. Ironbridge won most of them. Its visitor numbers increased to a total of around 400,000 in 1988, and over 1 million visitors a year were predicted for the last years of the century. Local authorities in the principal industrial cities established museums of industry. Birmingham's was opened in 1950, and closed in 1998. Those in Manchester, Sheffield, Leeds and Bradford all date from around 1980.

The opening of Wigan Pier in 1986 was an event of particular significance. The local authority, seeking to enhance the morale of a region where traditional industries were declining, used the reputation that the town had gained through the publication of George Orwell's *The Road to Wigan Pier* in 1936 to create a visitor attraction – a series of tableaux in former canal warehouses, staffed by actors, and a display of textiles alongside a mill engine preserved in situ in the Trencherfield Mill of 1907, the two being linked by a boat service. Wigan Pier was completely different from a traditional municipal museum, having started from ideas rather than a collection of artefacts. It was essentially a synthetic attraction – that word is not intended to be pejorative. It was successful as an educational venture and as a destination for excursions, and developed in interesting respects, not least in the establishment of a museum of the twentieth century based on Peter Opie's collection of printed ephemera. In this sphere it was the most imaginative example of local authority enterprise of the 1980s.

Another synthetic heritage destination opened in June 1985. Britannia Park, the 350-acre (140ha) creation of Peter Kellard, was located near Heanor in Derbyshire on the site of a former coalmine, overlooked by its winding house and steel headstock. It reputedly cost £18 million, and some leading retailers took leases of shops within the complex. The 'showcase of Britain', on a poster which featured Sir Winston Churchill and the footballer Bobby Moore, promised 'an unforgettable day out' and the 'experience of a lifetime'. The extent of support for the venture was shown by a fly-past by Concorde at the official opening. It was nevertheless a chaotic occasion – carpenters, painters and electricians were still working on many of the displays – brilliantly described by Richard Boston.[44] Britannia Park closed within a few months, although it was possible during 1986 to wander through to see such bizarre spectacles as a model of the Sydney Opera House abandoned to the weather, a grounded narrow boat, a pair of decaying aircraft, a suburban-style building that claimed to be a Cotswold farm, a fort that appeared to come from the set of a B-movie, and ironic signposts suggesting that a range of unfinished displays represented British genius. Britannia Park was a gentle reminder that the heritage industry needed a product beyond parking spaces, refreshments, clear signing, clean lavatories and retailing opportunities. The buildings, now occupied by the American Experience, are perhaps best interpreted as symbols of the post-Falklands jingoism of the mid-1980s.

A further indication in 1985 that heritage was becoming an industry was the opening of the first postgraduate course in heritage management in Britain at the University of Birmingham. Meanwhile, consultants from diverse backgrounds provided advice to local authorities and government departments about the establishment of visitor attractions, including those based on industrial heritage. The creation of 'another Ironbridge' was seen as a desirable objective in many regions suffering from industrial decline. The availability of funding from the National Lottery further stimulated both ambition and consultancy. It became evident in the 1990s that forecasting the popularity of industrial heritage attractions is as difficult as predicting the sales of a record by a talented but uncelebrated singer or the winner of a selling plate. Reports in the summer of 1999 showed that several very large projects with links to industrial heritage, including the National Glass Centre in Sunderland, the Royal Armouries in Leeds and the Earth Centre near Doncaster, were failing by substantial margins to reach their predicted numbers of visitors.[45]

Conclusions

Service industries change with tastes and fashions, and they became increasingly interdependent during the twentieth century. One of the ironies of the second half of the century was that as manufacturing industry declined, its heritage became a product of a new service industry, one that practised retailing, used techniques derived from the cinema, learned crowd-handling methods from sporting organisations, and formed part of holiday experiences. This is a paradox which raises questions about the nature of twentieth-century industrial archaeology that we discuss in Chapter 11.

Notes and references

1 P. Collins and B. Trinder, *The Archives of F. H. Lloyd & Co. of James Bridge, Wednesbury: A Report Compiled for the Triplex Lloyd Group*, Telford: Ironbridge Institute, 1988.

2 We are grateful to Sam Mullins, then (1986) of Leicestershire Museums Service, for access to this collection.

3 The section on chainstores draws principally on P. Mathias, *Retailing Revolution*, London: Longman, 1967.

4 R. Kinchin-Smith, 'A Survey of Sites in Cheshire and Merseyside Relating to the Alkali Industry', Ironbridge Institute assignment, 1993.

5 S. D. Chapman, *Jesse Boot of Boots the Chemists*, Nottingham: Boots, 1974.

6 The section which follows is based on A. Briggs, *Marks & Spencer 1884–1984: The Originators of Penny Bazaars*; A. Burns and B. Hyman, *Marks & Spencer 1894–1994: 100 Years of Partnership*, London: Marks & Spencer. We are also grateful for information from Angela Burns, formerly archivist with the company.

7 R. Graves and A. Hodge, *The Long Weekend: A Social History of Great Britain 1918–39*, London: Faber, p. 172.

8 A. Bennett, *Journals*, ed. F. Swinnerton, Harmondsworth: Penguin, 1971, p. 380

9 M. J. Stratton, 'New Materials for a New Age: Steel and Concrete Construction in the North of England, 1860–1939', *Industrial Archaeology Review*, 1999, vol. 21, pp. 15–16.

10 We are grateful to Angela Burns and Audrey Collins for information on William Whiteley and on department stores generally.

11 M. J. Stratton, *The Terracotta Revival*, London: Gollancz, 1993, p. 121; J. Birchall, *Co-op: The People's Business*, Manchester: Manchester University Press, 1994.

12 J. K. Walton, *Fish and Chips and the British Working Class 1870–1940*, Leicester: Leicester University Press, 1992.

13 G. Orwell, *The Road to Wigan Pier*, Harmondsworth: Penguin, 1962, p. 91.

14 Material on Sainsbury is drawn from B. Williams, *The Best Butter in the World: A History of Sainsbury's*, London: Ebury, 1994, and J. Boswell, *JS100: The Story of Sainsbury's*, London: J. Sainsbury, 1966.

15 L. Esher, *A Broken Wave: The Rebuilding of England 1940–1980*, London: Allen Lane, pp. 29–40; K. Richardson, *Twentieth Century Coventry*, Coventry: City of Coventry, 1972, pp. 297–300.

16 Burns and Hyman, op. cit., pp. 49–55.

17 Williams, op. cit., pp. 184–5.

18 P. Hall, *The Industries of London*, London: Hutchinson, 1962, pp. 59–71; Watford Corporation, *Watford Industrial Exhibition*, Watford: Watford Corporation, 1947, pp. 33–43; S. Barson and A. Saint, *A Farewell to Fleet Street*, London: English Heritage, 1988. We are grateful to Dr Derek Merfield for information on Salfords.

19 A. Forsyth, *Buildings for the Age: New Building Types 1900–1939*, London: RCHME, 1982, pp. 69–88; A. Jackson, *Semi-Detached London: Suburban Development, Life and Transport 1900–39*, London: Allen & Unwin, 1973, pp. 176–81. The section on cinemas also includes data from the National Monuments Record.

20 Forsyth, op. cit., pp. 89–91; N. Pevsner and E. Williamson, *The Buildings of England: Buckinghamshire* (2nd edn), London: Penguin, 1994, pp. 274–5.

21 Orwell, op. cit., p. 72.

22 Stratton, op. cit., pp. 135–41.

23 S. Inglis, *Football Grounds of Britain* (3rd edn), London: Collins Willow, 1996; D. Twydell (ed.) *Aerofilms Guide: Football Grounds*, London: Dial House, 1996; M. Heatley and D. Ford, *Football Grounds Then and Now*, London: Dial Press, 1994; K. Miller, *The History of Non-League Football Grounds*, London: Polar Print, 1996. The section on sports facilities also includes data from the National Monuments Record.

24 R. Pearson, *The Bass Railway Trips*, Derby: Breedon, 1993, pp. 17, 49–54.

25 Lewis Carroll, *Alice's Adventures in Wonderland*, London: Macmillan, 1958, p. 24.

26 B. Goodall, 'Coastal Resorts: Development and Redevelopment', *Built Environment*, 1992, vol. 18, pp. 5–11.

27 Reminscence of Kath Hands of Telford, BBC Radio Shropshire, *The Century Speaks*, November 1999.

28 J. K. Walton, *Blackpool*, Edinburgh: Edinburgh University Press, 1998, pp. 66–9, 97–102; see also J. K. Walton, *The Blackpool Landlady: A Social History*, Manchester: Manchester University Press, 1978.

29 Stratton, 'New Materials for a New Age', op. cit., pp. 19–20.

30 Forsyth, op. cit., pp. x, 64–5; Lindsay Anderson, *Oh Dreamland!*

31 Stratton, 'New Materials for a New Age', op. cit., p. 21, Forsyth, ibid., pp. 52, 60–3.

32 *Architectural Design & Construction*, May 1938.

33 D. Hardy and C. Ward, *Goodnight Campers! The History of the British Holiday Camp*, London: Mansell, 1986, pp. 45–7. This paragraph also draws on

photographs in the CPRE collection in the Museum of English Rural Life, Reading.

34 J. Betjeman, *John Betjeman's Collected Poems*, London: John Murray, 1983, pp. 409–12.

35 B. Poplett, *Peacehaven: A Pictorial History*, Chichester: Phillimore, 1993; D. Hardy and C. Ward, *Arcadia for All: The Legacy of a Makeshift Landscape*, London: Mansell, 1984, pp. 71–91, 275–76.

36 M. Lyons, *The Story of Jaywick Sands*, Chichester: Phillimore, 1996; Hardy and Ward, op. cit., *Arcadia for All*, pp. 138–62.

37 Hardy and Ward, ibid., pp. 118–32; G. Barsby, *Canvey Island*, Stroud: Tempus, 1997; B. E. Cracknell, *Canvey Island: The History of a Marshland Community*, Leicester: Leicester University Press, 1959; F. McCabe, *A History of Canvey Island*, Hornchurch: Ian Henry, 1985; S. White, *History of Canvey Island: Five Generations*, Canvey Island: The Bookshop, 1994. We are grateful also to Catherine White for information on Canvey Island.

38 A. McRae, *British Camping Coaches*, Stockport: Foxline, 1999.

39 This account of holiday camps draws chiefly on Hardy and Ward, op. cit., *Goodnight Campers!*.

40 We are grateful to Brian Malaws of RCAHMW for assistance with fieldwork in the Rhyl area. For the LMS camp, see *The Builder*, 30 June 1939.

41 D. St J. Thomas and S. R. Smith, *Summer Saturdays in the West* (3rd edn), Newton Abbot: David & Charles, 1983; R. Woodley, *The Day of the Holiday Express*, Shepperton: Ian Allan, 1996.

42 *Daily Mail*, 25 May 1931.

43 J. Allan, *Berthold Lubetkin: Architecture and the Tradition of Progress*, London: RIBA Publications, 1992, pp. 199–250.

44 *Guardian*, 17 June 1985.

45 *Guardian*, 31 July 1999.

Chapter eleven

Reaching conclusions

One of our objectives in writing this book has been to provide a trail guide through the confusing industrial archaeological legacy bequeathed by the twentieth century. The trail guide was an interpretive technique of the 1970s, pioneered at Cromford, Broseley and Ironbridge. Best practice in such a guide was to show to the user some points to look for, and then to provide a clear point-by-point itinerary, explaining what could be seen at a succession of stops. We hope that Chapters 2–10 have provided some themes worth pursuing, as well as some detailed studies. It is not our intention to grade towns and cities in the style of Baedeker, but rather to show how archaeological evidence may be used to enhance our understanding of the recent past – and this is done most effectively through a disciplined approach to the principal categories of archaeological evidence.

Classes of evidence

First, we have drawn attention to *artefacts*, principally to collections in museums, like those illustrating gas and electricity supply in Manchester, flameproof diesel locomotives in Leeds, plastics in the Science Museum and roadside furniture at Amberley. Nevertheless, many twentieth-century artefacts, particularly vehicles, are held in private collections, and collectors' organisations exist for almost every make of motorcar, from the Rolls-Royce to the Austin Seven. Rallies bring together Tiger Moths, traction engines, steam and diesel lorries, buses and motorcycles, military vehicles as well as oil engines, plastics, lawn mowers, tiles and teddy bears. The interests of private collectors have often foreshadowed those of the great museums. The value of disciplined collecting is illustrated by the displays at Wigan and Gloucester of the printed ephemera amassed by Robert Opie, which illuminate almost every chapter in this book.[1]

Second, we trust that we have shown our awareness of the enlightenment that can come from studying the *images* created in the twentieth century, just as it can from those of other historical periods – the reliefs of classical

Greece or the paintings of fifteenth-century Flanders. Our indebtedness to photographers of the stature of Bedford Lemaire, Eric de Maré and Denis Thorpe, as well as to those who took the snapshots which comprise the CPRE collection in the University of Reading, should be evident throughout this volume. We have also gained much from the study of the images of factories, like those in the annual reports of the Co-operative Wholesale Society or on the packets of Welgar Shredded Wheat, and from the work of the official war artists of the great conflicts of the twentieth century. Moving images provide a particularly potent record of the twentieth century, and we hope that we have shown something of what can be learned from the works of Sir Arthur Elton, Humphrey Jennings and Edgar Anstey.

The characteristic *structures* of twentieth-century industrial society have become evident in most chapters – pylons, cooling towers, tower blocks, control towers, steel-framed sheds clad with corrugated iron or anodised sheeting, cinemas, Klönne gasholders, motorway intersections and catalytic crackers. We have analysed *sites*, groups of associated structures, perhaps of different date, which make up power stations, motorcar factories, airports or marshalling yards. Structures and sites are elements of the *landscapes* – industrial estates, Radburn housing, Royal Ordnance Factories, garden suburbs – that are made up of the buildings wherein people eat, sleep and play, as well as those where they earn their livings. We have been aware of the need for the archaeologist to attempt to animate landscapes, and, where activities have ceased or changed, to utilise imagination to repopulate them. At one level this can take the form of sophisticated professional recording, like the work of the Welsh Royal Commission at Taff Merthyr Colliery (*see Chapter 3*), or the records of Mass Observation. It can involve seeing the past through the eyes of poets or essayists – our debts to John Betjeman, George Orwell and J. B. Priestley are evident throughout the book. Animation can utilise also writings that some might despise, like the memories of working people, or the trainspotting notes of Benjamin Brookshank which so effectively bring to life a wartime afternoon at Ashchurch (*see Chapter 7*).

Boundaries of the discipline

We have come to appreciate in this study the frontiers between industrial archaeology and several other disciplines – the histories of science, technology and transport, social history and urban history – and the different time scales that apply in these diverse disciplines. We have tried to be aware of the questions that scholars have raised about the twentieth century, and to highlight the contribution that can be made to discussion through the analysis of material culture. Nevertheless, we have been disturbed by the lack of attention to material culture that we have observed in many standard works on the history of twentieth-century Britain. Some business histories display no awareness of the factories that companies operated, while some social and economic histories reveal a disturbing ignorance of basic British geography.

We consider it particularly important to be aware of the distinctive contributions that can be made to human understanding by both industrial archaeology and the history of architecture. Just as some places recur from time to time in the book in different contexts, so do the names of some architects. Sir Owen Williams (1890–1969) was responsible for the Boots factory at Beeston, the British Airways hangar at Heathrow, Wembley Stadium and the first phase of the M1 motorway. Wallis, Gilbert & Partners designed many of the most innovative buildings of the 1930s, factories along the Great West Road and at Slough and the Victoria Coach Station.[2] Sir Frederick Gibberd (1908–84) is best known as the architect of the Roman Catholic Cathedral at Liverpool, but he also designed the BISF prefabricated house (*see Chapter 8*), Terminal 3 at Heathrow (*Chapter 9*), and the first generation of housing in the New Town of Harlow (*Chapter 8*). Lord (Norman) Foster (1935–), the son of a machine painter at the factory of Metropolitan Vickers, Trafford Park, encapsulates much of twentieth-century industrial archaeology, both in achievement and in attitude. Among his works in Britain are innovative houses in Milton Keynes (*Chapter 8*), Reliance Controls' factory and the Renault Parts Distribution Centre at Swindon (*see below*), the terminal at Stansted (*Chapter 9*), the USAF museum at Duxford and Maclaren's motor-racing team headquarters at Woking. He admires aircraft

11.1
Exterior detail of
the Renault Distribution
Centre, Swindon, by
Foster & Partners.

(Photo: Norman Foster)

company that published a high proportion of the first generation of the literature of industrial archaeology. Textile mills, providing large areas of floor space that could be rented cheaply, provided particularly good settings for other industries, some of them innovative. A commentator on industrial Lancashire in the 1980s recalled:

> A wave of mill conversions that broke over every textile town from the mid-1950s and brought very welcome employment diversity as an indescribable variety of firms, great and small, established and newly-born, adapted sound and very cheap premises on a scale that did much to redress the hostile influence of regional policy.[5]

From the 1960s the adaptive re-use of industrial buildings became a more conscious policy. One of the most imaginative conversions was that of the malting complex at Snape, Suffolk, which closed in 1963: it is now the concert hall on which the Aldeburgh Festival, created by Benjamin Britten and Peter Pears, is centred. The conversion was carried out by Arup Associates between 1965 and 1967, and after a fire in 1969 the buildings were re-opened in 1970.[6] Bush House in Bristol, a warehouse of 1832, restored to accommodate an art gallery and offices, became the archetype for waterfront developments – of which the Albert Dock in Liverpool was the most substantial. Subsequently the restoration of the Dean Clough mill complex at Halifax and Saltaire Mill near Bradford demonstrated that the restoration of industrial buildings could bring economic and social regeneration.

hangars and barns, buildings regarded by many architects simply as sheds, and regards the Boeing 747 as his favourite building. He has confessed that his work is rooted in industrial heritage: 'like many boys I was fascinated by aircraft, locomotives and machinery. Manchester was one of the workshops of the world at the time, so it would have been hard not to be.'[3] What has been made or built in twentieth-century Britain in its turn derives from and is intricately bound up with the legacy inherited from earlier generations. How the inheritance is interpreted shapes evaluations of present achievements, and determines whether the future is regarded with trepidation or confidence.

Recycling

Industrial buildings and sites have always been recycled.[4] We have shown how in the course of the twentieth century bicycle factories and shell-filling works were used for the assembly of motorcars, how the first Ford factory in Britain came to be used for storing timber, and how new uses were found for wartime airfields, shadow factories and redundant railway warehouses. Indeed, the railway station buildings of 1926 at Newton Abbot (SX 867712) were, for about twenty years, the base for the

Special places

The various chapters in the book identify some places as unique – Letchworth, Trafford Park, Gretna, Stanlow, Southampton Docks, Heathrow, Blackpool and Canvey Island are all discussed above. Such places are of relevance to most of the themes discussed in this book. Slough is another example. The military base of the First World War was the source of many of the vehicles on which commercial road transport

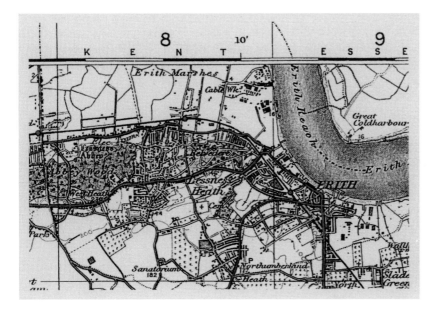

11.2

A place of significance
in twentieth-century
industrial history:
Erith as depicted on the
Ordnance Survey 1-inch
map of 1929.

(Authors' collection)

was founded. The trading estate on the site set a pattern for many others, and was the source of such characteristic twentieth-century artefacts as the Mars Bar, the Aspro, Chappie food for dogs and the Citroën DS. The kerbside double yellow line prohibiting parking also originated in Slough. Another area, less easily defined, is along a line of no more than five miles, to the south of Bedford, where there is an extraordinary coincidence of important twentieth-century sites: the brickworks and model village at Stewartby (*Chapter 8*), the Royal Ordnance Factory at Elstow (*Chapter 7*), the housing of the First World War at Shortstown and the Cardington airship hangars (*Chapter 7*). Sites like this are twentieth-century equivalents of Cromford, Blaenavon and New Lanark.

The book has highlighted also some good examples of certain types of structure, site and landscape: the former Royal Ordnance Factories at Wrexham and Thorp Arch, the archetypal Southern Electric suburb of Petts Wood, the New Towns of Harlow and Telford, the plotlands of Dungeness. The coming together of investigations into different topics raises questions about other places. We have not been able to undertake detailed research on Erith, and when we commenced the work we would not have included it on a list of the most significant places, but our exploration reveals that some of the key developments in synthetic fibres were made by the British Viscose Company, based there from 1892; that it was the location of oil-

processing works crucial to the development of margarine production in Britain (*Chapter 4*) from 1907; that the British Fibro-Cement Company, one of Britain's principal sources of plasterboard (*Chapter 8*), operated there from 1913; and it was the site of a Vickers armaments works that employed 14,500 people in the First World War. Other products of this site during the twentieth century included copper cables, mining equipment, asbestos, pre-cast concrete building components and Mobo toys. Similar questions arise about Dumfries, not the most heavily industrialised burgh in Scotland but nevertheless the location of the Arrol-Johnston motorcar factory (*Chapter 5*), of the Carnation creamery (*Chapter 4*), and of an ICI explosives works of the Second World War, alongside which the company built a synthetic fibres plant that was later modified to produce plastic films.

Much of the industrial archaeology of the twentieth century must be sought on old sites, places that have been concerned with mining and manufacturing since the eighteenth century but which underwent successive changes in the twentieth. In the central part of the Black Country around Tipton and West Bromwich one aspect of the twentieth century was the steady decline of coal mining and ironmaking which had flourished during the Industrial Revolution, but another was an extraordinary vitality. New industries were continually built upon the ruins of old ones, to the extent that, apart from the canals, most of the surviving industrial archaeological evidence in 1999 was from the twentieth century. J. B. Priestley famously drew attention in 1934 to 'Rusty Lane' in West Bromwich, which has been identified as Grice Street on the west side of Spon Lane. Priestley visited a steel warehouse, in an area that he found mean and squalid, and mused:

> In the heart of the great empire on which the sun never sets, in the land of hope and glory, Mother of the Free, is Rusty Lane, West Bromwich. What do they know of England who only England know? The answer must be Rusty Lane, West Bromwich.[7]

The area has changed since the time of Priestley's visit. The remnants of the last blast furnaces and the last collieries were cleared, together with the buildings that once housed the factory of Patent Borax Soap. The coal-fired power station at Ocker Hill had closed, and had been replaced in 1995 with an oil-fired peak-load generating plant, while the gasworks using important natural gas delivered by rail had but a short life in the 1960s (*Chapter 3*). Palethorpes converted a brewery in 1890 into a model factory making Royal Cambridge Sausages that were distributed throughout Britain in six-wheel railway vans, until the factory was relocated to rural Shropshire in 1968 (*Chapter 4*). Other characteristic twentieth-century products made in Tipton included Tan-Sad prams, Bean cars, Triplex grates and Vono bedsprings. There was a Royal Ordnance Factory on West Bromwich's eastern boundary during the Second World War. The area is criss-crossed by motorways that are among the most congested in Britain. Perhaps the area's most significant contribution to the technology of the latter part of the twentieth century was the development of lightweight steel framing by Hills and Co. and by J. Brockhouse & Co. for use in housing, and in the CLASP (Consortium of Local Authorities Special Programme) system employed in the construction of schools and on the Heslington Campus of the University of York.[8]

Wigan also was characterised by coal, iron and cotton, the trades of the Industrial Revolution, and was highlighted in the 1930s not by a paragraph in a book but by a whole volume, George Orwell's *The Road to Wigan Pier*, an attempt by a writer from a privileged background to empathise with those in a region whose economy was deeply depressed.[9] The opening of Wigan Pier in 1986 (*Chapter 10*) was very much an attempt by the community to confront its unglamorous past. Some of the displays are located in Trencherfield Mill – itself a twentieth-century building, erected in 1907. The adjacent Swan Meadow Mill, one of the largest cotton-spinning complexes in Lancashire, had long been tenemented, but was being converted to what is recognisably an industrial estate in 1999. Elsewhere in Wigan there was much evidence of fundamental social change in 1999. Wigan Rugby League Club, an institution for which the town was rightly famous, finally came to be acknowledged as an asset, and in the closing months of the century the JJB Sports Stadium was opened, providing accommodation also for the town's Association Football club. It is set in a North American landscape of shopping malls and fast-food outlets, along a ring road on the western side of the town, powerful evidence of the role of the service industries in the closing years of the twentieth century.

Coventry is a special case. The bombing of the city centre and the reconstruction of the cathedral made Coventry a symbol of the widespread regeneration necessitated by the Second World War. Coventry epitomised also the prosperity brought by full employment in the 1950s and 1960s, itself a signifier of the continuing importance during those years of the motorcar, aircraft and synthetic fibre industries. The Precinct (*Chapter 10*) was the first shopping centre of its kind in Britain. The railway station (*Chapter 9*) was the best that was produced by the nationalised rail industry. The city's housing estates include examples of many of the characteristic types of post-war house (*Chapter 8*). All this was historically determined.[10] Coventry was a city whose inhabitants developed through watchmaking and through building and working looms for ribbon weaving, through unusual skills in mechanical engineering, which were applied in the twentieth century to the construction of bicycles, motorcars, aircraft and munitions. Those skills led to the location of shadow factories in Coventry, in spite of its openness to air attack, and the creation of space for post-war expansion.

The Dalmuir and Kilbowie areas of Clydebank, on the north side of the river, 8 miles north-west of Glasgow and near to the western terminus of the Forth & Clyde Canal, similarly encapsulate many aspects of twentieth-century industrial archaeology. The first significant industry in what had been a rural area was a company that until the 1940s extracted iodine from seaweed. In 1871 James and George Thomson moved their shipbuilding concern from Govan across the Clyde to a site at the confluence of the River Cart, which stimulated the construction of four-storey tenement blocks to accommodate their workers. In 1899 the yard was taken over by the Sheffield steelmakers John Brown & Co., concerned to ensure markets for their armour plate. Subsequently the *Aquitania*, the *Queen Mary* and the *Queen Elizabeth* (*Chapter 9*) and many warships, including HMS *Hood*, were built in the yard. In 1884 the American company Singer moved its factory from Glasgow to Kilbowie, where it soon gave employment to over 5,000 people. In 1896 another Glasgow company, D. & J. Tullis, moved to Kilbowie, where it became one of the largest manufacturers of laundry machinery in Europe. Thus by 1900 three firms of international significance were established at Clydebank. They were joined in 1901 by the firm of William Beardmore, who established a shipyard that officially opened in 1906 with the launching of the battleship HMS *Agamemnon*. Subsequently Beardmore became involved with the building of submarines, artillery, airships, aeroplanes, locomotives and iron prefabricated houses (*Chapter 5*). In 1905–6 Robert ('Concrete Bob') McAlpine began to construct housing for shipbuilders in the Garden City style, and in due course completed 2,000 dwellings. The yard closed in 1929 but was revived, partly as a Royal Ordnance Factory, during the Second World War. Industry at Clydebank shrank considerably in the second half of the twentieth century, with the closure of Singer and the complete cessation of manufacturing on the Beardmore site. The rail services through Clydebank, fast and frequent electric trains running between Glasgow and Helensburgh, are part of one of the most successful schemes implemented under the British Railways modernisation plan of 1955. While some manufacturing sites have been cleared, in 1999 much housing that reflected the different periods of industrial expansion remained, and Clydebank's museum holds large collections of artefacts from Singers and from the shipyards.[11]

Industrial archaeology characteristic of the twentieth century is powerfully displayed along the 50-mile railway that follows the coast of North Wales between Chester and Conwy.[12] On the western edge of Chester is the factory where Wellington bombers were built during the Second World War (*Chapter 7*) and which continues to made sub-assemblies for airliners. Between the railway and the banks of the Dee, separating the former stations at Sandycroft (SJ 336672) and Queensferry (SJ 318683), are many of the buildings, some of them distinguished structures, of two munitions factories of the First World War, and about a mile to the south are the houses built for the factory by Sir Raymond Unwin. On the opposite side of the Dee is the Shotton coating plant of British Steel (*Chapter 2*), once an integrated blast furnace, steelmaking and pipe-making plant. An oil-fired power station (*Chapter 3*) commissioned in 1996 stands on the site of a former coal-fired generating plant at Connah's Quay. Flint was one of Courtaulds' principal rayon-manufacturing plants (*Chapter 2*) in the inter-war period. To the south of the railway, the site of the mills was occupied in 1999 by a retail park, while on the north side Castle Industrial Park included some well-designed industrial buildings of the early twentieth century, and retained a formal boundary fence with rusticated brick piers crowned by concrete cap-stones. The centre of Flint is dominated by two fifteen-storey tower blocks. To the west are traces of pit mounts and some surviving colliery buildings. The ferry steamer *Duke of Lancaster* (*Chapter 9*), built for the service from Heysham to Belfast in 1956, lay beached in 1999 at Mostyn, the site of blast furnaces and a steel plant in the early years of the twentieth century. The wharf where manganese was unloaded for steelmaking was still in use in 1999, two small diesel locomotives being employed to shunt its sidings. At Point of Ayr (SJ 1284), the site of the last working colliery in North Wales had been cleared by 1999, but derelict buildings remained of a liquid solvent extraction plant for the production of motor spirit from coal. It had been designed in response to the oil crises of the 1970s, but did not come on stream until 1986, and closed, made redundant by the fall in world oil prices, in 1995. Near to the site of the colliery is the terminal for gas produced in Liverpool Bay, from which sulphur is removed at Point of Ayr before it is pumped to the power station at Connah's Quay or supplied to the National Gas Grid. A lane, about half a mile long, lined by what would have been called 'bungaloid sprawl' in the 1920s or 1930s, leads to the resort of Talacre, which appears to have originated as a plotland settlement. At its centre is the Smugglers' Inn, part with a rather debased Bauhaus Modernist appearance, and part in the Hacienda style. A scatter of wooden huts which probably date from before the Second World War remains, but caravans comprise the greater part of the settlement. Thereafter caravans become an increasingly dominant feature of the landscape. At Prestatyn there are several holiday camps between the railway and the sea, one of them LMS's camp of 1939, which sixty years later was falling into dereliction around its landmark tower (*Chapter 10*). The railway station at

Rhyl is a monument to the working-class seaside holiday, a huge and spacious site, with space for four tracks, now with only three, very long platforms and an exceptionally wide footbridge. Only one of the two signal boxes, dating from before 1923, remained in use in 1999. West of Rhyl, around Kinmel Bay, are more holiday camps. The front at Colwyn Bay is distinguished by the spindly remains of a pleasure pier, while the streets lining the seafront towards Penrhyn Bay are richly rewarding for the student of inter-war housing, containing many characteristic dwellings of the 1930s, including several in the Modernist style. The modest concentration of industry at Llandudno Junction includes the depot that supplied locomotives for the many holiday trains of the 1950s, a cold store of the Second World War, and a factory making domestic appliances.

Paddington to Swindon

In 1999 the Department for Culture, Media and Sport issued a tentative list of places in the United Kingdom that might be proposed for designation as UNESCO World Heritage Sites. Among them was the Main Line of the Great Western Railway between Bristol and London, authorised in 1835 and opened in 1841, proposed because it was conceived by its builder, Isambard Kingdom Brunel (1806–59), as 'the finest work in the kingdom' and because, with its termini at Bristol and Paddington, its various bridges over the Avon and Thames, the Swindon Railway Works and Village and its stately passage through Bath, it is 'the most complete railway of its date in the world'. We contend that the Great Western Main Line is of equal historical value as a section through twentieth-century industrial archaeology, encapsulating some of its myths, and revealing something of its reality. We examine this contention in the context of the 77 miles of the railway between London and Swindon.[13]

A fictional journey from Paddington to Swindon was a persistent feature of the Great Western Railway's marketing of the inter-war period. Concepts of quality and service came to be encapsulated in the words 'Great', 'Western'

and 'Railway', inspiring an affection that did much to persuade decision makers to devote resources to industrial heritage. Much of the popular impression of the line was created by the engravings of John Cooke Bourne (1814–96), published in 1846,[14] which gave an heroic quality to the viaduct at Hanwood, the elliptical bridge over the Thames at Maidenhead, and even to wayside stations like Pangbourne. Publications like *Caerphilly Castle* of 1923, *Brunel and After* of 1925 and *The King of Railway Locomotives* of 1928 did much to create the myth of the Great Western Railway,[15] which tended to conceal that not many trains ran as fast as the Cheltenham Flyer or the Cornish Riviera, that some lines and stations received sparse and inconvenient services, that much of the railway's revenue was derived from the unromantic carriage of coal, and that its labour relations policies were not above criticism. Public perceptions of the line's importance were further enhanced by L. T. C. Rolt's biography of Isambard Kingdom Brunel, published in 1958,[16] which gave its subject an heroic status that few of his contemporaries accorded him. The journey thus has a mythical quality as part of the means by which industrial heritage was created, which is itself part of twentieth-century industrial archaeology.

The present Paddington station (TO 265815) dates from 1850–52, but it was repeatedly altered in the course of the twentieth century. The former Great Western Hotel, which forms the station's Chateau-style frontage to Praed Street, with a pediment embellished with scultures illustrating Peace, Plenty, Industry and Science, was being redeveloped in the late 1990s, but bronze panels bearing the legend 'GWR 1932' were being retained, evidence of its twentieth-century rebuilding with Art Deco features. Another substantial change was made in 1998 when blue-and-grey electric trains with charcoal-tinted windows began to operate the Heathrow Express service linking central London with the airport. In 1999 almost every service to Swindon was worked by a High Speed Train unit, often seen as a re-assertion in the early 1970s of traditional railway practices and values against the imaginative aircraft-derived engineering that produced the Advanced Passenger Train (*Chapter 9*). In 1900 all the trains operating from Paddington belonged to the Great Western Railway. In 1999, following the privatisation of the system a few years earlier, trains were worked by four different companies.

Activity around the throat of the station would have been more animated in the first part of the century than in more recent times. The country end of Platform 1 was used for many years for unloading milk churns, a practice that from the late 1920s diminished as glass-lined tankers were used to convey milk to bottling plants like those at Cricklewood and Wood Lane (*Chapter 4*). The canopies above the extension of the platform where parcels were handled remained in 1999. After passing beneath Bishop's Bridge Road, an elevated section of Westway, the A40(M) motorway slashes through the area once occupied by the Paddington freight depot and runs parallel to and then crosses the Main Line beyond Westbourne Park Station. The brick infill below the motorway is the Westbourne Park bus depot. Nearby, and also on the north side of the tracks, is Ernö Goldfinger's Trellick tower of 1968–72, the highest block of council flats in London and a much sought-after place of residence in 1999 (*Chapter 8*). On the south side of the tracks, a little before Westbourne Park, was Ranelagh Bridge Yard, where steam locomotives from provincial depots were turned, coaled and watered before backing on to the trains on which they were to return. The yard was laid out in the last quarter of the

nineteenth century on the site of the ornamental grounds of a mansion called 'Westbourne Lodge', and in 1999 was used for parking cars. On Hammersmith & City's line, London Transport's trains, which have run on tracks parallel to the main line, swing southwards at Westbourne Park. To the south of the main line on Barlby Road is the Clement Talbot car factory (*Chapter 6*), while to the north is the site of Kensal Green's gasworks (TO 235824), marked in 1999 by two surviving gasholders, and by Kensal Green House, the 'flagship' of public housing provision of the mid-1930s, designed by Maxwell Fry (*Chapter 8*). After passing through a pair of bridges, one carrying Scrubs Lane, the other the West London Railway, the carriage and locomotive sidings of Old Oak Common spread out to the north, bounded by the one-time Great Western route to Banbury and Birmingham, which is now served principally from Marylebone Station. The Old Oak estate, the first Garden City-style housing built by the London County Council (*Chapter 8*), lies to the south around East Acton Station on London Transport's Central Line, which the Main Line crosses west of the junction with the line to Banbury. South of the Main Line extends the lengthy depot where Eurostar trains, running to Paris and Brussels from Waterloo, are maintained.

Within a short distance the Main Line is crossed by Western Avenue, which leads northwards towards the Park Royal industrial estate (*Chapter 7*), to the factory built by Wallis Gilbert & Partners for Hoover in 1932, the frontage building of which is now adapted as a supermarket, and to Charles Holden's showpiece Underground station at Hanger Lane (*Chapter 9*). Beyond the Western Avenue bridge are Acton sidings (TO 195825), where the predominant traffic in 1999 was roadstone from Somerset, most of it hauled to London by diesel locomotives built by General Motors in North America. Great Western's book for boys of the inter-war period drew attention to what were then ultra-modern factories which could be seen on the next stretch of line, including AEC's works, south of the tracks beyond the bridge over Uxbridge Broadway, which built many of London's twentieth-century buses, and Nestlé's UK headquarters, where instant coffee went into production in 1939 (*Chapter 4*), which remained in operation in 1999, a building by

11.3
The country end of Platform 1 at Paddington in the early twentieth century, with milk churns being unloaded from siphon vans.

(National Dairy Council)

Wallis Gilbert & Partners alongside the Grand Junction Canal being recognisable from the train. On the northern side of the Main Line the HMV (His Master's Voice) factory, which made gramophones and records, remained in 1999 although with nothing to indicate its identity. The company's advertisements used a memorable image of a dog listening to a horned phonograph. The factory's machine shop of 1912 is an early work of Sir Owen Williams, built while he was working for Truscon. HMV products, together with Scott's Emulsion and Tickler's Jam, were among 'the well-advertised products whose names are household words' mentioned in a GWR book of 1923. To the south of the Main Line was the site of the GWR works where sleepers used to be impregnated with creosote, a task made unnecessary by the substitution of concrete for timber sleepers on main lines, and in the far distance the tower of the factory designed for Gillette by Bannister Fletcher in 1937 marks the route of the Great West Road.

The former Great Western Railway locomotive shed (TO 132800) at Southall was the base for a preservation project, and some graffiti-covered Pullman carriages were visible there in 1999. To the north of the tracks is the site of a gasworks marked by three surviving gasholders in 1999, one of them of the Klönne type. The line twice crosses the Grand Junction Canal, to which it runs parallel past West Drayton Station, before the canal swings north up the valley of the Colne. The M25 London Orbital Motorway (*Chapter 9*) passes over the line east of Iver Station (TO 041800), beyond which, on the north side of the tracks, is one of Britain's relatively few remaining rail-served oil depots, with its tank farm. Most oil products travelling long distances in 1999 went by pipeline. Iver Station was built in the 1920s to serve an intended Garden City that never materialised. The nearby Pinewood film studios of 1935 were built around Heatherden Hall, a Victorian house that included some furnishings from the Cunard Line's first *Mauritania*. To the west of Iver is a Bison concrete works (*Chapters 2 and 8*), while at Langley is the site of a one-time aircraft factory that was used for the assembly of Ford vans until the 1990s, and to the south on most days travellers are able to view a procession of airliners taking off westwards from Heathrow.

The approach to Slough (SU 9788021), junction for Windsor, is marked by the extensive ICI Paints plant to the north of the tracks. Beyond the station is the crenellated factory (SU 972803) erected by William Horlick in 1908, supposedly modelled on his company's works in Wisconsin, for the production of malted-milk drinks. Beyond, and also on the northern side, are the remnants of the connection to the rail system of Slough Trading Estate, parts of which can be seen from the train. Until the early 1960s railway wagons were loaded and unloaded at many of the factories on the estate. Near Burnham (SU 940813) is an example of the bungaloid sprawl that greatly distressed members of the CPRE in the late 1920s (*Chapter 8*), but by the 1990s it had been engulfed by later housing. The line crosses the Thames on Brunel's elliptical brick arches, then passes through Maidenhead, 24 miles (40km) from Paddington, and after another 2 miles reaches open country for the first time. That open country extends for only about 4 miles, and includes White Waltham airfield (SU 850788). Twyford (SU 790758) is the junction for the branch line to Henley-on-Thames. The train passes through a landscape of gravel pits in the Loddon Valley, and near to the site of Woodley airfield, where the first moving assembly line for manufacturing aircraft was installed at the Miles factory in 1938 (*Chapter 5*). The deep cutting at Sonning was recorded in one of John Cooke Bourne's engravings, and in many fine photographs by Maurice Earley, now held in the National Railway Museum.[17] West of the cutting is an extensive trading estate with many multi-storey blocks, including one occupied in 1999 by Microsoft.

Great Western's pre-war books for boys draw attention to Reading's two principal industries of the first half of the twentieth century: Suttons' nurseries, producers of seeds, a site vacated in 1962 that came to be occupied by insurance offices; and the biscuit factory of Huntley & Palmer, from which production moved to Huyton, Merseyside, in 1977 (*Chapter 4*), although the collected artefacts relating to the company remain in Reading. The prominent coal-burning power station at Earley, typical of the large generating plants of the 1930s, has also disappeared from the landscape, and supermarkets now stand among the gravel pits to the east of the station. The junction with the lines of the former Southern Railway (SU 7220738), which were installed during the Second World War, remained in use in 1999, but Southern's Reading South Station had been replaced by a car park. The third rail electric units which have worked to Reading from Waterloo since 1939, and the diesel units which since the 1980s have run to Gatwick, were diverted to a cramped platform at the side of the former GWR station.

West of Reading an industrial estate extends along the south side of the main line for most of the way to Tilehurst, and hidden among its factories is an angular brick cold-storage plant of the kind built during the Second World War (*Chapter 7*). On the opposite side of the tracks, on the banks of the Thames, are several clusters of small, smartly painted, prefabricated bungalows which probably originated as plotland settlements (*Chapter 8*). Tilehurst was, until 1968, the terminus of a corporation trolley-bus service. The next station serves the Thames-side resort of Pangbourne, a 'favourite resort of river folk' according to a GWR publication of the 1920s, whose original station was depicted by Cooke Bourne. Its coal yard, like most of those on the line, was by the 1990s a car park for commuters. Brunel's railway passes the entrance to the park at Basildon (SU 610781), where the great house, designed in the eighteenth century by Carr of York, was the home of a characteristically twentieth-century industrialist, Julius Salter Elias, Viscount Southwood (1873–1946), who expanded the printing industry of Watford (*Chapter 10*) and owned *John Bull*, the *People*, a share in the *Daily Herald*, the *Sporting Life*, *Illustrated* and *Woman*. Near Goring there were troughs from which steam locomotives could pick up water. In 1999 the tracks of the 3-mile branch line from Cholsey to Wallingford, where a preservation society has its base, remained intact. The silhouette of the concrete silos of the maltings at Wallingford is visible from the main line.

A hawthorn-covered rabbit warren now fills much of the site of the marshalling yard constructed during the Second World War at Moreton Cutting (SU 545896), just east of Didcot, junction for Oxford. At Didcot the Great Western Society occupies the former locomotive depot between the station and the avoiding line used by express and freight trains to and from Oxford. The shed is well preserved, retaining its

characteristic Great Western coaling stage, as are the locomotives, carriages and wagons that can be observed from passing trains.

For a distance of more than 2 miles, between Didcot (SU 525905) and the bridge carrying the A34 dual-carriageway from Oxford to the south coast, the train passes through an industrial landscape twice transformed in the twentieth century. In the inter-war period the area was occupied by Great Western's fodder depot, from which hay and grain were supplied to the horses that shunted wagons and operated road-carting services all over the company's system, and by huge Ordnance Depots built for the army and the RAF during the First World War. Lengthy sidings were shunted by the pannier-tank locomotives, with bulbous spark-arrester chimneys, that were based at Didcot. From the 1960s the site was occupied by one of Britain's largest coal-fired power stations (*Chapter 3*), whose six cooling towers provide a recognisable landmark for transatlantic air travellers bound to or from Heathrow. The power station originally drew its coal from the midlands by merry-go-round trains (*Chapter 9*). Much of it was delivered in 1999 by the same kinds of train, but was imported through the port of Avonmouth. Part of the power station is fired by natural gas. Beyond the power station's sidings is the Milton Park trading estate, with many Modernistic warehouses and factories.

Following the concrete structure that carries the A34 is the bridge of the B4017, the old route of the Oxford–Winchester road, marking the site of Steventon Station (SU 473916), at which, when the line was first opened, passengers for Oxford transferred to road transport. About 3 miles to the south lies the atomic energy research establishment at Harwell (*Chapter 3*). West of Steventon the line runs alongside one of the few remaining stretches of the Wiltshire & Berkshire Canal that is still in water. Wantage Road (SU 410913) was, between 1875 and 1925, the terminus of a 2-mile tramway to the town of Wantage, for most of its life worked by the locomotive *Shannon*, which in 1999 was displayed by the Great Western Society at Didcot. Buildings adjacent to the station site were occupied in 1999 by the Williams Formula One racing team. The former station at Uffington (SU 311904) had been the terminus of a branch line to the little town of Farringdon, 3 miles to the north, while the village of

Uffington lies more than a mile to the south. The importance of the military in twentieth-century Wiltshire is shown by the presence of the Royal Military College and Watchfield Depot at Shrivenham, once served by a station (SU 239875) on the Main Line.

Swindon is among the sites along the Great Western Main Line highlighted in the tentative list of World Heritage Sites, because the village built by GWR for its employees, with houses designed by Brunel,[18] has been well preserved, and because there are extensive remains of the company's locomotive works, which at its peak employed 14,000 people. The oldest parts, dating from the 1840s, are now occupied by the National Monuments Research Centre, while the many acres of sheds, erected from the 1870s when GWR began to build and maintain standard-gauge rolling stock at Swindon, have been put to diverse uses, ranging from a retailing centre to workshops for the repair of preserved steam locomotives. Some of the buildings of the 1840s were rebuilt as drawing offices in the early twentieth century. The GWR's most celebrated locomotives were designed there, and the rooms now accommodate researchers at NMRC. The lofty steel-framed A-shop, where for much of the last century locomotives were built and repaired, was demolished following the closure of the works in the 1980s.

If Swindon epitomises the demise of those large twentieth-century industries with roots in the nineteenth century, it illustrates also many characteristics of the industries that grew after 1900. Large factories were built there during both world wars with capital supplied by the government, and much benefit was derived from 'overspill' programmes designed to accommodate people from London in the 1950s and 1960s. As the train approaches Swindon from the east, terraces of tunnel-back houses around the football ground give the town a Victorian appearance, which is contradicted by the multi-storey office blocks around the station and the nearby Brunel shopping centre, generally regarded as one of the best-designed in Britain. The principal cluster of twentieth-century industrial sites is to the east of the station, alongside the branch line to Highworth. In 1916 the Ministry of Munitions established at Stratton a factory for producing ammonium nitrate, managed by

Brunner Mond (*Chapter 5*), on the west side of the Highworth branch line, near the junction with the main line. The explosive was taken 300 yards by aerial ropeway to a filling factory, on a site later occupied by a tobacco works. The sidings alongside the explosives factory were used in the early 1920s for the storage of fifty of the 2-8-0 locomotives, built to the design of J. G. Robinson during the First World War (*Chapter 7*), prior to their sale to GWR in May 1925. Part of the factory remained in use as a military stores depot until the mid-1960s, but the northern portion was opened by Plessey in 1942 to produce hydraulic components for aircraft, and in peacetime for combine harvesters. It remained in use until 1966. Another factory characteristic of the 1950s was that of the Garrard company, which made record changers, gramophone motors and ticket machines. Pressed Steel Fisher's works at Stratton St Margaret, now part of the Rover Group, was designed by H. W. Weedon & Partners, and opened in 1958 (*Chapter 5*). In 1999 it was still producing body panels for cars, many of which were despatched by train to Longbridge. The Vickers Armstrong Supermarine factory at South Marston was established during the Second World War, when it built Spitfires, and subsequently built Swifts and Scimitars and made parts for Vickers airliners assembled at Brooklands. In the mid-1950s the company desperately needed skilled workers, and to attract employees claimed that its factory was 'in a garden setting', that its machine shops were among the finest in the country, and that the facilities for personnel included a sports association, a dance hall and a flying club. Honda's car factory was built on the South Marston airfield, and began to produce cars in 1992. Swindon abounds with industrial buildings dating from 1960 that have gained icon status among architects: Reliance Controls' factory with its unfenestrated steel walls, designed by Team Four (the partnership of Norman Foster and Richard Rogers) in 1965–67; W. H. Smith's warehouse, comprising three linked hangars, designed by H. F. Bailey, also in 1965–67; and Renault's Parts Distribution Centre, designed by Foster Associates in 1983, of which one critic wrote: 'this breathtaking building has to be one of the most remarkable ever constructed in the United Kingdom'. An unusual advertising campaign by Honda during the summer of 1999 highlighted the advantages of living and working in Swindon.[19]

GWR's Main Line passes Windsor Castle, the Icknield Way, Wittenham Clumps and the White Horse. This terrain could be used as a section through almost any period of English history, but it illustrates the industrial archaeology of the twentieth century particularly well – providing references to every chapter in this book. The same kinds of features may be observed in most parts of Britain. If this book helps its readers to recognise in the landscape the evidence for the varied and paradoxical history of the twentieth century, and to link that evidence with collections of images and artefacts, it will have achieved its purpose.

Notes and references

1 R. Opie, *Remember When: A Nostalgic Trip through the Consumer Era*, London: Mitchell Beazley, 1999.

2 J. S. Skinner, *Form and Fancy: Factories and Factory Buildings by Wallis, Gilbert & Partners 1916–1939*, Liverpool: Liverpool University Press, 1997.

3 *Guardian*, 2 January 1999.

4 M. Stratton (ed.) *Industrial Buildings: Conservation and Regeneration*, London: Spon, 2000.

5 B. Rodgers, 'Manchester: Metropolitan Planning by Collaboration and Consent', in G. Gordon (ed.) *Regional Cities in the United Kingdom*, London: Harper & Row, 1986, p. 50.

6 H. Carpenter, *Benjamin Britten: A Biography*, London: Faber, 1992, pp. 454, 473.

7 J. B. Priestley, *English Journey*, London: Heinemann, 1934, p. 114; *Victoria History of Staffordshire*, vol. 17, 1976, p. 10.

8 J. Brimble and K. Douglas, *Britain in Old Photographs: Tipton*, Stroud: Sutton, 1995; *Britain in Old Photographs: Tipton: A Second Selection*, Stroud: Sutton, 1997; A. Saint, *Towards a Social Architecture: The Role of School-Building in Post-War England*, London: Yale University Press, 1987, pp. 214–22.

9 George Orwell, *The Road to Wigan Pier*, Harmondsworth: Penguin, 1962.

10 B. Lancaster and T. Mason, *Life and Labour in a Twentieth Century City: The Experience of Coventry*, Coventry: Cryfield Press, 1987; K. Richardson, *Twentieth Century Coventry*, Coventry: City of Coventry, 1972.

11 I. Johnson, *Beardmore Built: The Rise and Fall of a Clydeside Shipyard*, Clydebank: Clydebank Libraries & Museums Department, 1993; J. S. Childers, *Robert McAlpine: A Biography*, Oxford: Oxford University Press, 1925.

12 We acknowledge with gratitude the assistance of Brian Malaws, RCAHMW, with the fieldwork on which this paragraph is based.

13 Department for Culture, Media and Sport, *World Heritage Sites: The Tentative List of the United Kingdom of Great Britain and Northern Ireland*, London: Department of Culture, Media and Sport, 1999, pp. 58–61.

14 J. C. Bourne, *The History and Description of the Great Western Railway*, London: Bogue, 1846; A. Elton, 'The Paranesi of the Age of Steam', *Country Life Album*, London: Country Life, 1965.

15 W. G. Chapman, *The 10.30 Limited*, London: GWR, 1923; *Caerphilly Castle*, London: GWR, 1924; *The King of Railway Locomotives*, London: GWR, 1928; *Cheltenham Flyer*, London: GWR, 1934; A. Williams, *Brunel and After: The Romance of the Great Western Railway*, London: GWR, 1925.

16 L. T. C. Rolt, *Thomas Telford*, London: Longman, 1958.

17 C. Garratt, *Great Railway Photographers: Maurice Earley*, Newton Harcourt: Milepost, 1996, pp. 20–1.

18 J. Cattell and K. Falconer, *Swindon: The Legacy of a Railway Town*, London: RCHME, 1995; A. S. Peck, *The Great Western at Swindon Works*, Poole: Oxford Publishing Company, 1983.

19 M. Arloe, *Swindon: A Town in Transition: A Study in Urban Development and Overspill Policy*, London: Heinemann, 1975, pp. 60–85; P. Murray and S. Trombley, *Modern British Architecture since 1945*, London: Muller, 1984, pp. 136–9.

Appendix

Number	Site	Grid reference	Start	Notes
1	Barnbow, Crossgates, Leeds	SE 3834	1915	
2	Aintree, Liverpool	SJ 3698	1915	Bland Park Farm
3	Perivale, Willesden, London	TQ 1682	1915	
4	Georgetown, Paisley	NS 4568		
5	Quedgeley, Gloucester	SO 8213	1915	Part in military occupation; part industrial estate
6	Chilwell, Long Eaton, Notts.	SK 3135	1915	
7	Hayes, Middlesex	TQ 0879	1916	
8	Sumner Street, Southwark	TQ 3280	1915	
9	Banbury	SP 4541	1916	Most of site used for grazing. M40 cuts through western edge
10	Foleshill, Coventry	SP 3582	1915	
11	Abbey Wood, Kent	TQ 4779	–	
12	Cardonald	NS 5165	–	Retained after 1918 and re-used in Second World War
13	White Lund, Morecambe	SD 4563	–	
14	Ocean Quay, Devonport	SQ 4555	–	
15	Lightcliffe	–	–	
16	Rotherwas, Hereford	SO 5338	1916	Retained after 1918 and re-used in Second World War. Part returned to agriculture; part industrial estate
17	Horley, Sussex	TQ 2843	–	
18	Pembrey, Pembrokeshire	SN 4100	–	Adjoined explosives factory. Retained after 1918 and re-used in Second World War
22	Gainsborough, Lincolnshire	SK 8189	1917	
23	Chittening, Henbury, Bristol	ST 5381	1916	
24	Watford	TQ 1197	–	
28	Greenford, Middlesex	TQ 1684	–	

Table A1
National Filling Factories established during the First World War.

Sources:
NMRC; *History of the Ministry of Munitions*; fieldwork

Name and Grid reference	Type	Authorisation, start of production	Notes and present state
Aycliffe No. 9 Filling Factory NZ2822	Filling	May 1940, July 1941	Extensive industrial estate, part of a New Town. Filled 700 million small arms cartridges.
Birtley NZ2755	Made cartridges	Summer 1938	First World War works held in care and main- tenance, and recommissioned. Large Belgian labour force in WW1 lived in Elizabethville – huts replaced by 1920s council housing. Part of factory is still owned by British Aerospace; part is in ROF occupation, but unused.
Bishopton NS4371	Explosives	April 1939, April 1941	3 factories: Bishopton 1, 2 and 3. Approved 1937 as replacement for Waltham Abbey. Principal source of cordite, also made tetryl and RDX. Remains in British Aerospace ROF use.
Blackburn SD 7025	Explosives	1937, summer 1938	Made fuses. Now British Aerospace Royal Ordnance, Lower Darwen.
Blackpole SO 8657	SAA	July 1940, February 1941	North of Worcester. Extensive industrial estate.
Brackla No. 11 Filling Factory SS 9181	Filling	February 1940, December 1940	Satellite for Bridgend – to the north. Industrial estate.
Bridgend No. 2 Filling Factory SS 9279	Filling	1938, February 1941	Industrial estate. Factory employed 29,000 at peak.
Bridgwater ST 3342	Explosives	February 1940, March 1941	Made RDX and tetryl. 700+ acres. Much of the land is below sea level and thus difficult to drain. Making slabs for Airey Houses in 1949. Whole site remains in British Aerospace ROF occupation.
Burghfield No. 18 Filling Factory SP 6868	Filling	November 1940, July 1941	Atomic Research Establishment.
Chorley No. 1 Filling Factory SD5619	Filling	1935, January 1939	900 acres. Employed 28,000 at peak. Designed to replace filling capacity at Woolwich. Own railway station, at Euxton, 2 miles from Chorley. Intended as permanent ROF – not a wartime expedient. Making slabs for Airey Houses in 1949 as well as concrete railway sleepers, plus army and RAF uniforms. Remains in British Aerospace ROF occupation, but some buildings cleared.
Drigg SD0698	Explosives	November 1939, March 1941	On Cumbrian coast. Took water from Wast Water, 6 miles away. Made TNT. Now a dumping site for nuclear waste.

Table A2
Royal Ordnance Factories concerned with explosives and filling during the Second World War.

Sources:
W. Hornby, *History of the Second World War: Factories and Plant*, London: HMSO– Longman, 1958; C. M. Kohan, *History of the Second World War: Works and Buildings*, London: HMSO–Longman, 1952; I. Hay, *ROF – the Story of the Royal Ordnance Factories 1939–48*, London: HMSO, 1949; NMRC; fieldwork

Name and Grid reference	Type	Authorisation, start of production	Notes and present state
Elstow No. 16 Filling Factory TL 0547	Filling	November 1940, August 1941	Elstow storage depot, entered from B530, and Wilstead Industrial Park. At least ten hangars, numerous brick buildings and large areas of earth banks, together with some rail track, remain.
Featherstone No. 17 Filling Factory SJ 9205	Filling	December 1940, July 1941	Part is HMP Featherstone; part British Aerospace Royal Ordnance Speciality Metals Ltd; part is derelict, including buildings of prime archaeological interest.
Glascoed No. 3 Filling Factory SO 3501	Filling	1938, February 1941	Made 25-pounder shells and 40mm Bofors shells. Making slabs for Airey Houses in 1949. Remains in British Aerospace ROF use.
Gretna NY 3668	Explosives	–	Re-activated First World War works. Made TNT. 1,950-acre site in Second World War.
Hereford No. 4 Filling Factory SO 5338	Filling	1939	First World War factory on 350 acres, purchased June 1916, working by November 1916. Sold off in 1924 but recommissioned from 1931; operating by September 1939. Made big bombs and 15in. naval shells. Rotherwas Industrial Estate.
Irvine NS 3137	Explosives	March 1939	First World War factory recommissioned. Made TNT.
Kirkby No. 7 Filling Factory SJ 4399	Filling	February 1940, March 1941	Filled 14 million shot for 6-pounder guns and 20 million fuses for anti-tank mines. Leased by Liverpool City Corporation for industrial estate 1946.
Pembrey SN 4101	Explosives	July 1938, December 1939	Nobel factory taken over by government in First World War and recommissioned in Second. Principal source of TNT, tetryl and ammonium nitrate. Employed 3,000 at peak. After 1945 employed in destruction of surplus ammunition.
Queniborough No. 10 Filling Factory SK 6413	Filling	November 1940, November 1941	Few obvious traces. Site is now East Goscote Industrial Estate and housing.
Radway Green SJ 7854	SAA	December 1939, February 1940	Making 12 million rounds of ammunition a week in 1942. Made electric cookers after the war. Adjacent to Alsager. Part remains a British Aerospace ROF; part converted to industrial estate.
Ranskill SK 6687	Explosives	Late 1940, 1942	Made cordite.
Risley No. 6 Filling Factory SJ 6692	Filling	November 1938, March 1941	Engineering base of Atomic Energy Authority. Now HM Prison.

Table A2 *(continued)* Royal Ordnance Factories concerned with explosives and filling during the Second World War.

Sources: W. Hornby, *History of the Second World War: Factories and Plant*, London: HMSO–Longman, 1958; C. M. Kohan, *History of the Second World War: Works and Buildings*, London: HMSO–Longman, 1952; I. Hay, *ROF – the Story of the Royal Ordnance Factories 1939–48*, London: HMSO, 1949; NMRC; fieldwork

Name and Grid reference	Type	Authorisation, start of production	Notes and present state
Ruddington No. 14 Filling Factory SK 5733	Filling	1940, July 1941	Transit sheds, now used by Great Central Railway based at Loughborough.
Sellafield NY 0203	Explosives	1941, March 1943	Made TNT. Became Calder Hall Nuclear Power Station.
Southall TQ 1209	SAA filling	June 1940, February 1941	–
Spennymoor NZ 2533	SAA	July 1940, February 1941	Industrial use
Steeton SE 0344	SAA	July 1940, February 1941	–
Summerfield SO 8373	SAA filling	September 1940, May 1941	Part is still a British Aerospace ROF.
Swynnerton No. 5 Filling Factory SJ 8534	Filling	October 1939, March 1941	Over 1,000 acres. Station at Cold Meece, now a Department of Transport testing depot. Two substantial industrial estates. British Telecom training centre. MOD training range.
Theale SU 6470	Engineering	October 1940, March 1941	Made fuses.
Thorp Arch No. 8 Filling Factory SE 4446	Filling	May 1940, July 1941	Filled 162 million 20mm cartridges. Site now includes industrial estate, shopping centre with children's playground, prison and National Lending Library. Many Second World War buildings, single-storey piered brick walls, corrugated asbestos roofs, some protected by earth banks, with rail tracks still in situ.
Walsall No. 15 Filling factory SP 0199	Filling	December 1940, May 1941	Satellite to Swynnerton.
Waltham Abbey TL 3701	Explosives	Ancient	Bombed in Second World War and became research centre. Full report by RCHME.
Woolwich TQ 4479	Filling; engineering	Ancient	1,400 acres. Some functions moved to other sites before and in the early stages of the Second World War. Continued to make fuses – 120,000 a week by 1945. Maximum labour force of 46,000. In 1949, was re-rolling Anderson shelters to make usable steel, and making railway wagons.
Wrexham SJ 3749	Explosives	November 1939, February 1941	Made cordite. Now a vast industrial estate, with some Second World War buildings remaining.

Table A2 (continued)
Royal Ordnance
Factories concerned
with explosives and
filling during the
Second World War.

Sources:
W. Hornby, History of the
Second World War:
Factories and Plant,
London: HMSO–
Longman, 1958; C. M.
Kohan, History of the
Second World War: Works
and Buildings, London:
HMSO–Longman, 1952;
I. Hay, ROF – the Story of
the Royal Ordnance
Factories 1939–48,
London: HMSO, 1949;
NMRC; fieldwork

1900	139.7	1924	131.2	1948	245.9	1972	319.3
1901	139.7	1925	174.2	1949	197.7	1973	294.1
1902	153.8	1926	222.3	1950	198.2	1974	269.5
1903	156.9	1927	254.9	1951	194.8	1975	313.0
1904	136.6	1928	206.8	1952	239.9	1976	315.2
1905	127.4	1929	212.2	1953	318.5	1977	303.3
1906	130.6	1930	202.4	1954	347.8	1978	279.8
1907	121.3	1931	120.0	1955	317.4	1979	244.4
1908	100.9	1932	218.1	1956	300.6	1980	233.7
1909	98.8	1933	275.1	1957	301.1		
1910	86.0	1934	336.7	1958	273.7		
1911	67.5	1935	350.5	1959	276.7		
1912	53.4	1936	365.0	1960	297.8		
1913	54.2	1937	362.2	1961	296.1		
1914	48.3	1938	359.1	1962	305.4		
1915	30.8	1939	255.6	1963	298.9		
1916	17.0	1940	95.1	1964	373.7		
1917	–	1941	23.4	1965	382.3		
1918	–	1942	12.9	1966	385.5		
1919	–	1943	9.5	1967	404.4		
1920	29.7	1944	8.1	1968	413.7		
1921	76.1	1945	13.8	1969	366.8		
1922	84.5	1946	138.5	1970	350.4		
1923	66.1	1947	186.0	1971	350.6		

Table A3
Houses built in
Great Britain 1900–80
(in 1,000s).

Source:
B. R. Mitchell and P.
Deane, *Abstract of British
Historical Statistics,*
Cambridge: Cambridge
University Press, 1976

Location	Date	Notes
Gretna and Eastriggs	From June 1915	287 brick houses and 29 brick hostels, later converted into houses, laid out by Raymond Unwin for workers at Gretna munitions plant.
Well Hall, Eltham		Estate of 1,200 dwellings for workers at Woolwich Arsenal, designed in ten days by Frank Baines.
Mancot Royal, Queensferry, Chester		191 brick houses and six hostels designed to be convertible to houses, laid out by Raymond Unwin.
Dormanstown, Middlesbrough	1918	Dorlonco steel-framed houses with rendered panels, designed by Adshead & Ramsey for workers at the Dorman Long steelworks. Lay-out by, inter alia, Sir Patrick Abercrombie.
Shortstown, Bedfordshire	From 1917	Built by Short Brothers, near to the airship hangars at Cardington. Later became RAF housing.
Crayford Garden Village, Barns Cray, Kent	From 1914	Built for munitions workers employed by Vickers, with some post-1918 extensions. Some concrete-block houses.
Hamble, Hampshire		A 'Garden City' alongside the factory built by Fairey for the assembly of flying-boats. The intention had been to build 350 houses, but only 24 were completed.
Longbridge, Birmingham	Completed by October 1917	50 brick houses, 199 American prefabricated timber bungalows, and three large hostels.
Roe Green, Hendon	1917–19	Houses and cottage flats for workers employed by Aircraft Manufacturing.
Chepstow		Houses constructed of concrete blocks for shipyard workers.

Table A4
Some government housing developments during the First World War.

Sources:
M. Miller, *Raymond Unwin: Garden Cities and Town Planning*, Leicester: Leicester University Press, 1992;
M. Swenarton, *Homes Fit for Heroes: The Politics and Architecture of Early State Housing in Britain*, Oxford: Clarendon Press, 1981

Further reading

General introductions

The best introduction to the history of the first half of the twentieth century is Charles Loch Mowat, *Britain between the Wars 1918–1940*, London: Methuen, 1955. A. J. P. Taylor, *English History 1914–45*, Oxford: Oxford University Press, 1965, and Arthur Marwick, *Britain in the Century of Total War*, London: Bodley Head, 1968, are also essential reading. The second half of the century, or most of it, is well covered in K. O. Morgan, *The People's Peace: British History 1945–1989*, Oxford: Oxford University Press, 1990. *The Rebirth of a Nation: Wales 1880–1980*, Oxford: Oxford University Press, 1981, by the same author and, on the first half of the century, T. C. Smout, *A Century of the Scottish People*, London: Collins, 1986, provide broad views of their respective nations that are refreshingly free from the obsession with Westminster politics that pervades much writing on 'British history'. On social history, John Benson, *The Rise of Consumer Society in Britain 1880–1980*, London: Longman, 1994, is a sound introduction, while Robert Graves and Alan Hodge, *The Long Weekend: A Social History of Great Britain 1918–39*, London: Faber, 1940, remains a stimulating and well-informed guide to the inter-war period. Robert Opie, *Remember When*, London: Mitchell Beazley, 1999, is a delightful introduction to the century's popular images, while Alastair Forsyth, *Buildings for the Age: New Building Types 1900–1939*, London: RCHME, 1982, is a pioneering study of the industrial architecture of the first part of the century.

Industrial archaeology

Barrie Trinder (ed.), *The Blackwell Encyclopedia of Industrial Archaeology*, Oxford: Blackwell, 1992, is international in its coverage and includes much that relates to the twentieth century. The standard guides to industrial archaeology in Britain tend to concentrate on the eighteenth and nineteenth centuries, but include some twentieth-century material. The best of them are: Sir Neil Cossons, *The BP Book of Industrial Archaeology*, Newton Abbot: David & Charles,

1993; Keith Falconer, *Guide to England's Industrial Heritage*, London: Batsford, 1980; John Hume, *The Industrial Archaeology of Scotland*, vol. I: *The Central Lowlands*, London: Batsford, 1976; John Hume, *The Industrial Archaeology of Scotland*, vol. II: *The Highlands and Islands*, London: Batsford, 1977; and D. Morgan Rees, *The Industrial Archaeology of Wales*, Newton Abbot: David & Charles, 1975. The first books specifically on twentieth-century industrial archaeology were by Kenneth Hudson: *Food, Clothes and Shelter*, London: John Baker, 1978; *Where We Used to Work*, London: John Baker, 1980; and *The Archaeology of the Consumer Society*, London: Heinemann, 1983. Michael Stratton and Barrie Trinder, *The English Heritage Book of Industrial England*, London: Batsford, 1997, is thematically arranged and considers twentieth-century buildings alongside those of earlier periods. Regional surveys that include significant material on twentieth-century sites include: David Eve, *A Guide to the Industrial Archaeology of Kent*, Telford: Association for Industrial Archaeology, 1999; Pamela Moore, *A Guide to the Industrial Archaeology of Hampshire and the Isle of Wight*, Southampton: Southampton University Industrial Archaeology Group, 1984; and Barrie Trinder, *The Industrial Archaeology of Shropshire*, Chichester: Phillimore, 1996.

A new material culture

The best introduction to iron and steel technology remains W. K. V. Gale, *Iron and Steel*, London: Longman, 1969, which can be supplemented by the excellent pamphlets published by British Steel (now Corus) on current operations at their plants. Frank Newby (ed.), *Early Reinforced Concrete*, Aldershot: Ashgate, 1999, brings together some important papers on concrete technology. The development of constructional techniques is covered in Michael Stratton, 'New Materials for a New Age: Steel and Concrete Construction in the North of England, 1860–1939', *Industrial Archaeology Review*, 1999, vol. 21, pp. 5–24. Susan Mossman, *Early Plastics: Perspectives 1850–1950*, Leicester: Leicester University Press, 1997, is the essential introduction to the history of plastics.

Twentieth-century power and energy

The coal industry is comprehensively analysed in three volumes of the official history: Roy Church, *The History of the British Coal Industry*, vol. III: *1830–1913: Victorian Pre-Eminence*, Oxford: Clarendon Press, 1986; Barry Supple, *The History of the British Coal Industry*, vol. IV: *1913–46: The Political Economy of Decline*, Oxford: Clarendon Press, 1987; and William Ashworth, *The History of the British Coal Industry*, vol. V: *1946–1982: The Nationalized Industry*, Oxford: Clarendon Press, 1986. The industry's archaeology at the time of its demise is portrayed in Stephen Hughes, Brian Malaws, Medwyn Parry and Peter Wakelin, *Collieries of Wales: Engineering and Architecture*, Aberystwyth: RCAHMW, nd, and Robin Thornes, *Images of Industry: Coal*, Swindon: RCHME, 1994. N. Dennis, F. M. Henriques and C. Slaughter, *Coal Is Our Life*, London: Eyre & Spottiswoode, 1957, is a classic sociological survey of a mining community, while R. J. Waller, *The Dukeries Transformed: The Social and Political Development of a Twentieth Century Coalfield*, Oxford: Oxford University Press, 1983, elucidates the development of Britain's principal twentieth-century coalfield. T. I. Williams, *The History of the British Gas Industry*, Oxford: Oxford University Press, 1981, provides an excellent account of the industry up to and through the period of conversion to natural gas. The technology of oil extraction and refining is clearly explained in the BP publication *Our Industry*, of which there are many editions. Michael Stratton, *Ironbridge and the Electric Revolution: The History of Electricity Generation at Ironbridge A and B Power Stations*, London: John Murray, 1994, is a broader view of the industry than the title suggests, while R. Cochrane, *Landmark of London – the Story of Battersea Power Station*, London: CEGB, 1984, is a sound study of the most celebrated of British power stations.

The international transfer of technology: the case of the food industry

A broad survey of the industry, with an extensive bibliography, is provided in Barrie Trinder, 'The Archaeology of the British Food Industry, 1660–1960: A Preliminary Survey', *Industrial Archaeology Review*, 1993, vol. 15, pp. 119–39. On biscuits, the most useful works are: T. A. B. Corley, *Quaker Enterprise in Biscuits: Huntley & Palmer of Reading 1822–1972*, London: Hutchinson, 1972; and Margaret Forster, *Rich Desserts and Captain's Thin: A Family and Their Times 1831–1931*, London: Chatto & Windus, 1997; and for biscuit tins, see M. J. Franklin, *British Biscuit Tins*, London: New Cavendish, 1979. A sound regional account of the dairy industry is provided by Peter Sainsbury, *Tradition to Technology: A History of the Dairy Industry in Devon*, Tiverton (privately published), 1991. For Trafford Park, see R. Nicholls, *Trafford Park: The First Hundred Years*, Chichester: Phillimore, 1996.

Cars, ships and aircraft

Paul Collins and Michael Stratton, *British Car Factories from 1896*, Godmanstone: Veloce, 1993, is the essential starting-point for a study of the archaeology of the motorcar industry. Of the many books on the history of the industry, two recent publications are recommended: James Foreman-Peck, Sue Bowden and Alan McKinlay, *The British Motor Industry*, Manchester: Manchester University Press, 1995; and Roy Church, *The Rise and Decline of the British Motor Industry*, Cambridge: Cambridge University Press, 1994. The archaeology of aircraft manufacture is analysed in Michael Stratton, 'Skating Rinks to Shadow Factories: The Evolution of British Aircraft Manufacturing Complexes', *Industrial Archaeology Review*, 1996, vol. 18, pp. 223–44, and the series of studies of individual aircraft manufacturers published by Putnam is recommended.

The age of science

W. J. Reader's two volumes, *Imperial Chemical Industries: A History*, vol. I: *The Forerunners 1879–1926*, Oxford: Oxford University Press, 1970, and *Imperial Chemical Industries: A History*, vol. II: *The First Quarter-Century 1926–1952*, Oxford: Oxford University Press, 1975, are essential reading, although they are not archaeologically based, and do not cover the greater part of the sixty-seven-year history of ICI prior to the demerger of 1993. F. A. Kirk, 'Twentieth Century Industry: Obsolescence and

Change: A Case Study: The ICI Coal-to-Oil Plant and Its Various Uses', *Industrial Archaeology Review*, 1998, vol. 20, pp. 83–92, is excellent as a case study, and also as an exploration of the appropriate means of recording a complex twentieth-century plant.

The century of total war

The social and economic history of the First World War is detailed in the official *History of the Ministry of Munitions*, and that of the Second World War in the several volumes of the official civilian history of the war. Arthur Marwick, *The Deluge*, London: Bodley Head, 1968, and Angus Calder, *The People's War*, London: Jonathan Cape, 1969, are the best social histories of the two world wars. D. Edgerton, *England and the Aeroplane*, London: Macmillan, 1991, is a challenging analysis of the influence of military ambition on twentieth-century industry. Robert Buderi, *The Invention That Changed the World: The Story of Radar from War to Peace*, London: Little, Brown, 1997, is an enlightening account of how the pressures of war influenced technological development. One of the best books on the social history of the Second World War that reflects in several respects on industrial archaeology is David Reynolds, *Rich Relations: The American Occupation of Britain 1942–45*, London: HarperCollins, 1995.

The great rebuildings

Twentieth-century housing is best approached through the study of particular topics. Works to be recommended are: M. Glendinning and S. Muthesius, *Tower Block: Modern Public Housing in England, Scotland, Wales and Northern Ireland*, London: Yale University Press, 1994; Dennis Hardy and Colin Ward, *Arcadia for All: The Legacy of a Makeshift Landscape*, London: Mansell, 1984; Alan Jackson, *Semi-Detached London: Suburban Development, Life and Transport 1900–39*, London: Allen & Unwin, 1973; Anthony King, *The Bungalow: The Production of a Global Culture*, London: Routledge & Kegan Paul, 1984; M. Miller, *Raymond Unwin: Garden Cities and Town Planning*, Leicester: Leicester University Press, 1992; Paul Oliver, Ian Davis and Ian Bentley, *Dunroamin: The Suburban Semi and Its Enemies*, London: Barrie & Jackson, 1981; Phillip Riden, *Rebuilding a Valley: A History of Cwmbran Development Corporation*, Cwmbran: Cwmbran Development Corporation, 1988; Andrew Saint, *London Suburbs*, London: Merrell Holberton, 1999; Mark Swenarton, *Homes Fit for Heroes: The Politics and Architecture of Early State Housing in Britain*, London: Heinemann, 1981; Brenda Vale, *Prefabs: A History of the UK Temporary Housing Programme*, London: Spon, 1995. Works of particular note on building materials include: John Woodforde, *Bricks to Build a House*, London: Routledge & Kegan Paul, 1976; Michael Stratton, *The Terracotta Revival*, London: Gollancz, 1993; Tony Herbert and Kathryn Huggins, *The Decorative Tile in Architecture and Interiors*, London: Phaidon, 1995; and Tony Crosby, 'The Silver End Model Village for Crittall Manufacturing Co., Ltd.', *Industrial Archaeology Review*, 1998, vol. 20, pp. 69–82.

Changing horizons: the archaeology of transport

Gordon Jackson, *The History and Archaeology of Ports*, Tadworth: World's Work, 1983, is the best general introduction to British ports, while R. McAuley, *The Liners: A Voyage of Discovery*, London: Boxtree, 1997, is a full and up-to-date history of the liner trade. John Hibbs, *The History of British Bus Services*, Newton Abbot: David & Charles, 1968, and G. Charlesworth, *A History of Britain's Motorways*, London: Thomas Telford, 1984, are valuable contributions to the history of road transport. Jack Simmons, *The Railway in England and Wales 1830–1914*, vol. I: *The System and Its Working*, Leicester: Leicester University Press, 1986, provides a full picture of the railway system in the early years of the century. Much of the history of the railways in Britain after 1914 has to be assembled from the many published writings by railwaymen of different grades. The key books on transport in London are T. C. Barker and M. Robbins, *A History of London Transport*, vol. 2: *The Twentieth Century*, London: Allen & Unwin, 1974; O. Green and J. Reed, *The London Transport Golden Jubilee Book*, London: Daily Telegraph, 1983, and Christian Barman, *The Man Who Built London Transport: A Biography of Frank Pick*, Newton Abbot: David & Charles, 1979. For air transport see Kenneth Hudson, *Air Travel: A Social History*,

Bath, Adams & Dart, 1972; L. Marriott, *British Airports Then and Now*, Shepperton: Ian Allan, 1993, and G. Hayter, *Heathrow: The Story of the World's Greatest International Airport*, London: Pan, 1979.

Expanding services

General introductions to retailing are provided by Michael Winstanley, *The Shopkeeper's World*, Manchester: Manchester University Press, 1983, and J. B. Jeffreys, *Retail Trading in Britain 1850–1950*, Cambridge: Cambridge University Press, 1954. More detailed studies include: P. Mathias, *Retailing Revolution*, London: Longman, 1967; Asa Briggs, *Marks and Spencer 1884–1984: The Originators of Penny Bazaars*, London, Marks & Spencer, 1984; Angela Burns and Barry Hyman, *Marks & Spencer 1884–1994*, London: Marks & Spencer, 1994; Bridget Williams, *The Best Butter in the World: A History of Sainsbury's*, London: Ebury, 1994; and John Walton, *Fish and Chips and the British Working Class 1870–1940*, Leicester: Leicester University Press, 1992. For cinemas, see D. Atwell, *Cathedrals of the Movies*, London: Architectural Press, 1980. John Walton's many works on Britain's principal twentieth-century seaside resort are summed up in his book *Blackpool*, Edinburgh: Edinburgh University Press, 1998. Dennis Hardy and Colin Ward, *Goodnight Campers! The History of the British Holiday Camp*, London: Mansell, 1986, is also essential reading on the seaside holiday.

Towards conclusions

The most recent and comprehensive guide to the adaptive re-use of industrial buildings is Michael Stratton (ed.), *Industrial Buildings: Conservation and Regeneration*, London: Spon, 2000. Great Western Railway's works at Swindon is thoroughly analysed in John Cattell and Keith Falconer, *Swindon: The Legacy of a Railway Town*, London: HMSO, 1995.

Index of Names

including companies and brands

Taff Merthyr 23–4, 200
Talacre 191, 204
Taunton 160, 195
Team Valley 5
Telford 102, 139, 177, 202;
    see also Ironbridge
Tenterden 160
Teesside 10–11, 29, 77, 80–4, 86, 151;
    see also Billingham, Middlesbrough,
    Newport, Redcar, Stockton on Tees,
    Wilton
Thaxted 160
Theale 157, 214
Theddlethorpe 32
Thirsk 116
Thorp Arch 105–6, 202, 214
Thorpe Marsh 40
Thurrock 183
Tilbury 148–51
Tilmanstone 27
Tipton 31, 57, 202–3
Tonbridge 37, 116
Tongland 39
Torquay 188–90
Torrington 162
Totnes 52
Toton 166–7
Towester 160
Trafford Park 3, 5, 8, 13, 15, 30, 33, 43–7,
    53, 63, 65, 68, 87, 107, 141, 174, 183,
    187, 200–1
Trawsfynydd 38, 40
Tredegar 24, 27, 137
Treforest 5, 11, 70
Treharris 23
Trostre 11
Tummel 39
Tutbury 51, 55
Tuxford 40
Tyldesley 22
Tyne Dock 10

Uffington 208
Upminster 130

Verny Junction 166, 195

Wakefield 24m 103, 159;
    see also Caphouse
Wallasey 135
Wallingford 208
Wallsend 37, 77, 84
Walsall 12, 102, 127, 138, 214

Waltham Abbey 96, 102–3, 214
Walton, Yorkshire 30
Wantage 208
Ware 89
Warrington 14, 40, 110, 139, 186
Warwick 113
Washington, Co. Durham 15, 139
Watchett 151
Waterhouses 52
Watford, Hertfordshire 47, 183–4, 208, 211
Watford Gap, Northamptonshire 159
Wath 167, 177
Weald & Downland Museum 196
Wednesbury 11, 37, 177
Wellesbourne Mountford 112–13, 119, 159
Wellingborough 10, 46, 166, 168, 183
Wells next the Sea 168
Welwyn Garden City 47, 89, 200
Wem 111
Wemyss Bay 148
Wenvoe 90
West Bromwich 24, 31–2, 156, 202–3
West Burton 40
Westbury, Wiltshire 133, 160
Westfield 30
West Molesey 130
Weston super Mare 107, 136
Wetherby 169
Wexham 13
Weymouth 100
Whaley Thornes 24
Wharncliffe Silkstone 28
Whetstone 115
Whipsnade Zoo 136, 195–6
Whitchurch, Shropshire 179
Whitehaven 4
Whitemoor 167
Whitesand Bay 130
Whitland 52, 54
Whitley Bay 189–90
Wick 160
Widnes 15, 79–80, 178
Wigston 113
Wigan 24, 57–8, 131, 185, 196, 199, 203
Wilton, Teesside 79–80, 85–6
Winchester 116, 153, 159, 179, 208
Windsor 158, 207
Winfrith Heath 40
Winnington 81–2
Wissington 49
Witham 134
Withernsea 130, 162
Woking 200

Wolverhampton 17, 36, 75, 104, 117, 124,
    136, 141, 153, 156, 169, 171
Woodford, Cheshire 76
Woodford Halse 116, 162, 167
Woodhead Tunnel 166
Woodlands 26–7
Wootton Pillings see Stewartby
Worcester 34, 179
Workington 10
Worksop 24, 169
Worthing 130
Wrenbury 53
Wrexham 38, 47, 88–9, 104, 115, 117, 119,
    127, 137, 202, 214
Wytch Farm 33

Yaxley 133
Yeadon 171
Ynysmaerdy 23
York 36, 40, 55, 105, 115–16, 123, 125, 162,
    168–9, 174–5, 203, 207–8

Subject Indexes

Air transport

airliners 170–3
airports 75, 169–75
air terminals 170
car ferry services 173–4
flying boats 170
See also Mechanical engineering:
      aircraft manufacture

Chemicals

biotechnology 97
coal as chemical feedstock 28–9, 84–6
dyestuffs 86–7
ethanol crackers 85
explosives 81, 87, 99, 103, 106–7
Haber–Bosch process 83
oil as chemical feedstock 84–6
pharmaceuticals 89, 109
phosphorus 88
plastics 16–17
saltworks 79
Solvay process 80–2

Civil engineering

bridges 154, 159–60
concrete, constructional uses 12–13, 46, 65,
      82; *see also* Housing
steel, constructional uses 8–9
tunnels 150, 154, 159–60

Communications

computers, 79, 90
photography 90
printing 184

radio and television 19–90
telecommunications 89–90

Factories

architectural style 5
industrial estates 3, 43–5, 104–5, 112–13,
      159
see also Food industry; Manufacturing
      industries; War and society: Royal
      Ordnance factories, Shadow factories

Food industry

bacon 57
baking 46–7
beer 56
biscuits 48
breakfast cereals 45, 47–8, 104
chocolate and cocoa 55–6
coffee 55, 58–9
cold storage 113, 115, 146
corn milling 44–6
dairy products 50–5
edible oils 44–5
fish 58
ice cream 59
margarine 49
pickles 57–8
sugar 49
wine 56–7

Housing

building materials 132–5
bungalows 130, 143
diversity in twentieth century 121, 128
concrete construction 123–4, 127–8, 137–8,

140–3
Garden City style 123
local authority housing 122–6, 139, 140–3
modernist style 129–31, 136
plotland developments 131–2, 190–3
prefabricated houses 135–8
private developers 128
slum clearance 127, 143
statistics 215
steel construction 127
timber construction 125
tower blocks 140–3
see also War and society: housing

Industrial communities

company housing 82, 131
Garden Cities 123–5
mining villages 24–7
New Towns 139, 143

Iron and steel

Bessemer process 8, 10, 102
government involvement 7–8
LD process 10
iron ore, sources of 9–10
open-hearth process 10, 101–2
rolling mills 10–1
stainless steel 12
steel casting 11
tinplate manufacture 11–12
tube mills 11

Manufacturing industries

Bricks and tiles 17, 132–3, 135, 158
Furniture and wood products 17, 109

Glass 17
Metal windows 133–5
see also Food industry;
    Mechanical engineering

Mechanical engineering

aircraft manufacture 61–4, 66, 68–9, 71,
    74–7, 100–1, 106–9, 119
bicycle manufacture 71–2
commercial vehicle manufacture 69–70,
    109, 114
hydraulics 94
lift manufacture 109
motor car manufacture 61–74, 100–1,
    106–8, 119, 126

Minerals

aluminium smelting and processing 13–14
asbestos 15
cement manufacture 133
plasterboard manufacture 135
potash mining 86
tungsten mining 109
uralite 15, 123

Power and energy

coal exports 106
coal-fired power stations 3, 32, 36–41
coal gas 30–1
coal mining 19–30
coke production 28–9
gas-fired power stations 40–1
hydro-electric power 14, 38–9
natural gas 31–2
nuclear power stations 38–40, 106
offshore oil 35
oil pipelines 34
oil refineries 33–5, 85–6, 88
onshore oil production 33
open-cast coal production 28
shale oil 32–3, 88
steam engines 29–30

Rail transport

bridges 160
Channel Tunnel 150, 160
coal carrying 166–7
electric traction 163–4
extent of system 159–61, 168–9
freight depots 165–6
Great Western Main Line 205–10
locomotive depots 167–8
marshalling yards 167
North Wales coast line 204–5
passenger stations 160, 168
Pullman services 161–2
streamlined trains 164–5
steam locomotive technology 162–3
train ferries 95, 148
underground railways 164
war and railways 110–11, 114–18

Road transport

bridges 154, 159
bus and coach stations 156–7
by-passes 153
filling stations 3, 155–7
motor bus and coach services 156–8
motor car showrooms 152–3, 155
motorways 158–9
roadhouse pubs 154–5
roll-on roll-off ferries 150
tramways 156
trolley buses 156
tunnels 154, 150
urban road building 152–3, 158
see also Mechanical engineering:
    commercial vehicle manufacture,
    motor car manufacture

Seaside holidays

entertainments 189–92
holiday camps 113, 191, 193–5
hotels and boarding houses 188–9
plotland settlements 190–3
railway services 162, 187–8, 195
retailing 190

Sea transport

containers 151–2
ferries 148, 150
freight handling 151–2
liners 146–9, 151
passenger terminals 149–51
wet docks 145–6, 151
wartime ports 117
warehouses 145

Service industries

chain stores 178–80, 182, 190
cinemas 27, 185–6
co-operative stores 178–80, 182, 190
department stores 180–1
financial services 177
fish and chip shops 181–2, 190
open-air museums 196
retail parks 177
sport 177–8, 186–7, 195
supermarkets 182–4
town centre shops 182–3
zoos 195–6
see also Communications; Seaside holidays

Textiles

Ardil 84
cotton 15, 197
nylon 15–16, 84–5, 108
rayon 15, 17
terylene 85

Theory and interpretation

adaptive re-use 201
architecture, history of 200–1
collections 199
images 199–200
industrial archaeology 2–5, 199–201
industrial museums 196–7, 199
landscape history 2–3, 200, 202
international transfer of technology 43–60,
    70–1

Transport

see Air transport; Rail transport; Road
transport; Sea transport

War and society

airfields 112–13
air transport 171–2
American material culture 118–19
chemical plants 84, 87
cold storage depots 113, 115
hostels 113–14
housing 102, 106, 114, 118, 125, 216
military depots 95–6, 110–11, 118
national factories 75, 96–102, 211
oil industry 34
plotlands, effect on 132
Royal Ordnance factories 47, 70, 78, 98,
    102–6, 118, 212–14
shadow factories 73–4, 76, 106–9